*Shelby Foote*

# Shelby Foote

## A Writer's Life

C. Stuart Chapman

*University Press of Mississippi*   *Jackson*

Willie Morris Books in Memoir and Biography

www.upress.state.ms.us

11  10  09  08  07  06  05  04  03     4   3   2   1
∞

Library of Congress Cataloging-in-Publication Data
Chapman, C. Stuart.
    Shelby Foote : a writer's life / C. Stuart chapman.
        p. cm. – (Willie Morris books in memoir and biography)
Includes bibliographical references and index.
    ISBN 1-57806-359-0 (cloth : alk. paper)
    1. Foote, Shelby. 2. Novelists, American–20th century–Biography.
3. Historians–Southern States–Biography. 4. Southern States–Historiography.
5. Southern States–In literature. 6. Foote, Shelby. Civil War. I. Title. II. Series.
    PS3511.0348 Z625 2003
        815'. 54–dc21                                        2002006901

British Library Cataloging-in-Publication Data available

Very strange, looking back on a life once the pattern
has emerged. What in God's name will they make of ours
someday, if they take the trouble?

—*Shelby Foote to Walker Percy, January 22, 1974*

# CONTENTS

Acknowledgments                                                    IX
Author's Note                                                       XI
Introduction                                                      XIII

1. Roots                                                             3
2. Beginnings, 1916–1935                                           21
3. College Days, 1935–1937                                         50
4. Writing and Fighting, 1937–1945                                 70
5. First Successes, 1945–1951                                      94
6. First Failures: "Two Gates to the City" and *Jordan County,*
   1952–1954                                                      139
7. *The Civil War,* Volume I, 1954–1958                           157
8. *The Civil War,* Volume II, 1958–1963                          179
9. *The Civil War,* Volume III, 1963–1974                         195
10. After the Deluge: *September September,* 1975–1978            221
11. Turning Home, 1978–1990                                       238
12. A Star Is Born, 1990–                                         257

Afterword                                                         270
Notes                                                             272
Index                                                             309

# ACKNOWLEDGMENTS

Although it would be four more years before I conducted the first interview and six more years before I put down word one, this book began on a January day in 1991, an afternoon on which I donned coat and tie and made a three-mile pilgrimage to Shelby Foote's Memphis home. After working as a reporter for *The Clarksdale (Mississippi) Press-Register* during 1990, I was back at Rhodes College for my final term. Three months before, Ken Burns's *The Civil War* series had aired on the Public Broadcasting Service (PBS), turning Foote into a national icon. When Mrs. Foote opened the door on that warm day, I'm sure she assumed that I was part of the wave of people who suddenly wanted a little piece of her husband. Any assumption that my interest was a product of the PBS series was wrong, however, for during those months in the Mississippi Delta, I had lived in a place so sparsely furnished that a mattress, much less a television set, would have been a luxury. Consequently, when I journeyed forth to the Foote house, I had not yet seen any of the series' episodes. But during a marvelous five-week period that fall, I did feast on the 3000 pages of Foote's Civil War trilogy, reading them before work, during lunch hours, and late into the night.

Mesmerized by Foote's magnum opus, I felt the need to pay my respects upon returning to Memphis. Mrs. Foote ushered me into the den where Foote held off his vicious dog while I scrambled for refuge not on—but *in*—the sofa. Viewed from the distance of ten years, the thirty-minute conversation that followed was not particularly rich or enlightening—in fact, it was rather superficial. Nevertheless, as had been the viewers of *The Civil War,* I somehow also became hooked by the man's aura. Returning back to my Gothic-plated campus, I digested all of his novels over the next few weeks, but my interest in Foote and his work increased exponentially after reading Jay Tolson's 1992 biography of Walker Percy, *Pilgrim in the Ruins,* which advanced the importance of Foote in Percy's life. From the day I finished Tolson's biography, I knew that I was going to write a biography of Foote.

It would be three more years before I began to interview Foote's friends and enemies, and even from that date, it has taken me more than five years to write *Shelby Foote: A Writer's Life,* mainly because I wrote it and rewrote it, ad nauseam, while working on a Ph.D. at Boston University. Along the way, I have received enormous help of all kinds, not merely from the more than sixty people whom I interviewed, most of whom did not know me from Adam, but from old friends such as Frank Howell, Charles Mitchell, and David Waguespack, who generously offered me sofas when I found myself in their respective necks of the woods. Moreover, I appreciate the efforts of several friends who read versions of the manuscript or provided valuable editorial information, including Charles Wright, Stephen Crockett, Lee Hall, and particularly David Marut. I am also greatly indebted to my advisor, Jack Matthews, who until recently had not read a copy of this manuscript, but whose influence on my scholarship in the area of Southern literature and culture appears on every page. And to Dr. Mike Shirley, who cultivated and refined my interest in Southern history and culture. Countless other people—too numerous to name—have provided valuable photographs and materials for this study. I also thank the Southern Historical Collection at the University of North Carolina in Chapel Hill, which provided a travel grant that enabled me to study Foote's papers, and the staff of the Greenville Library, particularly Kay Clanton.

Although they too have provided a great deal of financial support, my mother, father, and brother have been particularly generous with their emotional comfort, all of which, weak mortal that I am, I have absorbed in enormous amounts. Because of our family's relentless sarcasm, I often do not let them know how important they are to me. I do now.

Finally, I dedicate this book to a wonderful woman, Wendy Wyeth, who, having come into my life more than two years ago, has not necessarily changed me completely, but has completely changed my perspective on life. No longer do I, like Percy's Will Barrett, merely try to get to the next Wednesday afternoon, but I have begun to realize that life indeed may be, to quote a line from a Foote letter, "a wonderful thing . . . a Godgiven wonderful thing." For her, I am eternally grateful. She has made my Wednesdays brighter.

## A U T H O R ' S   N O T E

For reasons that I cannot fully explain, Foote consistently employs irregularities in his spelling, particularly in terms of the punctuation of contractions. In all cases, I have followed the manuscripts of his letters.

Like its namesake's reputation, the park named after Nathan Bedford Forrest occupied a dubious place in the Memphis landscape. Manifested in the weeds encroaching along its edges, Forrest Park's demise was due in great part to its location on Union Avenue, formerly the city's grand showpiece, but now reduced to an umbilical cord tying together Memphis' downtown area with the city's ever-eastward expansion. One mile west stood the city's modest skyscrapers, high on a bluff overlooking the Mississippi River. For decades, the river had invited settlers from the East to populate its banks. People had spread out over its floodplain, establishing the agricultural dynasties whose offspring now filled the banking and agribusiness offices of those downtown buildings. In the opposite direction ran a 15-mile corridor of primarily white residential expansion, initiated with the urban flight of the 1960s and then repeatedly sustained by a momentum that had long since displaced inert resistance. In its wake, around Forrest Park, stood sloughs of poverty.

But on this hot Sunday in July 1996, Forrest Park once again occupied a focal point in Memphis' cultural life. In the back part of the park—otherwise unnotable except for the bronzed horse and rider at its center: stocky and unkempt for a traditional statuary subject—a bevy of uniformed men went about their business of readying for the day's birthday celebration. By day, these men were lawyers, accountants, and police officers; but come Saturday and Sunday, they became Sons of Confederate Veterans, donning the butternut gray to participate in battle reenactments. Following on the heels of the enormous and well-received Civil War centennial celebrations of the early 1960s, interest in the bitter conflict surged. The reproduction of the war offered an opportunity for many

Americans to reengage with their past. But, as Tony Horowitz argued in *Confederates in the Attic*, the Civil War reenactment industry also channeled anxieties that many reenactors—a group dominated by white rank-and-file workers—have about racial tensions and growing economic disparities.

Given this impulse, the resurgence of such groups as the Sons of Confederate Veterans had not come without costs. Opposition to the annual ceremony had been visible and vocal in past years. In 1994 one of the matriarchs of the civil rights movement, Rosa Parks, who had refused to give up her Montgomery bus seat in 1955, had spearheaded the protest. Side by side with Parks on that day had been D'Army Bailey, a high-profile activist in the Memphis black community. Now a contentious and controversial Shelby County Circuit Court Judge, Bailey had fought civil rights battles during the 1950s and 1960s in the South, Boston, and Oakland, where he had served as a city councilman and adviser to Congressman Ron Dellums, the standard-bearer for race reform in the Bay Area.

On the eve of the event two years earlier, opponents spray-painted the Forrest statue with "head of the KKK," "slave trader," and "racist murderer." Although that incident had prompted the Nathan Bedford Forrest camp to hold an all-night vigil around the statue and the graves of Forrest and his wife, a protester at the 1995 event dared to show up, flagging motorists along Union Avenue. On one side, the protester's sign read "Native White Protestant Supremacy"; on the other, next to a photo of a lynching, the protester wrote, "Invisible Empire of the South—When Will the Hatred End?"

Who was Nathan Bedford Forrest, a man who could simultaneously elicit such lionizing and demonizing, such evangelical worship and blinding hatred? Who was the person who was both a cultural icon worthy of emulation and a demon to be spat on? Who was the man behind the statue? That man, or at least his reputation, had become a test case for Southern culture in the twentieth century, and his stock had risen and fallen depending on the respective era's governing ideology. In the 1930s Forrest's reputation soared as the Nashville Agrarians championed his cause.

Espousing a South rooted in Jeffersonian republicanism, Agrarians such as Forrest biographer Andrew Lytle argued that Forrest's affinity with the soil had produced his climb from impoverished beginnings into the Memphis ruling class. (Forrest served as a Memphis alderman in the 1850s.) Forrest's reputation also continued to rise in the 1950s and 1960s with the revival of the Ku Klux Klan, an organization he founded in 1866.

The same elements that boosted his image also provided fodder for his detractors. Forrest's emergence into prominence during the antebellum period came not merely through owning plantations, but through slave-trading. In a system steeped in injustices, it was the slave-trader whose traffic in black bodies made him persona non grata, the despicable unfeeling man who exposed the economic underpinnings of a paternalistic system passing itself off as generous and altruistic. Moreover, Forrest's racism continued to dog him during the Civil War, in incidents that twentieth-century Southern blacks repeatedly brought to the public's attention. If Forrest was a man for all seasons, no one knew whether the next solstice would bring summer or winter.

As the July morning ripened into an early afternoon of torturous Memphis humidity, rising almost to the point where it would trigger booming thunderstorms, a crowd of four hundred people gathered around the base of the monument—many wearing Civil War regalia, antebellum hoop skirts, or Confederate uniforms. Although some visitors occupied the folding chairs set out near the statue, most people stood in an arc around the front of the statue and graves, which were bedecked in flowers and bouquets. It was just minutes before the ceremony would begin, a service that would feature the Covington, Tennessee, mayor as the keynote speaker. With the exception of a civil Bailey, who stood quietly among the crowd, no dissenters were in sight on this day. Amid the reverent murmur of the gathered crowd, a car pulled up and slipped into one of the metered spaces. The door opened and out of the car slumped a bearded, slightly bent-over man whose long arms suggested a once-greater height, before old age had stolen several inches. Disentangling himself for a moment, the man stood surveying the crowd. He was stylishly informal, suggesting even in mufti a customary grace. Where on most occasions he appeared in public in conservative suits, the man now wore khaki walking shorts, white tube socks, and sneakers. He wore a gray t-shirt that read, "Honor the Old Warrior!" The only sign that the man belonged to an earlier era lay in a foppish gold watch chain that peeked out of his shorts.

Although the man had become as closely identified with the Civil War as any American, several moments passed before the audience recognized Shelby Foote. After all, the seventy-nine-year-old had not been expected. Although Foote had himself been a Forrest Camp member until the 1950s, when he resigned in protest against Alabama Governor George Wallace's speech to the camp, he had spoken at the Forrest celebration several times, including the previous year. Even though he had expressly declined the camp's invitation for this year's event, as Foote walked toward the monument, the uniformed soldiers rushed over to meet him with deep, genuflective gestures. Quickly, the ceremony was rearranged. With clouds increasingly threatening, the proceedings began in haste: Foote was introduced, and when he was, the crowd gave him the warm, comforting applause that he had grown accustomed to over the previous five years. Foote shuffled up to the podium, raised his head, and peered out over the crowd. A body of almost all white faces met his gaze, a desert broken only by the oasis of Bailey's black face, a man who since 1978 had been Foote's intellectual sparring partner and friend. Overhead, the Jehovah-like mien of ominous clouds glared, and he began to speak.

Shelby Foote usually decried public appearances. As a private and even reclusive man for most of his life, Foote kept to himself, regimenting his days strictly in accordance with his writing routine. On any other afternoon, he would just be emerging from the book-lined study of his Tudor house, three miles east of the present battleground. Two decades had passed since Foote's last novel, *September September*, but the methodical man still followed the same schedule that had governed his entire working life. Up by seven, coffee, a light breakfast, then in his study by eight, working steadily—with a short break for lunch, during which he watched *As the World Turns*—through the afternoon until early evening. Publicly, he claimed that he was working on the white whale that had eluded him in both the early 1950s and late 1970s, "Two Gates to the City." In actuality, though, he puttered about his study in his pajamas, reading, listening to Mozart and Beethoven, and at all times laboring to keep his ever smoked-out pipe filled.

His private routine had been compromised after Ken Burns's 1990 *The Civil War*, a nine-part series broadcast on PBS. Until the documentary, Foote had toiled in relative obscurity. When his novels appeared in the 1940s and 1950s, they had been met with lukewarm receptions, quickly going out-of-print. Although he had received recognition for his three-volume, 1.2 million–word *The Civil War: A Narrative*, it was not the best-seller that Foote had hoped for. Burns's television series changed all that. The series broke all PBS viewership records, and as viewers tuned in, they saw Foote—lots of him. Foote appeared in almost ninety spots, substantially more than the other commentators in the series. Added together, his appearances represented almost one hour of the eleven-hour series. Foote's combination of knowledge about the war, his gentlemanliness, and his honeydewed mellifluous voice gained him a coast-to-coast following. Hundreds of news outlets ran stories on Foote, and organizations rushed to sign him up for speaking engagements. Trying to capitalize on this Foote frenzy, Random House printed thousands of copies of his novels. The publishing house had even greater luck with the sale of Foote's trilogy. In the first eight months following the television series, Foote earned more than $750,000 in royalties. The soft-spoken, punctilious man had charmed a nation.

Suddenly, Foote became the country's expert on the Civil War and even its caretaker of History. In such issues as Disney's proposal to build a historical theme park in Manassas, Virginia, just miles away from the crucial Civil War battles of First Manassas and Second Manassas, Foote served as a de facto spokesman for protecting the country's historical sites and the appropriate administration of history. Forrest, however, represented a much more difficult case. Based on his past calls for racial integration—even as early as the mid-1930s—Foote presumably would have anxieties championing anyone who had exploited blacks. Although his feelings about integration had cooled somewhat in the wake of affirmative-actions programs, which he thought stunted blacks' initiative, Foote still understood the injustices suffered by Southern blacks. In a C-Span interview just two years before the Forrest event, Foote said, "Slavery is a huge stain on us [Southerners]. We all carry it. I carry it deep in my bones, the consequences of slavery." He also knew the personal costs of such a system. As he told another interviewer, "There was not a morsel of food in my mouth, not a shred of clothes on my back, not an hour of education that I ever had that didn't come out of exploiting some black somewhere or other."

Foote also knew that racial incidents tended to cling to Forrest. In one of the most controversial incidents of the entire Civil War, Forrest was involved in what became known as the Fort Pillow Massacre. Forrest's troops pinned black Union soldiers on a Mississippi River bluff 50 miles north of Memphis. The Union troops faced the daunting choice of jumping off the 300-foot bluff or placing themselves at the mercy of Forrest's bloodthirsty troops. Neither choice offered sanctuary. Those who jumped were riddled with gunfire from the cliff, and those black soldiers who surrendered were shot. For *The Civil War*, Foote quoted a Confederate sergeant's letter about the Fort Pillow incident: "The poor, deluded negroes would run up to our men, fall upon their knees and with uplifted hands scream for mercy, but were ordered to their feet and then shot down."

Even worse, Forrest's creation of the Klan, an organization that Foote had always manifested particular disgust and hatred for, should have sufficed to tip the scales against him. As a close friend to the Percy family, Delta patricians who had always prided themselves on their opposition to the Ku Klux Klan, Foote had a hatred of the Klan instilled in him from an early age. During the 1960s, Foote, as he advertised during later interviews, had gotten "crossways" with the Klan.

\*\*\*

The contradictions that Foote felt in evaluating Nathan Bedford Forrest had structured his entire life. He hated the injustices of the South, but he still longed to be a part of the culture's elite, as had been his millionaire grandfathers before they lost their money in the 1910s and early 1920s. Foote reconciled these contradictions, ultimately, by conceiving aristocracy not as a money-based grouping, but as a rubric signifying good judgment and breeding—"civilization," in the words of Daniel Singal's account of a typical New South reaction to modernity. Foote also escaped these dilemmas by taking flight into his private world of art, which had long since served as his "religion." Not unlike one of his literary heroes, the French writer Marcel Proust, who retired to his cork-lined room, Foote wanted to push the world away and just work. Such a posture was, to some extent, predetermined. Foote lived in an era whose governing aesthetic was formalism, a principle that claimed that artistic language was distinctly different from everyday language. He subscribed to a notion of the word as being in the world, but not of the world. Art, in other words, provided Foote a refuge that he was all too ready to find.

In spite of Foote's best efforts to stave off the cultural dilemmas of his era, the politics of Southern life constitute the very heart of his work. At its best, Foote's writing dramatized tensions related to racial and regional identity. At its worst, it fell back on the cold social prescriptions of Southern paternalism. That war between the suppression of politics and its unintentional reemergence appears nowhere more clearly than in *The Civil War: A Narrative*. Foote's trilogy dramatizes the plights of individual soldiers, but it does so at the expense of the historical and political events surrounding the war, events that were tearing Foote apart by the region's internecine crisis. He escaped by returning, ironically, to a nineteenth-century historical event, one made even more distant by whittling it down to just sabers, avoiding the political elements responsible for the rattling of those weapons.

Yet, what is striking about *The Civil War* is its active engagement with the events of the civil rights movement. Just how closely these events affected his own writing project are suggested in the bibliographical note at the end of volume II, *Fredericksburg to Meridian* (1963), where he attacked Alabama Governor George Wallace, Mississippi Governor Ross Barnett, and Arkansas Governor Orval Faubus for "reproducing, in their actions during several of the years that went into the writing of this volume, much that was least admirable in the position my forebears occupied when they stood up to Lincoln." To read *The Civil War* in this way is not to diminish its accomplishments, only to qualify its impetus. Read through the lens of Foote's contemporary politics, the trilogy becomes more tortured—and maybe, finally, more heroic.

In the face of the oncoming storm, Foote began to speak, and when he did, he reflected a strategy that had governed his retreat into his art. Torn between the poles of vilifying Forrest, which the protesters had done, or absolving him, which the Confederate reenactors were doing, Foote staked out a limited position and subscribed to it so faithfully and fervently that he could talk past not only dissenters' questions, but also past any questions lingering in his own conscience. At the celebration, Foote judged Forrest solely on the merits of his military skill. By framing the argument in this way, Forrest could be easily defended, for although his tactics were unorthodox at best, capricious at worst, military leaders around the globe recognized him as a brilliant tactician, the only soldier on either side of the Civil War who had risen from private to general. As Foote told the crowd, "He would be a study in any command school." Foote's criterion of military genius did not apologize for Forrest's slave-owning activities, but neither did it put the general in the protesters' noose.

Foote even made allowances for Forrest's Klan activities. A year earlier at this same event, Foote had declared that although he despised the twentieth-century Klan, Forrest's Klan was far different. Whereas the present-day Klan espoused an extremist nativism that demonized blacks, Jews, and Catholics—threats to Anglo-Saxon superiority—Forrest had only been interested in rooting out Northern carpetbaggers. "The Klan of the 19th Century is not the Klan of today," Foote told one Forrest supporter.

To be sure, Foote's opinion of Forrest had not been crafted to avoid the protesters' slings and arrows; but, writ large, this act revealed how Foote had avoided deep ambivalences about the South, history, and the present. However strategic the lauding of Forrest's military accomplishments were, they could not conceal his anxieties about defending Forrest. During his speech, Foote almost acknowledged the validity of the protesters' claims: "I have enormous respect for him—*no matter what your politics are or the color of your skin."*

Like some Greek chorus responding to the oracle's declaration, thunder clapped and rumbled, lightning blazed, and within moments, a violent storm swept across the field. Hoop-skirted women and gray-clad lawyers sprinted for cover. Foote himself scrambled into one of the tents yards away, followed by a group of people, including Bailey. In the midst of the blinding storm, brutal with its lightning and downpour, Bailey questioned Foote about how anyone could respect Forrest. Others in the tent listened quietly to the spirited debate about Forrest raging between them, until, mutually, "they agreed that they disagreed."

Within twenty minutes the storm had abated, its only remainder the drip, drip of the rain running from the trees to the tents. Emerging from the tent, Foote saw that the crowd had scattered and dispersed. With few people around, Foote said his good-byes, hurriedly scurried out to his car, and headed home, back to the quiet privacy of his study. In the midst of an era that has increasingly seen the South not as a home for cotton, but as a host for national corporations, Foote has become, according to Bailey, the "last of a dying breed."

*Shelby Foote*

# CHAPTER ONE

# Roots

The gods visit the sins of the fathers upon the children.
—Euripides, *Phrixus*

It is not only what we have inherited from our fathers that
exists again in us, but all sorts of old dead ideas and all kinds
of old dead beliefs and things of that kind.
—Henrik Ibsen, *Ghosts*

JUST AS SHELBY FOOTE had an enormous inheritance yanked
from under him, so too did Foote's great-great-great-grandfather
have a fortune stolen from him. Whereas Foote's grandfathers lost
their money through poker playing and crop speculation, George
Foote II's mid-eighteenth-century loss—a "major crisis," according to
a family historian—came after cousins refused to give the Footes land
that they considered themselves entitled to. Their loss amounted to
hundreds—perhaps thousands—of acres of some of the richest tobacco
land in Prince William County. Although he could have stayed in
Brent Town and enjoyed a comfortable tobacco-growing existence,
without the additional land, George feared some corresponding
diminution in his family's social status. As much as any place in the
American colonies, Virginia society depended on extravagant display,
and such exhibitions themselves required money and the cachet available only to the largest landowners.

The Footes had been accustomed to fraternizing with the best of
Virginia society for almost a century—since Richard Foote, grandfather

of George, settled in the colony's Northern Neck region in 1688. Born in 1666 to a prominent mercantile family, Richard traveled to the New World as an agent for his father and uncle, Nicholas Hayward, an absentee owner of Chotank, a Virginia plantation. The two Footes and Hayward seized an opportunity presented by France's increasing intolerance of Protestants under the reign of Louix XIV, bought 30,000 acres, and established a French Huguenot settlement in Brent Town, 35 miles inland from Chesapeake Bay. Only a handful of French families arrived on Virginia soil, however, as the Huguenots waited to see whether a possible English victory against France in the 1688 War of Succession might usher in Protestantism in France.

As manager of an empty American settlement, the bachelor Richard suffered through a decade of bleak years. Things took a turn for the better in 1698, however, when Foote inherited Chotank after his uncle's death. Suddenly wealthy, Foote built a large house, Cedar Grove, on the grounds of Chotank. From his newly established position as a large plantation owner, Foote now became part of the "social whirl" of the Prince William County plantocratic world, socializing and fox hunting with the leading Virginia families, such as the Washingtons, Fitzhughs, and Marshalls, people who would go on to be cornerstones of American democracy.

With his wife, Elizabeth, Foote had five children over the course of the next decade, including his second son, George I, born around 1706. Under primogeniture, second was of no more importance than last, and while his older brother, Richard, inherited Chotank and its surrounding lands, George had to settle for 2200 acres of the Brent Town land, which was in the process of being divided between the Foote and Hayward families. In 1737 George took his wife, the former Frances Berryman, and his two sons, George II and Gilson, born in 1734 and 1736, respectively, to Brent Town at the extreme southwestern corner of Prince William County. Although they were farther away from the county's social life, George, and later his sons, did well financially.

After George I's death in 1759, things began to sour for the family. A Chotank uncle, Richard Foote III, believed that he had been shortchanged 1450 acres in the Brent Town division of land. When he lost that suit, Richard "unjustly . . . proposed to recover a part of the land . . . by sharing the loss with George's descendants." George II fumed. Not only had his father's acreage been divvied up among the family, creating even smaller tracts on which to plant tobacco, but now his uncle demanded that he cut deep into his own holdings to pay for a division of land that he had not even been party to. George II initially refused to honor his uncle's request, but after an arbitrator ordered George II and his brother to pay Richard £100 for the disputed land, Foote made preparations to exit Virginia, a place where his possessions no longer could keep pace with his name.

George II quickly sold his land, using some of the money to pay the judgment and some to pay for the moving of his family 275 miles deep into the hinterlands of North Carolina, where they could start anew. After a lengthy trip with his wife, Margaret, and their four children, they decided to settle in what would become Hillsboro. North Carolina, however, was no Canaan.

Like Virginia, Foote's new colony had its own problems. In a place where there was no established social order, as there had been in Virginia, George II found himself having to walk a tight line between his English sympathies and the North Carolinians' aggressive colonial attitudes. Nevertheless, in this hotbed of conflict, George II's money and his ability to talk himself out of difficult situations enabled him to survive and flourish. By 1779 he had amassed more than 1000 acres and owned slaves. His wealth no doubt influenced the colony's assembly and governor to name him, in 1777, to the prestigious position of justice of the peace for Caswell County. Before Margaret died, at some point during the Revolutionary War, the couple would have three more children, the first of whom—the family's fifth—was William. Born around 1772, William would be the great-great-grandfather of the future writer Shelby Foote.

Although he had garnered substantial wealth in North Carolina, George II was as unsettled as ever. In 1788 the fifty-four-year-old Foote moved yet again—125 miles to the northwestern part of South Carolina, in an area of Chester County called Brushy Fork Creek. When his family reached South Carolina, William and his brother James struck out on their own. Buying land and five slaves, they farmed together until 1805, when William moved to neighboring Union County and married Nancy Sanders Rice McDaniel, a widow.

William Foote did well over the next few years, amassing a sizable amount of land and slaves and owning a tavern. When he built a two-story house several years into his marriage, Irish stonemasons were imported to construct its exterior. William and his wife needed a large house because they had a growing family. After two daughters were born to them, on December 11, 1813, their first son, Hezekiah "Henry" William, was born.

Henry's first professional interest would not be farming, as had been the case for every generation since Richard Foote first stepped onto Virginia soil; instead, he indicated at some point in his teenage years that he wanted to be a lawyer. Soon afterward, his father made arrangements for Henry to begin "reading law" under Colonel Z. P. Herndon, the customary practice of the day for aspiring attorneys. Even while he pored through law books, Henry Foote, as he would reveal throughout his life, had a nose for opportunities. In 1832 when the state's nullification crisis developed, in which South Carolina stood poised to secede from the Union, Foote, out of civic duty or out of some hot-blooded Byronic response, quickly raised a volunteer company and was commissioned as a first lieutenant by South Carolina Governor Robert Y. Hayne.

After President Andrew Jackson threatened the South Carolinians, the crisis soon played itself out, but Foote's blood was up. Agitated, he craved adventure, and he was not alone. The country was streaming west. "From 1815 to 1850," according to James McPherson, "the population of the region west of the Appalachians grew nearly three times as fast as the original thirteen states." Provided one had the right amount of pluck and skullduggery, opportunity beckoned. One of the principal routes lay virtually beneath Foote, as residents from the Carolinas tumbled over the Appalachians in pursuit of unclaimed lands in Alabama, Mississippi, and western Tennessee.

Along with friend James Harrison, Henry Foote joined this horde in 1833. For weeks they traveled westward. Finally, in early 1834 they reached the town of Columbus in northeastern Mississippi, a Tombigbee River town that predated Mississippi's statehood in 1817. Close to the edge of the developed territory, Columbus would be the place where Harrison put down roots, but Foote would not settle there. Hearing news of the creation of a new town just 30 miles south, he pressed on. Noxubee County was carved out of lands ceded by the Choctaw Indians under the 1830 Treaty of Dancing Rabbit Creek, and had been created by the Mississippi legislature on December 23, 1833. Foote apparently arrived in the midst of the discussions for the development of Noxubee's county seat, Macon, held between February and April 1834. When Macon was formally established on April 8, 1834, Foote was one of the first landowners, purchasing several lots southeast of the courthouse. At twenty-two, he had settled into the town that he would call home for the rest of his life.

After arriving in Macon, Foote became a member of the Mississippi bar. Foote wasted no time; he ran for Noxubee County Circuit Court clerk in 1835 and was elected. Now in a position of prominence, Foote believed that he needed the social status equal to his political position. Although the Mississippi social pecking order was still an undefined mass, certain names carried a great amount of weight. One family, in particular, moved Foote: the Dades. Not only were Colonel H. C. and Catherine Lewis Dade originally Virginians, but they had a lineage that tied them to one of the new country's founders: Catherine Dade's grandmother was George Washington's sister. As importantly, they had an attractive daughter, Frances Lucinda Dade. Foote proposed, and they were married on November 15, 1836.

With his family life in order, Foote began his career as circuit court clerk. In this position, he administered legal disputes in the highly litigious society of the Mississippi frontier. With cotton prices having steadily increased since the 1830s, Mississippi enjoyed boom times, ushering in an influx of people both eager and desperate to get a share of the windfall. Although he was overwhelmed with work, Foote handled the pressure with great skill. According to one commentator, he "discharge[d] the trust . . . honestly, faithfully and capably." His success did not go unnoted. When he ran for office again in 1839, not only was he reelected, but his salary kept pace with his success. By the end of his tenure, county officials had boosted Foote's salary to $6000. Although this figure represented roughly one-third of what the wealthiest Mississippi planters were making at the same time, it was a "very lucrative" figure for a Mississippi civil servant, significant enough to be noted in an 1884 *Planters' Journal* article.

Foote's early success signaled that greater things stood in the offing. After he left the circuit court clerk's position in the 1840s, he began his own law practice, and in just a few years, area residents recognized him as a leading lawyer, a product of his "brilliant intellect." Like many other men of the period, Foote also had farming interests on the side. During the 1840s and 1850s he purchased two Noxubee County farms and one hundred slaves. Nine miles east of Macon stood his 500-acre cotton plantation, which was supplied with horses and mules raised at his 1000-acre stock farm, his "special pride," two miles south of Macon.

Although his career steadily moved forward, Foote soon had to deal with tragedy. After giving birth to eight children, two of whom died in infancy, Frances had yet another pregnancy—her last. While delivering Huger Lee Foote on January 25, 1856, Shelby Foote's great-grandmother, Frances, died of what was called child-bed fever, a bacterial infection that usually resulted from unsterile obstetric procedures.

With seven motherless children, Henry Foote felt compelled to marry again. Within a matter of months, he had "contracted" a marriage with Mary Foote, a marriage that in a later era and place would have raised eyebrows. Mary was the cousin of his first wife (the two mothers of the brides were sisters), and she was also the daughter of his cousin, Gilson Foote. In a frontier region driven by practical concerns, Henry Foote felt no compunctions about wedding Mary, and by the end of the same year in which Foote's wife died, the two were married. Their union would produce one daughter, Mollie Frances, before Mary Foote died on November 2, 1859.

During his tenure as circuit court clerk, Foote had joined the Whig Party, a strong presence in the Deep South in the decades before the country would become a two-party system divided along strictly regional lines. With its principle of industrious work as the royal road to wealth, the Whig philosophy particularly appealed to upwardly mobile entrepreneurs such as Foote. His allegiance ran so strong that in the 1840s he even established a Whig newspaper, the *Macon Intelligencer.*

By 1850, however, the Whigs began to wilt as the party struggled to articulate a consistent position on expansionism and slavery. Scrambling, Southern Whigs reintroduced themselves as the Constitutional Union Party, a group that declared national unity a constitutional imperative, even though detractors called the machinations of this "Old Gentleman's Party" an attempt to maintain the economic status quo. Foote joined the Constitutional Unionists in 1851, and he ran as the Unionist candidate for the county's Mississippi House of Representatives seat in 1856. In winning the seat, Foote became part of a Unionist renaissance in the South—particularly in large cotton-growing areas.

A nationwide recession that began in 1847 and extended into the 1850s increased demand for cotton by English mills and New England factories; the recession drove cotton prices up more than 50 percent to 11½ cents near the end of the 1850s. Cotton production, in turn, surged. The 1858 crop was particularly heavy; at four million bales, it was double the annual average. Such prosperity strengthened the Unionists' philosophy of economics dictating politics. Ironically, however, the party became the victim of its own successes. Particularly because the North suffered an economic downturn in 1858, the South's good fortune emboldened fire-eaters. As South Carolina Senator James Hammond told the U.S. Senate in late 1858, Southerners were "unquestionably the most prosperous people on earth, realizing ten to twenty per cent on their capital with every prospect of doing as well for a long time to come. The slaveholding South is now the controlling power of the world. . . . No power on earth dares . . . to make war on cotton. Cotton is king."

In the face of this bombast, Unionists tried to quell swelling Southern nationalism, especially strong in the aftermath of John Brown's failed slave rebellion at Harpers Ferry, Virginia, in 1859. The platform for the 1860 Constitutional Union presidential candidate, John C. Bell, a wealthy Tennessee planter, signaled their growing distance from the Southern and American populace. While Republican and Democratic platforms ballooned in this tension-filled election, the Unionists forewent formal policies, adopting instead a resolution claiming "to recognize no political principle other than *the Constitution . . . the Union . . . and the Enforcement of the Laws.*" Although he ran well in certain Southern plantation-holding areas, including Noxubee County, Bell ran a distant fourth behind Republican Abraham Lincoln, Southern Democrat John C. Breckinridge, and Northern Democrat Stephen Douglas. In the hostile postelection climate, the Unionists fought a war of survival, but even in their strongholds, they could not stem the tide set off by South Carolina's December 1860 separation from the Union. At the county's January 1861 convention called to debate Mississippi's secession ordinance, Foote, as Noxubee County's leading politician, had the privileged place of making the final convention speech. Rising to the occasion, Foote "opposed secession with all the fervor of his mature manhood." But mere words were not enough to slake the imaginations of men lusting after martial glory: Like most of the rest of the state, Noxubee County voted for Mississippi to secede from the Union.

If Henry Foote's pride was hurt by the vote, he did not grieve long. Anticipating the loyalty that Robert E. Lee in a few weeks would display in forsaking the top U.S. military post for service for his native Virginia, Foote quickly raised a company, Foote's Mounted Men, "composed of many of the best citizens of Noxubee." When the Confederate government incorporated the company, they became the 1st Mississippi Cavalry, with Foote as its colonel.

The 1st Mississippi was assigned to home regiment duty, which involved ensuring that slaves did not form a fifth column. By the end of 1861 Foote's troops were called up for service, where they were organized in the corps of General Leonidas Polk, the "Fighting Bishop." Union General Ulysses S. Grant had successfully pierced Tennessee's Cumberland River defenses of Fort Donelson and Fort Henry, and now Union corps had spread out over the Mid-South. The Union Army soon moved to capture Cairo, Illinois, which stood at the confluence of the Mississippi and Ohio Rivers. Fending off those efforts, the 1st Mississippi Cavalry fought Grant at Belmont, Missouri, a minor battle in which Confederate troops retreated initially and then later recouped their losses.

After the winter encampment, the 1st Mississippi Cavalry continued to play a part in the pursuit of Grant. In the early spring of 1862 the Confederate Army attempted to pin Grant against the Tennessee River near a southern Tennessee church called Shiloh, a site that had little value other than in its proximity to the Confederate-held railroad center of Corinth, Mississippi. On April 6, Confederate General Albert Sidney Johnston launched a surprise attack, which included Foote and the 1st Mississippi. Over the two bloodiest days in American military history until that point, the Union armies suffered 1754 killed, 8408 wounded, and 2885 captured, while Confederate losses amounted to 1723 killed, 8012 wounded, and 959 missing. The total of 23,741 killed, wounded, captured, and missing soldiers represented an aggregate surpassing all of the casualties for the nation's first *three* wars. Although Foote somehow emerged unscathed, he came close to suffering injury when Union soldiers shot his horse's tail off.

After Shiloh, Governor Charles Clarke recalled Foote, asking him to organize the state militia in the eastern part of Mississippi. Foote accepted the offer gladly. Not only was he weary from the long year of soldiering, but his children needed looking after. Over the next few months, Foote raised thirteen cavalry companies, which became a 1300-member regiment. This new 1st Mississippi Cavalry, which was under state control, provided homeland defense. During the final three years of the war, Foote only had one more combat experience.

In April 1863 Union Colonel Benjamin Grierson and his 1700 men set out from Memphis on an overland trip aimed at diverting attention from Grant's stratagems against Vicksburg. The "ubiquitous blue column," as Shelby Foote would later describe Grierson's phantomlike movements, cast shadows in every direction, but seemingly bore no substance. Eastern Mississippians who had been previously spared military action, clamored for safety, and newspaper editors, in stories that trailed the colonel's moves, screamed for his defeat and capture. In the face of Grierson's destruction stood Foote and his brigade. "He was probably shaking in his boots," his great-grandson later laughed. Although Foote's brigade set out to capture Grierson's troops, they found themselves doing little more than filling up his wake, giving chase until Grierson was well past them. After Grierson's 1863 raid, Foote's Civil War fighting was over. The western theater had moved eastward, as General William Tecumseh Sherman moved his troops toward Atlanta. For the rest of the war, Foote would hole up with his troops around eastern Mississippi, watching for any new Grierson to come down the pike.

Two years later, the end of the war brought bittersweet peace for Foote. As was the case for many Southerners, the war had cut deep into his personal property. Not only had he lost his slaves, but his land had gone virtually unattended for several years. In spite of the fact that he had been in the vicinity of his farm, skeins of weeds and tares littered his fields. Doubt flooded Foote, now well into his fifties, as he questioned his next move. Yet, he began mustering the same tornadic energy that had marked his arrival in Mississippi three decades earlier. Now he had the support of a new wife, Sybilla Messinger, likely a war widow, whom he had married in December 1863. Drawing on this new source of strength, Foote began reasserting himself as one of Macon's major players. Foote's friends urged him to run for Mississippi's 6th District Circuit Court judgeship, although the position was held by a popular judge. In spite of his opponent's strength, Foote saw the election as an opportunity to revive and resuscitate himself. He ran for the seat and beat the incumbent. As a circuit court judge, Foote traveled the roads of the district, moving from town to town as the various court terms dictated. According to the *Planters' Journal,* Foote "administered justice with an even hand" and the "frequent affirmance of his decisions by the supreme court attested his profound knowledge and astute judgment of the noble science of law."

In his reelection bid four years later, Foote received a challenge from the man whom he had unseated. Foote won again, but this four-year term would be far more trying. With the congressional reconstruction acts taking effect, the dynamics of the South were inverted almost overnight, as blacks had been given not only the suffrage, but wider rights to property. The situation smarted for wealthy white Southerners, who found their decades-long way of life threatened. As an ex-Confederate colonel and now a public judicial figure, Foote felt targeted; but the opportunistic Foote knew how to turn demonization into gain.

In 1871 the Mississippi state government, run by former Union General E. O. C. Ord, demanded that Foote take the oath of allegiance. He cavalierly refused. Foote received the request again from Ord's office, and again he refused. Finally, at the end of a court term in Columbus, Foote ceremoniously stepped down from the bench. Whether his intention had been some principled attack against the government, a selfish promotion of himself, or both, Foote's ploy worked. Three years later, his star was in the ascendant. Foote joined the Democrats, who had become the vehicle for a Bourbon-tinged white supremacy, and was elected in 1875 to the Mississippi State Senate to represent a district that included parts or all of Noxubee, Kemper, and Neshoba Counties.

Henry Foote did not invest all of his energy into his political affairs, however. During the years after his resignation of his judgeship, Foote revitalized his farming interests. Far from being the weed-infested lands that greeted him after the war, his property had regained its antebellum magnificence. Nor was he content to farm just in Noxubee County. Sybilla's deceased husband had bequeathed her a 3000-acre plantation in the Mississippi Delta, the 200-by-50-mile magnolia leaf–shaped region tumbling south from the Memphis bluffs down to the Vicksburg hills. As the beneficiary for centuries of a runoff that swept the continent from the West Virginia plateaus to the highest points of the Rocky Mountains, the Delta boasted a rich, deep topsoil. In fact, when state geologist E. N. Lowe surveyed the region in 1857, he predicted that the land was so rich that all of the continent would someday be oriented around this area, which was not even the size of New Jersey. "Whatever the delta of the Nile may once have been," Lowe wrote, "will only be a shadow of what the alluvial plain of the Mississippi will then be."

By 1860 Lowe's prediction had already come true. The interior of the Yazoo-Mississippi Alluvial Delta, as it was more properly known, was "practically roadless and altogether malarial . . . a melange of impenetrable canebrakes, swamps, and wilderness, the haunt of panther and bear and alligators," as Shelby Foote would later describe it. However, the settled areas closest to the Mississippi River boasted a handful of the country's richest counties: Bolivar, Coahoma, Issaquena, and Tunica. Together, these four counties had an average per capita income of $18,438, a figure far above the $4,380 per capita average for all Southerners. In the southwestern Delta, tiny Issaquena County claimed the region's greatest concentration of wealth. With a per capita worth of $26,800, Issaquena was the second wealthiest U.S. county.

Even with these success stories, Delta farming had grown especially difficult after the Civil War. The emancipation of slaves created a labor shortage for the region, and many former plantations had fallen into disrepair. According to Delta planter and U.S. Senator James L. Alcorn, the region had "reverted back to substantially the condition of waste from which it had been reclaimed in the [eighteen] fifties." Furthermore, as owners of vast amounts of land, Delta farmers suffered particularly harshly under the high tax rate of the reconstruction governments, and bankruptcies loomed on many doors. "Every year my capital gets less and less," George Collins wrote. "There is nothing to live for here."

By the mid-1870s—around the time of Henry Foote's election to the Mississippi Senate—the financial and labor woes of Delta planters had bottomed out. Thanks to the advent of various forms of sharecropping, climbing cotton prices, and a sympathetic Democratic state government, the Delta "soon produced enough success stories to reclaim its reputation as the most profitable cotton-growing region in the South." In this new era, Henry Foote began his Delta farming operations.

He was not ready to take on the challenge personally, however. More than sixty years old now and comfortable in Macon, the paterfamilias did not want to take on the awesome task of growing cotton in the Delta, particularly on a tract that was among the largest in the region. Instead, his youngest son, Hugh, would do the honors. Whether Hugh volunteered for his father's farm duty is unclear. Possibly the job fell to him because, at the time, Hugh had been the only son without a career. (His brothers had gone on to be lawyers or planters.) In any case, beginning in the early 1870s Hugh submitted to a decade-long educational odyssey. While many sons of wealthy Mississippians landed at Yale, Princeton, or the University of Virginia, Hugh had a more practical education thrust upon him: Bryant and Stratton's Commercial College, a Cincinnati school known for its instruction in bookkeeping and management. After Hugh graduated in 1872, his father sent him to Poughkeepsie, New York, where he spent three years at the Eastman College, graduating in 1875. Yet even with these degrees under his son's belt, Henry Foote did not think Hugh quite ready to tame the Delta. Henry Foote wanted his son to have more experience, so he had Hugh engage in "cotton merchandising" in Macon before he sent him to study operations at a Haney Grove, Texas, farm that was the size of the Delta plantations. By 1877 Henry considered him ready to take on the family's little corner of the Delta.

Hugh Foote was only one of Shelby Foote's grandfathers making an entry into the Delta about this time. A Viennese Jew, Morris Rosenstock, was a nobody when he stepped off a riverboat onto the Greenville shore. Not unlike William Faulkner's Thomas Sutpen in *Absalom, Absalom!* who "first rode into town out of no discernible past," Rosenstock seemingly materialized out of thin air. Yet in the years to come, Rosenstock would grow, if not as notorious as the fictional Sutpen, almost as wealthy.

Many of the facts related to Rosenstock's birth, origin, and immigration are hazy. Although his date of birth is unclear, the Foote family believes that he was born sometime between 1856 and 1858. In the 1880 U.S. census, Rosenstock lists New York as his birthplace; that claim seems to have been part of a fiction that he employed not only to ease employment possibilities, but also possibly as a ploy to evade government officials. With the Prussians combing over central European villages in the early 1870s to pick up able-bodied men for their war with France, Rosenstock may have left Austria to avoid conscription. As well as his birthplace, Rosenstock's parentage also seems at issue. In the same 1880 census, Rosenstock claimed that his mother was Austrian, but he failed to list any nationality for his father.

Although Rosenstock could not claim the family inheritance that the Footes could, his life in rich, cosmopolitan Vienna provided him with a cultural background, however nascent, that the frontier Foote ancestors could not claim. As Mike Gold would later write about New York's Jewish immigrants, "These Jews came from the world of peasant Europe, where art is inherited with one's father's farm, and is a simple fact of life." At the very least, Shelby Foote's grandfather's connection to Vienna provided the writer with an attributable source for his own artistic interests. If his own proclivities were the product of any family member, Foote later claimed in an interview, his "grandfather Rosenstock" bestowed them upon him.

Rosenstock's route from New York to Greenville and Washington
County, Mississippi, is unknown; like one of the characters in Shelby
Foote's *Jordan County,* he may have ridden a steamboat down the Ohio
and Mississippi Rivers, disembarking in Greenville, which had become
the central port for the Delta. However he arrived, by 1880 Rosenstock
was working as bookkeeper on Avon Plantation in southern Washington
County, a plantation formerly owned by a Dr. Peters. Depending on
the hour of the day, Peters was a county surveyor, a practicing doctor,
and a planter. When this "old southern gentleman of the Delta" died
in 1875, he gave each of his four daughters one of his four plantations.
His youngest daughter, Minnie, inherited Avon Plantation, where
Rosenstock worked. Before long, Rosenstock parlayed his bookkeeping position into a courtship with his mistress. "How a Jew bookkeeper
managed to marry the daughter of a planter, I don't know," Shelby
Foote later said, "but he swung it somehow." On April 9, 1886 they
were married in a ceremony at Minnie's mother's house. No longer an
outsider, Rosenstock had become a card-carrying Deltan.

While Rosenstock farmed Avon, Minnie began delivering babies.
Within several years of their marriage, the couple had four daughters.
The first daughter, Claire, died two months after she was born in 1887,
but the next two lived: Maude, in 1888, and Lillian, the writer's
mother, in 1894. In the process of delivering her fourth child, Minnie
died of child-bed fever. Devastated, Rosenstock named the daughter
after his fallen wife.

In several years, Rosenstock would marry a Greenville woman by
the name of Mathilde (Kelly) Hafster, but for now he sought to work
his way into the exclusive Delta planter membership. In addition to
owning Avon Plantation, by 1898 Rosenstock also had part ownership
in Sunnyside, a plantation across the river from Greenville in Arkansas.
Suggesting the status that he had achieved, his two partners ranked
among the most important figures in the town, if not the region: O. B.
Crittenden was an important Delta planter and businessman and
future U.S. Senator LeRoy Percy, called the "Gray Eagle of the Delta,"
was the patriarch of a clan that was arguably the leading Delta family.

Membership in that elite club did not turn out to be so fortuitous—
the three men would be cited by the U.S. Department of Justice as

guilty of "debt peonage" in 1907. For a decade, the three owners had imported Italian workers, in what they considered an "experiment," a novel way to deal with the Delta's ongoing labor shortages. The three owners advanced the Italian immigrants money for travel to Arkansas, but then used that debt as an ongoing lien against their labor. When the workers complained to federal officials about this slavery, the Department of Justice sent in Mary Quackenbos to investigate. Over the complaints of Rosenstock and the other owners, Quackenbos determined that there had indeed been criminal wrongdoings. As titular head of the company, Crittenden was arrested and taken to Washington, D.C., where he avoided prosecution only because Percy coerced his friend President Roosevelt to call off the investigation. Although Roosevelt did not condone the practices of the O. B. Crittenden Company, the president felt beholden to the hospitality that Percy had shown him on a Delta bear hunt in the early 1900s. Pressured by the president, the Department of Justice then agreed to call off the investigation, but only after the Sunnyside owners agreed to release their Italian workers.

No matter how much training he endured, no amount of preparation could have fully equipped the twenty-two-year old Hugh Foote for the responsibility of managing a 3000-acre plantation. Coupled with this burden was deep sadness. In Macon on March 1, 1878 Foote had married his longtime love interest, Mattie Cavett, and he brought his new bride to Sharkey County. Mattie was not long for the Delta—or for this world—as she died six months later. Although it is not clear what the cause of death was, given the epidemic raging through the Mississippi Valley that year, she may have died of yellow fever. Depressed, Foote channeled his bereavement into his work.

While others in the wild Delta found "clearing the land . . . so arduous and expensive that many purchasers quickly gave up and sold out," Foote seemed to thrive on it. Henry Foote liked his son's results, and figuring that he could deliver similar results on even more land, Henry began looking to buy other plantations. Geologically rich though it was, Delta land was still inexpensive into the early 1880s because the region lacked flood control and an inland transportation system. Forty-acre sections of land were sometimes "swapped for livestock or rifles." Henry Foote took advantage of these low costs to snap up two other Delta plantations: Council Bend and Egremont. The former legislator no doubt knew that land values would soon be increasing because the Louisville, New Orleans, and Texas Railway planned to build a railroad system that would carry cotton quickly to the New Orleans and Memphis exchanges. Even better for Delta landowners, New York investors backing the proposed railroad demanded assurances from state and federal officials that flood control would be forthcoming.

With these improvements promised, demand for land soon mushroomed. Between 1879 and 1889 acreage in cultivation doubled and production boomed. The Delta's 1889 cotton crop represented a 160-percent increase from the 1879 crop. The Footes joined the land grab, leveraging their plantations for three more in Washington and Sharkey Counties: Mounds, Hardscrabble, and Mount Holly. Of the three, Hugh had a special fondness for Mount Holly. It stood on a rise several feet higher than the surrounding land, enough to make a difference during any floods. But it was Mount Holly's plantation house that served as its glory. Located on the northeastern shore of Lake Washington, a Mississippi River oxbow lake, the house crowned a rise above the lake full of ancestral cypress trees, whose knobby knees played host to herons and pelicans. The house itself mirrored the scenic vista. Based on models produced probably by Calvin Veaux or the Philadelphia architect Samuel Sloan, the twenty-room Italianate house featured seven bedrooms, a parlor, and a ballroom large enough to hold an orchestra. Mount Holly was a perfect place to host the social events expected of Foote and his new wife, Kate, whom he had married in 1882. Hugh loved Mount Holly so much that he set up a series of installment payments to buy it from his father. There, he began to fill up its rooms as his wife gave birth to Katherine and Huger, before giving birth, in 1890, to Shelby Dade Foote, the writer's father. A fourth child, Elizabeth, was born later.

There would be plenty of social occasions to fill Mount Holly, as Foote became more and more of a public figure. In 1885 he was elected as Sharkey County sheriff, a position that under Mississippi state law gave him substantial power. Far different from his father's assertive style,

Hugh led by example, and community members gravitated to that solid stability. In 1887 they reelected him as sheriff, and in 1889 they elected him as state senator from Mississippi's 20th District. There was, reports one source, "no solicitation on his part" for the Senate seat; even so, he was "nominated by acclamation."

By the time that his father died in 1899, Hugh had almost completely paid for Mount Holly. Henry Foote's bequeathment to his youngest son was Mount Holly and the rest of his Delta plantations. Almost overnight, Hugh became sole owner of one of the region's largest farming operations. Journeying back to Macon for the funeral, Hugh Foote found that, even in death, his father wanted to let family members know that he was still the polestar for their compasses. Theatrical to the end, the colonel had a special assignment for his fourth wife, the former Eleanor Curtiss, a younger woman whom he had married in the 1880s. Henry Foote insisted that his wife erect a cenotaph for his tomb. On one side Foote was buried, and on the other sides would now rest his previous three wives.

After his father's death, Hugh Foote continued to farm the five Delta plantations. With the demand for cotton still strong in the 1910s, Foote amassed great amounts of wealth, a net worth that his grandson would later peg at "close to a million dollars." Times had never been better—or so they seemed. Although it may have motivated him earlier, money, seemingly limitless as it had become, had now lost its appeal. Hugh Foote needed new thrills, stimulations commensurate with the excitement he had earlier received from his herculean conquest of the Delta plantations. At first, Foote had been able to stave off his need for novelties through activities—hunting, in particular—and Foote had gained a reputation for his crack marksmanship. In Shelby Foote's *Tournament,* which is based on his grandfather's life, during a cross-country odyssey of winning shooting contest after contest, Hugh Bart is told that he had the "most spectacular style . . . ever seen." Given Hugh Foote's hunting acumen, not surprisingly, when he invited Theodore Roosevelt down to the Delta to hunt bear in the 1890s, LeRoy Percy asked Foote to serve as their guide.

But even hunting soon lost its appeal in the thick lethargy that settled around him. In 1910 Foote put Mount Holly up for sale and moved with his family to Greenville. Among other things, the town offered Foote a new opportunity: gambling. Although he had played cards recreationally throughout his life, Foote's card playing soon bordered on the pathological. He began gambling everywhere, including Memphis card parlors, but he usually played at the Greenville Elks Club, a Greek-colonnaded building two doors down from the Greenville Methodist Church. In this temple the million-dollar fortune that Hugh Foote and his father had amassed began to hemorrhage. At first, Foote gambled with a certain discipline. Similar to Hugh Bart's insuring that "he came out farther ahead on a winning night than he trailed behind on a losing one, for he followed a rule by which he must quit when he had dropped two hundred dollars in a game," Foote knew, initially, when to head home.

Drinking and his ego, however, gradually displaced his inveterate rule, and over a period of several years he began losing large sums. As he lost, he gambled more, sure that the next turn of the cards would rescue him. Even his wife could only helplessly watch his slide. Near the end of his life, with cancer rampaging through his stomach, the ailing Foote sat on a pillow to provide as much comfort as possible while he bet on his hands. By the time he died on July 18, 1915, he had proven himself enormously successful in squandering the family's fortune. Hugh Foote had become living proof of the roller-coaster ride that frequently characterized the life of the Delta, a place, "where the credit is easy and the crashes are hard." Over the course of two generations, he and his father had been able to assemble a tremendous fortune; that same fortune, however, had fallen fast—almost as if propelled by its sheer size and weight. It was an end that came too soon for a grandson who would spend his life and writing career poised pregnantly between a wish to have been part of the Southern elite and a thankfulness that his grandfather had saved him from the privilege of that rank.

# CHAPTER TWO

# Beginnings
## 1916–1935

For rebellion is as the sin of witchcraft, and stubbornness is
as iniquity and idolatry.
                                        —I Samuel 15:23

Poetry is man's rebellion against being what he is.
                                —James Branch Cabell, *Jurgen*

JUST AS HUGH FOOTE'S life ended, Shelby Sr.'s began. Growing up
among the comforts of a plantation lifestyle, replete with servants
and money, Shelby Foote Sr. assumed that he would not have to work,
that he would own his father's plantations. "He had every reason to
expect," his son said later, "that everything was going to run smoothly
for the rest of his life. He could have done what he wanted to do: play
cards, go hunting, all that kind of thing." After his family's money
dried up through his father's thin poker hands, Shelby Sr. nevertheless
continued to live the planter's life. While his friends left for Eastern
colleges to begin their apprenticeship into adulthood, Foote wandered
about town. He "didn't do anything," claims his son.

In the last months of his father's life, Shelby Foote Sr. finally got on
track. That wake-up call coincided with his interest in Lillian Rosenstock.
Lillian had returned home to Greenville after spending a year in the
early 1910s at Randolph-Macon Women's College in Lynchburg,
Virginia, a finishing school for women of a particular caste. According

to one local newspaper, she was "exceedingly popular in Greenville's social circles." Financially well-off beaux fought for her hand, but she expressed little interest. Finally, one man caught her attention: Shelby Foote. Although they had known each other for years, Lillian and Shelby did not start dating until sometime around 1914. When Morris Rosenstock learned that they were seeing each other, he objected vehemently. Rosenstock was not concerned about the financial disparity between the two families, although with Hugh Foote having lost all of his money, such an opposition on these grounds could have easily been justified. Instead, thanks to his second wife's devotion to the synagogue, Rosenstock's own faith had become essential to his identity, and he wanted his daughters to avoid marrying a Gentile. The pool of Jewish candidates was large in Greenville, and Rosenstock had already seen his oldest daughter, Maude, marry Mic Moyse, a member of one of the local Jewish families.

Such a demand for racial purity was not supposed to arise in Greenville, which touted itself as an oasis of tolerance in the xenophobic South—particularly in its supposedly seamless relationship between Christians and Jews. Greenville not only had a vibrant Jewish community, but was run, in great part, by Jews. Two of the town's three department stores, Tannenbaum's and Nells and Blum, were Jewish owned. Jews also served in important government positions. As Shelby Foote recalls, "I remember being amazed to discover that they didn't take Jews in the Country Club in Greenwood. I couldn't believe that, because in the Country Club at home, there were probably more Jews than there were Baptists."

Reflecting the inclusion of Jews in Delta life, it was Rosenstock, not Hugh Foote, who objected to the budding relationship. Aware of her father's objections, Lillian made sure that their affair was conducted *sub rosa*. At the various parties that she attended, accounts of which appeared almost daily in the local newspapers, Foote almost never attended. They continued to meet outside the public eye, but by the summer of 1915 they were ready to get married. Knowing that her father would not approve of any public event, Lillian suggested that they have a secret wedding. On July 1, 1915, just two weeks before Hugh Foote died, Lillian and Shelby, along with several friends, gathered at the home of Greenville Presbyterian Church's Reverend Frederick Graves to be married. A few hours later, they boarded a midnight train bound for New Orleans, where they would celebrate their honeymoon.

When they returned a week later, Rosenstock was still "mad as hell" about his daughter's insubordination. At the same time, he knew that the damage had been done, and when Shelby began looking for a job to support his new wife, Rosenstock, as a peace offering, tried to help his new son-in-law. Even as powerful as he was, Rosenstock could not do much with a candidate who had no work experience and was saddled with a reputation for laziness. The best that Rosenstock could do was to get Foote a job as a lowly shipping clerk at the Greenville office of the Chicago-headquartered Armour Meats and Company.

The importance of the Delta's cotton crop had only grown over the last few years, as area farmers stepped up production in an attempt to capitalize on the lower yield of boll weevil–ravaged states, a plague that the Delta avoided. In 1910 the region—accounting for one-tenth of the area of Mississippi—had produced 28 percent of the state's cotton crop. Five years later, with the European powers needing wartime supplies, demand mushroomed exponentially. In that year, the tiny region produced one-half of Mississippi's cotton crop, a figure that represented one-tenth of the country's cotton production.

Seven months into their marriage, Lillian was pregnant. It was an untimely pregnancy because she was to give birth at the end of autumn, right at the height of the cotton-picking season. During October and November every year, her father disappeared, his attention commandeered by his kingdom of fifteen gins. It was not surprising, then, that when Lillian began experiencing labor pains on November 16, 1916, her husband was 25 miles away, in Rolling Fork, helping out at a friend's father's gin. Despite Shelby's absence, Lillian managed to make it to the Greenville Sanitarium on Washington Avenue. After she checked herself in, Lillian sent a telegram down to Rolling Fork. Shelby received the news and hopped aboard the Yellow Dog, the familiar name of the Yazoo and Mississippi Valley Railroad. Slow as the train was, Foote nevertheless was with Lillian as she gave birth to Shelby Jr. on the morning of November 17.

The next day's *Daily Democrat* "In Society" column reported that, in what would become an unprophetic prediction, the young Shelby Jr. was a "nice boy."

After several days' stay at the sanitarium, Shelby Sr. took Lillian and Shelby Jr. back home. They were not there long. Beset with the new caretaking responsibilities for his wife and son, Shelby Sr. "suddenly caught fire" in his job. Championed by one of Armour's regional executives, Foote began racking up a series of promotions—advancements that would require moves to new offices. The Footes first moved to Jackson, Mississippi, and then Vicksburg, Mississippi. Within another year, the family moved to the Florida panhandle, where Shelby Sr. did a stint in the company's Pensacola office.

While her husband devoted himself to his work, Lillian focussed her energies on her son. Displaying the devotion and indulgence that she would bestow on him for the rest of her life, Lillian began marking her place. At first, her hand was most evident in Foote's clothing. Developing a sartorial interest that would last him for the rest of his life, Lillian turned him into a little Lord Fauntleroy, dressing him in stylish jackets and headware. Pictures from even the earliest age show Foote dressed in suits. In one photograph, taken when he was about four, Foote wears a leather aviator jacket and dark pants that have a military stripe running down the side, topped off with black shoes. On his head, he wears a hat that is something between an aviator's hat and a toboggan.

Because her husband was so engrossed in his work, Lillian and Shelby Jr. enjoyed plenty of time together. By 1922 Shelby Sr. had done so well that he was named manager of all of the southern Armour offices—likely his last stop before the company's Chicago headquarters. In the late summer of 1922 the Footes packed their belongings yet again to move to Mobile, where Shelby Sr. had assumed his managerial position. Shortly after the family's move to Mobile, however, tragedy struck. Shelby Sr. entered the hospital for minor surgery on his nose, but failed to tell the doctor that several days earlier he had had a wisdom tooth extracted. Not aware of this dental work, the doctor gave Foote a sedative, which infected the exposed area around the extracted tooth. Septicemia, an invasion of pathogenic bacteria into the bloodstream, quickly set in. After he began complaining of chest pains, Lillian rushed her husband to the hospital, where he survived for just a few days, as the bacteria slowly congested his heart.

During Shelby Sr.'s last days, several family friends attended to young Shelby. When word came that the boy's father had died, the guardians debated about how to break the news to the five-year-old. Knowing the possible repercussions of such a traumatic moment, they wanted to proceed with care. Finally, a man by the name of Watts agreed to take the responsibility. He approached the young boy tentatively and tried to console Foote, "Your father has gone to heaven." Little Shelby, however, saw through the mirage: His father was dead. Of greater importance for Foote were those concerns that he had heard batted about in conversations. Precociously echoing the general obsession of his culture, he asked Watts, "Who will get his money?" Although his comment revealed that Foote was too young to fully understand the significance of his father's death, the effects and consequences of that loss reverberated throughout his development, until Foote recognized it as the "most important event of my life."

The death of Foote's father also made available a freedom that sons in patriarchal cultures rarely enjoy. In these societies, fathers serve as symbolic and real guardians of acceptable ideas and avenues of action. Some male children, as Foote would later discover, could not accept such pressure; in fact, one of his Greenville friends would commit suicide because he could not measure up to his father's excessive academic demands. Free of such paternal pressure, Foote would have the opportunity to carve out his own identity, a possibility ripe with productive missteps and successes.

All the consequences of the medical oversight lay yet in the future; at present, he and his mother had to transport Shelby Sr.'s body back to the family cemetery at Mounds Plantation. While Lillian and Shelby Jr. were in Greenville, Mic and Maude made them an offer: If the Footes would move back home, they could live in the couple's two-story home. The invitation was a godsend. Not only did Lillian want to return to the comfort of familiar surroundings in this time of crisis, but she also had little money, rendering moot Shelby Jr.'s question about the fate of his father's assets.

Nor could her own father provide much aid. Like Hugh Foote, Morris Rosenstock had managed to lose almost everything that he had labored years to earn. But where it had taken the Footes two generations to transform nothing into something and then reverse the process, Foote's maternal grandfather did it in only one. At least Rosenstock's falling from the ranks of Delta giants was not solely his own doing, but part of the 1921–1922 Farm Depression. In the spring of 1921 he and other cotton factors found themselves buying cotton that had soared to nearly $1 per pound—the fabled dollar-cotton figure. By the time the crop was picked that fall, prices had plummeted to 30 cents. Rosenstock's former empire of land and gins disappeared, sold off at auction prices.

Within days of her return to Pensacola, Lillian made arrangements to move their belongings from Mobile to the Moyses' 1400 Washington Avenue home. Lillian easily could have fallen into despair, a state exacerbated by the fact that even though equipped with few marketable skills, she now had to earn a living for two people. Until her husband's death, the idea of working, as it was for most American women of the 1920s, stood at the farthest remove. Now she had no choice. Desperate to earn some money, Lillian opened up a makeshift gift shop in Greenville, where she sold a number of her possessions. From the shop's initial proceeds, she purchased a tombstone for Shelby Sr.'s grave. At the same time that she ran the shop, she also began studying shorthand to equip herself for secretarial work.

While his mother began her own career, Shelby started school at the Starling Elementary School, just a few blocks from the Moyses' house. Starling was a beginning step in a school system that, for whites, was considered the best in the state. That education came at a high price, however. Whites in Delta counties benefitted mightily from state laws that allocated education money based on the total number of school-age children, white and black, in a county. State officials did not check whether the money was spent in proportion to the racial divisions. Under this "don't ask, don't tell" policy, white county officials "simply diverted a great percentage of the money that should have gone for black schools to the education of white pupils," according to James Cobb. Like most other school systems in the Delta, where blacks outnumbered whites, the Washington County system took full advantage of this fiscal freedom. In 1929–1930, several years after Foote started at Starling, officials recorded the ratio between per pupil expenditures for whites and for blacks as seven to one, even though there were equal numbers of black and white students in the county schools.

If he was not conscious of the deprivation blacks suffered, Foote was hyperaware of the South's oppression by the North. As a young boy, he knew "reams of obscene doggerel about Lincoln" and had been instilled with the idea that "the South, founded on the highest ideals . . . [was] never guilty of the slightest strain or smudge." In the popular myth of the Lost Cause, the morally superior South had "perished because of the oppression of a stronger power," and the culture, like some penitent, wore this defeat proudly. As the grandson of two Southern planters, Foote had a special role to play: "I was given clearly to understand as a child that I was a Southern aristocrat."

Partisan though Shelby was taught to become, he was still a child, albeit a strange one. Even at this age, his fellow students considered Shelby an enigma. His classmates often did not know how to take his combination of friendliness and bombast. One student who did like Foote's unpredictability was Louie Nicholson, a mischievous boy whose actions bordered on the rambunctious. From the first grade on, the boys' antics seemingly fed off of each other and, at times, were even directed against each other. During one third-grade episode, Nicholson stabbed his friend with a pencil, injecting a ball of lead into Foote's arm. Over the next decades, the lead worked its way up Foote's arm until it rested just below his elbow.

Foote's grandfather Rosenstock also served as one of his companions and the first in a series of surrogate father figures. Rosenstock was short, and he dressed neatly and with splendor, topped off with poinsnez and chain, an appearance that signified his planter status even after had lost his money. When Rosenstock's wife and daughter went away on vacation, the young boy stayed with his grandfather. "We were very close," Foote said. "I liked him very much." The two of them slept together on Rosenstock's big featherbed, and in the mornings they ate breakfast at the downtown Log Cabin restaurant, afterward marching the two blocks to Rosenstock's cotton office on Broadway Avenue, where his grandfather tried to reassemble another fortune.

Meanwhile, Foote's mother plugged away at her secretarial work for several Greenville employers. An offer for steadier work came in 1925, from her husband's former company, Armour. Unfortunately, the position was in the company's Pensacola office, so once again she and Shelby, who had just finished the third grade, would be relocating—his fifth move in eight years. Pensacola offered a different experience from that of the Delta, where, as Hortense Powdermaker suggested in *After Freedom: A Cultural Study in the Deep South,* "almost everyone boasted about having an ancestor who had been a Colonel in the Confederate Army, and tried to give an impression of being descended from men who had big plantations with a large number of slaves." Not saddled by such brevetted imagery, Pensacola, an overgrown fishing village, oriented itself simply toward the yawning Gulf of Mexico at its feet. As he could only articulate later, Pensacola's escape from the unwritten regulations of the agrarian South gave it an ethos that appealed to Foote.

The move to Pensacola also tested and ultimately forged the bond between Shelby and his mother, who were now living by themselves for the first time. As close as they became, their relationship always seemed unorthodox to others around them. Although the two would become hermetically connected, neither was easy to get along with. In the coming decades, friends and family members would usually cite Shelby as the difficult one, but living with Lillian was not easy. She was generous to a fault; nevertheless, she excited easily. Betty Carter, newspaper editor Hodding Carter's wife, remembers that "she used very profane language." Lillian's anger and frustration were not always channeled into spates of curses. More often, she redirected those anxieties by indulging her son every liberty: "She had the idea that no one could love anyone more than she did." Shelby soon began to understand that almost anything he did would be tolerated by his mother. "A lot of bad things happened to me and she stood by me through all of them," Foote remembers. "She got discouraged I'm sure from time to time, but she never reproached me for any of my mistakes. I could see her disappointment. But she never said what I would have said in her place: 'There you go again. You're always acting like this.' She never did that."

In the summer of 1927, after Shelby's fifth-grade year, the Footes received word that Rosenstock had contracted tuberculosis. Greenville had been on their mind constantly during the previous months. Through newspaper accounts, they had followed the death and destruction of the 1927 flood, a monstrous disaster that was quickly labeled one of the catastrophic hundred-year floods. Rosenstock's illness, however, was not flood related. After a relentless cough vexed him throughout the spring, Shelby's grandfather finally visited his doctor. Unaware of the dangers of tobacco, the doctor told Rosenstock that his problem might be alleviated by changing cigarettes: Lighter Chesterfields would be more salubrious than the Camels that he had been smoking. Rosenstock changed cigarette brands, but the prescription did not eliminate the coughing. By the middle of the summer, his condition had worsened, and in July the doctor sent Rosenstock to a tubercular sanitarium at McGee, Mississippi, 60 miles southeast of Jackson. Hearing the news, Mrs. Foote quickly gathered the ten-year-old Foote from a summer camp, where he had developed an intense sunburn. Shortly after their arrival in McGee, Rosenstock died. When he saw his supine grandfather, Foote started crying. The adults around Foote refused to believe that a child could show such emotion—they assumed that Foote was reacting to his burns. No one seemed to understand how Foote had relished his grandfather's compassion, friendliness, and dramatic successes and failures. In a statement that captured the rise and fall of both of his grandfathers, Foote later said, "Though they were both extremely rich in the course of their lifetimes, they barely had the money at their deaths to pay for the shovel that buried them."

When the family transported Rosenstock's body back to Greenville, the Footes went along, a journey that enabled them to see firsthand the destruction that had leveled Greenville, Washington County, and the rest of the Delta. All the information that they had received from relatives and newspaper stories did not prepare them for the horrid scene before them, a scene all the more appalling because they had not witnessed the gradual progress of the destruction. With Greenville's face scarred and cracked, its air filled with the stench of dead animals and people, the ten-year-old knew even then that he was face to face with something sublime, something that he would later describe as "the greatest disaster this country has ever suffered."

What elements conspired to wreak such havoc? After heavy winter snow and rain had swollen the upper Mississippi well beyond its full pool capacity, the river began trundling its load south. In spite of the record amounts of rainfall, many Deltans doubted that they were in danger. The lower Mississippi, with its deeper and fuller channel, usually absorbed any excessive rainfall, and the U.S. Corps of Engineers had greatly fortified the existing levee system over the previous two decades. By early April, the river was on the boom; Deltans read about the crest reaching St. Louis, then Cairo, then Memphis itself. In front of Greenville, the river climbed steadily. Boats sucked down the river ran level with the town's 30-foot-high levee, seemingly walking on top of Greenville's downtown district. White women and children who had not already relocated elsewhere quickly rushed south to Vicksburg or north to Memphis, where they filled hotels or friends' houses. On April 21, as they waited for the highest waters to pass by Greenville, the river broke through the levee at Mounds Landing, Mississippi, 10 miles north of Greenville. A wall of water "three-quarters of a mile across and more than 100 feet high" rushed through the cut; the 468,000 cubic feet of water represented "triple the volume of a flooding Colorado [River], more than double a flooding Niagara Falls, more than the entire upper Mississippi ever carried." Seventy-five miles away in Yazoo City, at the southeastern edge of the Delta, water covered the rooftops.

Butting up to the river, Greenville was inundated. "Of all the counties in the entire flooded region, from Illinois to the Gulf of Mexico, Washington County was the single one that suffered the most devastating losses," noted John Barry. Floodwaters washed away 2200 buildings and damaged thousands of others. At least 240 people drowned. Because it lost more property than any other U.S. county, Washington County received twice as much federal aid as any other Mississippi county, triple the amount of any Louisiana county, quadruple that of any Arkansas county, and double the aid received by Missouri, Illinois, Tennessee, and Kentucky combined.

By the time the Footes arrived in July, the town had dried out. Wide cracks in the ground revealed the water's violation of the town's soil, and "chocolate bands," as Foote described them in "Tell Them Good-by," striped the houses and trees. Through these residual emblems, Foote for the first time found himself facing the complex relationship between the Mississippi River and the Delta, a Faustian pact that both provided the region's blessed bounty and guaranteed its periodic destruction.

Although the Footes planned to return to Pensacola and Armour after Rosenstock's funeral, Greenville exerted a magnetic pull, as did the Moyses. The childless couple also had a deep affection for their young nephew. "Mama Maude," as Foote called his aunt, "was about as much my mother to me as was my own mother. I loved her very much and she was very fond of me and we were very close." Lillian decided that if she could find work, she and Shelby would remain in Greenville. She soon got a break. Through friends, Lillian learned that lawyer Billy Wynn needed a secretary. She took the job, and soon the Footes were headed to Pensacola to pack their belongings. For Shelby, who would begin sixth grade in a few weeks, the return to Greenville marked a return to a world that was familiar to him, a place for which he held a great fondness. Greenville, he remembers, "was a great place to grow up in."

Later declarations aside, Foote's junior high school years were hardly halcyon and green. On the contrary, they were downright troubling. Still not sure about how to forge relationships with others, Foote struggled to fit in. Repeatedly, he found that he had no desire to be a part of any organized group. Neither did he allow himself to conform to accepted standards of dress, and his awkwardness about fitting in produced iconoclastic extremes. While other male students wore traditional chinos, Foote insisted on wearing plus fours, or knickers—apparel considered too formal by his fellow students. His peers "would tease him about wearing the plus fours," according to one classmate. "He looked absurd in them."

Rather than being offended by such criticism, Foote revelled in it. When the Moyses planned to host a tea party for Foote and his friends,

Foote asked Mic Moyse to buy him a tuxedo because he wanted to be the center of attention. It did not matter than few adults owned tuxedos, much less children. "Shelby," said LeRoy Percy, with only slight exaggeration, "was the only boy in the state of Mississippi at that age that had a tuxedo." Nevertheless, Foote's expensive prop did make him the party's focal point. When his date, Sarah Farish, arrived, she laughed uproariously, a response repeated by other party-goers.

The year 1930 ushered in a new individual who would temper Foote's dramatics, a person who taught him that it was okay to be different and that it was okay to explore the world of books. On a warm spring day, William Alexander Percy approached Foote at the Greenville Country Club. "Dreadful golfer" though he was, Percy was golden in just about everything else he touched. He came from good stock. Since 1841, when Charles Percy arrived in the Delta, the family had worked to ensure that they were always on solid ground. These "giants," as Barry called them, not only made Greenville, but, in a sense, the Delta and even Mississippi. Through their tireless efforts to interweave capital, art, and politics, the family "led both the South and the nation."

Percy knew the young Foote only through Lillian, Wynn's secretary in the office next to his own law office. However, Percy sought out Shelby because he needed a young boy to shepherd his new charges, the sons of his cousin, LeRoy Percy, who had recently committed suicide. The family—Mattie Sue; Walker, the future novelist; LeRoy Jr.; and Phinizy—had been without a husband and father since Percy shot himself at their Birmingham home the previous year. Wanting her boys to be around some father figures, Mrs. Percy accepted Will's invitation that they come stay with him. With the Percy boys soon moving into his house, boys whom he would later adopt after Mrs. Percy's fatal car crash in 1932, Will Percy sought companions for his cousins.

On that day at the country club, Percy told Foote, "Some kinsmen of mine are coming here to spend the summer with me. There are three boys in the group and the two older boys are about your age. I hope you'll come over to the house often and help them enjoy themselves while they're here." Foote agreed to take them "under his wing." Because Foote and Walker Percy would become lifelong friends, the two participants of a correspondence that ranks among the richest in American letters, the meeting between Will Percy and Foote has an apocryphal air about it. But as LeRoy Percy Jr. makes clear, Will Percy's request that Foote play ambassador for the boys was little more than mere chance: "It had nothing to do with any particular attribute of Shelby." It had, instead, everything to do with where Percy's and Wynn's offices were located.

Even if there were other boys whom Percy could have asked, he could not have done much better than Shelby Foote. At fifteen, younger than Walker by a little less than a year and slightly older than LeRoy (often called Roy), Shelby was just the right age to serve as their companion. (The third son, Phinizy, or Phin, was ten at the time of the move.) According to LeRoy, "He was the first boy we met in Greenville. Shelby introduced us all around." Foote's gracious hosting revealed the satisfaction that he derived from the Percy boys. For the first time, he had discovered the brothers that he never had. Their friendship blossomed, and almost immediately Foote made Will Percy's Broadway Avenue house his own. "Shelby spent almost as much time at our home as he did at his own home," LeRoy Percy remembers.

Even at their young age, Walker and LeRoy were very different people, and Foote's respective relationships with each boy tapped into one of the competing halves of Foote's developing personality. Shy and reserved, Walker was given to cerebral activities. LeRoy, on the other hand, was boisterous, boasting a disposition that not made him one of the popular figures among Greenville youths, but would also enable him to serve later in life as one of the region's political and agricultural leaders. Initially, LeRoy was Foote's more frequent companion: "Shelby and I, the first year or two, spent way more time together than he did with Walker." With LeRoy, Shelby could play the brash swashbuckler. The two boys delved into the physical and romantic activities that the Delta society encouraged in its males: sports, chasing girls, and having a good time. "Shelby liked to," as LeRoy Percy said, "hell around the Delta." Foote had increasingly become a welcome figure for the girls that he and LeRoy courted. His sharp and well-defined features had now been complemented by his height: After a growth spurt near the beginning of his high school years, Foote reached his ultimate 5 feet

10 inches. Never one to miss a chance with the ladies, Foote seized on these opportunities with a combination of bravado and courtliness.

But the showmanship and bravado that made him popular at dances also manifested itself in more damning ways. Known around the neighborhood as "Dennis the Menace," Shelby liked "to stir things up," remembers one Greenville resident. Some of these pranks represented boyhood fun that spiraled out of control. On one occasion at Will Percy's house, Shelby suggested that the boys place tennis balls into a trough that encircled the dining room's Venetian chandelier, an exquisite piece Percy had bought while traveling in Europe. Knowing their Uncle Will's reverence for the chandelier, Walker and Roy refused to take part. Only Phin played along with Shelby. The fun ended quickly, however. After a few balls had been placed in the trough, a quick ripping noise came from the ceiling. Under the weight of the tennis balls, the delicate chandelier fell, shattering into pieces over the hardwood floor. After some deliberation, the boys sent a delegation of Shelby and Roy to break the bad news to Will Percy. The innocent Roy's presence would hopefully temper Percy, whose stoic persona hid a vesuvian anger. When the two boys arrived at Percy's office, Will listened to them for only several minutes before he blew up. Not caring about clients in his office, Percy began cursing the boys, yelling that they were the "most ungrateful people he had ever known."

Foote's pranks caused Greenvillian parents to become uneasy about Foote, many of whom decided that "he was the wrong kind of boy to have your youngsters hang around." One afternoon in front of neighbors Mary Jane Zeiser and her mother, Foote brandished a 32-caliber Smith and Wesson pistol that had been his father's. Without provocation, Foote began playing a mock Russian roulette with Zeiser's wire-headed terrier, whom Foote remembered as one of "those yappy little dogs." Over the cries of Zeiser and her mother, Foote repeatedly pointed the gun at the dog, thinking that all of the gun's chambers were empty. Foote discovered too late that the gun was loaded: He had blown the dog's head off. Thinking that Foote had intentionally shot the dog and fearful that he would turn the gun on them, Mrs. Zeiser and Mary Jane sprinted around the corner, yelling for help. Foote apologized, but the damage had been done. It was, as one Greenville resident remembers, a "serious" incident, one that blackened Foote's reputation around town.

Other pranks followed. According to several people, Foote reportedly went to a high school party dressed as a woman. After the drag queen broke in on a dancing couple, the boy who found himself dancing with the new "woman" recognized Shelby. Infuriated, the boy pulled Shelby outside the dance hall to fight. Visitors wandering by the alley subsequently discovered an unusually tall, well-dressed woman beating up the boy, just one of many fights that Foote fought during the course of his youth.

Horrible as these pranks were, they represented Foote's overcompensation for a private side moiling within him, a feeling that had been building since his exposure to *David Copperfield* at age twelve. Reading Dickens's novel made him realize "that there was a world, if anything, more real than the real world. There was something about the book that made me realize what art is." Subsequently, Foote's intellectual interests uneasily existed side by side with his public activities. Ironically, it was often through the very practices meant to indoctrinate him into prescribed avenues of behavior that this cerebral facet emerged. While others saw guns as a means to an end—the hunt itself—Foote only enjoyed all the elements of the hunt's preamble. It was not that he had no inclination toward hunting: As a descendent of Hugh Foote, he was presumably equipped with the tools that would have made him an excellent shot. Yet, the idea of sitting in a deer stand or a duck blind did not appeal to Foote, and he never accompanied Roy or any of the other Greenville boys on their hunts. "He liked to fool with guns," reported LeRoy Percy, "but he didn't like to hunt." What intrigued Foote was the romantic idea of the hunt.

To cultivate these intellectual interests, Foote turned to Walker Percy. Quite different from the gregarious Roy, Walker had little interest in attending parties. He lived, as his biographer Jay Tolson claims, in a "shell": "Quiet, self-conscious, he was always on the fringe, following what others were saying or doing, occasionally offering some wry comment on what was going on, a witty phrase or a name summing up a person." Walker's introspection stirred the cerebral side of Shelby, and the boys began to symbiotically forge their common interests.

In the odd, angled-off rooms upstairs in Will's house, the two found small alcoves where they could engage in their interests. Initially, they built model airplanes: Spads and Sopwith camels. Even at this early point in their lives, Tolson astutely claims, their respective planes betokened their intellectual bent. Whereas Walker built planes that were operational, adumbrating his later belief that art did make things happen, Foote built planes that did not fly, but were to be exhibited on a shelf. Presaging his later beliefs in formalism, Foote's planes were showcase pieces, self-contained and bereft of utilitarian value.

With Walker, Foote also gained access to Will Percy and his cosmopolitan sophistication, an oasis in the 1920s and 1930s South. During this period, Southerners promoted religion at the expense of intellectual inquiry, a disposition nowhere more apparent than in the 1925 Scopes Monkey Trial, in which religious conservatives rallied and defeated a Dayton, Tennessee, instructor teaching evolution at the town's high school. By comparison, Greenville took on a Maecenean role in fostering the development of education and the arts. Not only was its white school system the best in Mississippi, but in 1930 this small town of 16,000 people—merely the sixth largest in Mississippi—boasted an opera house that hosted many of the famed New Orleanian and other national opera companies. Such an environment would produce more than thirty writers, including Foote, Will Percy, Walker Percy, classmate Charles Bell, and another friend, Josephine Haxton, who writes under the pen name Ellen Douglas. Describing the town's special qualities, Foote said, "That was amazing. I don't know how to explain it. I guess the hand of God reached out and touched Greenville. Or the hand of whatever."

To some extent, Greenville avoided the myopia of other Southern towns because of its role as a commercial center. Much like New Orleans to the south, Greenville's site as a crossroads for trade provided ingress for pluralistic elements. Among others, immigrant Chinese, Assyrians, Lebanese, and Italians made the Delta "a great melting pot . . . a conglomeration." As Foote claimed, "The Delta has been more liberal than the [Mississippi] hills because of this co-mingling, at least for one thing, so they are more sophisticated or whatever you want to call it. At least they are aware of an outside world and ties with the

Old World." Notwithstanding the town's location at this crossroads, it was the Percys who orchestrated the town's success. In Foote's early childhood, the paterfamilias had been LeRoy Percy, the former U.S. senator who ran the Delta with an iron fist. Percy was well known throughout the region, but he gained wider national recognition in 1922 after he single-handedly defeated a budding Greenville Ku Klux Klan klavern trafficking on growing racial unrest. Although the Percys' motives toward blacks were tangled up in a complex relationship of paternalism and economic self-protection, they were seen as liberals in their treatment of blacks. The family considered blacks as the South's form of noble savages, a belief that earned the Percys, in the Mississippi of the 1920s and 1930s, the tag of being Negro sympathizers. As Walker Percy later encapsulated these monikers, "Will Percy was regarded in the Mississippi of his day as a flaming liberal and nigger-lover and reviled by the sheriff's office for his charges of police brutality." According to Foote, the community "thought Mr. Will was practically a 'mixer.' They didn't think it was right that he would receive Negroes in his home. . . . That was looked on as a pretty wild thing to do in those days." To be sure, the Percys believed in a scale of Darwinian progress, in which blacks had historically demonstrated themselves to be inferior beings. Within that schema, the family bestowed blacks with only as much respect as they felt they could extend to naturally inferior beings.

Like his father, Will Percy was very involved in the governing of Greenville. A graduate of Harvard Law School and a lawyer by trade, Percy was everything else by choice: a philosopher, an art patron, and a poet. According to Tolson, Percy was "a magnificent composite of types . . . [p]art solitary *penseroso*, part Romantic artist, part chivalric knight." As part of his noblesse oblige code, Will Percy felt compelled to do what he could to raise the culture of his town. Where his father had bent the ear of state and national politicians, Percy spearheaded artistic and cultural projects. In 1936, when he and other Greenville residents became disenchanted with the local gossip rag, *The Delta Democrat,* Percy took it upon himself to provide a more sophisticated newspaper, convincing Covington, Louisiana, editor Hodding Carter, a fervent Klan opponent, to take the reins of a new publication. Percy put up most of the initial money to get the *Delta Star* underway; how-ever, lest it appear that Percy and the other investors were assembling their own public relations organ, the investors signed an agreement indicating that they would not attempt to influence Carter's editorial decisions.

Gracious to friends, Will Percy always tried to play willing host, and his two-story bungalow house was an open hostel where people came and went. In 1932 David Cohn told Percy that he needed a quiet place to write a memoir about his life in the Delta, a work that became *God Shakes Creation*. Percy told him to come stay for the weekend. Two years passed, yet Percy never told Cohn that he had outworn his welcome. That hospitality extended to others beyond his immediate circle. When Northern intellectuals and literati of all stripes traipsed through Mississippi, they gravitated toward the white house at the corner of Percy Street and Broadway Avenue. Many had known Percy at Harvard, some knew him through his position as editor of the Yale Series of Younger Poets from 1925 to 1930, and others carried intro-ductions from Eastern friends. Regardless of their means of entry or their politics, Percy welcomed everybody, leading Phin Percy to think that his house frequently "resembled a hotel." It may not have been, as John Barry claims, "a salon visited by people of international renown," but the Percy guest list could serve as a chapter in a *Who's Who*, as writers such as Vachel Lindsay, Sherwood Anderson, Dorothy Parker, and Stephen Vincent Benet stayed there.

There were limits to Percy's generosity, however. When visitors pub-licly upstaged him or flouted his beliefs, he felt insulted and offended—his hospitality had not been returned with the proper amount of respect. On one occasion in the 1930s, when Percy introduced Langston Hughes to a Greenville black church, he spoke of the way that Hughes had "risen above race." Yet, when Hughes stood up to speak, concilia-tion was not his text. Instead, between what Walker Percy remem-bered as "the most ideologically aggressive poetry you can imagine," Hughes lectured the blacks on how the whites oppressed them. Percy squirmed in the front row, fuming as he figured out how to distance himself from Hughes. Leaving, he knew, would only embody and exacerbate the poet's harangue. He stayed, but he was quick to dismiss

Hughes's words as a "communist speech." Around town, Percy also denied volunteering for the event. He soon let it be known that "he was furious at having been drawn into introducing a radical like Langston Hughes."

The attack on Hughes exposed a fundamental contradiction in Percy's makeup and, more generally, the Southern plantocratic ethos, a collision between the benevolence of the gentleman planter and a racial stratification that enabled such graciousness. According to James Cobb, "The stability of Delta society depended on an intricate network of customs and control mechanisms that guaranteed the fundamental socioeconomic supremacy of all whites over all blacks, while assuring as well that the Delta's white planter elite would remain at the very top of the region's socioeconomic and political pyramid." When Percy could walk the line between benevolent patrician and a race-based superiority, he shone. When challenged, though, by someone such as Hughes, Percy fell off the high wire.

Foote would increasingly wrestle with Percy's views during the next few years, but at this young age, he was captivated by Percy's artistic interests. For Percy, the arts were part and parcel of daily existence. He would often leap into a discourse on a Browning or Keats poem. "He could read you a poem of Keats that, by the time he finished reading it, made you want to run home and be with Keats by yourself," said Foote. Under Will Percy's tutelage, Foote also began to develop what was to become a lifelong interest in classical music. An accomplished amateur pianist, Uncle Will's love of music ran deep—his music collection was easily the largest in Greenville. Percy was also the first Greenville resident to own a Capeheart, one of the first automatic record players. Frequently, the Capeheart malfunctioned, and when it did, Percy had to listen to the repetitive clack of the machine until his servant, Ford Atkins, fixed it. In spite of his technological shortcomings, he made sure that music filled his house. Sunday afternoons were spent listening to radio broadcasts of Arturo Toscanini directing the NBC Symphony Orchestra or the New York Philharmonic, while at other times, Percy put together his own concerts, performances distinctly nineteenth century: Bach concertos and Brahms symphonies dominated the selection. As Walker remembered, "Uncle Will wasn't much for twentieth-century music. He would play Stravinsky's *Le Sacre du printemps* and shake his head."

Foote and Walker also availed themselves of Will Percy's library, the largest in Greenville. The two took down copies of Shakespearean plays, divvying up the parts and reading them aloud in a boisterous collaboration. More than just engaging with Uncle Will's books, Foote met the writers staying there, including Parker, Lindsay, Benet, and Oxford native Stark Young.

Will Percy also informed Foote about Faulkner, the man whom he would grow to admire. Unlike the other guests, Faulkner did not traipse through Percy's home before Foote's eyes. He could not, because Percy had banished Faulkner several years earlier from his home. Unwittingly, Percy had piqued the young Foote's curiosity. Disgusted with Faulkner's behavior, Will Percy shared his animosity toward Faulkner with a story that had Percy "shake his head about it every time he would remember it." On an afternoon in the late 1920s a friend ushered the barefooted Faulkner to a small party at Percy's home. Faulkner had already been drinking, and shortly after his arrival some of Percy's friends called for a tennis game at Will's backyard court, a sport that, unlike golf, he played fairly well and took seriously. The revved-up Faulkner eagerly volunteered. His game, however, showed all of the accuracy of Don Quixote's windmill-tilting. Encapsulating his cousin's story, Walker Percy remembered, "Whether distracted by literary inspiration or by bourbon, he never managed once to bring racket into contact with ball." Faulkner "made a fool of himself," Foote later laughed. Such irreverence flew in the face of Percy's strict code of behavior, and after that afternoon Percy could never bring himself to mention Faulkner as a great writer. "Faulkner never had Mr. Will's admiration as a writer or a man or anything else after that display on the tennis court," Foote said. "He didn't think anything good could come from anybody who would do a thing like that."

The exposure to these literary figures inspired Foote to believe that it was not only acceptable, but heroic, to be a writer—even in a culture where masculinity and artistic interests often butted heads. Even more than before, Foote sunk himself into a reading project that for a person of any age would be remarkable, in the process making himself into what his writer-friend Bern Keating would call "the greatest con-versationalist that I have ever known." Beginning at the age of sixteen, Foote read "quite literally almost everything that I had any reason to think was solid and worthwhile that I could get my hands on . . . clas-sical literature, Greek and Roman, [before I] moved on to all the Frenchmen and the Englishmen and the Russians." His quest had the air of an investigation. When Foote discovered that a Greenville women's group, the Tuesday Study Club, had its own collection in one of the upstairs library rooms, Foote began raiding the room. There he found "many books that I had never heard of." Stealing them, Foote "would read them and take them back . . . when I went for others."

There were other books that he had been told about but could not find at the Tuesday Study Club's library. According to Walker, Will Percy said the three most important works of their time were James Joyce's *Ulysses,* Thomas Mann's *The Magic Mountain,* and Marcel Proust's *Remembrance of Things Past.* Foote ordered *Ulysses* and *The Magic Mountain* immediately, and upon receiving them, he spent the next six weeks inhaling them on his front porch swing during this "big summer of his life." All three would prove monumental for his work: "I have reread those three books . . . I've reread them and reread them."

Several months later, for his seventeenth birthday, his mother gave him the Proust, and the experience of reading the seven novels that make up *Remembrance of Things Past* was "what, if anything, made me an author." *Remembrance of Things Past* provided responses to many issues and questions roiling about in Foote's mind—both in terms of its language and aesthetic formulations. Foote was mesmerized by the rich language of Proust, the "Shakespeare of our time," as Foote fre-quently called the French writer. Reading Proust made him feel "like a colt in clover."

But Proust also had another appeal for the young Foote. Proust's claims about memory provided the young Foote with ways of coming to terms with past and present, which seemed to exist side by side in his culture, a society that could not look forward for fear of sprain-ing its neck. Coming from a region where young boys such as Faulkner's Quentin Compson could be "two separate Quentins now—the Quentin Compson preparing for Harvard in the South . . . and the

Quentin Compson who was still too young to deserve yet to be a ghost," Foote struggled to reconcile past and present. Proust's answer: a crystallization that tied together the memory of the prior event and the agent's present position. In *The Past Recaptured,* the final book of *Remembrance,* Marcel rediscovers the past through a chain of seemingly insignificant associations such as the smell of steaming tea and the sight and taste of madeleines: "The grandeur of real art . . . is to rediscover, grasp again and lay before us that reality from which we live so far removed and from which we become more and more separated as the formal knowledge which we substitute for it grows in thickness and imperviousness."

Reading Proust was a monumental experience for Foote, and in the future he would reserve *Remembrance of Things Past* as a "prize" for finishing a book, but another literary mentor filled in those skeletons with flesh. Not 130 miles northeast of Greenville—about a three-hour drive away—Faulkner was writing what are now considered three of the greatest American novels, *As I Lay Dying, The Sound and the Fury,* and *Light in August.* Nevertheless, Faulkner's work at that time went underappreciated, and saddled with financial obligations, he found himself cranking out stories and even prostituting himself as a Hollywood screenwriter to eke out a living for his wife and daughter. In Greenville, though, Foote gobbled up every Faulkner work he could find. His appetite had been whetted by his reading of *Light in August,* which had supplied an experience unlike any that he had known before. After reading it, Foote felt dazed and disoriented. He later remembered how "different" the novel "was from what came before it and how it just knocked you off your feet."

Although Foote appreciated Faulkner's experimental techniques, what attracted him to the writer was his resistance to making the region a *Gone with the Wind* saga. Instead of romanticizing the Southern caste and slavery systems, Faulkner exposed their ugly underbellies. Faulkner, Foote later said, "was showing me a country I knew well, and showing me how really little I knew it compared to him." In the next few years, Faulkner would not only become a friend, but a palpable influence who often handicapped Foote's efforts to find his own literary voice.

Foote's forays into the world of literature dug deeper for him the renegade channel that he had already cut. Foote naturally wanted to live in the artistic world that he had discovered. That realm lured with him with possible fame and publicity, and, more immediately, it gave him an opportunity to express his unorthodox self. Like most budding writers, Shelby was sure that the world around him did not quite understand his thoughts and feelings. Consequently, his personal cosmos and the mundane world began to blur. Extending the dramatization of fictional characters into his own life, Foote played out the roles of the characters he had been reading about. At times, Foote may even have been developing for himself the leading role in some future novel that he would write. Whatever the cause of his rebelliousness, Foote began extending his earlier recalcitrance into problems with authority figures, a struggle that would plague him well into his adult life. Telling his classmates that he was a "miracle worker . . . a genius," Foote believed that he had license to challenge his elders. At times, these confrontations involved serious intellectual inquiry. For instance, Foote frequently got himself into debates with Miss McBrayer, a Greenville High School history teacher. She often sparred with Foote over various historical questions. After one such debate, McBrayer heatedly told her student, "Shelby Foote, you would argue with the Lord!" Without missing a beat, Foote responded, "That's right. Whenever I get with him, we're going to have at it."

While the debates with McBrayer were largely good-natured, other encounters bore more malice. With no one was this more apparent than Greenville High School's stern principal, E. J. Leuckenbach, fictionalized in *Jordan County* as Professor Frozen Back, who "walked with a stiff Prussian carriage as if he were pacing off the distance between barriers for a duel." Leuckenbach's demanding nature rubbed many of his students the wrong way, but his relationship with Foote was especially strained. In one notable incident, Leuckenbach found Foote in the school newspaper office, where a physical education teacher had permitted him to go. Foote had told the gym teacher he had work to do on the newspaper, but Foote's work during that hour involved reading *Ulysses,* a novel whose American ban for its pornography had been declared unconstitutional by the U.S. Supreme Court in 1933. When the principal barged into the office and saw Joyce's novel in Foote's hands, Leuckenbach went crazy. No student of his was going to read pornography. Foote calmly let Leuckenbach finish his tirade. With great flourish, he responded, "Mr. Leuckenbach, this novel is not only not obscene, but it is one of the few literary texts on which the U.S. Supreme Court has issued an opinion." Stung by Foote's obstreperousness, Leuckenbach slapped the student with a suspension.

These encounters with authority figures represented Foote's struggle to forge his own voice. At some point during his freshman or sophomore year of high school, Foote began writing poetry. Walker Percy later claimed to have launched Foote's career when, during one study hall, Percy passed Foote his own poem, "In Somnium: in the Manner of Poe." Although the two friends would laugh later about how bad their poems had been, at the time Foote took his poetry very seriously.

One available vehicle for his writing was the Greenville High School newspaper, *The Pica* (pronounced, idiosyncratically, as "pee-kah"). While some high schools struggled to enlist enough students just to get a newspaper out, *The Pica* held an honored place in the school's life. In a series of tryouts and interviews each spring, Greenville students vied for places on the newspaper's staff. Not a typographical error-laden compilation of gossip, *The Pica* was a slick, award-winning newspaper that featured stories; essays; book reviews; and stinging editorials about not only school matters, but important local, state, and national issues. Named Mississippi's best high school newspaper for five consecutive years (1931–1935), *The Pica* also reaped regional awards. In a 1934 contest, Mississippi Valley High School Publications Association rated the paper the third best high school newspaper in Tennessee, Alabama, Kentucky, Arkansas, and Mississippi, an award proudly displayed on the newspaper's banner.

Foote began writing for *The Pica* during 1932–1933, his third year of high school. Although his actual reporting during that year was minimal, he did publish poems. In November, "Embers" appeared, marking the first time that he had any work published, and throughout the rest of the year, Foote continued to publish his poems in *The Pica*. In 1933–1934 Foote played a more active role in the paper's production.

Beginning the year as a staff writer, the paper's editors quickly promoted him to features editor. In this position, he handled many of the paper's interviews, including a 1933 jailhouse interview with Washington County prisoner Jessie Scott, who was to be electrocuted on the next day for murder.

During his next year with *The Pica* and his fourth year of high school, Foote fully exhibited the writing talent and renaissance versatility he had developed. In addition to writing the majority of the paper's feature stories, Shelby also wrote hard news and book reviews. Recognizing his talent, the Mississippi Valley High School Publications Association named Foote the 1933–1934 high-point winner in the overall category, the first literary honor that he would ever receive.

Given his future literary career, all of Foote's early journalism work is important—if only as a precursor of things to come. In particular, the poetry that he published in *The Pica* deserves special consideration because it was this work that paved the way for his later short stories and novels. Although there were moments of artistic maturity, the poetry more frequently bore artificiality. "Death Took My Love," which appeared in the February 1934 issue, represents some of this conventionality: "Death took my love / Away from me / And left me not / A trace of her; / He lay her on the heavy bier / With cloth over / The face of her." Likewise, in a collection of poems entitled "Five Images" (an obvious takeoff from Wallace Stevens's consideration of blackbirds), the narrator mundanely claims that "all the grass was spectrum colored / As the sun played with the dewdrops / That were clinging to the alfalfa."

Part of Foote's lack of originality may stem from his vehement belief in the generative powers gained from the intense study of literary forebears—even to the point of imitation. As Foote would later suggest, the first novels of "most of the best writers I know of are written under the obvious influence of some one particular writer." Foote once cited Robert Louis Stevenson's advice to would-be writers, "Pick some writer whom you admire . . . and imitate him. . . . Having learned to do that, develop your own style." Too often, though, Foote's literary fathers dominated his work, and his poems became merely a palimpsest of the poetry that he had been reading. "Her Knight Comes Riding," for instance, relies exclusively on Browningian dramatic monologue, and

"Jeremiah Jones" was little more than a transcription of E. A. Robinson's "Richard Cory":

> Jeremiah Jones was a man we could depend on;
> No finer man was there in all of Linden.
> His face was honest and his eyes were clear;
> His talk was all straightforward and sincere.
> He was the president of the leading bank
> In which our bonds and currency we sank.
> We trusted him to keep them safe and sound
> Down to the last six pence and bottom pound.
> We had no thought but that they were secure
> And of his honesty we all were sure.
> But Tuesday Jeremiah caught a ship
> And sailed away with thousands in his grip.

At the very least, though, Foote's impulse to study his masters provides a clear sense of which poets he was reading. Browning was a significant influence on the young writer, and, in a review of Alfred Kreymborg's *An Anthology of American Poetry: 1630–1930*, Foote mentioned by name Robinson, Robert Frost, and T. S. Eliot.

At its best, Foote's early poems could transmute imitation into something fresh. Like Shakespeare's Sonnet 130, Foote's poetry could poke fun at the conventionality of traditional courting procedures. In "Madrigal (Almost)," he wrote:

> If I loved you, I'd whisper low
> Endearing words of love,
> I'd kiss your hand with a bow
> And swear by gods above
> That till our dying day
> My love would still be true:
> Then low I'd softly say
> That 'twas you and only you
> Each of those I'd surely do,
> And other sentimental rot;
> If I were in love with you.
> But, as you see, I'm not.

Even while he labored to develop his literary skills, Foote still enjoyed the social activities of his peers. He continued to be thought of as arrogant, as evidenced in a *Pica* article matching up students with Hollywood titles, where he was deemed "The Man Who Played God." Nevertheless, Foote had many friends, particularly among the ladies. "Shelby," read one anonymous notice in a *Pica* gossip column, "is still running around with all these girls; you think that he'd realize that he couldn't have them all." Among others, he dated Anne Hargrave, Virginia Gibbons, and Mary Elizabeth Yates. Even though Foote referred to Hargrave as "my girl," on one three-week trip to Brinkwood, the Percys' Monteagle, Tennessee, house, Foote was paired with Yates. The trip was organized by Foote's regular group, which included Sarah Farish, Margaret Kirk, and the Percy boys, a clan that managed to have its own dynamic in spite of the fact that four of the members of the group were dating: Walker sometimes went out on dates with Kirk, while LeRoy and Sarah had been a couple for several years. Accompanying the teenagers on the trip was Mrs. Farish. At first, everybody got along, but after several days, cabin fever set in. Swinging Yates in a hammock one day, the Foote started pushing her dangerously high. Although Yates asked him to leave the hammock alone, Foote persisted, until she began yelling at the top of her voice. At that point, "Everybody turned on Shelby," remembers one person who was there. Ill feelings simmered among the group, and after a shopping trip, the girls returned to find the three boys flinging grapes at a photograph of Sarah. The next day, Mrs. Farish carted the three couples back to Greenville. "It's amazing that we survived that trip," one of the group said. "We hated each other at the end of it."

While all of his friends were heading to college at the end of the summer, Foote would return for one more year at Greenville High School because he still needed a few credits to graduate. During this fifth year, Foote served as editor of *The Pica,* an honor that he considered one of his greatest achievements: "I don't know what literary distinction I may achieve in my lifetime," Foote said later, "but there's one thing they can never take away from me—in 1934 and '35 I edited the best high school newspaper in the United States." Frequently parked at his newspaper desk, which reportedly housed a whiskey bottle and a gun, Foote sat for hours, focused intensely on the novel before him as students tramped in and out of the office on their way to classes. When he wrote, his editorials were daring and ambitious— even preachy. In the February 1935 issue, Foote urged his classmates to undergo the liberation that he felt that his reading had provided him: "You *must* see that, staying here [Greenville], you have no chance to become even slightly cultured *except through reading*. This is your only chance to raise yourselves above that all-too-low standard set by your parents and others who have gone before you." That year of reading and writing should have prepared him fully for an illustrious college career, for it would be at the higher academic level that Foote would encounter minds who would challenge him. To the contrary, his final year of high school ended sourly. In the months leading up to the end of the school year, both Maude and Mic Moyse died. After Maude's death in January, Mic suffered from depression for several months before collapsing in the bleachers at a local baseball game in May, the victim of a massive heart attack.

For Foote, the deaths of the Moyses marked but one in a series of tragic events. Late in the year, a Greenville High School teacher accused Foote of making "untoward advances" toward her. False as it was, the accusation gave Leuckenbach a pretext to rid himself of Foote, for the principal was tired of being the victim of Foote's editorial harangues. (In what was almost certainly the work of Foote, the paper's annual lampoon issue featured a story headlined by "Leuckenbach Hangs at Dawn.") Consequently, Leuckenbach expelled Foote for the rest of the year. Even blinded by his anger, Foote instinctively knew who in town had the power to get things done: Will Percy. After hearing the story, Percy walked over to Lillian's office to ask if Shelby could stay at his house until the matter was resolved. While Percy intervened on his behalf, Foote sat in the library at 601 Percy Street, reading C. M. Doughty's *Travels in Arabia Deserta* and Richard Burton's edition of *The Arabian Nights*.

Percy did get to the bottom of the situation, entreating Leuckenbach to reinstate Foote after a one-week dismissal, but only after one of Foote's favorite teachers, Miss Louise Hawkins, protested at a faculty meeting that the accusation was "unfair and ridiculous." With some fear that his decision might upset school operations, Leuckenbach soon had to reinstate Foote. (As evidence of Foote's innocence, the accusing teacher soon resigned, afterward checking herself into an insane asylum.) Nevertheless, Leuckenbach would have his chance for revenge— when Foote sought admission to the University of North Carolina.

Under the direction of President Frank Porter Graham, a Southern liberal who allied himself with Roosevelt's New Deal programs, North Carolina had become one of the region's most progressive schools. Graham refused to buckle under growing pressure to reinstate biblical creation theory, championing instead the empirically driven science of UNC sociologist Howard Odum. In what was a weird twist of his inveterate conservatism, Will Percy had insisted that Walker attend North Carolina. A year after Walker matriculated at Chapel Hill, LeRoy followed.

Foote wanted to join his friends at Chapel Hill, and by the spring of 1935 he had sent in his application materials. As was the practice of the day, the UNC Office of Admissions wrote the applicant's principal for an opinion of the student. Leuckenbach must have relished the chance to trash Foote. Although it is not known exactly what he wrote, Foote's encapsulation of his principal's claim seems an accurate summation: "By no means allow this dreadful person in your school." In an era when so much depended on the recommendations of academic authorities, Leuckenbach's directive led to Foote's rejection from Chapel Hill. A subsequent letter from UNC dashed Foote's hopes of joining his friends: "We are sorry to inform you that you have not been accepted into the University of North Carolina." After his May 31 graduation, Foote settled into a job at the town's U.S. Gypsum mill. While boys from the wealthier families spent their summer lounging about at the Greenville Country Club, Foote slaved away at the Chicago Mill, as it was known locally in recognition of the company's headquarters. Under the heat of a 140-degree humidifier, Shelby guided wallboard after wallboard through a micrometer, simultaneously eating "salt pills by the handful and drinking about a quart of water an hour" to make up for the streams of sweat pouring off him. Shelby Foote was presumably headed nowhere.

# College Days
## 1935–1937

> He saw the heads of his classmates meekly bent as they
> wrote in their notebooks the points they were bidden to
> note, nominal definitions, essential definitions, and exam-
> ples or dates of birth or death, chief works, a favourable and
> an unfavourable criticism side by side. His own head was
> unbent for his thoughts wandered abroad and whether he
> looked around the little class of students or out of the win-
> dow across the desolate gardens of the green an odour
> assailed him of cheerless cellardamp and decay.
> —James Joyce, *A Portrait of the Artist as a Young Man*

N O ONE AT THE Chicago Mill mistook the cover-alled youngster
for the boy genius he proclaimed himself to be. No one even
cared. But thankful to have a job in the depths of the Depression,
Foote could not complain. The Depression had hit Greenville hard.
Although the city's businesses were beginning to feel the trickle-down
effect from New Deal programs by 1935, the town's recovery was still
slow, and residents continued to scale back their pre-Depression level
personal expenses.

Foote and his mother found themselves not merely struggling to get
by, but now laboring to pay an expense that they had not paid for in
almost seven years: rent. After the Moyses died, Lillian insisted that her
brother-in-law had promised his house to Shelby. But the accountant

Mic Moyse had died intestate, and without any documentation substantiating her claim, the Moyse relatives successfully turned back Lillian's challenge. With no house, the Footes scrambled to find an affordable home, and they settled into a unit at the Allen Court Apartments at 222-A Washington Street.

While Foote punched the clock, Walker Percy "drift[ed]," reading, among other books, *The Magic Mountain* and listening to music. Although Will Percy encouraged the Percy boys to travel during their breaks (Walker had spent the previous summer traveling in Europe, including a walking tour through Germany), Walker wanted to cast anchor this summer in Greenville. The two friends' different schedules served as an ever-present reminder of their different economic strata. Being a Percy equated to having opportunities that Foote could never hope for, and Shelby's awareness of this deficit bordered on envy. "He would have loved to be in the Percy family itself," said Bunt Percy. "It was as if that was what he was always interested in."

In the evenings after work, Walker and Shelby often got together, "helling around," in Foote's oft-invoked phrase. Their summer also took on a sentimental quality, as both friends sensed that this would be the last period of time that they would spend together for possibly many years. Thanks to Leuckenbach's letter, the UNC administrators had snuffed out a Chapel Hill reunion. When Walker returned to UNC to resume his medical school preparation, Foote would remain in Greenville, gritting his teeth as he dutifully arrived at the mill each day with his lunch pail. Although Shelby could derive some consolation for his rejection by attributing it to Leuckenbach, the upshot was that he was not going to college.

Percy's talk about the UNC campus unwittingly sparked Foote's desire to go to Chapel Hill, however. Knowing that he had absolutely nothing to lose, Foote began hatching a plan. His modus operandi, he decided, would consist of an unannounced, preemptive strike. Rationalizing that the Depression would keep some admitted students from enrolling, Foote assumed that he could fill one of the vacant spots. His surprise arrival, further, would disarm school officials. With him on site, these officials would not have the opportunity to coldly deny his written request for admission. Confident that his plan would work, Foote soon shared his intentions with his friends, who were quick to express serious doubts about it; LeRoy Percy even told Foote that any unexpected appearance would only antagonize UNC officials. Yet, these friends also knew Foote—they knew that deterring Foote's stubborn monomania was nearly impossible. "We knew he was coming," said Roy Percy, "but we didn't think he had a chance in hell of getting in."

He *was* coming. Just a few days before the fall quarter began on September 20, Foote threw his books and suitcases into Donald Wetherbee's car to begin the two-day, 600-mile quest. Walker and LeRoy had already departed for school, where they were meeting their Sigma Alpha Epsilon fraternity brothers for a few days of preschool fun. Like Walker, Wetherbee was beginning his junior year, and during their freshman year he and Percy had roomed together. After a night spent in a Knoxville hotel, Foote and Wetherbee arrived in Chapel Hill the next afternoon. While Wetherbee moved his things into his dorm room, Foote headed for registration, queuing up in the line for incoming freshmen. When the admissions official asked for his name, Foote gave it to him. The official finally located his file and, after quietly reviewing it, told Foote, "We told you not to come." With something between bravado and ignorance, Foote responded, "I know you did, but I couldn't believe you meant it." Angry, the admissions official told Foote that he had not been accepted and should step out of the line. Foote refused, pleading, "I know that you have classes that you can't fill. I came up here all the way from Mississippi. Give me a chance." After an afternoon of haggling, the admissions staff decided that Foote's vehemence trumped Leuckenbach's scathing criticism. When he paid his $150 tuition, he would be admitted—but only conditionally. He would not be considered a degree student, but a "special student." It was a compromise that Foote could live with.

Over the next few days, Foote took the battery of placement exams for incoming freshmen. As if to snub the admission staff's initial decision to reject him, Foote posted stellar results. In the mathematics placement test, not his greatest strength, Foote scored a B. More significantly, in a class of more than five hundred students, Foote scored one of the four highest grades on the aptitude test. While these scores were impressive, Foote's greatest accomplishment involved his admission to the school's advanced level of composition. On the strength of his entrance essay, the school named him a member of the Flying Squadron, a designation that enabled him to take whichever English classes he wanted. (Two years before, Walker and Wetherbee had earned the same honor.) Foote wasted no time in informing Leuckenbach of his accomplishments. He sent a letter to the new *Pica* editor, Kenneth Haxton, asking him to place the results of his entrance exams in the next issue of the newspaper.

By the time the fall quarter began, Foote had his schedule in order. For his first term, he had few options—Foote signed up for classes in English composition, math, biology, and hygiene, and he had to take a new social science course that was offered for the first time during Foote's freshman year. The brainchild of Howard Odum, the course incorporated government, sociology, and economics into the school's traditional freshman history course.

Even though Foote attended almost all of his English lectures, he made it to other lectures infrequently—at best. Other things commanded his attention. Although Greenville may have been more worldly than most Mississippi cities, it still paled in comparison to the world that Foote was stumbling through in progressive Chapel Hill. During Foote's first term, the leader of the Communist Party addressed a campus that had one week prior had been visited by the Imperial Wizard of the Ku Klux Klan. Foote at least knew of the Klan, but the communists were a foreign bunch, even though many of his writer-heroes, including John Dos Passos, Edmund Wilson, and Sherwood Anderson, openly expressed their communist sympathies. Although he certainly knew of the pervasiveness of communism among the literati, Foote also grew up hearing Southern conservatives brand communists as threats to the region's social and racial structures. As Foote said, "You can't be a Communist in Mississippi. There's no party down there to join." But at Chapel Hill, where the memories of the violence against the Gastonia mill workers in 1932 still boiled blood, there were communists "all over the campus: students and professors—lots of Communists." At The Intimate Bookshop, where Foote often bought books, owner Ab Abernathy printed communist propaganda.

Intrigued as he was by the these political issues, Foote especially invested himself in the treasures of UNC's five-story library. Although Will Percy's collection was the largest in Washington County, if not the Delta, Foote had never seen anything the size and scope of UNC's library. Like an archeologist walking among the ruins of an uncovered city, Foote wandered up and down the vast library's aisles, hour after hour. "I was absolutely amazed at the Carolina library," Foote said. "I had never seen anything like those eleven floors of stacks . . . and that excited me a lot." Although that image would grow greater and greater in his mind over the years, so that "eleven" floors replaced the actual five, Foote often missed classes to entomb himself there—even spending the night there on one occasion.

Serious though he was about these new intellectual avenues, Foote was no loner. Through the Percy boys, he met a number of new people, many of whom were the Percys' SAE brothers. On football game weekends that fall, Foote and his friends took dates to Kenan Stadium. Afterward, they often went to dances at the Tin Can Gymnasium, where bands, including Tommy Dorsey's, would play. On other weekends, the group would drink at the Sir Walter Raleigh Hotel in Raleigh before slinking off to places frequented by none of their football dates. Prostitution, as Joel Williamson reports, was a way of life in the South well into the twentieth century, the product of a culture that delicately reconciled sexual desire with social custom, what Walker Percy once called "a genteel repressed Southern Presbyterian sexuality." In the virgin-whore complex dictated by patriarchal cultures, nowhere more apparent than in the 1930s South, unmarried women of high social standing could not provide sexual favors, but prostitutes could. "Every city of any size had its brothels, and the larger the city the more brothels there were and the more openly they operated," Williamson writes. In the Chapel Hill–Durham-Raleigh metropolis, an area that boasted UNC, Duke, and North Carolina State, whorehouses abounded, and Foote availed himself of them frequently. Alone and with his friends, he regularly visited such dens as Katy Mae's on the outskirts of Chapel Hill. When he won The Intimate Bookshop's $25 first prize for the largest student book collection, Foote did not use that award for new books. Instead, he thanked Abernathy for the prize, departed the downtown bookstore, and minutes later was heading "straight to the whorehouse in Raleigh."

The virgin-whore dynamics that dictated the existence of brothels also governed Foote's categorization of women into two groups: for him, women were either sexual objects unworthy of respect or beings whom he paralyzed with attention. As he would tell Percy in a 1950 comment that captures these two poles, "Women I'm no good with, except in the sack. . . . The reason, I suspect, is that I have no real respect for them and they know it—except when Love enters the picture, when the reverse is true: I respect them too much, and they naturally resent having to measure up to all those expectations." So ingrained was this attitude that it would be decades before Foote could imagine a woman as both a desirable object and an autonomous agent. Until he made such concessions, his relationships would border on the disastrous.

Because he felt comfortable with the people around him at UNC, Foote's arrogance diminished. For the first time in his life he began to be able to laugh at himself. In one biology class, Foote's Delta accent, a deep bass Southern drawl that coddled vowels, broke up a class. When asked to discuss the characteristics of a particular crawling creature, Foote pronounced "earthworm" as "eahthwuuuhmmm." Class members roared, with Foote joining in.

Given his friendship with the Percys, Foote wanted to pledge SAE when UNC's fraternity rush began. With their backing, Foote seemed a shoo-in. But even at an institution hailed for its liberalness, the xenophobia of the 1930s was deeply ingrained. During rush, the fraternity's president, its Eminent Archon, announced that Foote would be blackballed: The fraternity had discovered that Foote's mother's family was Jewish. It did not matter that Foote did not practice Judaism and had not been regularly to synagogue since he was eleven. In fact, when Foote went to religious services at all in Greenville, he attended St. James Episcopal Church. Walker found the president's decision to blackball Foote "a decision extremely difficult . . . to accept." Percy knew his friend's religious history, or lack thereof, and he argued the decision with the SAE leadership. But no amount of pleading could change the Eminent Archon's decision: Foote the Jew was tainted, damned by genetics.

When Walker realized the finality of the decision, he asked for permission to tell Foote himself. After several tries, though, he found that he could not bring himself to explain his organization's decision to his friend. He palmed the task off on his younger brother. At least on the surface, Foote accepted the decision. Under what seems to be a tacit understanding, Foote and his friend never discussed the blackballing, perhaps aware that any discussion might challenge their friendship. In fact, within a number of days, he had turned his attention to Alpha Tau Omega, one of the few national fraternities in the 1930s that did not discriminate on the basis of religion. The fraternity wanted him, and after Foote became an ATO pledge, he moved from Steele Hall into the ATO house at 303 East Franklin Street.

If Walker indirectly repudiated Foote, he also had opened up doors for his friend by introducing Foote to Charlie Poe, an SAE who was editor of the *Carolina Magazine,* the school's national award–winning literary publication. (Percy sometimes contributed pieces for the monthly issues.) Published since 1884, for decades the magazine was a perfunctory, unambitious college publication, until Terry Couch, later the director of the University of North Carolina Press, assumed the editorial reins in 1924. Couch began taking on campus, state, and national political issues with an aggressiveness rarely seen on Southern campuses. Couch not only wrote stories attacking the resurgent Southern fundamentalism, but he published unedited letters from anti-evolutionist Fundamentalist preachers whose bumbling, reactionary rhetoric served as its own self-parody. With such irreverence, the magazine "soon became a prime topic of conversation not only on campus but out in the state as well." North Carolina legislators lambasted the publication for its incendiary philosophy.

After Poe encouraged Foote to submit some pieces, Shelby wasted no time in putting together what were his first fictional works. Although Foote may have previously envisioned himself as the next Keats, he soon discovered that poetry did not offer a large enough canvas to relate the complicated culture that he wanted to depict. Prose, on the other hand, offered an opportunity for issues to surface and crystallize. As Foote once summarized succinctly, prose offers "a way to get in there and move around." Beginning with "The Good Pilgrim: A Fury is Calmed," which appeared in the *Carolina Magazine*'s November 1935 issue, Foote contributed fiction to five of the eight 1935–1936 issues. In its December issue the magazine published "Sad Hiatus: A Short Short Story," and in January, "The Old Man that Sold Peanuts in New Orleans: A Story." "The Village Killers: A Story" followed in February, and in April, "This Primrose Hill: A Short Story." Although these pieces lack the polish and maturity of Foote's later novels, steeped as they are in an excessive Wolfean erudition (in "This Primrose Hill," Lurlyne Brighton's mother is characterized as a "malarial valetudinarian"), they also reveal a maturity well on its way toward blossoming. These stories presage the themes and material that would preoccupy him for the rest of his life.

Only one critic, Robert Phillips, has written on Foote's early stories. Phillips claims that Foote's themes in the *Carolina Magazine* stories provide "some obvious connections" to his later work. For Phillips, those connections lie in the stories' adumbration of "the failure of love in the modern world," which Phillips considers to be the primary theme of Foote's work. These stories, according to Phillips, spell out how love "would restore health, unity of thought and feeling, wholeness to modern man's fragmented psyche." To a certain extent, Phillips is right: These stories do involve isolation, or the lack of love, as individuals' best efforts to connect not only get thwarted but often turned against them. In "The Old Man That Sold Peanuts in New Orleans," a story about an unnamed peanut vendor's friendship with two prostitutes ("the only two people in all New Orleans who cared whether I froze or starved"), the paternal vendor discovers that even his best efforts to provide compassion redound against him. On the day after Christmas, the vendor goes to Maison Blanche, a New Orleans department store, where even with the donation of five cents from a neighborhood boy and the benefit of a half-price sale, he comes up nine cents short of the price of a pair of slippers he wants to buy for the two women. Tantalizingly close to the necessary figure, the man takes the slippers, thinking that he "can bring the nine cents next week." Moments later, the store detective predictably sweeps him up and arrests him. Handcuffed, the man sits laughing "like a fool" outside the store, overcome with a world gone wrong, a world where well-intentioned efforts become absurd failures.

A similar sense of alienation runs through "The Good Pilgrim," a story about two former Parchman Prison inmates who, after serving their sentences, seek to become successful sharecroppers. Although the narrator's crime is not revealed, Ray, the narrator's friend and now sharecropping partner, has killed three women during his lifetime. The rage that engulfs Ray and produces these murders, though, is not premeditated. Rather, it spontaneously ignites: "It came furiously out of nowhere into being, the cased fury of dead worlds, pent-up fury down the long tunnel of lines and wires." On one occasion that rage leads Ray to kill a dog, not unlike Foote's earlier shooting of Zeiser's dog, as a way of staving off his inner suffocation: "He knew what he had to do and lifted the gun horizontally before him. . . . The clear eyes of the dog did not wince and not a muscle moved. He watched it a moment and pulled the trigger. The dog dropped heavily onto its side and lay solidly there; it did not whimper; it did not even twitch."

More than just a dramatization of futile efforts to find love in an inscrutable modern world, Foote's early stories began to engage with the racial and social issues that lurked around him and had constituted his development. (Phillips does acknowledge that in addition to exploring the "conditions of love," the *Carolina Magazine* stories feature themes of "sex [and] race.") In particular, Foote had begun exploring the constitution and even artifice of Southern racial and social hierarchies. The anger that Ray feels in "The Good Pilgrim," for instance, stems specifically from the racial oppression that he has suffered. Not only does he live in "the harsh unpainted cabins of his race," but the "cased-fury of dead worlds, pent-up fury" specifically comes "whirring down the icy tundras and sweltering jungles of times past, the silent screams of his race before it was subjugated to cotton and mules and saxophones and dice." The sense of unarticulated subjugation reverberates through Ray's body, the symbolic location on which slavery enacted its power: "Sitting there he felt his guts turning and his heart pumping: it got louder and stronger till he thought it would burst his chest and crack the white ribs underneath." As the beating grows "louder and stronger till it was throbbing violently in his ears," Ray starts to fear that his viscera will serve as some return of the repressed: "he was afraid all the dead, now resurrected, demons would come out," through his "white ribs," a color designation that, articulated at all, suggests that Foote associates Ray's malady with the distinctions between white and black. Because this connection between Ray's violence and the racial oppression he suffers from is only suggested in the one outburst in the middle of the story, it appears that Foote's understanding and awareness of this relationship was just developing. Nevertheless, clearly, the tension that Foote felt in his desire to be and not be part of any Southern hierarchy of wealth based on racial injustices was already coming through.

Like Faulkner, Foote was also interested in how, even within the white community, power depended on an oppressive social structure. In "The Village Killers," a title that is an obvious takeoff from Ernest Hemingway's short story "The Killers," an oppressive social structure ensures that Francis, who transports liquor from Louisiana to Mississippi for the bootlegger Pozzy, will fall victim to a swindler's suggestion that he use the money Pozzy gives him to buy booze for easy horse-track wins. Not surprisingly, Francis wins and wins, until he bets all the money entrusted to him—and loses for the first time. Returning to Clayton, Mississippi, Francis is beaten unmercifully: "Francis felt no-feeling run into his legs and did not know how he was standing. He felt one of the men slapping at his face with the flat of his hand; hard quick blows. He tasted blood. He hung limp between the two men, Ferry still kicking and Pozzy hitting at the boy's back and neck with his short arms. He was shouting in a strange tongue now. Francis let his head hang down. *I am numb now I am numb now.*" Francis's misguided efforts to escape his lower-class background end up earning him a place in a ditch.

By the end of his freshman year, Foote's challenge to his region's demand for orthodoxy came through clearly. In "This Primrose Hill," Foote's final story for the 1935–1936 school year, he spelled out the complexities of Southern economic hierarchies. Set in the 1930s, "This Primrose Hill" explores the way that money begets claims of aristocracy. Will, the protagonist, comes from a pretentious family whose labor in getting that wealth cannot easily be concealed: It was "accumulated over a period of fifty years in a land where fifty years could hardly be expected to obliterate the fact that his grandfather came down the river on a raft during the late Reconstruction and it being common knowledge . . . that this same grandfather was a carpetbagger." Exploring other fictions of the Southern ruling order, "This Primrose Hill" shows how the culture's efforts to raise women to an ideal paralyzes, not honors, women. The parvenu Will seeks to marry Lurlyne Brighton, a nubile young woman whose noble bloodlines should provide her with opportunities, but instead, make her, paradoxically, into a cultural victim. Because she is both economically and sexually desirable, she becomes the love interest of the town's men. Yet, even though these men desire her, she cannot, under her class's demand for pure women, fulfill their wishes. Lurlyne becomes the walking contradiction of having to be an object who produces desire—in others and for herself—and yet have superhuman will to stave off that desire.

Trapped between acting on these pleasures and living up to her family's reputation, Lurlyne gives in to her sexual impulses, and soon she had "acquired something of a reputation." According to the narrator, "On our way back to our farms we would see her emerge from unfrequented, notorious roads in ramshackled Fords with the boys of the town—not always with one, sometimes with two or three and even more." As one of the workers in the barbershop where some of the story takes place claims, "If that's blueblood, I'm glad I didnt have none to pass on to my daughter."

What Foote's story makes clear is that Lurlyne is not the only person victimized in this culture of contradictions—everybody is. Beset by the loss of his money and hence his claims to being part of the Southern elite, Lurlyne's father is a drunk, or at least "not so much a hard drinker as a poor one, he was perpetually in a rosy glow of alcoholic agreeability and good will toward men." Completing the picture, Lurlyne's mother seeks to hold on to her former position of prestige. A "clinger-on of the upper stratum, a lady of the first degree, proud and empty with the uselessness of her kind," the mother finds herself obsessed with questions of her family's worth, particularly in monetary terms. She "was filled with the sense of family and inwardly conscious of the scorns of time but blamed her position on the dark diceman Fate, constantly ruminating on what would have been and living in the splendor of the past."

Weighted down by these societal pressures, Lurlyne suffers an emotional breakdown. She wants, as she tells her father, people to hate her, which would at least justify her discomfort: "Nobody hates me. They dont even hate me." Richly, Foote's story signals the way that culture's ills rely on avoiding complete exposure and full disclosure. At the end of the story, Lurlyne pulls up short in voicing fully her relationships with the boys. Her father's response: a return to the anesthetization that enables the system of contradictions to persist: "He picked his way downstairs in the clear moonlight and made his way to the sideboard, the decanter and the glasses faintly clinking."

"This Primrose Hill" indicates just how deeply ambivalent Foote's understanding of his native region had become. Like Faulkner before him, Foote had begun to understand the personal and societal costs involved in the claims for Southern grandeur. He wanted to believe the tales of glamour that had been instilled in him from the cradle, but he also knew "way back then that there was something dreadfully wrong about his culture." Writing became his way to engage in the dialogue between his warring impulses. Writing also introduced him to the injustices that constituted that society, and because that structure constituted him, writing introduced Foote to his own complicity in the injustices. Writing was indeed both balm and poison.

Foote's writing cut into his academic performance, however. On the way to being inducted into Phi Beta Kappa that year, Walker Percy earned As and Bs in advanced chemistry, physics, and zoology classes, while Foote struggled to get past the most basic courses. To be sure, the first term at UNC was a difficult one—in some years, the drop-out rate ran as high as 40 percent. Nevertheless, Foote earned Bs in social science and English, Cs in biology and hygiene, and a D in math. Although UNC did not determine a student grade point average, Foote had earned the equivalent of a 2.4 GPA.

His grades did not provide his only shock that Christmas break. Invoking a legend that in a leap year, as was the approaching 1936, women could ask men to marry them, Anne Hargrave, who was back home from Mississippi State, proposed to Foote on New Year's Eve. Flattered, Foote nevertheless had his wits about him: "I don't think we should go get married until one of us can afford it." Back at school several days later, Foote received a letter from his mother saying that Anne had gotten married on January 2. The shocked Foote went straight out and bought a quart of whiskey. Drinking almost half of the bottle within a hour, Foote stood up to reach for water to mix with the liquor. He never made it. Instead he fell over on his face, passing out.

The loss of Hargrave was just one of several strange events that occurred during the final two terms of his freshman year at Chapel Hill. When Foote and Walker Percy started out on a bus trip to New York during their spring break, they almost did not reach their destination. With Franklin Roosevelt's 1936 reelection bid beginning, the two not surprisingly talked of the sitting president. Pleased with Roosevelt's social and economic agenda, Foote vehemently defended Roosevelt. Percy, however, found Roosevelt unstomachable. Echoing Uncle Will's sentiments, Walker thought that Roosevelt's concern for the average man made him a traitor to his class. The discussion took a more damning turn as they begin to talk about rights for Southern blacks. Foote suggested that the South and the United States should "raise them up to be just like anyone else." Smarting from Foote's overzealous advocacy of Roosevelt, Percy found Foote's proposal for racial integration anathema. If Foote's logic were carried out, Walker shot back, it would lead to racial chaos, the likes of which the South had never seen. With Shelby espousing these heretical views, Walker wondered whether they were brethren: "Do you call yourself a Southerner, man?" Percy then moved off to another part of the bus where he could cool off.

Exhausted by their feuding, the two boys checked into the Sloane House on West 34th Street and immediately went to bed, sleeping through much of the next day. When they awoke, their rift had diminished, and they set out to see the city. On that trip, Percy and Foote attended a performance of Arturo Toscanini's New York Philharmonic, but the rest of their six-day trip was not restricted to highbrow culture. In addition to visiting tourist sites, the two moved north toward Harlem, where they danced at the Copa Cabana Club. Even more exotically, these two boys, who several days earlier had argued about the place of blacks, made their way north of Central Park, where they listened to jazz at the Ubangi Club on Harlem's 7th Avenue.

Back at Chapel Hill, Foote's growing reclusiveness led to trouble with the ATO leadership. Although he had been eager to join a fraternity, he realized over the course of that year how much he detested Greek life. "I had no use for it," he said later. "I thought it was all a bunch of foolishness." The ATO brothers soon tired of Foote's apathy and insolence. At meals, they got angry when Foote refused to properly invoke God—both an honest intellectual dilemma for Foote and an opportunity for him to goad the fraternity members. Fearful that he was becoming a cancer for their organization, the Worthy Master called Foote in. During the interview, the fraternity leader claimed that "he had heard that Foote had a Jewish grandfather and they didn't like my attitude anyhow—the way I said the blessing and things like that." He then produced a litmus test, "So how do you feel about Jesus Christ?" In a deadpan tone, Foote responded, "I'm all for him. My biggest problem is with his father." Although Foote chuckled at his own response, which was for all of its humor an assertion of his atheism, the Worthy Master found nothing funny about the comment. "We don't want you to come back next year," he told Foote.

Foote's apathy was not limited to his fraternity. He had also lost interest in taking any classes other than those he wanted: "I hadn't been on the campus more than two or three months before I knew that I did not want to get a degree. I also had serious doubts about how long I wanted to stay there." After his first-term 2.4 GPA, Foote's grades plunged. He did earn four more As during the year—two in English classes, one in social sciences, and one in history—but his other grades were deplorable. During the winter and spring terms of 1936, Foote earned two Ds in biology and a D and an F in hygiene. Even in math, where he had fared so well in his entrance exam, now he earned an incomplete and an F. While Foote's performance in these classes was probably commensurate with the time and energy he invested, his F in a French class during his spring term was more surprising. With his interest in language and his love of Proust, one would have expected a much better grade. In any case, Foote was certainly right when he admitted that "I have very small smatterings of German and French and Spanish and Latin. I never stayed with one of them long enough to learn it." When Foote returned to Greenville in mid-June, he toted a dismal 1.9 GPA.

Fortunately for Foote, Walker had also chosen to return that summer to Greenville, where he would work under Dr. E. T. White, the chief pathologist at Gamble Brothers and Archer Clinic. Unfortunately, Walker had returned, in great part, because of Uncle Will's illness. Several months before, Walker had been visiting Will at Brinkwood, where one evening Will's speech suddenly became garbled. Recognizing the juxtaposed speech as an aphasic response to a stroke, Walker knew that his uncle needed help, and several days later they took a train to Baltimore to have the doctors at Johns Hopkins examine Percy. It was a fruitless trip: the Hopkins staff told Will that no great discoveries had been made in the field of aphasia. Although these last years would serve as a catalyst for the production of Will Percy's autobiography, *Lanterns on the Levee,* the aphasia would prove to be a "particular hell on earth." The attacks would come without warning. During the next year, when Foote was at the Percy house, he heard Will juxtapose several words. Instinctively, Foote laughed. In control of his faculties almost immediately, a sign that he probably suffered from what doctors now call expressive aphasia, Percy reprimanded him, "You mustn't laugh when I make mistakes. I have an ailment that makes me make those mistakes."

In Greenville that summer, Foote resumed his old position at the U.S. Gypsum Company. It was a summer spent negotiating the poles of Southern society, seeing in real terms what he had been exploring and exposing through his writing. He still longed to be part of the social elite, however, and during that summer Foote attended several events at the Memphis Country Club, the bastion of Memphis high society. At the same time that he attended these formal occasions, Foote continued to develop his perception of the travesties that befell blacks in Southern life, a culture that he would later call "perhaps the most racist society in the United States." One incident that summer etched itself indelibly into Foote's mind. While helping out at the Percys' Trail Lake Plantation, Foote witnessed the stabbing of one of the workers, a friend. On the following day, Foote went by the Greenville Colored Hospital to see his friend and take him some cigarettes. Inside the hospital, which he had never visited, Foote found patient beds jammed together almost on top of each other. Visitors barely had room to walk in between the beds. Medical attention was similarly remiss, as few nurses or doctors attended the patients. The hospital seemed more like a tomb than a station for repair and rejuvenation. Viscerally disgusted, Foote hurried out of the hospital, leaving his friend for the safety of the streets. The episode, Foote remembers, was one of the "experiences about race that hit me hard. I couldn't believe what I saw. That was one of the first shocks I had in terms of what was done to blacks."

By September, Foote was bound for Chapel Hill again. Far more than the previous year, where he had been anxious just to get admitted, he returned now with a purpose. Almost from the day that he moved into his off-campus boarding house, Foote worked tirelessly to groom himself for what he believed was a future writing career. Even under this regimen of reading and writing, his grades actually improved because, having completed the basic curriculum requirements, he could now take what he wanted. Of his eleven classes during 1936–1937, five were in English and four were in history. In the English classes, Foote shone, earning As in three undergraduate classes and an A and a B in two graduate classes. However, he struggled in his history classes—an irony for someone who would later make his mark as a Civil War historian—earning a C, E, D, and B. For the year, Foote earned a 2.6 GPA.

Foote's grades were not merely a reflection of his growing indifference to—and even distaste for—the classroom, but also a reflection of the time he invested in writing for *Carolina Magazine*. Contributing even more than he had done the previous year, Foote wrote five stories for the magazine during 1936–1937. The magazine staff also added new responsibilities to his workload: book reviews. In January, Foote reviewed John Dos Passos's *The Big Money*, and a month later, he reviewed Tucker Brooke's edition of Shakespeare's sonnets. For the May edition, Foote reviewed Caroline Gordon's *None Shall Look Back*, a novel whose "canvas of war and peace" touched him to the core.

Foote's review both suggested his own nostalgia for the Civil War, as well as how he considered modernity a threatening force:

> The heroes are all dead now. But in such works as this novel, and in the daguerreotypes, bearded and sternlipped, with all the braid and insignia of post and clan, they are like foreigners who never knew our land, or visitors who came and went and left after them only the memory of a passing: a few faint scars on the ignoble grass and ghostly echoes down the long halls houses had then, talking fine horses and fine whiskey with a sort of emotional disregard which the automobile has killed.

Foote's most impressive review appeared earlier, in December 1936: a two-page review of Faulkner's *Absalom, Absalom!* Although "The Literature of Fury" was ostensibly about Faulkner's novel, Foote's review quickly leapt from *Absalom* into a retrospective of all of Faulkner's work. He understood Faulkner's intention of employing seemingly incongruous lexical combinations as "dry vivid dusty" and "speculative, urgent, intent": "The contrasting word is put between two that are similar, so as to call especial attention to it: words which to a superficial glance seem not only contradictory but impossible, but which, nonetheless, create precisely the mood at which it is evident he is aiming." The power of Faulkner's novels, according to Foote, involved his willingness

> to look deep into the bowels of the human brain and come up with horrors past some folks' bearing . . . in all of them the final impression is the same: there are the same emasculated lusts and spent desires when the tales have spun their lengths, and the reader is left with the feeling that someone—sometime during the last few pages—has stolen his insides and left him suspirant on the beach of tragedy, with the tale of fury done and the fine proud tall figures gone to dust.

It would be ten years before older, wiser critics on this side of the Atlantic began to discern and appreciate what the college sophomore already realized.

It is one thing to praise one's literary hero, but it is another to steal his ammunition. As he would for years, Foote found it difficult to separate his own work from Faulkner's. One of Foote's stories, "Bristol's Gargoyle," which appeared in *Carolina Magazine*'s February 1937 issue, is so patently Faulknerian in theme, characters, and even style that one wonders whether Foote could have in good conscience claimed that he produced the work. Foote's Miss Esther Weathers combines two Faulkner characters: Miss Rosa Coldfield from *Absalom, Absalom!* and Miss Emily Grierson from "A Rose for Emily." Just as Mr. Grierson threatens to ward off all of Emily's suitors, including the Northern contractor Homer Barron, Colonel Weathers refuses to allow Esther to marry an outsider, the Virginian Porter Merritt. With her love interest thwarted by her overbearing father, Weathers, like Coldfield, withdraws into a bitter spinsterhood. After being pent up for decades, the sulfuric silence brims over poisonously—and with Faulkner-like voluminousness. Weathers tells the father of the story's narrator that the town understands her as "the vacuous mandacity [sic] moiling the surreptitious concomitant advocacy of their acrimonious vilification of what they are pleased to call one poor old defenseless woman." When she does act, Esther exercises a weird punishment on the neighborhood and her father by attempting to keep her father's death from the public, not unlike Grierson's decades-long sequestration of the dead Barron. Weathers mirrors Coldfield and Grierson so much that one wonders whether Foote was not self-consciously trying to provide future readers and critics with the road map of his literary heritage. If this is true, Foote bore all the subtlety of an anvil-striking blacksmith.

Although Foote succumbed to the dangers that often befall young writers, he had also begun to carve out his own voice by the end of his sophomore year. "And the Gay and the Blue," which appeared in the *Carolina Magazine*'s April 1937 issue, reveals the conflict between forming individual identity and, as a minority, having to heed the culture's demands. Eben Jaynes is a black swashbuckler whose masculine, carpe diem philosophy proves deficient when the voracious sexual appetite of his lover, Kate Mae Tanner, inverts Eben's assumptions about the delicacy of females and the supposed invincibility of males. He is unable to endure both Tanner's sexual demands and the loss of his male superiority: "the soul leaving me, like it was a leak in between my ribs where it would scape, like a punctured tire does: I could almost hear it going sssssss: slow and whispering sssssss." Jaynes finally lashes out at Tanner and kills her.

The story's tension involves the conflict between the rich sophistication of Jaynes and a white culture that denies subjectivity to blacks. Armed with an unwavering view of blacks as incapable and immoral, whites, as Foote suggested, fail to take into account the complex existence of the black characters, a richness depicted throughout Foote's story. Instead, Jaynes is conscious of the way that his hanging would be justified by "them pale-eyed bleach-haird country whitefolks." They would think, he assumes, "One less nigger, hey?"

By the spring of 1937 Foote knew that his time at Chapel Hill was coming to an end. One incident that spring encapsulated for him that his Chapel Hill years were a "funny experience." While taking a class on English novels under Dr. Dougald MacMillan, a teacher whom he later recalled with great fondness, Foote discovered that he was not enjoying reading Sir Walter Scott's *Quentin Durward*. Foote subsequently sought MacMillan out and told him, "Dr. MacMillan, I'm having real trouble with this book. I honestly don't like it and don't want to read it. Do you take that into consideration at all?"

MacMillan responded, "Well, if I were you, I wouldn't read it. No, if that's the way you feel about it, do that."

Based on MacMillan's advice, Foote put Scott's novel aside. When the examination on *Quentin Durward* came up, Foote wrote at the top of the test, "I have not read this book and it was with your permission I didn't read it, if you remember." When the test was returned, he had received an F. Foote approached MacMillan only to have the professor tell him, "That's right, you didn't have to read it. I admired your attitude and I think you were right not to read it, but, of course, as you know, I had to fail you. You couldn't get a passing grade without reading the book."

UNC had clearly outlived its use for Foote. When he left for home in June, he would not return, but the motivation for his departure was something that he misrepresented for years. In interview after interview in the following decades, Foote insisted that the greatest catalyst for his leaving involved his belief that war was imminent: "One of the reasons I didn't go back to school . . . was that the war was heating up in Europe. We all saw it coming." War *was* coming—in fact, it had already come. On the Iberian Peninsula, the Spanish Civil War had raged for more than a year, and in the middle of the continent, Germany occupied the Saar in 1935 and invaded the Rhineland in 1936. Tensions mounted. What previously had been dismissed as no more than a bad dream now awakened European rulers. Hitler's actions probably resonated with Foote far more than with the average American. As a product of the Lost Cause, Foote had studied military history since his childhood. "I read . . . Civil War things when I was a boy, practically the way other people read detective stories," he once said. From Ernest Hemingway's writings about war, Foote also believed that it offered golden opportunities for budding writers. Given these influences, news of the European battles and campaigns stirred him, and Foote and Louie Nicholson reportedly entertained thoughts of fighting in Spain. But Foote's claim that he left UNC because of the war is specious. Although hindsight provides perfect vision, there were still several high-water marks to be reached before a second world war would commence. When Foote left UNC, the annexation of Austria, the 1939 Munich Conference, or, later that year, the invasion of Poland had not yet taken place, events that would first have to occur to dislodge the United States from its isolationist neutrality.

Although Foote's claim that he wanted to fight Hitler was real, it was not the primary reason for his departure from UNC. Foote himself alluded to the dubiousness of this claim when he told James Newcomb that he went "indirectly" into the service following his departure from college. The real reason involved his belief that he was now ready to become a professional writer. Having served years of what he thought of as an apprenticeship, Foote now considered himself ready to blaze his own trails. Although his friends chuckled at his quixotic notions, with the experience of writing for the *Carolina Magazine,* Foote sensed that it was time to journey out into the realms where he would forge in the smithy of his soul his own identity and the identity of his region. He wanted to go home, close his bedroom door to the world, and write. As he would acknowledge from the sanctuary of his later success, "That's the real reason I went home, to write the novel."

# Writing and Fighting
## 1937–1945

War alone brings up to its highest tension all human energy
and puts the stamp of nobility upon the peoples who have
the courage to face it.
> —Benito Mussolini, *The Italian Encyclopedia*

War brings out the worst and best in men, and combat can
be a valuable experience for a writer.
> —Shelby Foote, 1968 interview with *Roanoke (Va.)*
> *World-News* reporter Bob Mottley

To be always ready for war is the surest way to avoid it.
> —François de Salignac de La Mothe Fénelon, *Telemaque*

NO FATTED CALVES AWAITED the prodigal son when he returned
to Greenville in June 1937 to launch what he alone believed
would be an illustrious writing career. Under any occasion, the town's
former troubled child would not have been showered with homecom-
ing greetings; cotton season was in high gear, and Greenville residents
were engrossed in the rituals of the early cotton season. Such practices
seemed especially welcome that year because, just months before, the
town had avoided a flood almost as serious as that of 1927. Watching the
river swell upstream, to the point that Paducah, Kentucky, disappeared
under a wall of water, displacing 230,000 residents, Greenvillians
anticipated the worst. Somehow, though, the newly reinforced levees

held back the water. When Foote arrived home, the relief was still palpable, and residents happily watched the cotton pierce the soil and make a stand—routine had reasserted its hold on madness.

Flood or no flood, Shelby had not been looking for any sort of royal welcome. He merely wanted to get to "know [my homeland] better, year-round." While he roughed out his first novel in his head, he worked at a number of jobs, the experiences of which became for him, "at least as valuable as what I got in Chapel Hill." For thirty cents an hour, Foote served as a carpenter's helper on the construction of a bridge connecting Greenville to the Arkansas side of the river. It was no job for the faint of heart: 90 feet above the Mississippi, Foote carried lumber on exposed catwalks. During the harvest, Foote also worked in cotton gins, where alongside Delta blacks and sharecroppers, he weighed cotton being brought in by area planters.

Once the bridge was completed, Foote took up his old job at the town's U.S. Gypsum mill, until a few months later, when a job at the *Star* opened up. Hodding Carter needed a copy editor, and Foote took the position. At the *Star*, Foote was at the beck and call of Carter; his wife, Betty; and Donald Wetherbee, who was now the managing editor. Humorously characterizing the pecking order, Foote claimed, "It was Hodding himself who worked harder than anybody, unless maybe it was his wife Betty who worked harder than he did, and then Donald Wetherbee . . . who worked very hard, then I was the [copy editor] who did not work very hard." According to Betty Carter, Foote characterized himself accurately, and the Carters refused to give him too much responsibility because he manifested so little initiative. "He was a terrible worker," said Carter. "You never knew if he was going to be there." As Wetherbee said, "I wouldn't bet my last dollar on him being there to read copy if it got in the way of writing. He was irreverent and insolent, but in a charming way."

Foote's poor work ethic at the *Star* stemmed from his frustration about having to earn his daily bread. Not only was he saving his energy for his own work, but the romantic Foote felt slighted that others did not appreciate his literary potential. Consequently, he maintained a simmering resentment that had no definite direction in its release: Anyone could become fair game for his antics. On several

occasions, Foote allowed mistakes in newspaper copy to go by uncor-
rected, as if to revenge himself on a world that failed to recognize his
genius. Once, Foote's "oversight" led Greenville residents to discover
that the day's weather forecast was "partly cloudy with shitty winds."
When writing *Follow Me Down* a decade later, Foote remembered his
former jokes. In that novel, Russell Stevenson, the *Clarion*'s managing
editor, allows the newspaper's society editor to embarrass herself by
overlooking copy about one bride's wedding dress collar being made of
"white lice." At its worst, Foote's subversiveness became rebellious. In
1940, while Hodding Carter held a one-year Nieman Fellowship at
Harvard University, Foote prodded Wetherbee to push for more auton-
omy and responsibility. Then Foote attempted to enlist other newspaper
employees in his cause. Running the paper in Hodding's absence, Betty
Carter feared that Foote's actions could cause a mutiny. Interceding in
time to quell any revolt, she berated the young insurgent for his actions.

In spite of this half-baked mutiny, Foote invested the minimal
amount of time and energy in the *Star* job, focusing instead on his
novel. As is the case with many first-time novelists, he had turned to
autobiographical material. In Foote's case, that meant mulling over not
merely his family, but the person who had siphoned off its fortune and
consequently its prestige, his grandfather, Hugh Foote. "I wanted to
learn what it was that had made him lose all of his money," Foote later
said. Questioning his grandfather's motives became a rich source of
inquiry for him, and he began gleaning information and stories from
family members and friends. As *Tournament* emerged over the next few
years, its focus would not surprisingly be squarely on Hugh Bart, a
thinly veiled portrait of his grandfather. It was, Foote candidly admitted later, "a young man's attempt to deal with what he imagined might
have been his grandfather's life."

Before he started what he at first called "Courtyards Where
Jamshyd Glared and Drank Deep," a title taken from a line in Edward
Fitzgerald's *The Rubáiyát of Omar Khayyám*, Foote felt that he needed to
make a pilgrimage to Oxford, Mississippi, to see Faulkner, his greatest
model—and his greatest anxiety. That was no easy task: Faulkner had
a reputation of being aloof and uncompromisingly private. But driven
by his usual audacity, Foote overcame any reservations he had about

intruding. In mid-June 1938, with Walker home from Columbia Medical School and the two of them bound for Brinkwood, Foote told his friend that he wanted to stop at Faulkner's home, Rowan Oak. Percy did not want to. Having not yet come under the spell of Faulkner's work and fearful lest Faulkner connect him to Uncle Will, Walker asked his friend on what grounds he would make his visit. Foote said that he would ask Faulkner where he could purchase a copy of *The Marble Faun*, Faulkner's first book, a 1924 collection of poems that had not sold well and was now out of print. Percy thought the pretext specious, and when they drove up the gravel driveway at Rowan Oak, he refused to go in: "I don't know that man and he doesn't know me and I'm not going to bother him." After Foote responded, "He's a writer. It's all right, we'll go see him," Percy came down even harder: "Well, *you* can go knock on his door. *I'm* not going to do it." Percy said that he would stay in the car and read either *Gone with the Wind* or the Raymond Chandler novel he had brought on the trip.

Foote stopped the car and "waded" through the pack of dalmatians, fox terriers, and bird dogs littering the yard. A few moments after he knocked on the door, a bearded Faulkner appeared. Suddenly struck dumb, Foote somehow exhaled, "Mr. Faulkner, I'm from Greenville and I'm wondering where to get a copy of your first book, *The Marble Faun*." Faulkner thought for a moment before telling Foote, "I don't know where you can get one. Maybe Leland Heyward [Faulkner's agent] could find you one. I can give you his address." Quickly warming to the young Foote, Faulkner walked around the yard and grounds with him, telling Shelby that he had "just finished a book about your country over there." (The book was *If I Forget Thee, Jerusalem*, or as it was initially published, *The Wild Palms*, whose "Old Man" half chronicled the 1927 flood.) Happy perhaps that his novel was finished, Faulkner was unusually talkative, chatting for two hours while Walker melted in the sweltering car.

When he rose to leave, Foote told Faulkner that "Will Percy's nephew" was in the car. If Faulkner remembered the drunken afternoon on the Percy tennis court, he did not acknowledge it. In fact, he said that he would come outside to greet Walker. Percy and Faulkner exchanged pleasantries, and then the two boys resumed their trip to

Brinkwood. Although Walker and Faulkner would never meet again, the visit marked the first of a series of visits between Foote and Faulkner. Nevertheless, it was this first visit that was monumental for Foote. "For Shelby," writes Patrick Samway, "the chat with Faulkner provided a pivotal moment in his life; he had met one of America's most famous novelists at the peak of his career." (However epiphanic it was to meet a writer unlocking the convoluted dynamics of the South, those lessons came slowly. Just hours after meeting Faulkner, Foote and Percy saw D. W. Griffith's *Birth of a Nation,* the work often cited as the inspiration for the twentieth-century rebirth of the Ku Klux Klan.)

Now energized, Foote returned home to begin his novel. In the late summer or early fall of 1938, he took the step of generating a fictional cosmos for which he was going to be sole owner and proprietor. In the *Carolina Magazine* stories, he had already identified fictional towns that constituted his imaginary Jordan County, including Bristol, the county seat. Now, like Thomas Hardy and Faulkner, Foote provided a visual matrix—a map—for the locales that appeared in his stories. Actually, two maps accompanied the manuscript, one of the entire county and one an inset of Bristol. Those maps laid out a geographical schema that coincided closely with the real Greenville and Washington County: "Jordan County was laid down, Bristol was where it was, Ithaca was where it was, the lake [Lake Ferguson] was where it was." Foote's preparation for the novel went a step further than the creation of the maps. In a practice that James Newcomb would later call a "rage for symmetry," Foote created his first novel outline. That outline spelled out an eight-chapter structure, each of which would have seven subsections. Foote even identified how many words would constitute each chapter and event, for unlike a writer who allowed stories to develop organically, Foote needed to know what scene he would be writing on any given day, even weeks and months before he reached that point in the book.

By February 1939 Foote felt confident enough to begin. Working not only on weekends, but before and after his copy editing at the *Star,* Foote plugged away at depicting the effort of Asa Bart, his novel's narrator, to understand the life of Asa's grandfather, Royal Bart (a character whose name would later be changed to Hugh Bart). As Asa states, "It was in . . . talking to others who knew Bart while he came and strove and went, that I learned the full story [and] grew to know [him]." "When all the facts were marshaled," Asa says moments later, "and all the opinions counted, I emerged with the complete figure." Throughout 1939 Foote maintained a hermeticism that his Greenville friends found comical. When LeRoy Percy would drop by Foote's apartment and try to get him to play golf, Foote refused. "He kept saying that he was going to have a novel published, but we laughed, and said, 'Shelby, there's no way.'" While Percy laughed, Foote worked, and as he did, he reveled in the experience of daily putting down words on paper. *"Tournament,"* as Foote later said, "was a sort of thrashing around in the English language, a discovering that maybe I could write." If he could write, Foote still labored under a Faulknerian yoke that he could not shake. In describing the mansion Solitaire in the novel's first draft, Foote wrote,

> Its dusty brick rainstreaked, its low pillars garbled, itself gutted, despoiled, vacant now for two years, the land not even planted this season, with an air of febrile advocacy, a charivari of grandeur, possessing grain for grain the texture and stuff of the dregs of nothing more that backwardyearning hope, recapitulant, somnolent, tinted by the red rising sun behind it, the panache of dust and desire, now off to the mansion surmounted a slope which rose from the lake to the road and seventy five yards beyond.

Furthermore, Solitaire's slave quarters had "whitewashed walls blistered and scaled and peeled as if by disease or perhaps just longevity like the cosmeticcaked cheeks of dropsical dowagers, they squatted in grim remise of pristine licitness, spared or overlooked by yankee firebrands." When a planter named Cassendale Tarfeller dies in a duel defending his daughter's honor, "all that remained was a dustfouled suit covering the deathmisshapen bundle of weary bones and flesh." For a while, Foote had Wetherbee read his work, but Wetherbee acutely realized how much of an albatross Faulkner represented for Foote. After he told Foote that the novel sounded too much like Faulkner, Foote would never again ask him for any help.

Foote's words signified Faulkner in another way. Like Faulkner's novels, Foote's "Courtyards Where Jamshyd Glared and Drank Deep" explores the region's past, specifically the creation of the Delta. At points, the novel veers out of its way to explore the founding of the county. Isaac Jameson, Royal Bart's father-in-law, "had been the region's first settler and . . . at one time owned nearly all the land on the eastern shore of Lake Jordan." While the novel repeatedly turns to explore the county's past, what may be the most interesting element of the narrative is the way that Asa's focus on the past and the plunge into his grandfather's life serves as a refuge from the present. Asa's view of the town is less a general phenomenon of town replacing country than it is a reflection of the 1930s cultural milieu. In this period of "historical unrest . . . the railroads had out-done the river packets; the motion picture and the automobile had altered all conceptions of leisure and love; the electric light and the telephone no longer were gadgets—all these, and more, were part of a new and different life." Within the town itself, a "four-block business section" represents an "intricate and highly effective snare."

To its credit, Foote's novel does not simply view these changes as isolated phenomena. Instead, Foote understands how these changes dramatically affect the culture's social and racial dynamics. This new town culture has led to a highly intense social flux. Writing about the girl whom Hugh Jr. marries, Kate Bateman, Asa indicates that her appeal is not merely tied up with her beauty, but with the fact that she "represented one of the leading families" of Bristol. Such pressures from boys wear her down. As she tells her father, "I'm so tired. . . . So tired of coming in night after night with my mouth all slick and weak from kissing." Kate's behavior reflects the novel's insistence on the town's immoral behavior, reflected nowhere more clearly than in the preachers' admonitions to their congregations about the consequences of Haley's comet: "It was coming soon, and sinners had better get right." Any failure to rectify their actions would mean that they "would all be burnt to cinders in their beds or choked by the poisonous gases."

If the town's capitalism produces social strife, *Tournament* goes even further in suggesting that the town's commercial structure produces racial anxieties amid its de facto integration. Bristol's four-block business section includes "banks and saloons, law offices and markets, but mostly they were clothing stores." As Grace Elizabeth Hale notes in

*Making Whiteness,* clothing stores were especially pregnant with the possibility of racial mixing because such arenas not only called for the common touching of goods, but perhaps the purchase of the same clothing, a signifier of an unsanctioned equality: "Whites and blacks could meet the other wearing the same hat or dress." These Bristol clothing stores, which are run by whites, such as the children of Abe Wisten, feature "facades . . . slashed with banners flaunting ruin and opportunity in foot-high letters: FIRE SALE! BANKRUPT! FORCED TO SELL! BUY NOW!" Although the lack of racial-specific language here seemingly refers to both white and black consumers, in another place, Foote refers to the downtown snare as one "baited mainly for Negroes."

The novel's sense of an impending crisis comes through strongly in its depiction of the 1903 flood. As Michael Denning claimed, "Metaphors of natural disaster were deeply embedded in popular discourses about the Depression." Denning's statements seem tailor-made for Foote's novel: The flood becomes a metaphor for both the crisis facing 1930s Southerners and the extraordinary means needed to resolve it. As Hugh Bart rows from place to place in an attempt to save stranded Deltans, he finds the "old landmarks" submerged and erased: "There was a strange new countryside all around them. Roads, fences, shrubbery, the old landmarks, the lake itself, all were gone. Now there was only the limitless stretch of water, littered with flotsam and dotted at random with barns, houses, tree tops, and a line of telegraph poles marching in even progression beside the submerged railway." Not coincidentally, moments after the description of the featureless landscape, Bart finds himself with a potential race riot, writ small, on his hands—one of the most disturbing scenes that Foote would ever write. In an effort to sink the makeshift casket for Major Dubose's body, Bart orders several nameless black men to jump overboard with the coffin to send it clear of the boat. The men protest: "Captain, I aint lying: I caint swim." Nevertheless, Bart tells them, "Youre going to do it, all right. Youre going to do it, if I have to capsize you myself." When they do not move fast enough, Bart threatens the men: "He took out the derringer" and "cocked it," saying, "I'm tired of talking. . . . Stand up now, both of you."

On one level, Bart's actions may have been abhorrent to a writer who was at least sympathetic to the New Deal's efforts to create a more democratic South. On another level, however, Foote could justify Bart's actions as appropriate for the restoration of societal order. Attitudes toward the New Deal and Roosevelt had changed dramatically even in the two years since Foote had returned from UNC. Like many Americans, Southerners had grown disenchanted with Roosevelt's authoritarian attempts to pack the Supreme Court. In what Pete Daniel calls the "conservative revolution," some Southerners claimed that the New Deal had "metamorphosed" the South by replacing "the old paternalistic system and bec[oming] the master of Southern agriculture."

Out of this impulse, many apologists, such as Will Percy, instituted an imaginary return to the plantation as a remedy for the social and political ills. Just before and during the time that Foote wrote "Courtyards Where Jamshyd Glared and Drank Deep," Percy was writing *Lanterns on the Levee,* his infamous defense of Southern plantocracy. As Percy wrote of the supposed loss of the region's traditions, "We of my generation have lost one line of fortifications after another, the old South, the old ideals, the old strengths." For Percy, the country's post-Depression zeal for democracy spelled trouble: "In time we are all good democrats; in the manger we look the same and in the grave. But at this particular time and place, viewed not from a peak in eternity but from the ephemeral now, I rejoice to be of a caste which, though shaken and scattered, refuses to call itself Demos."

Although in coming years Foote would disavow Percy's views on Southern paternalism, in the late 1930s he was enormously influenced by them. "I didn't develop any opinions of my own until about the time he died," Foote acknowledged in a 1980s interview. So impressionable was *Lanterns on the Levee* for the young man that in at least one place in his own novel he virtually copied Percy's words. Percy had written of one of his father's workers crying out after his father's death: "The roof is gone from over my head and the floor from under my feet. I am out in the dark and the cold alone." In the final lines of his own novel, Foote had Royal Bart mumble, "The four walls are gone from around me, the roof from over my head. I'm in the dark, alone."

Although *Tournament* may have enabled him to, as Foote said later, "look . . . at my homeland in a way I had never done before," given Percy's influence, it is not surprising that the novel would become an apology for Southern plantocracy. For Foote's narrative, Solitaire, or the imaginary return to it after the family moves to Bristol, represents that nostalgic solution. In one scene following the move into town, Royal Bart tells his wife that for her upcoming birthday she can have anything that she wants. Although she refuses to tell her husband precisely her wish, what she wants is her former home: "Solitaire, she almost said." Mrs. Bart's wish is not the only moment when the agrarian homeplace serves as a sanctuary removed from contaminating capital. In the chapter "Solitaire," Bart discovers that his money in Lawrence Tilden's bank has been funneled into a loan for a clothes merchant, Abraham Wisten. When Wisten cannot make his payments, an extension that Tilden rejects, the merchant commits suicide. Once Bart learns that his money was indirectly responsible for the suicide, Bart demands that his money be returned to him—at Solitaire. When the messenger arrives with the money, Bart, symbolically, refuses to touch the tainted cash. "Ernest," Bart tells his servant, "take the gentleman's satchel." After the exchange is made and after Bart finally touches the bag—but only after it is "partly covered by the big napkin"—Bart refuses a "receipt." The only residue of the transaction that he wants involves witnessing the cashier's cloud of dust as he leaves the plantation: "Get off this place. . . . Git!" In other words, Solitaire, as a retreat, becomes a means to inoculate Bart from the tragedies spawned by the practices of the consumer culture.

Foote's novel's endorsement of Southern plantocracy does not come without qualifications. At times, the novel echoes Cobb's claim that sharecropping was a "strategy in dealing with tenants . . . to keep them economically dependent enough to ensure that they would be ready to work whenever labor was needed." In spite of the fact that he was "too hard a worker," Patterson's "farming forty acres of another man's land with another's man's mules" ensured that he could not succeed. Consequently, Patterson was "foreclosed for his furnish," which the novel understands as a "common enough practice in the region."

But Royal Bart's nobler version of plantation-owning seems a more appropriate form of governance, something akin to Will Percy's claim that sharecropping "offer[ed] as humane, just, self-respecting, and cheerful a method of earning a living as human beings are likely to devise." After Patterson's bad experience, Bart enlists him as an overseer, and in that position, Patterson "began to know something like peace for the first time since he had lost his land." Moreover, Bart has compassion for his workers in a way that potentially alleviates racial strife. When Bart discovers that his black workers are "having women trouble," he sets himself up as "an expert on the subject": "Let her ramble if she wants," he tells them. "Dont make a move in her direction. She'll be back.'" Just as Solitaire's daily activity yields a "pattern" for Bart's life, so too does Solitaire seemingly provide order for the dilemmas of the 1930s.

Day by day, the draft of the novel grew; by early 1940 the manuscript weighed in at almost five hundred folio-sized pages. On March 11, just over a year since he had begun the novel, Foote finished a first draft of a hefty 651 pages. Driven by momentum, Foote immediately began a typescript of the manuscript, revising as he typed the novel, including dropping the title "Courtyards Where Jamshyd Glared and Drank Deep" for the simpler *Tournament,* a title that captured Bart's shooting events. By April, a 374-page bound typescript was ready to be sent off to a publishing house. Foote thought that Alfred A. Knopf was the logical place to send his work. Although he would later claim that Knopf had "the best-looking books in America . . . and I wanted mine to have all the advantages I felt sure that it deserved," he actually sent his manuscript there because Knopf's Harold Strauss was handling Will Percy's *Lanterns on the Levee.*

Out of respect for and obligation to Percy, Strauss began reading Foote's manuscript soon after receiving it. Strauss thought that the novel showed enough promise to have other editors read it. Like Strauss, these editors liked what they read and realized that Foote had talent; but they also believed that *Tournament* in its present form would not sell: It was "too experimental in nature." Several weeks after Foote submitted his manuscript, weeks that "surely [were] the longest two in my lifetime up to then," Strauss wrote the young man that Knopf could "publish it, at perhaps not too great a loss." Strauss feared, however, that the longer-term consequences of "being identified by the nation's bookshops as a nonselling writer—a curse that might well follow [him] all the rest of [his] writing life" outweighed any "fleeting satisfaction" of Foote having his novel published. Concluding the letter, Strauss suggested that Foote put the novel in "cold storage." "The best thing I could do," as Foote later remembered the letter, "would be to put it away and come back to it after I had written a second or possibly third novel which they would be most interested in looking at."

Dejected, Foote initially considered burning the novel. But before he did so, Foote realized that the Knopf editors had given him high praise, however qualified. Valuing that opinion, he took their advice and put the book away in his mother's linen closet. In the meantime, the war that Foote had been looking for since his Chapel Hill days had erupted.

In a December 31, 1951 letter to Walker Percy, Foote declared that he had no regrets about a war experience that for all of its initial promise of glory, defused disappointingly. "I don't regret that five-year chunk the war took out of my life," he wrote. With the letter coming on the heels of a six-year period during which Foote had published several short stories and four novels—enabling him, he claimed, to join the ranks of the "American writers of all time"—Foote's successes certainly colored his view of his wartime activities. Foote would spend, in one form or another, the rest of his life trying to redeem himself for the greatest disappointment of his life.

In 1940, though, his hope for martial heroism burned bright. Foote longed to fight, and Hitler's overreaching finally provided him with the opportunity to develop the heroic self fermenting in his imagination. After playing the acquiescing partner for several years to Hitler's waltz through central Europe, the Allied leaders finally found Germany's September 1, 1939 blitzkrieg invasion of Poland unstomachable. In the eyes of the Western powers, Hitler had overstepped the line in the sand, the 1938 Munich Agreement that British Prime Minister Neville Chamberlain had promised would bring "peace for our time . . . peace with honor." Although the United States did not declare war on Germany, many Americans responded to Hitler's growing rapaciousness by joining National Guard units. Short of enlisting in the regular armed forces, participation in the guard represented the closest step to military service. Nowhere was this response clearer than in the South, where enlistment in the National Guard soared. "That was something that we felt we should do," said Roy Hanf, a Greenvillian who was one of those enlisting.

In spite of the fact that he was in the midst of finishing the draft of *Tournament,* Foote too enlisted: "I felt very strongly that we should be in the war—to stop Hitler—so I joined the Mississippi National Guard." Along with most of the Greenville enlistees, Foote joined the National Guard's 31st Division, known as the "Dixie" Division, whose nickname came from its tradition of snapping to attention any time Dixie was played. Headquartered in Montgomery, Alabama, the division had four companies, two of which were located in Mississippi: one in Greenville and the other in nearby Greenwood. As with most of the enlistees, the Mississippi National Guard bestowed Foote with the rank of private.

Private Foote thought that federal mobilization would come quickly, but the United States continued to stick, at least officially, to its stubborn isolationism. Even though federal action was slow in coming, the Dixie Division worked to hone its skills: Division members frequently spent weekends on duty at the Greenville Armory, and in the summer of 1940 the division trained for two weeks at Camp Shelby in Hattiesburg, Mississippi. The stars seemed to favor Foote. Not only had he been promoted to sergeant, but when Foote entered Camp Shelby, he did not fail to realize that the camp was named after his relative Isaac Shelby, a man who was the governor of Kentucky, but more importantly for Foote's present mindset, a Revolutionary War hero.

Finally, the wait was over. In November 1940 the U.S. government called the Dixie Division into service. Now federalized, mobilization occurred soon afterward, and Foote was ready. With Douglas Southall Freeman's *Robert E. Lee* and G. F. R. Henderson's *Stonewall Jackson* in his pack, Foote and the Greenville company convoyed to Camp Blanding, a new military base near Starke, Florida—35 miles southwest of Jacksonville. The camp, they soon discovered, bore little more than a name. When Foote and DeBerry Turnipseed rode into camp, they saw no buildings or structures of any kind, only acres of sand dotted with stubborn palmettos. Turnipseed turned to Foote and asked, "Sgt. Foote, are we going to live here?"

Once they established quarters on the sandy soil, exercises began. Assigned to the 114th Field Artillery, Battery A, Foote soon shone because he, like his Major Barcroft in *Love in a Dry Season,* had spent so much time preparing mentally for its challenges and exigencies. According to Roy Hanf, Foote was an "outstanding soldier. He more than knew his job, and he could grasp anything they threw at him." In one artillery exercise, camp officials singled out Foote for his intelligence and skill in zeroing in on a target. Moments later, the officers called up Foote to a command post overlooking the target area—the "first and only time," according to Hanf, a Dixie Division noncommissioned officer was invited up to the post. "They wanted to see how he would perform," said Hanf. Foote executed his assignment perfectly, orchestrating a series of direct hits on the target.

For almost a year, the Dixie Division remained at Camp Blanding, grinding daily through military drills. At night and on weekends, Foote and his companions went off-base to Jacksonville, where they could drink and visit the town's red-light district. When they had longer periods of leave, they traveled back to Mississippi, trips often taken in Foote's new $1125 white Oldsmobile convertible. Charging $7 per passenger, Foote made his monthly car notes from his friends' fees.

As much as anyone in the company, Foote could mix it up; his quick wit and resourceful storytelling made others eager to include him. However, where others never rose above such play, Foote's mind knew a level of seriousness foreign to most of the other soldiers. As Roy Hanf remembered, in the middle of a conversation Foote would often make "some reference to something that Shakespeare had written or he might make some sort of reference to something musical or to someone in the musical profession."

With one Dixie Division soldier, Louie Nicholson, Foote let his guard down. As they had done throughout their boyhood, Foote and Nicholson spent a great deal of time together while they were at Camp Blanding. When Foote went off-base to Jacksonville, he was often with Nicholson, who had relentless energy. Nicholson lived recklessly and hard, drinking and womanizing with great gusto. "He lived," Foote remembers, "as if he was going to be killed. He had as much fun as he could." Toward the end of their time at Camp Blanding, however, Nicholson told Foote that he had decided to join the Air Force. Flying airplanes, he thought, would provide a thrill he did not find in the peripatetic artillery. "I'm going to get out of here," Nicholson told him. Foote began crying; not only did he not want to lose his friend's company, he did not want to lose his friend. Foote pleaded, "God Almighty, Louie, don't do that." When the two of them parted company several days later, they said good-bye for the last time. Nicholson would be killed several years later flying a mission on the dangerous Ploesti raids, Allied efforts to bomb German oil reserves in Romania. When Foote found out about Nicholson's death, he "cried for days." It would be, Foote once said, "the greatest loss I ever had."

At the end of 1941 Foote himself was leaving Camp Blanding—and the Dixie Division. Following the December 7, 1941 Japanese attack on Pearl Harbor, the Dixie Division readied for combat in the European theater, while the Army sent Foote to officer candidate school in Fort Sill, Oklahoma. His fellow soldiers considered Foote's assignment fitting. As one said, Foote was "a natural born officer because of his brilliant mind." On his way west, Foote detoured through Greenville to celebrate Christmas. There, he saw Walker, who would soon be heading back to New York for a pathology internship at Bellevue Hospital. Since his graduation from Columbia Medical School in June, Walker had been working at Gamble Brothers and Archer, where he could keep tabs on both Uncle Will and Bunt Townsend, a clinic nurse whom he had been dating for several years. Percy had met Bunt, from nearby Doddsville, several years before when he first worked at Gamble Brothers and Archer, and the two had become far closer than any of Walker's previous relationships.

Just before Christmas, Will Percy had suffered a cerebral hemorrhage, and when Foote arrived home from Camp Blanding, he found his mentor laid up at Greenville's Kings' Daughters Hospital. The strokes of the past years had beaten down his arteries, and his skin had shriveled up. A few months earlier, the Johns Hopkins doctors told him that "he had the oldest-looking body for a man his age that they had ever seen." Embarrassed by the exposure of chinks in his previously flawless armor, until his hemorrhage, Percy had confined himself to his own home, where he puttered around in his "coat," a kimono.

Friends and family members sensed that the end was near, and several came to spend that Christmas of 1941 with Percy. From New Orleans arrived former University of Tennessee star football player Bob Horton. From New York came Percy's former Sewanee roommate, Huger "Huggie" Jervey, formerly the dean of Columbia's Law School and now the director of Columbia's Parker School of International Studies. At Kings' Daughters they gathered, hoping desperately for some sort of miraculous recovery. It would never come. In his final days, Will Percy lost all ability to communicate, and on January 21, 1942 he died of a cerebral hemorrhage. Foote learned of Will Percy's death from a telegram his mother sent him at Fort Sill, where he had begun OCS training. Another one of his fathers had died.

The wheels of the nation's war industry slipped into gear as a country awoke to find war no longer imminent, but present. Through the intensive regimen of OCS training, Foote readied himself for leadership. His emergence into the officer ranks coincided with the country's preparation for warfare; the vague, unarticulated role he felt destined to play was finally being scripted. Like his great-grandfather, Henry Foote, he was going to lead men into battle.

Live combat was what Foote craved; but once again it proved to be a distant echo. After Foote completed the OCS course and was commissioned as a first lieutenant, the Army sent him back to Camp Shelby, Mississippi, where he served as an artillery instructor. His military service had taken an unusual trajectory; in returning to the place from where he had begun, he seemed to be regressing. Putting a good face on a disappointing situation, Foote at least used his skills in training young recruits. It was they who would be experiencing combat firsthand. Sitting continents behind the front lines, Lieutenant Foote would continue to tell green kids how soldiers should operate when under fire. The irony cut him deeply.

Of some consolation was Foote's proximity to Greenville, and he frequently made trips home. Foote wrote his friend that Greenville had "gone to hell"—full of pilots training at the U.S. Basic Flying School at the Greenville Airport, but emptied of most of those people with whom Foote had grown up. Although LeRoy Percy, who would ultimately be a bomber pilot in the European theater, was still at home, settling Will Percy's estate, his other friends had been flung to all corners of the globe. His former Dixie Division mates were bound for North Africa to force German General Edwin Rommell's troops across the arid desert into Egypt. In the South Pacific, Phin Percy, now an Annapolis graduate, would soon become a PT boat commander, serving in the same fleet in which John F. Kennedy would earn military distinction. Of Foote's friends, only Walker Percy had not joined the war effort.

As the months passed, Foote's desire to get into the war grew greater and greater. The war's ongoing campaigns tormented him. Craving activity, Foote took actions during this period that flew in the face of everything he had previously believed. An avowed atheist, Foote had himself confirmed an Episcopalian in 1942. His decision to convert was not based on any special belief in the Episcopal Church's interpretation of Christianity, for his attendance at Greenville's St. James Episcopal Church had been "worse than irregular." But remembering the problems that his Jewish ancestry had caused him at UNC, he wanted to make sure that no obstacles stood in his way when an opportunity for combat did arise. As he later said, "I had to make a decision somewhere along the line whether I wanted to be a Jew or a Christian. And I chose the Christian thing because I figured that life's hard enough without having to carry around that Jewish thing with you too." His conversion was, he admitted later, a "matter of convenience. . . . I didn't have any religious preference. So it wasn't a question of choosing between them as religions." So uncomfortable was he about his conversion, though, that he never told many of his closest friends.

Whether God was responsible for provoking the Army in his favor, Foote soon began moving toward combat. Late in 1942 he was sent to Camp Bowie near Austin, Texas, to captain Battery A of the 50th Field Artillery, 5th Infantry Division, which would soon set sail for England. After several months of preparation with the 50th Artillery, Foote started for Europe in July 1943. Although Foote's company rushed to New York, their transatlantic crossing was delayed.

With their embarkation several days away, Foote asked for and received leave to go upstate to see Walker, who was also in the midst of a religious conversion of his own. But where Foote had forsaken his atheism for a creed he did not subscribe to, Percy was in the beginning stages of a deep spiritual and intellectual odyssey that would reorganize his entire life. Shirking the positivistic materialism that he had formed out of his belief in the wonders of science, Percy had stumbled into an existential pilgrimage that would ultimately land him at the high altar of Catholicism. The move from scalpel to pilgrim's rod occurred after he contracted tuberculosis late in his first spring at New York's Bellevue Hospital. After suffering persistent coughs, head colds, sore throats, and chronic fatigue over the course of several months, Percy underwent an extensive physical examination. X-rays revealed a spot on his right lung. Although no vaccine had been developed, public education had enabled tuberculosis to drop from the first to the seventh cause of American deaths by 1937. Nevertheless, 600,000 people still contracted tuberculosis annually, 70,000 of whom died. Pathologists were particularly susceptible to the disease. Working around cadavers that often carried the bacteria, these doctors feared contracting the disease; by the time Percy discovered the tuberculosis in his lung, he had performed more than a hundred autopsies on tubercular patients. The greater chance of picking up the bacteria, however, came from living patients. In fact, Percy believed that he had contracted tuberculosis from an acquaintance, and he could list a handful of patients and family members stricken by tuberculosis.

Treatment began almost immediately. He was not yet a case of, as Percy and other Bellevue residents noted on charts, a patient who "went rapidly downhill and made his exitus," but neither was there time to dawdle. Doctors treating tuberculosis in the 1930s believed that a quick response significantly improved the chance for a full recovery. In June 1942 Percy had undergone a pneumothorax, a procedure in which air was injected into the chest cavity while the lung was collapsed. Throughout the summer, the pneumothorax was repeated every few weeks. By September, Percy left New York City for Saranac Lake, an upstate sanitarium located in the Adirondack Mountains. The cooler, more temperate air there provided patients with the opportunity to relax their lungs. While he convalesced, Walker embarked on a period of self-examination that had been far more characteristic of his friend's previous reading program. According to Samway, "He put aside Macleod's *Physiology* and Gay's *Bacteriology,* and took up the works of Soren Kierkegaard, Martin Heidegger, Gabriel Marcel, Jean-Paul Sartre, and Albert Camus." Percy had also undertaken an extensive study of the church fathers—Saints Augustine and Aquinas, among others.

Riven by these competing emotions of eagerness about his new discoveries and fear about what they held—if anything—Percy developed a sour-edged disposition that others had previously not seen. Arriving at Percy's "cure cottage," Foote quickly witnessed his friend's meager lifestyle and stern regimen. "Immediately struck by Percy's utter isolation," Foote now understood why Walker sounded so resigned in his letters. Only three people visited Percy on a regular basis: a doctor, the woman who delivered his meals, and the woman who bathed him. Although Percy was certainly glad to see Foote, his friend's presence also reminded him yet again of a world passing him by. Western civilization was locked in a heroic Armageddon, while Percy found himself holed up in an out-of-the-way sanctuary for sick people, its closest city, Montreal, in another country.

Following his short visit, Foote returned to New York, and with the rest of the division, soon set sail for England on the *Queen Elizabeth*. Arriving on the west coast, the 5th Division quickly moved inland and set up base in Birmingham, in the country's Midlands region. An industrial city, Birmingham held little allure for the soldiers when they had free time. But with London only "a fast train ride away," Birmingham's noxiousness did not matter much. Although it was rebuilding from the damage that had been suffered three years earlier in the Battle of Britain, Hitler's failed, preemptive strike to end the war early, London was still Britannia's imperial capital. When he visited London, Foote stayed with a friend he had previously met in training, who had a flat on Mount Street between Grosvenor and Barkley Squares. By his own admission, Foote's visits did not involve pilgrimages to such London monuments as Westminster Abbey or the National Gallery of Art. Those sites would have to be saved for another day and time. Instead, Foote's London visits were bacchanalian holidays, and he was "too busy drinking and helling around" to do much around the city.

In late 1943 the 50th Field Artillery moved to Northern Ireland. Foote and his battery began final preparations throughout the spring of 1944 for what they knew would be the invasion of Europe. Although he and his men did not know when that invasion would occur, Foote knew that the situation augured well. After so much military training, he was now poised to participate in what would become the largest military invasion the world had ever known. But as their preparations intensified, things grew heated for Foote in his own camp. When a lieutenant colonel upbraided one of the men in his battery for dubious reasons, Foote's insubordinate impulse flared up. Considering the reprimand unwarranted, he went over the lieutenant colonel's head to the batallion's colonel. The colonel agreed with Foote, and he subsequently overruled his subordinate's order.

Foote had nevertheless wronged a superior, and he was going to pay for his insolence. A West Point graduate, the tyrannical lieutenant colonel did not want a civilian to upstage him. From that point on, the officer began scrutinizing Foote's every move, seeking an opportunity to gain revenge. "He was keeping books," Foote remembers. He did not have to wait long. Several weeks later, Foote returned to camp after curfew. On that evening, he had been in Belfast, visiting Tess Lavery, an Irish woman he had begun seeing. On the return trip, the train broke down. When Foote finally reached camp two hours later, the battalion leader arrested Foote. Foote attempted to explain the reason for his absence, but the commander refused to listen to what he considered "alibis." When he finally learned that the train had indeed broken down, the unrepentant commander released Foote.

But the zeal with which the commander pursued Foote would not go unrewarded. He soon had another occasion to apprehend Foote, and this time the charge stuck. The camp where Foote and his men were headquartered lay just over 26 miles from Belfast, a figure insignificant other than the fact that camp jeeps were not supposed to be taken outside of a 25-mile radius. When off-duty soldiers took jeeps into Belfast, they technically violated this rule, but almost without exception, camp officials overlooked the transgression. With the commander tailing him, however, such minor infractions were not a luxury for Foote. On another trip to see Tess, one in which he had signed out a jeep, the lieutenant colonel arrested Foote for falsifying government documents.

Arrested on legitimate charges, Foote found himself court-martialled. The lieutenant colonel wanted him out of the Army. In any other month, Foote may have been able to defend himself successfully against the charges. But with the Normandy invasion looming, an attack that called for the strictest of security measures, the general commanding the battalion could take no chances. Insubordination of any kind represented a potential danger for the imminent invasion. The court martial found Foote guilty and ordered him stateside with the albatross of a dishonorable discharge. Short of death or incarceration, it represented the Army's worst punishment.

The verdict leveled Foote. Just weeks before his battery would arrive on the French coast, all of his efforts of the last five years had been thwarted. Once again, his unwillingness to tone down his brazen cocksureness with an authority figure had cost him dearly. But where his audacious act of showing up unannounced at UNC had proven cheeky enough to overcome Leuckenbach's objections, Foote had no available recourse with the inflexible Army. During the next few days, Foote stumbled around Belfast with Tess, wondering how he could have negated all of his preparatory work.

Blinded with disappointment and anger, Foote nevertheless was sober enough to understand that the dishonorable discharge could have serious future repercussions. He had Walker contact Huggie Jervey, whose position at Columbia provided him high-level government contacts. Foote himself soon called Jervey, who agreed to provide any help that he could. After contacting Army officials over the next few months, Jervey would be able to get Foote's discharge commuted to an "other than honorable" discharge. While this penalty did not alter the fact that he was permanently banned from the Army, it did not bear the stigma of the original punishment.

In the meantime, Foote had to decide where he would settle. Greenville was not an option because he feared that residents would look disfavorably on his seeming avoidance of the D-Day invasion, which had cost the lives of several Greenville boys. Notwithstanding the dubiousness of the charges levied against him, Foote was too embarrassed to return to Greenville: "I couldn't go home in disgrace." He was right: Many Greenvillians would later fault him for getting dismissed from the Army, accusing him of finagling his way out. "That was the story going around town," one Greenville resident later said. When Foote finally returned to the United States on the *Mauritania* in August 1944, he settled in New York. The city offered a number of advantages, but, principally, it provided one of the best places to get back into the war. Foote also hoped to get Tess Lavery to the United States so they could be married, and New York offered more of an identifiable locale for Tess to come to than some Mississippi town in the American hinterlands. The crisis of Foote's court-martial had precipitously catalyzed their several-months-old relationship. Thin though this reasoning would prove to be, it was enough for Foote to arrange for Tess to come to New York to become Mrs. Shelby Foote.

While he waited for his reenlistment and his marriage, Foote needed to find a job and a place to live. With the war having drained the city of residents, Foote found an apartment in one of Manhattan's toniest neighborhoods, the Upper East Side. Although his $9-a-week apartment at the corner of 86th Street and Park Avenue was small, it was superbly located. Sitting on a rise, Foote's apartment building offered a vista down into midtown Manhattan. Discovering that the Associated Press's New York bureau was short of reporters, Foote bought a new suit and went for an interview. With his previous *Star* experience, the news organization hired him to man the local desk at nights.

On one weekend off, Foote made a trip up to Saranac Lake. While there, he and Walker Percy caught up, tightening a bond increasingly centered around intellectual and literary matters. Foote welcomed Percy's new discoveries as fertilizer for his own interests, and during their walks around the lake they talked books.

In spite of this increased interest in the liberal arts, Percy still planned to resume his medical career. With X-rays indicating that his tuberculosis was in remission after two years, the sanitarium released Percy. Returning to New York, he moved into the empty servant's quarters at Jervey's 1150 5th Avenue home. Percy arranged an instructorship at Columbia that would begin in January 1945. During these months, Walker and Shelby spent time together around the city, going to a number of restaurants and cinemas. Late that year, they also traveled to Atlantic City, where Percy stayed for several weeks because he found the Jersey shore soothing.

Percy did not get back to New York until October, when Tess arrived to become Mrs. Shelby Foote. During the first days that the three of them were together, they went to movies and ate at excellent New York restaurants that Foote, the budding epicurean, had discovered. After acquiring their marriage license, Foote and Tess arranged to marry a few days later. It was an ill-advised decision. Although he did not verbalize his concerns about marrying Tess, they manifested themselves on the wedding day. Riding with Walker, his best man, to the Church of the Transfiguration, on 29th Street near 5th Avenue, Foote began whistling a rendition of Cole Porter's "Don't Fence Me In." Things did not improve upon meeting up with Tess, who was accompanied by Percy's friend and occasional date, Memphian Hope Galloway. When the minister saw Foote and Lavery looking pale and trembling, he told them, "I have never seen two people getting married look so solemn." Foote tried to shrug off his comment, but Tess could not. On two separate occasions, the service had to be stopped because she cried so violently. When the minister asked her if she wanted to go on with the service, Tess nodded her head through her tears.

In spite of this awful beginning, Shelby and Tess got along well in the months after the wedding. Finding a new apartment in Washington Heights, a neighborhood at the northernmost tip of Manhattan, they settled into a domestic routine. Soon afterward, though, Foote learned that the Marine Corps had accepted him. The Marines needed men— apparently even to the point of taking people whom other services had rejected. Foote did not care about the rationale behind their move; he appreciated their willingness to accept him. In January 1945 with the Allied troops racing toward Berlin, Foote reported to Marine boot camp in Parris Island, South Carolina. Tess traveled with him and lived in a trailer outside the camp.

Known for their rigorous demands and seeming superiority, the Marines at Parris Island scoffed at Foote's previous Army experience. "You used to be a[n Army] captain, didn't you?" one asked him. "You ought to make a pretty good Marine private." He did make a good Marine. At boot camp, his superiors quickly recognized his brains and sent Foote to intelligence school at North Carolina's Camp Lejeune. From Lejeune, he went to San Diego, where he worked on the construction of rubber boats for a possible invasion of Japan, an enormous undertaking that many said would require a million men. However, just when it looked like the door was open for him to see action, the United States dropped an atomic bomb on Hiroshima on August 6. Three days later, American pilots dropped a second atomic bomb on Nagasaki. The Japanese surrender followed. While others celebrated in the streets, Foote was devastated that World War II was over. According to Tony Horowitz, he had "missed the great trauma of his own generation's adolescence." Like Malcolm Barcroft in *Love in a Dry Season*, which Foote wrote in the years after World War II, he was disheartened. Having been rebuffed in his attempt to enlist in the Army for World War I, Barcroft headed home to Bristol on the train: "Rejected, dejected, he watched the scenery slide past the Pullman window." Despite spending six years in the armed services, war too had slid by Foote.

# First Successes

## 1945–1951

Success or failure lies in conformity to the times.
—Niccolò Machiavelli

NOT LONG AFTER THE war's end, Foote and Tess took off for Greenville. Whereas other soldiers were stuck at their military assignments for months, Foote's departure from the Marines came swiftly because he had accumulated such a large number of discharge points—one of the only benefits of his extensive military experience. Although he was still reluctant to return to Greenville, fearful of any comments that others would have about his supposed bowing out of the D-Day fighting, Foote did not want to refuse his mother's generous offer of having the couple live with her. Such an arrangement was hardly the best prescription for a new marriage, but he also did not want the burden of additional expenses.

In the weeks following his return to civilian life, which "afforded the unfamiliar triple luxury of sleeping, eating, and defecating, all under a single roof," Foote found a job with a local radio station, WJPR. In his new job, Foote produced advertisement spots to fill the few breaks in the station's never-ending music, which led Greenvillians to render the station's call letters as "We Just Play Records." At night, he and Tess often socialized with friends, including Walker Percy and Bunt Townsend.

Foote also quickly resurrected his writing. Years later, he would recast this return as a fortuitous accident: "Out of boredom and desperation, I reached up onto the top shelf of that hall closet and took down the typescript I had put there more than six years ago, back in that other world that had existed before the war." Hardly miraculous, Foote actively turned to his writing, in part, to redeem himself for his unsatisfactory war experience. Desperate to get something published, Foote began combing the 1940 *Tournament* manuscript for potential story material: "Some of it still looked pretty good to me and some of it looked God-awful." One of the sections that looked pretty good was "The Flood," which was about Royal Bart's efforts to bury the dead Major Dubose in the swelling waters of the 1903 flood. Alone for thirty years, Dubose, a former Civil War soldier, had turned to writing about the war as a way to alleviate the pain that racked him during the first years after his wife's death: "Major Dubose wept at night alone, and for five years he refused to be comforted." Writing constantly, Dubose had amassed what others believe to be 6000 pages of "microscopic characters" on the Civil War, an effort that makes him a curiosity. When someone sees a page 6403, another citizen claims, "Then I reckon he's through Shiloh," one said. "Shiloh? He must be taking his fiftieth whack at Appomattox by now."

While watching the flood waters rise around Solitaire, Royal Bart is visited by Dubose's servants, who declare that the major has had a stroke. When Bart arrives at the major's house, in a barely audible voice Dubose indicates that he wants his "Man you sep." It's too late—the water has already seeped onto the manuscript, something that Dubose never learns because he dies in the next few minutes. Ironically, Bart and the two black sharecroppers who try to sink Dubose's body into the raging waters weigh it down with the iron box that houses the manuscript. Their efforts to bury him would lead to the disturbing scene of Bart ordering the servants to jump out of the boat with the makeshift casket. In a novel plagued with narration, Foote had chosen a dialogue-filled section that bordered on the explosive, not merely for its inherent dramatic qualities, but for its showcasing of the dynamics between race and power in Southern paternalism, an issue that was making national headlines after several postwar murders of Southern black veterans.

These events infuriated President Harry S. Truman, triggering what would ultimately lead to proposed civil rights legislation.

Stealing away for precious minutes and hours, Foote scrawled in black ink over the 1940 *Tournament* typescript, deflating primarily the rhetorical excess of his earlier efforts. His labor was slowly teaching him how to "screw his ass to the bottom of the chair and write." Such concentration required shutting out those around him. Foote expressed indifference, at best, to most Greenvillians, and, at worst, he antagonized them. Residents remember Foote's disregard for even common courtesies. When he went into Nelms and Blum to visit Kenneth Haxton, who now had taken over the store for his family, Foote took his new white boxer, Bo. As Haxton remembers, "The dog would come into my store and scare everybody there." Nelms and Blum customers complained, but even after Haxton asked Foote to leave Bo outside, the boxer continued to march in with his owner, scattering shoppers in his path. Because of such behavior, Foote developed a reputation for being, in the words of one young Greenvillian, "that mean old man over on Washington Street." Sure about himself, Foote did not care how others viewed him. As a friend would later note, "He hasn't paid a lot of attention to codes of behavior."

Living so self-centeredly, though, meant shutting out even those closest to him. On a number of occasions when LeRoy Percy dropped by to ask Foote to play golf, Foote pleaded industry. More than just disregarding friends, Foote shirked his wife, and a relationship that was unstable at its outset, "quickly went from bad to worse." Tess had tried to fit in with the people of her new hometown, but in spite of her best efforts, she never struck the right chord. When the couple socialized at local bars—often honkey-tonks on U.S. Highway 61—Tess wore formal, full-length white gloves. Although the out-of-sorts Tess contributed to the relationship's decline, Foote's monomania for his writing irrevocably crippled their marriage. Driven by his inner demons, Foote refused to invest the time and energy necessary to make the relationship work. Marriage "galled" him, he later told Walker Percy, an attitude that virtually doomed any of his relationships.

By early 1946 their relationship was living out that promise. In February, Tess initiated divorce proceedings and Foote made no efforts to reconcile their differences. In the March 8 papers that finalized their divorce, Foote agreed to pay $25 per month in alimony, as well as 15 percent of his future royalties, an odd inclusion and one suggesting that because *Tournament* had earlier been rejected, he was not sure if he would have any future work accepted. Less than two years had passed since their horrible New York wedding. (In a final irony, Tess later married the bombardier from the *Enola Gay*, the plane that dropped the atomic bomb on Hiroshima.)

If Foote lost a wife, he gained a vocation. In the months preceding the divorce, he had set in motion the engine that would produce his first literary victory. Foote had asked Ben Wasson, now the *Delta Democrat Times*'s literary editor, to represent him. On the surface, Wasson seemed the unlikeliest of candidates to direct a new writing career. At best, his weekly "The Time Has Come" columns featured drum-beating for area authors, but more often they served as bulletin boards for local reading and music clubs. But before he had beat his retreat back to his native Greenville several years earlier, Wasson had been a literary agent in New York and Hollywood; for a time, he had also served as an assistant editor at Cape and Smith, where he edited his friend Faulkner's early work. (When Faulkner finished *The Sound and the Fury* at Wasson's New York apartment in 1928, the future Nobel laureate threw the manuscript down on the bed, saying "Read this one, Bud. It's a real son of a bitch.")

In April, when Foote finished a clean, twenty-six-page version of "Flood Burial," Wasson sent the story to Stuart Rose, the fiction editor of *The Saturday Evening Post*, often the first destination for writers' stories because of the magazine's generous payments. Rose liked what he read. "Flood Burial" met all the requisite *Post* criteria: it was humorous, not too erudite, action-filled, and—of great significance for a magazine known for its covers—it offered several scenes that could be easily illustrated. But "Flood Burial" was a little long. Rose wrote Foote that if he could shorten the story by two pages, the magazine would accept it. In a 1973 interview, Foote said that he refused to alter or omit one word from "Flood Burial," merely rearranging the story's appearance: "I re-typed it with two more lines on each page and sent it back." Foote's manuscript, however, tells a different story. Not only did Foote make a number of omissions, but he painstakingly recorded how many lines he cut on each page. At the bottom of the manuscript pages, Foote kept a running tally of how many more lines needed to be cut to eliminate the two pages that Rose called for.

Pared down, the revised story was sent back to the *Post*. Just a few weeks later, Foote received a letter saying that "Flood Burial" would be published in the magazine's September 7, 1946 issue. With that same letter came a $750 check, an amount almost large enough to buy a new automobile. Ecstatic, Foote ran over to Walker's garage apartment at the Percy place to celebrate the first professional literary achievement of what would ultimately be, between them, a raft of triumphs. The next day, Foote headed downtown. His first stop: Wasson's office, where even though Mrs. Foote complained that Wasson was "taking" her son's money, Foote gave him the customary 10 percent agent's fee. Afterward, Foote sailed through Greenville's downtown district on a shopping spree, landing a shotgun, a leather jacket, and a desk lamp. Later that day, he went by WJPR to announce that he was quitting. His new office would be a garage at the Allen Court Apartments, which he leased with some of the remaining *Post* money. Foote closed the garage door, nailed a rug over it, and installed a gas heater. While the rental of the study represented a certain confidence about his future work, the termination of his job signaled a cocksureness that bordered on the ridiculous. On the basis of the acceptance of one story, he had become, in his mind, a full-time writer.

Made brave by the first blush of success, the unemployed writer lost no time in working on another story. Not wanting to "pull any more out of the book *[Tournament]*," Foote set out to write something new: "Tell Them Good-by," one of his most moving stories and a piece that Foote would repeatedly incorporate into later works. Drawing on his exposure to the music he had heard in local juke joints and New Orleans venues, Foote had "Tell Them Good-by" follow the musical development of a self-taught black Delta cornetist, Duff Conway, whose talent serves as a passport out of the Delta to New Orleans bars, where he "develop[s] his final tone and style." From New Orleans, Conway moves to the New York club circuit, where his music haunts and captivates one white, would-be classical composer, Harry Van. Van tells himself, *"Something is happening that means everything I've done adds up to nothing."* As a result, Van shirks the classical pieces that he previously had composed. Ultimately, Duff Conway returns home, where he commits murder.

On the surface, the story seems to be about racial issues. Although race was always an issue in the South, Truman's advocacy of civil rights had infuriated Southern Democrats, some of whom would walk out of the 1948 Democratic Convention and nominate South Carolina Governor Strom Thurmond as their Dixiecrat presidential candidate. Foote's story seemingly reacted to these concerns as it featured a black man struggling to assert his own identity. In particular, Foote represented whites' reaction to the death of a black man. The revelling of the white jailer, Roscoe Jeffcoat, in Conway's electrocution suggests a hatred whites reserved for Southern blacks. Although Foote is careful to avoid having Jeffcoat explicitly identify Conway as black, perhaps afraid of how the *Post* would view such blatant racism, Jeffcoat's vitriolic remarks at the end of the story bespeak an underlying vengeance. After Conway is killed with the first jolt of electricity—the "deep, pulsing hum and the odor of burning"—Jeffcoat tells the assembled crowd, "Yair! Just one bump on the road to glory, and he never knew what hit him. Yair. Steady now and we'll hit him again; not because he needs it, but because the law says so. Yair!"

For all of the racial suggestions of "Tell Them Good-by," the story primarily focused on something else: a belief that an entertainment industry bent on earning profits has corrupted art. Young and idealistic, Foote held a steadfast belief in the purity of art. Already in "Flood Burial" Foote had suggested the way that Major Dubose's writing—his effort to express himself—had gone unappreciated. But in "Tell Them Good-by," Foote made this issue even clearer. Conway's "unique blare" gets compromised by a band leader, Rex Ingersoll, who transforms his sound into a counterfeit of its original purity. Ingersoll tells Conway that to keep the "icks" happy, he would have "to take some of the blare out of it. . . . On those passages that belong to you, go right on and ride it out. . . . But other times you have to hold back and melt into the others." In exchange for the new sound, Conway earns "two hundred and fifty dollars a week." Frustrated by Ingersoll's effort to make his music commercially viable, Conway tells the band leader that "my horn don't suit this town." Even worse, Foote directly connects Ingersoll's suggestion with the tuberculosis that Conway contracts. After "Rex put a mute in the horn and hung a tin derby over the end of it," Conway begins to suffer a cough. "My wind backed up on me," he tells Van of the initial tuberculosis symptoms. "What was supposed to be coming out the other end got choked back down my throat. I like to bust."

Foote adds one more component to this theme of the corruption of art—he attributes the source of this corruption to the North. Always an issue for Southerners, particularly with the emerging racial tensions, the North-South divide grew even wider after World War II. The belief that the North imposed its views on the South also had a parallel cultural component. As Allen Tate argued in "The Profession of Letters in the South," Southern writers can never fully express their concerns "so long as [their work] must be trimmed and scattered in the Northern magazines, or published in books that will be read as curiously as travel literature, by Northern people alone." This North-South divide did not escape Foote. He had already articulated a fundamental interregional difference in his Jordan County maps, suggesting that his "county in general is industrial in the northern part and agricultural in the southern part, so it's a microcosmos of the upper country, in a sense." Also, by sending his work to New York publishing houses, that gulf was only compounded in Foote's mind. Not coincidentally, in "Tell Them Good-by" Conway's sound is not muted when he leaves the Delta, nor is his music corrupted in New Orleans. In the Crescent City, Conway enjoyed "the years which made him what he was when, later, musicians who were supposed to know called him the best horn man of his time." It is only in New York that Conway's music gets compromised, which was, not coincidentally, the place where magazines and publishing houses compromised Foote's own work by editing it. Indeed, in several years, when he reached a point where he could make demands of editors, he would insist that his work not be edited—their only responsibility would be to publish it.

Page after page, this breakthrough story rolled off his typewriter. Foote would later claim that he focused on the story's length, wanting "Tell Them Good-by" to be twice as long as "Flood Burial." For a writer obsessed with the number of words that he could write in a given day, week, or month, such a claim was not far-fetched, particularly because magazines paid on a per-word basis. Whatever the reason, soon after he submitted the story to Rose, a letter from New York arrived at the Footes' house. As Foote remembers the letter, "We do not know whether this is a long short story or a short novelette, and we do not care. Our check for $1500 will come in the next mail." "Tell Them Good-by," Rose informed Foote, would appear in the *Post's* February 15, 1947 edition, whose cover would announce that the issue included "a complete novelette by Shelby Foote."

Foote's success bordered on the phenomenal. His first two postwar attempts to have something published had succeeded. Moreover, by publishing them in a national magazine, New York literary agents would see them. His stock rocketed skyward. Such success both excited and scared Foote, however. As he admitted to Walker Percy, he felt confident, but he also feared that as his work improved he would set the bar higher for himself: "The most heart-breaking thing about it is: the better you get, the harder youll have to work—because your standards will rise with your ability." Under such pressure, Foote knew that he needed some time off before he started another story, and when Percy suggested that he drive cross-country with him in the summer of 1946, Foote readily agreed. Struggling with decisions about whether to propose to Bunt Townsend, who was moving to New Orleans to work for an internist, Percy sought sanctuary. He was in love for the first time in his life. As Tolson writes, "His experiments with other women had convinced him that Bunt Townsend was the only woman he wanted to be with." But after losing two parents, Percy found it difficult to reveal his emotional inner sanctum, fearful that such exposure would again invite loss. Troubled, Percy wanted to go to New Mexico because the West, as Will Barrett says in Percy's *The Last Gentleman,* was "the locus of pure possibility." In the South, a person constantly ran up against "antecedents . . . ever the sense of someone close by." By comparison, in the West, "what a man can be the next minute bears no relation to what he is or what he was the minute before."

In early July, the two men left Greenville in Percy's green Packard convertible. As they motored west, Foote discovered that Percy's escape was not merely rooted in his indecision about marrying Bunt.

Percy hovered on the edge of converting to Catholicism, a huge move for a member of family who had been indifferent Protestants or non-believers. Moreover, Percy wondered whether his growing desire to write could be reconciled with the allegiance that he considered necessary for religious faith. Foote's atheism only compounded Percy's dilemma. As Foote would tell his friend several years later, "I seriously think that no good practicing Catholic can ever be a great artist; art is by definition a product of doubt; it has to be pursued." During one night of drinking in Santa Fe's La Fonda Hotel, where they had set up shop while Percy looked for a permanent place to live, Percy told Foote, "If you take the claims of Christianity seriously, then it seems to me that Catholicism is where you have to end up." Perhaps Percy's sincere religious enquiry reminded Foote of his own earlier conversion, for Foote lashed out at his friend, "Yours is a mind in full intellectual retreat."

Foote stayed with Percy for ten days, after which he flew home; unexpectedly, his friend followed close behind. Although he had found a place to live in Santa Fe, Percy had also found some answers for the questions plaguing him. After stopping briefly in Greenville, Percy soon headed south to New Orleans and Bunt. He moved with a sense of purpose and proposed to her a few weeks later. Eager to get on with their lives, they set November 6 as their wedding day.

A week before the wedding, Foote and Percy flew out to New Mexico to retrieve Percy's car. Although they needed to get back in time for the wedding, Walker and Shelby took a northerly route home so that they could see the Rocky Mountains. The sublime heights lost their appeal for Foote, however, as he came down with flu. When they arrived in New Orleans several days later, Foote's condition had worsened. He needed to collapse in bed for several days, but with the wedding less than twenty-four hours away, any extended rest loomed like some dreamlike fantasy. He pulled himself out of bed the next day and stood up for Percy as his best man. In spite of his ailments, Foote, "who was always with us," according to Bunt Percy, drove Walker's car the next morning 500 miles up to Chattanooga, Tennessee, while the newly-weds took the train.

When the Percys headed northward for Brinkwood the next day, Foote returned to Greenville. Never one to work in transit and now feeling better, Foote sat down to work on "Miss Amanda," a story that had been moiling around in his mind during the weeks of traveling. Although "Miss Amanda" would introduce an outside interloper, Charley Drew, it was strikingly similar to the stories of aristocratic families in decline that he had written for the *Carolina Magazine,* including "Bristol's Gargoyle" and "This Primrose Hill." Writing something familiar was ideal because Foote wanted to quickly crank out a long story. He not only assumed that his work would be accepted without question, but he assumed that the longer it was, the more princely sums he would receive. Consequently, Foote sat down and whipped off the story of Drew's attempt to marry into the Barcroft family. Within weeks, he had finished the seventy-page story, which he promptly sent to Rose. What he had not counted on was that the editors at the mainstream *Post* would believe that Foote's depiction of the insular Barcroft family had crossed the boundaries of propriety and good taste. With the return of his manuscript came a letter from Rose "informing . . . me that the *Post* did not publish stories containing implications of incest."

The *Post*'s rejection of "Miss Amanda" in late 1947 marked a turning point in Foote's career. In what is an understatement, Foote remembers that he had "kind of hurt feelings about it." Perhaps because his thirtieth birthday had come calling a few weeks earlier, on November 17, a "terrible day . . . one of the worst days of my life," now he knew that he would have to be even more committed to his work: "I settled down and realized that writing was an important thing and that I had better work very hard at it." If his previous work involved cloistering himself away, his subsequent work would be downright monastic.

Never one to shy away from hard work, Foote soon began a disciplined, daily writing schedule that featured all of the flexibility of Commencement Day at a military academy. He rose early each morning; until noon, Foote hunched over the door that, supported by two sawhorses, served as his writing desk. After a break for lunch, he returned to the desk until late afternoon or early evening, grinding away in pursuit of some crystallized perfection. Until Foote finished his work for the day, he was off limits. Incoming telephone calls went unanswered, and knocks at the door went disregarded. Day after day, week after week, the schedule continued. "A lot of people think we [writers] wake up in the middle of the night with something called inspiration," he would say later. "I think what you'd better do is get a good night's sleep. You've got a hard day ahead."

For a man who labored upward of fifty hours per week, Foote produced relatively little volume. While his hero Faulkner could churn out whole chapters in just a few days, Foote curbed any desire for speed in favor of thoroughness. Attempting to create a "little sonnet" in each day's work, a perfect combination of lexical reference and sound, Foote wrote no more than five hundred words per day. Juggling words, Foote gauged the candidacy of each phrase as he mouthed and sounded whether a lexical combination "provided the precise rhythm" he desired. Sometimes, he would spend as much as forty-five minutes trying to decide how a sentence should be completed. Foote even encouraged this deliberation by writing in an ideogram-like hand, what one reporter called "strange Oriental" script. His writing utensil also kept him from sprinting ahead too quickly—a dip pen, which constantly required refilling. In spite of this slow composition process, Foote actually produced novels as fast as other writers, if not faster. While other writers would rewrite manuscripts again and again, Foote revised little after he finished the day's work.

In early 1947 his meticulous efforts were directed toward the subject of war, not merely because he continued to feel "cheated, as though I was dealt out of the big adventure," but because he had planned to write novels on the three Civil War battles that had taken place in or just outside of Mississippi: Shiloh, Brice's Crossroads, and Vicksburg. Previously, those works lay in the future, but now, anxious to have a novel published, Foote accelerated the plan. Of the three battles, he naturally turned to Shiloh, the one major battle in which his great-grandfather, Henry Foote, had fought, and a place that he had visited many times: "For me, something emanates from that ground, the way memory sometimes leaps at you unexpectedly."

While *Shiloh* was still in the planning stages, Foote hatched a plan to bankroll himself while he wrote the book. Turning back again to the *Tournament* manuscript, he extracted a section from the "Solitaire" chapter about the efforts of a Jewish Bristol merchant, Abraham Wisten, to open a new store. (Wisten had been the beneficiary of money that Royal Bart invested in Lawrence Tilden's bank.) Like Foote's grandfather Rosenstock, Wisten was an Austrian Jew who left Vienna, in part, because of the conscription, but now he had landed himself among the gentry—or so he hoped. Wisten's emporium was to be "the finest, merchandise bazaar, between Memphis and New Orleans." When the store does not draw enough customers and Tilden refuses to extend the loan payments, depression sets in. "Ive lost my honor and all, all I own, and now I aint even pitiful. I'm apsurd," Wisten tells his wife just hours before he commits suicide.

Foote hired the *Delta Democrat-Times*'s Bill Yarborough to typeset "The Merchant of Bristol." He planned to sell the story's 260 copies—all signed—at $1.50, a project that would hopefully gross him almost $400. (In the process of producing "The Merchant of Bristol," Foote also indirectly launched the Levee Press, which was Foote's suggested name for a venture by Ben Wasson, Hodding Carter, and Kenneth Haxton. Over the next few years, the Levee Press published works by Mississippi writers, including Faulkner's "Notes on a Horsethief," Eudora Welty's "Music from Spain," and a collection of Will Percy's poems.) When "The Merchant of Bristol" was published on June 2, 1947 sales of the story disappointed Foote. At $1.50, Foote was asking people to choose between his story or a nice dress shirt. Clearly, he had overestimated his appeal.

Foote soon turned his attention to *Shiloh*. He realized that although he knew the time sequence and spatial configuration of the battle almost as well as any park ranger, he had no intention of merely transcribing these events with cold objectivity. He did not want his account of war to be like top-down historiographical accounts that were, as one character in the novel says, "written to be read by God Almighty, because no one but God ever saw it that way." Instead, in what would be the opening salvo for *The Civil War*, Foote wanted to render battle through the prism of individual experience, as Stephen Crane had done in *The Red Badge of Courage*.

As early as his 1937 *Carolina Magazine* review of Caroline Gordon's *None Shall Look Back*, Foote had indicated the importance of enlivening any account of war. More recently, in the years around the composition of *Shiloh*, two *Delta-Democrat Times*'s book reviews that he wrote outlined this combination of historical facts and poetic license. In a review of Fletcher Pratt's *Ordeal by Fire: An Informal History of the Civil War*, Foote highlighted the importance of adhering to historical facts, an observation that he found wanting in Pratt's book. "In the first of the 'Lee to the rear' incidents," Foote wrote of *Ordeal by Fire*, Pratt "writes that the General was 'majestic on his huge white horse,' though every schoolboy knows that Traveler was small and gray with a black mane and tail." However, if these historical details were not compromised, certain liberties could be taken. This "style," as he often termed this impulse, would avoid what he considered to be the general dry analytical nature of standard historians, and the modus operandi of the social historians coming into vogue in the post–World War II years. In his October 12, 1947 review of Stanley Horn's *Gallant Rebel*, Foote criticized that nameless historian: "When he turns novelist, it is asking too much to expect the historian also to be a stylist, to handle the English language as well as he handles the little three-by-five notes on which he makes his notes." But even such handling of the English language had its own potential land mines. In the *Ordeal by Fire* review, Foote suggested that Pratt's errors resulted directly from his high-flown rhetoric: "Mr. Pratt is apt to become carried away with himself, to reach for a colorful adjective whether it appears in the sources or not." As Foote would encapsulate his methodology in the bibliographical note to volume I of *The Civil War*, "Accepting the historian's standards without his paraphernalia, I have employed the novelist's methods without his license." Eloquent though that summation of his methodology was, it also protected him from criticism from either camp. Foote could be both novelist *and* historian without being accountable to either novelists *or* historians.

After a trip to Shiloh on April 6 and 7, 1947, the anniversary of the battle, where he slept on the battlefield and made a charge with a stick bayonet, Foote returned home to begin the novel, whose monologue chapters he grouped into what Helen White and Redding Sugg have called a series of "diptychs." In the first two monologues—the first diptych—Lieutenant Palmer Metcalfe, an aide-de-camp to General Albert Sidney Johnston, and Union Captain Walter Fountain provide background on not merely the events that led to the Civil War, but information on the generals involved in the battle. The Metcalfes claim Johnston as a family friend, while Fountain has known Grant as a fellow townsman from Galena, Illinois. The second diptych features alienated elements of both armies. Confederate Private Luther Dade is a poor white from Solitaire Plantation whose lack of education makes him unable to understand some of the military commands handed down from on high: On one occasion, Dade mistakes the "Austerlitz" of Johnston's battle order for "oyster itch." In the other monologue of the diptych, Union Private Otto Flickner joins the hordes of Union deserters fleeing from the battle. With the rest of the masses, Flickner hides under the Tennessee River bluff, "wishing," as do the others, "like Jesus they could walk on water." Finally, the third diptych represents a new-found respect for the generals who have proven themselves as fighting soldiers in Shiloh's baptism by fire. The various members of the 23rd Indiana Squad, who pass the narrative baton between themselves, repeatedly express satisfaction with the way that Grant proves his mettle in the fighting, while Confederate Sergeant Jefferson Polly, fighting under General Nathan Bedford Forrest, finds that Forrest is the "the first cavalryman of his time, one of the great ones of *all* time, though no one realized it that soon except men who had fought under him." (Forrest is the very general whom Foote would honor in 1996.)

Within the interlocking monologues, Foote combined objective data with subjective experience. In representing the events at Shiloh, Foote used the exact order of battle and the exact words of the principals, including those of Union Generals Ulysses S. Grant and William T. Sherman and Confederate Generals Albert Sydney Johnston and Nathan Bedford Forrest. "Historical characters," Foote wrote in the afterword, "speak the words they spoke and do the things they did at Shiloh." But the objective data ran hand-in-hand with the subjective responses of these monologists to those battlefield events. He wanted to create, as Foote has Union Corporal Blake say, "a book about war, to be read by men, [which] ought to tell what each of . . . us saw in our own little corner. Then it would be the way it was—not to God but to us." In a moment near the beginning of the novel, Foote perfectly emblematizes this kaleidoscope methodology of moving between the massed corps and the individuals who constitute those military bodies. While viewing the troops, Metcalfe thinks,

> Seen that way, topping a rise and looking back and forward, it [the Confederate Army] was impersonal: an army in motion, so many inspissated tons of flesh and bone and blood and equipment: but seen from close, the mass reduced to company size in a short dip between two hills, it was not that way at all. I could see their faces then, and the army became what it really was: forty thousand men—they were young men mostly, lots of them even younger than myself. . . . This was the third day out, and their faces showed it. . . . Their faces were gay now in the sunlight, but when you looked close you saw the sullen lines of strain about the mouths and the lower eyelids etched with fatigue.

In addition to this combination of objective facts and subjective experience, *Shiloh* represents one of the most important moments for Foote's writing career. In future decades this ability to combine facts and experience would prove to be a personal salve for Foote during the civil rights crisis, as well as make him the symbol of a late-twentieth-century understanding of the Civil War in nonpolitical terms. Foote's novel turned war from an event rooted in political and historical causation into an arena for individual bravery, devoid of political considerations. The novel does present the political causes of the war, but it does so for the sake of exorcising them. In his monologue, Fountain notes that Grant was "neither pro nor anti on the slavery question, though his father had been an Abolitionist and his wife had kept her two Negroes with her all through her marriage."

Whereas the allusions to Grant's ordeal represent the political and cultural issues behind the North's understanding of the causes of the Civil War, Metcalfe's monologue depicts and develops the prewar Southern context, a process inherently more difficult because Foote has to negotiate a culture rooted in slavery, a connection that threatened to doom his sympathetic treatment of the Southern soldiers. At several points, the novel suggests that the Metcalfe family's wealth may be rooted in slave-owning: The Metcalfes are friends with Johnston, who has a "plantation," and Metcalfe comments about the "Sully portrait" of his mother hanging over a mantle of "*the* house in New Orleans," suggesting that the family's New Orleans house may be a house in town that the family owns in addition to outlying plantations. Skirting the slavery connection, the novel instead focuses on Metcalfe's education, a safer way of signifying the Southern aristocracy. Metcalfe's speech is peppered with Shakespearean allusions. Moreover, as he writes out Johnston's battle order, punctuating it in the process, Metcalfe recognizes that it is based on Napoleon's orders.

Moving from these perspectives, Foote suggests that a representation of war should be exclusively focused on the bravery of its combatants. Throughout *Shiloh,* he repeatedly shows how soldiers should be valued not because of any social status they may be able to claim, but because of their desire to fight. On the Northern side, this judgment involves redeeming Grant and Sherman, who have been victimized by rumors and bad newspaper reports. Fountain notes that the "suspicion of insanity" about Sherman is trumped by his willingness to fight, which "changed our minds about him." The redemption of Grant is even more drastic. Because of Grant's militarism—embodied by his claim that "I have nothing to do with opinions. I shall deal only with armed rebellion and its aiders and abettors"—his earlier peccadilloes of drinking are erased. "The soldiers never put much stock in all the talk about him drinking and carousing," Fountain notes, "for we . . . knew that he had seen to it himself that the whiskey would not get him this time, the way it had done eight years before."

On the Southern side, this transformation of war is even clearer. The hero who best exemplifies this concept is Forrest, a figure who shows up in virtually every monologue. From this baseline, Foote had also grown to understand Forrest as a Civil War hero precisely because of his inclination to wage war. The redemption of Forrest involves avoiding his slave-trading stigma, and *Shiloh* instead emphasizes his work ethic and his lowly social status: Polly notes that he worked under "an uncle in a livery stable." The real focus on Forrest involves his aggressiveness on the battlefield. As Metcalfe thinks of Forrest, he was someone "who did not fight as if odds made the winner, who did not necessarily believe that God was on the side of the big battalions, who would charge a brigade with half a regiment of weary men and send that brigade stumbling back to its tents demoralized and glad to be let alone."

This emphasis on fighting also realigns the Civil War not as a contest between regions, but, in a sense, between combatants and noncombatants. What is striking about *Shiloh* is that the differences between the Northern and Southern armies are not so much emphasized as are the difference between the soldiers and all other outsiders. As Blake says two months before the Battle of Shiloh, when six men were killed at Fort Donelson, "the rebels were really on our side." At Shiloh, Blake expounds on his earlier claim: The rebels "wanted the same things we wanted, the right kind of life, the right kind of government—all that— but theyd been misled by bad men. When they learned the truth they would stop fighting."

Bringing all of the aspects of his newly established writing regimen to bear, Foote wrote *Shiloh* quickly, his thoughts clear in his mind as the first draft of the novel would be the cleanest he ever wrote. The heat of summer had arrived in May, but Foote bore onward. As always, he relished working in the heat, and just two months after starting *Shiloh,* he had finished a rough draft. So anxious was he to finish the book that he immediately began a typescript of the manuscript. On July 4, Foote cranked the last sheet from his typewriter drum—ironically, on the nation's Independence Day, he had finished a book inspired by his great-grandfather's efforts to achieve Southern independence. Preparing to send the manuscript northward, Foote tied the typewriter sheets together and bound them up in a cardboard cover. Now, though, he did not need Ben Wasson to call on his literary friends. On the strength of the *Post* stories, a number of agents had come bidding to do his services. After considering the candidates and their proposals, Foote chose the Jacques Chambrun Agency because he liked Chambrun's idea of serializing excerpts from *Shiloh* as a way of generating interest in the entire novel.

While he waited to hear about the progress of *Shiloh* from Desmond Hall, the Chambrun agent assigned to him, Foote found himself involved with another issue. For several months, he had periodically gone to Memphis to socialize and drink. "He was a disciplinarian when it came to writing," said LeRoy Percy, "but that was about the only thing that he was a disciplinarian with." A social and commercial center,

Memphis, the "capital of the Delta," was the place to which Deltans gravitated: "People came from the Delta to Memphis the way Japanese go to Tokyo, the way Frenchmen go to Paris." At the center of this omphalos was the Peabody Hotel, a grand hotel filled with Italian chandeliers and Baroque marble fountains. Popular since its establishment in 1869, the Peabody had been immortalized in David Cohn's 1935 claim that "the Mississippi Delta begins in the lobby of Peabody Hotel in Memphis and ends on Catfish Row in Vicksburg." "When I was a boy," Foote has said, "there was a common saying . . . that you could go into the lobby of the Peabody, and if you sat perfectly still for five minutes, you'd see at least three people that you knew from [your] town. And you would."

In addition to being a host for out-of-towners, the Peabody Hotel served as a gathering place for Memphis' young social set. "It was the place to go," recalls Fred Smith, the founder and chief executive officer of Federal Express. It was the place where Foote went, developing relationships with rising Memphians such as Smith and Lucius Burch, a dynamic lawyer, who would later carry the torch in the Memphis white community for civil rights. More than just meeting men, however, Foote set out for conquests of women. His suave courtliness and good looks were all the currency that the impoverished writer needed among the wealthy Memphis belles.

Knowing that he could have anyone he wanted, Foote only chased the prettiest women. One of the women Foote charmed was Marguerite Dessomes de Maurigny Stinson, a twenty-six-year-old beauty from a prominent Memphis family. Peggy, as she was called, was the daughter of an otolaryngologist, a former president of the Memphis and Shelby County Medical Society, and the soon-to-be chief of staff and president of one of Memphis' largest hospitals, Baptist Medical Hospital. After one of Foote's 1947 trips to Memphis, the two started dating. Perhaps Foote provided the romantically inclined Peggy her starving artist. What Foote saw in Peggy seems clearer. A stunning blonde, she provided the looks that Foote always sought in his women. And whether he permitted himself to articulate this, Peggy's family, like his own grandfathers, commanded social prestige because of their money.

Before long, though, their relationship bore unexpected fruit: Peggy was pregnant. Just as he had felt compelled to marry Tess, now, too, Shelby did not hesitate to ask Peggy to marry him, even though they had not known each other long. Livid, the Stinsons denounced Foote and Peggy's plans to marry. They expected their daughter to wed someone on their economic and social level—if not a captain of industry, then at least someone more respectable than a writer stigmatized by a divorce. Until this point, Dr. Stinson had never been crazy about Foote, but under the circumstances, their relationship grew downright icy. Attempting to dissuade Peggy from marrying Foote, Dr. Stinson threatened to cut Peggy off. The tactic did not work. Perhaps because she was so eager to get away from her mother, who drank heavily and was addicted to prescription drugs, Peggy insisted that the wedding go forward. In spite of whatever embarrassment the family might suffer, she intended to have her wedding in Memphis.

The Stinsons relented, but they did their best to muffle the event. While other Memphis debutantes enjoyed grandiose weddings, the reports of which were splashed boldly across the society pages of the Memphis newspapers, Peggy had to settle for a short, quiet ceremony and a small *Commercial Appeal* article about her wedding to "William Shelby Foote." The Stinsons also successfully steered the August 30, 1947 ceremony away from their own Evergreen Presbyterian Church to the study of Reverend William S. Evans, minister at Highland Heights Methodist Church. On that Saturday family members gathered in Evans's office, where they watched the suit-clad Foote exchange vows with Peggy, who wore a champagne-colored satin dress with a corsage of purple orchids, topped off by a small hat of foam green satin. Following the wedding, the Stinsons held a small reception at their home. A few days later, the couple moved in with Foote's mother. Within a week, thanks to a reception that the Carters held for the couple at their Feliciana home, Peggy met Foote's Greenville friends, including Bern and Franke Keating and Kenneth and Josephine Haxton.

As the new couple settled in, Foote waited to hear news from New York about the sale of the *Shiloh* chapter and the entire novel. With tensions escalating between the United States and the Soviet Union, however, war was not a marketable subject. In early 1948 Hall sent

*Atlantic Monthly* the excerpt. While Foote suffered "twitches and jumps" waiting to hear the magazine's response, he assembled "Initial Seven," a collection of intermediate drafts of his stories up to that point. He also began work on a new novel, which he was calling "Vortex" (a manuscript later published as *Follow Me Down*). After four months, the *Atlantic* staff rejected the *Shiloh* chapter. Disappointed but still hopeful, Hall kept "peddling it all over New York," where it continued to be, as Foote told Walker Percy, "admired but not accepted." Finally, in late June 1948 *Blue Book Magazine* bought the excerpt for $500 and planned to publish it in the magazine's June 1949 edition.

The negotiations for the chapter had gone on so long that by the time *Blue Book* bought the story, the fate of the novel had been sealed. Hall had given Random House first dibs at the novel, but the press rejected the manuscript because the editors feared that with "women readers constitut[ing] about 75% of the bookbuying public," a war novel would not sell. Hall then passed *Shiloh* on to the smaller Dial Press. After reading the novel, Dial executives Bert Hoffman and George Joel asked Foote to come to New York in June 1948.

Arriving early one morning after the two-day train trip, Foote trudged over to lunch with Chambrun and Hall, where he briefed them on his work. Buoyed by a few drinks, Foote then tromped over to meet with Hoffman and Joel. The two Dial executives told Foote that they were interested in *Shiloh*, but, as Random House had claimed, they believed that in the current environment it would not sell. Eager nevertheless to make Foote part of their stable of writers, they asked whether he had ideas for other novels. The question could not have been more favorable for Foote. Not only did he have *Tournament* in storage, but he had already started "Vortex." Because *Tournament* had previously been rejected by Knopf, common sense would dictate that he talk about the new novel. But Foote defied conventional wisdom, trotting out an idea he had "in mind," which was none other than the plot of *Tournament*. Hoffman and Joel bought Foote's plan hook, line, and sinker. "It sounded like a good subject," the Dial editors told him. When asked how long he would need to get the manuscript ready, Foote told them, "Six months." Betting that he could produce a winner and assuming that they could take him at his word for this "new" novel, Hoffman and Joel offered Foote a $750 advance to be paid in $125 monthly installments. Elated, Foote left the meeting thinking that "my first written novel," the one that had been stored in the linen closet for almost a decade, "was to be my first published novel after all."

It did not take six months to whip *Tournament* into shape, it took three. Ecstatic about having money, which enabled him to pay back some loans from Percy, Foote spent the summer of 1948—a summer "hot as blazes"—rewriting *Tournament.* "I'm writing my Bart book, going strong," Foote reported just a few weeks after meeting with the Dial editors. "It's going to be good, good: really good!" Foote was "simplify[ing]" it, "so that the story comes out better." Other than dropping a few incidental scenes and changing two names ("Royal Bart" to "Hugh Bart" and "Huger" to "Clive"), however, Foote changed little. The novel's plot still focused on the accumulation of Bart's wealth and its loss through gambling. Moreover, the revised novel, as had the original, still advanced Solitaire's plantation ethos as a solution for the 1930s ills, including the advent of racial crises, a commercial culture, and the increasing heterogeneous makeup of the South. Acknowledging these nonchanges, Foote told Percy, "Essentially it's what you read rewritten."

The changes Foote made were on the level of form. Upon rereading the manuscript, he realized that he needed to get rid of the literary footprints that had dogged the original version: "I revised as I went along, removing nearly all the Joyce, most of the Wolfe, and some of the Faulkner; what Proust I encountered I either left in or enlarged on." Where in the earlier manuscripts, Solitaire had been described as "gutted, despoiled, vacant now for two years, the land not even planted this season, with an air of febrile advocacy, a charivari of grandeur, possessing grain for grain the texture and stuff of the dregs of nothing more than backwardyearning hope, recapitulant, somnolent," in the new version it was "vacant now for two years, the land not even planted this season, with an air of febrile advocacy, possessing grain for grain the texture and stuff of the dregs of nothing more than hope, somnolent." In describing a skeet shooting tournament, Foote had earlier rendered Dr. Tidings's missed shot as "then apparently without reason and confounding concatenation as if in a hiatus of volitionless fate, the doctor missed his 23rd target." While revising the manuscript, Foote not only found that sentence so horrible that he omitted it, but the sentence elicited a rare margin note: Underneath an exclamation mark pointing to the sentence appears "oh oh." Even after his efforts to peel away the stylistic excesses, the novel still wore his literary mentors like some albatross. In his *New York Times Book Review* of the novel, Michael Ravenna pointed out that the book featured strained rhetorical flourishes as well as a thirty-two line sentence, excesses expected, Ravenna claimed, because "after all, Mr. Foote is Mr. Faulkner's neighbor." Even Foote later admitted its sophomoric overwriting when he reread the novel in later years; he found that he "need[ed] a dictionary to look up some of the words."

When Joel and Hoffman received the manuscript in late 1948, the Dial editors began reading *Tournament,* anxious to see what they had invested in. By early 1949 they accepted the novel for publication, scheduling the release date for September 12. When the book appeared, it was met with mixed reviews. Other than Hodding Carter's excessively laudatory review in the *Delta-Democrat Times,* Ravenna's *New York Times*'s piece offered the most praise. Ravenna called the book a "moving, many-sided narrative . . . [Foote's] novel moves swiftly and holds the interest." Although "it cannot be said that Mr. Foote has made use of any new or striking material," Ravenna wrote, "he has demonstrated that it is still possible to write of his region freshly and effectively." In the *Saturday Review,* Frederick Rutledge Smith Jr. praised the novel's skill at fleshing out the historical backdrop of Bart's activities. Smith wrote, "This is . . . a felicitous insight into the mores and manners, the out-of-step code of a period and of a place unique in the history of America." In *Sewanee Review,* Cudworth Flint praised Foote for the "vividness, more intense than in the rest of the book, with which the flooding of the Mississippi over plantation lands after a break in the levee is described."

More critics were less liberal with their praise; many found fault, in particular, with Foote's depiction of Hugh Bart. At this point in his career, Foote had a Jamesian obsession with character, but in *Tournament,* Bart himself seemed to be a problem. As the anonymous *International Herald Tribune* reviewer wrote, "Hugh Bart is never fully illuminated from the inside. The novelist depends on floodlights—a melodramatic glare unrelieved by warmth or significant shadow." Similarly, Flint questioned the motivation for Bart's actions: "The book gives no clear indication that he possesses any specific abilities beyond energy, strength, determination, and a kind of luck with things and people. He expresses no aims beyond wealth, dignity, and security, and these he attains until he throws them away." Flint also identified another troubling feature that would haunt Foote over the next few years—his unwillingness to sacrifice authorial intelligence for the sake of narrative drive: Foote's book, according to Flint, is littered with "episodes . . . [that] seem to be included because the author knew of similar occurrences and could not resist mention of them." Ultimately, the book was seen as a failure. Not only did Flint call it a historical novel that "belongs . . . in the class of those which do read like a novel, but like a disappointing one," but the *International Herald Tribune* reviewer claimed, "Mr. Foote has evident gifts, but he is not yet master of his medium." The novel was, as Foote himself later characterized it, a "young man's novel."

The poor reviews did not help sales. Dial sold only 2054 copies of the novel, 750 of which were bought in Greenville. Many Greenvillians read *Tournament* as a roman á clef, seeking some town model for each fictional figure. While getting a haircut soon after the novel was published, Foote heard two women in the adjacent beauty parlor debating whether his Hugh Bart had been an exact copy of Hugh Foote. Over the loud roar of a hair dryer, one woman yelled, "They say it's about his grandfather. But I knew his grandfather, and he was a nice man." In spite of the disappointing sales, Joel assured Foote that the numbers were "quite respectable for a first novel." Foote appreciated his publisher's kind words, but he knew, as he told Percy, that "it's not going to make us rich." If Foote was going to avoid being "a poor boy all my days," he needed to develop his skills and broaden his canvas.

Even with its modest reception, *Tournament*'s publication gave Foote the confidence that he had enjoyed in 1946 when *The Saturday Evening Post* published "Flood Burial" and "Tell Them Good-by." Suddenly, the world burst green and a plethora of ideas whorling in his head fought for his attention. Not coincidentally, his relationship with Peggy had hurdled past its awkward beginning. To use the terms that he would use in a letter to Percy, "Love entered the picture," and consequently, he had more "respect" for Peggy. Perhaps they came to enjoy each other's dynamic personalities. At the very least, their love was tied to an event of early 1948: the birth of Margaret on March 16. From the day she was born, Foote spoiled his daughter in a way that recalled his mother's indulgence of him. The proud father thought she was beautiful and extraordinarily smart, praises that he was not reluctant to share with others.

Bolstered by this increased good feeling about his family, Foote returned to "Vortex" soon after revising *Tournament*. As he conceptualized that novel, it would be radically different in subject matter from *Tournament*. Whereas *Tournament* had focused on the trials and tribulations of Hugh Bart, the owner of Solitaire, "Vortex" would trail the life of a Solitaire sharecropper, Luther Eustis. Foote had previously shown an interest in exploring this underbelly of Southern culture in some of the *Carolina Magazine* stories, but it was his recalling of the 1941 Greenville murder trial of James Floyd Myers that now provided him the impetus to write about poor whites at length. A Jasper, Alabama, chimney painter, Myers had left his wife and family in the summer of 1940 to run away with Imogene Smothers, a Works Progress Administration library assistant. Escaping their western Alabama community, the two ran west to Mississippi, finally stopping at Lake Ferguson. After hiding out for two weeks, Myers began feeling guilty about abandoning his family, his burden translating into his drowning Smothers in the lake. Because it occurred within Washington County, the murder received a great deal of attention in the *Delta Democrat-Times*. The case seemed so clear-cut that initially no Greenville lawyer was willing to defend Myers. Finally, local lawyer Ben Wilkes, on whom Foote's Parker Nowell would be based, took the case. When it came to trial in July 1941, Wilkes skillfully persuaded the jury to declare Myers insane. Instead of being electrocuted, Myers was sentenced to life at Parchman Prison.

During one of his leaves from Camp Shelby, Foote had attended Myers's trial. For his account of Luther Eustis and Beulah Ross, the fictional equivalents of Myers and Smothers, he drew heavily on the account of the murder that had emerged in the trial proceedings. Although he pushed the setting of the novel forward to 1949, the same gory details that had emerged in court found their way into Foote's novel. The authorities find Ross's body virtually unidentifiable, the product of "bream and minnows holding old home week and sending word out to the channel cats to come get in on the fun." At the same time, the actual crime became only a leaping-off point for Foote, as he chose to focus more on the reception of and the conditions that produced the murder.

Much had changed for Foote. It would be several years before he would read Albert Kirwan's landmark study of the manipulation of race in the plantocrats' exploitation of Southern poor whites, *Revolt of the Rednecks: Mississippi Politics, 1876–1925,* a book that would profoundly change Foote's thinking about social and racial dynamics in the South. But in the nine years that had passed since he first began *Tournament,* Foote had come to understand how the plantation system victimized sharecroppers.

Because of his habit of reading literature as apolitical, Foote never explicitly articulated the social and political dynamics of his new novel. When asked by interviewers about the book, he frequently spoke about it in broad, moral terms. On one occasion, Foote told an interviewer that the novel reflected "a sad world in which people live under nearly unbearable pressures." Even while writing the book, Foote told Percy that his novel had "taken on implications . . . nothing less than the Fall of Man; [it] entails a complete analysis of the sense of guilt in a man's soul, from all angles as well as from inside it."

Underneath these ahistorical claims, though, Foote had created a novel that very much reflected the historical context in which he was writing. Similar to Asa Bart's fear of a commercial culture in the South, Nowell claims that the Bristol business district is "a brick- and glass-walled canyon, an oversized trap laid by merchants (and by doctors and lawyers, too) for the Negroes and country oafs blundering in with money clinched in their fists." In "Vortex," the trap was not just limited to the immediate buying and selling of goods. Instead, in a broadening of this theme, Foote suggests that a more metaphorical trap also exists through the rhetorical elements associated with the print industry.

As Lawrence Schwartz has argued, the production of paperbacks and magazines exploded during and after World War II, "creating a mass market." Treatment of the Myers case participated in this new market, as three detective-story magazine articles were written about the Myers case and investigation. Foote himself had already critiqued the paralyzing culture industry in "Tell Them Good-by." In that story, Foote had suggested that the oppressiveness of this dynamic had a specific North-South polarity. In his new novel, however, he was more interested in the way that the rhetorical hegemony depended not on region but on participation in the new market, a set of cultural conditions that dispossessed even further those, including the Southern sharecroppers, who did not have access to those tools.

That sense of the dispossessed being spoken *for* came through as early as the outline that Foote created for the novel. Paralleling his efforts in *Shiloh* to marry objective data with subjective experience, the new novel was structured around a series of monologues that, all in all, conveyed the details of the murder through subjective lenses:

1—I—the bailiff (trial scene)

2

3—II—a news reporter (finding of body)

4—III—the dummy (informing of sheriff)

5

6—IV—the murderer (how he met & killed her)

7

8—V—the murdered (life seen backward)

9

10—VI—the murderer's wife (his background)

11

12—VII—the fisherwoman (life on island)

13

14—VIII—the lawyer (defense plea; man after crime)

15—IX—the turnkey (jail scene)

Significantly, Foote's structure embedded the murderer and victim within a cast of people who reported on and carried out the consequences of the murder. Foote intimated this connection when he told an interviewer that the novel's structure enabled the reader to "get deeper and deeper involved by people who are more and more aware of what happened, where the very heart of it was. . . . And then, as you come out of it, you get less and less involved until you're back out in 'the world' again."

In particular, that control occurs through the journalistic work of Russell Stevenson, the *Clarion* reporter. Stevenson tends to exaggerate details for the sake of selling newspapers. When he learns of the murder, he thinks that the crime has all "the angles": "It was almost too good to be true. Black magic, the lurid element: everything any story ever needed." Capitalizing on this material, Stevenson intends to create for his readers an account that would "jerk them back in their chairs when they flipped the paper open after supper." At first, his work merely involves frilling up relatively inconsequential details of the murder. Stevenson decides to change the time of the discovery of Beulah's body from 9:00 A.M. to 8:45 A.M. "to make it sound more accurate." Increasingly, though, Foote has Stevenson create new material about the murder, transforming the indistinguishable Beulah into a "beautiful blonde." When a copy boy asks Stevenson how he could know whether she had been a blonde, Stevenson responds, "They all are, once theyre murdered. Besides maybe she was."

Stevenson's sensationalizing of the murder does not represent an isolated instance of journalistic license. Instead, Foote suggests that his efforts mirror the way that print culture exploits news. On the day before the *Clarion* reporters learn of the murder, Stevenson has allowed the paper's society editor to embarrass herself by letting the mistake about the bride wearing a "collar of white lice" go to press. Stevenson plans to send the mistake to the *Reader's Digest*'s "Slips That Pass in the Night" section, where he hopes to receive "ten sweet bucks." The murder of Ross presents even greater opportunities for Stevenson, as he plans to send his slick account of the murder to a detective-story magazine, "one of those with a babe on the cover's got half her dress ripped open and a knife in her hand dripping blood." Stevenson wants to beat his colleagues to the punch, as he imagines earning "a good fifty, maybe sixty bucks."

Moreover, the novel suggests that this magazine culture has changed the region's social dynamics. Specifically, *Follow Me Down*, as Foote now called his novel after a line from Leadbelly's "Fannin Street," suggests that this dynamic has created two new groups of power in Southern culture, groups that upset the South's traditional connection between power and a land-based wealth. The first group represents those purveyors of print, such as Stevenson. Significantly, Stevenson's social status is not merely that of a lowly newspaperman, but through his weekly golfing outings, he presumably rubs elbows with the local planters. More specifically, Stevenson's tales of experience come to replace real experience. His Sunday "farm page" does not involve actual conversations with farmers about their crops; instead, he merely "rigs together . . . releases from the County Agent and canned junk off the clip sheet." From these, Stevenson becomes a farming authority even though he never lifts a hand to a plow. Brilliantly, Foote has Stevenson declare that "I'm an expert farmer with a pair of scissors."

The second group that emerges from this new cultural dynamic is an increasingly intellectualized Southern ruling class whose high-culture currency demarcates it from the low culture of the detective-story magazines. This high-culture impulse is seen most clearly in Nowell, who represents a literalization of the myth of the educated Southern aristocrat. Far different than any other character in the story, Nowell invests himself in intellectual enterprises: During the first five pages of his monologue, he refers to or quotes Mozart, Shakespeare, and Emerson. Nowell's interest in the arts is sincere. When he sees a Bible, he wants to read it because "I have a desire to open every book that I see." At the same time, Foote also suggests that Nowell's preoccupation with high culture serves as compensation for a commercial world he finds alien. When Nowell sees a billboard for a movie starring Rita Hayworth, "low-bosomed in a strapless gown, being embraced about the knees by a young man with patent-leather hair," as a form of escape his mind immediately runs to the "lover on Keats's urn."

What matters most for the Southern poor is that they have neither Stevenson's rhetorical tools nor Nowell's intellectual fund to draw from. Lacking these opportunities, their own economic and social deficits grow even greater. In the late 1930s Foote may have agreed with Will Percy's defense of sharecropping, but by the late 1940s Foote had grown to believe that the fate of the poor had not improved, but had actually declined. Consequently, *Follow Me Down* repeatedly shows them seeking various means to alleviate their plight. Central to this desire for relief is Eustis's religion. Although he himself had little faith in any transcendent belief system, in general, Foote presents Eustis's religious zeal sympathetically. Luther wants to "rise up out of . . . sin and iniquity," and he wants to "pray forgiveness" for the "wrong[s]" he has done."

Yet, for all of the sustaining power that religion provides for Luther, it is his religion that ultimately does him in. Literally, this downfall occurs when Dummy, the mute on the island to which Luther and Beulah escape, recognizes "Solitaire Plantation" on the flyleaf of Luther's Bible. More broadly, the novel suggests that Eustis's religion comes to serve as justification for the actions that he takes. Luther abandons his wife and family because "I believed that what had drawn me [to Beulah] . . . was an ache to save her soul," an act that represents what Robert Phillips calls his "dedicat[ing] his penis to what he felt to be the Lord's will." Eustis's religion, in other words, provides no salvation for his economic predicament. In Nowell's words, the Bible has "betrayed him."

Religion is not the only false hope for the sharecroppers. Indeed, any effort for relief paradoxically works to further their enslavement. Given Foote's fascination in writing about the Civil War, what may be the most interesting moment in the novel involves the fraternal gatherings of Civil War soldiers. On the island where he later escapes with Beulah, in 1907 Luther had attended one of these "yearly spree[s]." That day of barbecuing and passing around the "demijohn" provided temporary relief: Here, they could be the brevetted officers to which they have promoted themselves, as "all the veterans were officers by then." Significantly, Foote suggests that this gathering involves solely people of little social significance. The general who organizes the reunions was only a "provost guard lieutenant" during the war, suggesting that even this most important veteran at the gatherings did not enjoy the sort of social position that would have commanded him a place on the front lines.

Luther's retreat to the island repeats the same process of control that his grandfather and his fellow privates have labored under. From that Confederate reunion, Luther has remembered the island as "a promised land." He thinks of it as a place free of the regulations and restrictions that govern him on the mainland plantation. What he finds there, however, is a cast of misfits, including Dummy and his mother, Miz Potts, a woman whose botched hysterectomy has made her features masculine, which led her husband to abandon her. Given this collection of pariahs, the island is no Eden, but actually a marker of the effects of the governing hegemony. Moreover, in a novel that features a publishing world that is seeking to capitalize on grotesqueries, the misfits represent not merely the people who have been shunned but those who are now candidates for the demonization that the magazine industry feeds on.

By the middle of 1949 Foote had finished a draft of *Follow Me Down*. Through the rest of the summer and early fall, he turned that manuscript into a typescript, sending off the finished copy of the novel to the Dial editors in late October. After a careful review of the novel, Hoffman and Joel set July 1950 as the publication date. When the book appeared, Foote again found himself the recipient of mixed reviews. Several reviewers were quick to praise his work. As J. J. Maloney wrote in *The Chicago Sun*, "On the whole, Mr. Foote handles this complex structure quite adroitly." Even greater praise came from Seymour Krim: "Very few young writers are able to write as sharply or as shrewdly as Shelby Foote. 'Follow Me Down' is this young ex-marine's second novel, yet it is written as confidently as if it were his twenty-second."

But there were continued complaints, particularly about his inability to give each speaker individual subjectivity. For all of its attempts to present multiple perspectives on the murder, the novel sounded strangely as if it had come from one voice: Foote's. According to Maloney, "Shelby Foote brings nine points of view to play in 'Follow Me Down,' but they all reflect his own. Even unusual words and odd mannerisms of style are repeated by characters who have nothing else in common." Maloney continued, Foote "does have the irritating habit of reporting the same slight incident as seen though the eyes of first one and then another of his characters without ever differentiating enough between the accounts to justify the repetition." In *The Chicago Sunday Tribune*, R. L. Blakesley echoed Maloney's sentiment. He wrote, "Presenting a story in such fashion calls for considerably more polish than Mr. Foote exhibits in 'Follow Me Down.' It is bogged down by repetition. . . . But as a straight story it would have been first rate." Finally, an anonymous *Time* reviewer criticized Foote's continued Faulknerian yoke: "All that keeps him from writing a really first-class novel is an unfortunate tendency to borrow over-much from the verbal mannerisms of Neighbor William Faulkner."

The very person whose work haunted Foote's efforts would echo this point. Although he did not explicitly suggest Foote's style was too imitative of his own, Faulkner found Foote's novel lacking. During a January 1951 visit to Greenville that Faulkner made to sign copies of the Levee Press publication of "Notes on a Horsethief," Faulkner told Foote that *Follow Me Down* was a "good book." But then Faulkner told the young writer, after he "looked at me rather piercingly," "Do better next time." Although he appreciated the fact that Faulkner was reading his work, Foote's reaction to Faulkner's criticism echoed how he felt about the reviews. As he told Walker Percy, "I should have told [Faulkner] the plain truth: that I never do less than my best: but as it was, I just said I would and he said 'Good.'" To his friend Foote could acknowledge that "perhaps . . . [*Follow Me Down* was] a tour de force that doesnt quite come off," but he still expressed defensiveness about not receiving better reviews. "If you could read all the reviews," Foote wrote Percy, "you would see why I say a writer can write only for himself, hoping that the time will come (after he is dead, alas) when some student will do a critical study that has value. Small hope, I assure you."

Foote did not have to worry about whether there would be a "next time," but, with several options available, merely what would constitute that next project. Although he may have given some thought to resurrecting *Shiloh*, by early 1950 Foote had turned his attention to a collection of stories that he was calling "my CHILD BY FEVER collection," a series of seven stories (one short novel, two long stories, four short stories) running from the present backward to a fictionalized initial cross-cultural encounter between Delta Indians and the Spanish. Several of the works, including "Ride Out" (a slightly revised version of "Tell them Good-by") and "Child by Fever," had already been written.

"Ride Out," of course, had been published in 1947 in the *Post,* and Chambrun had unsuccessfully shopped around "Child by Fever" after Foote completed it in 1948. In between these pillars, Foote still had the four short stories to write. Of these, three were going to be vignettes, but the fourth of the short stories, "The Sacred Mound," would be longer and would, representing the historical encounter, serve as the final story in the collection. By May, Foote had finished a draft of "The Sacred Mound," but he was not happy with it. Foote sent the story to Percy, asking his friend to read and critique the piece and to determine whether the medical issues featured in the story were accurate, including whether the murdered trappers' hearts would "smoke" in cold weather.

Whether "The Sacred Mound" continued to present too many difficulties or whether Foote merely found that he wanted to begin something else, by July 6 he had begun a new novel whose working title was "The Arms You Bear," after a line from A. E. Housman's "Be still, my soul." On that day, Foote reported to Percy, "I am happy to report myself 'with book,' I broke ground this morning. A tremendous undertaking, very different from my other two." This new novel was, in fact, not new; instead, it built on "Miss Amanda," which had more recently been revised as "The Enormous Eye" for "Initial Seven." As with the earlier versions of the story, the novel would feature the Footean obsession with an old Southern family in decline, the Barcrofts.

Barcroft's money enables him to enjoy the military title, Major, that he has longed for, but, after being rejected by the Army for both the Spanish-American War and World War I, never realized. "And mind you," the traveling salesman Charley Drew is told, "don't call him Mister. Call him Major." As with his title, Barcroft's obsession with preserving the family name produces disastrous results. After his wife has nearly died giving birth to their second daughter, a doctor advises that any future conception would probably kill Mrs. Barcroft. The major is so eager to have a son, however, that he demands that his wife conceive again; predictably, she dies in childbirth. The major gets his comeuppance when, after pushing his twelve-year-old effeminate son into hunting, a friend accidentally blows the boy's head off with the 460-gauge shotgun that Major Barcroft has given his son. Now sonless, the major guards his daughters, sure that any suitors are not interested in his reclusive daughters but merely in the family's money. That vigilance anticipates Drew's efforts; as in the earlier stories, the St. Louis salesman courts Amanda Barcroft for the sake of inheriting her fortune.

While "The Arms You Bear" would again feature Drew's assault on the House of Barcroft, a new subplot would dramatically change the story. A counterpoint to the Barcroft material, the new plot featured a sex-obsessed Fitzgeraldian New South couple, Jeff and Amy Carruthers. Among other aspects of their tobacco fortune, these stepcousins inherit a Mississippi Delta plantation house, which they return to restore. This inclusion of the New South couple enabled Foote to explore the fictions of both eras. Previously, Foote had expressed a disdain for what he saw as modernity's commercialization; thus, it was not surprising that the Carruthers would become so ridiculous as to be farcical, a parvenu American wealthy class whose interest lay in the showy display of money. But juxtaposing the Carruthers against the Barcrofts also paved the way for a critique of the Old South. Foote had heretofore considered the Old South as the imaginary refuge that he could always return to in the midst of the abysmal present day. In *Tournament* he *had* pecked at the shortcomings of agrarian aristocrats, and in *Follow Me Down* he began to question the manipulation of poor whites. But in both cases, Foote pulled his punches, refusing to admit to himself that there was not something desirable about Southern aristocracy. In "The Arms You Bear," however, Foote looked squarely at his region. For the first time what he saw was an Old South run, like the New South, by an obsession with maintaining the purity of family lineage.

Even though Foote's novel would develop this social criticism, rigid formalist that he was, he still described the breakthroughs of his novel in terms of technique. For the first time, he was focusing more on the construction of plot rather than the development of character: "This time the hero is the Story: I'm trying what I can do with the old system of making the reader want to turn the page to see what happens next." Abandoning the first-person perspective of *Shiloh, Tournament,* and *Follow Me Down* for a third-person omniscient perspective, Foote created new opportunities for himself. For most writers, the third-person perspective would introduce detachment, as any information would come not from the characters themselves, but from some outside observer or voice. For Foote, however, the third-person perspective was a godsend because, as reviewers had noted, his monologues had been homogeneous. Foote still maintained a narrator, a character whom Phillips called "a man of learning and intelligence," who "places himself among the townspeople and reports their views," but now the voice was consistent, the product of a self outside of Foote, and that resident's voice was also noticeably unobtrusive.

Ironically, creating an exciting plot enabled Foote to develop, as he told Percy, "characters who live in their own right. . . . This book has really got *people* in it; they live and breathe." One of those living, breathing characters was Charley Drew. Foote may have intentionally toned down his character for "The Enormous Eye" to get the story past the censorious *Post*, but in the new novel, Drew would become the liveliest figure that Foote had ever depicted. At the most basic level, Drew served as a literary device, tying the two plots together. While continuing to pursue Amanda and the Barcroft fortune, he becomes, as an executive at a local bank, financial advisor and friend to the Carruthers, a position from which he engages in a lengthy affair with Amy. More than just a mechanical link, Drew is a Iagoean master manipulator. Drew's rhetorical legerdemain manifests itself, for instance, when he gains a position as a salesman for the St. Louis cotton company of Anson-Grimm, after he extracts a position from Mr. Anson, the father of a fallen soldier with whom Drew fought in Europe but "barely remembered."

Foote brilliantly connects Drew's rhetorical ploys with his effort to overcome the regional and ethnic stigmas that he bears. As a foreigner to the South, a "Yankee 'carpetbagger,'" according to Phillips, Drew has to be more excited than everyone else about the Southern ethos. When he attempts to justify to Amanda his decision to leave his sales positions for the job at the bank, Drew adroitly trots out the well-worn praise of Southern life: he "had fallen in love with the Deep South. . . . Elsewhere it's so frantic." Even richer, in "The Arms You Bear," Foote made Drew a member of a Polish immigrant family. Whereas "The Enormous Eye" identifies him only as being from an Ohio shopkeeping family, Foote now made his name "Druvashevaki," a family whose members were part of the "steel-mill labor gang" of the Youngstown steel mills. Drew realizes that he has to outrun his past, and one of his first acts after he leaves Youngstown for World War I is to change his last name.

Working at his normal pace of five hundred to six hundred words per day, Foote sailed through the novel for the first few months. He was "feeling good," he wrote Percy, "because the writing goes so well." In the middle of October, however, he ran into a dry spell—precisely at the beginning of section two of the three-sectioned novel. Not surprisingly, that point in the novel represented Foote's deviation from the narrative drive that had motored the novel thus far and reverted back to the analytical mode that had plagued him earlier. His work, consequently, had been "hellacious": "Ive never written so slowly, so tediously. A page a day, at a crawling rate."

His writing problems were not only related to what was going on with his new book, but also what was not going on at home. Foote and Peggy had experienced "problems from the beginning," as he would later tell Percy. Part of their problems again lay with Foote's devotion to his work. But Shelby was not solely responsible for the marital difficulties: Peggy had some mental problems. She would sometimes scream for minutes at a time, her shrills lacing the entire apartment complex. As one friend remembers, she would lie in bed for days clad in cashmere sweaters.

Although Foote was reluctant to talk to Percy about Peggy, on one occasion he let slip his growing disgust with his wife. In a letter during the same month that his writing had become hellacious, Foote told Percy that Peggy claimed that she had "pus on her kidneys." Dr. Foote's diagnosis was different: "What she really wanted was to go into a schizophrenic huddle with herself while somebody minds the baby." Peggy's mental problems were compounded by the fact that she missed her family and her friends, and at every opportunity, she found some pretext to go to Memphis. As Foote mocked one of her visits, Peggy had gone to Memphis for "three weeks [of] dental appointments."

Regardless of the reason for her absences, Foote relished them. When Peggy and Margaret were gone, he could work without disturbances.

"Peg and Margaret are still in Memphis: will be up there all month,"
Foote wrote Percy in October 1950, "but I sure am getting some work
done. . . . This is the way a man ought to live." In the summer of 1948,
when they had gone to Memphis for several weeks, Foote had written
Percy that "I'm baching," a pun that both captured his musical interests
and his joy about temporarily being a bachelor.

Foote continued to plod along through the middle section of the
novel, carving out one page per day until one December morning.
"I approached work sluggishly," Foote told Percy about this Monday,
"and all of a sudden something took me by the hair." That yanking
unleashed a gusher, and Foote had to "hold back to keep from covering reams of paper with gouts of words." Over the next few days, Foote
cranked out not the two thousand words that he would normally have
written over a four-day period, but five thousand "of the best words
I ever wrote." What he had done was to get past the clunky historical
material and return to the theatrics of Drew, the Barcrofts, and the
Carruthers. "I'm past the midpoint of the novel," Foote reported. "It
should go easier the rest of the way, downhill. Plot, plot, plot." As he
would write Percy near the completion of the novel, "I'll stand or fall
by this one as far as plot goes; if the reader can limp through that long
dry middle section, he'll have quite a lump in his gut by the time he gets
done. He'll damn well know he's been in the presence of an artist."

What Foote's statements do not reveal, however, is how much of this
farce has a political component—it is an attack against the Southern
ruling order. Close to the time that he wrote the novel, he read Kirwan's
*Revolt of the Rednecks*. Although Kirwan's book focused on the way
that Southern plantocrats used race to, in Foote's words, "pit . . . the
rednecks against the negro," Foote keyed on Kirwan's questioning of
the ulterior motives of Southern plantocrats, "the ones we have been
raised to respect, the sincerely honorable men." Although Foote was still
several years away from calling the plantocrat "the son of a bitch who
set the system up so he could rule the roost," at this point Foote agreed
with Kirwan's claim that these "sincerely honorable men . . . are
devoted to . . . the vested interests (the railroads and the bankers, the
planters and the money men in general), in a belief (false, I think, and
he thinks too) that such interests are what make our country great."

However self-evident Kirwan's claims are now, at the time they represented a huge revelation for Foote, a discovery that was not merely
academic, but deeply personal. Not only had he and Percy wrestled
with their views about Southern aristocracy on a theoretical level, but
Foote's sense of his exceptionalism was tied up with his identification
with "the son[s] of a bitch who set the system up." Kirwin had demonstrated that the Old South was not merely corrupt, but actually a myth
advanced for ideological reasons. This discovery represented a road-to-
Damascus experience for Foote, and throughout his life Kirwin's book
would continuously crop up as a reference point.

Given the fact that it proved such a lightning rod for Foote, Kirwan's
argument would not surprisingly find its way into Foote's new novel,
as the book ironized the way that the "sincerely honorable men . . . are
. . . devoted to the vested interests." Foote mocked the efforts of the
wealthy to adhere to noblesse oblige, the responsibility that the wealthy
had historically given themselves as part of their high position. Major
Barcroft flouts this principle even while he seems to adhere to it. After
his death, the town discovers that his sole living child, Amanda, has
not inherited the "three or four millions," she was expected to inherit.
Instead, all that her father has left her of his vast estate is $4000 and a
quarter interest in a downtown office building: "For Amanda," a note
over the stack of bills reads, "This is All." Amanda receives only a frac-
tion of the major's estate because, in the months before his death, he
made a "donation" to the Tennessee military academy he had attended.
Ostensibly, this gift enacts the benevolence of Southern paternalists;
but what becomes apparent is that the donation represents a fulfill-
ment of his personal wishes. Because Barcroft had never been able to
enlist for any war, being reduced to following campaigns on a map in
his study, the money "was sent to endow a library of military history
and tactics."

The Carruthers' violation of this obligation is far grosser. In fact,
they do not merely violate this principle, they specifically invoke
this rule for the sake of justifying their own desires. Perversely, they
"translated as an obligation inherited by the rich to behave as the poor
expected," the narrator notes, "if only for the sake of giving the
poor an opportunity to envy the rich by reading of their doings in the

Shelby Foote
*(Courtesy of William Alexander
Percy Memorial Library)*

Foote (front row, center), editor of the award-winning *Pica*, with
newspaper staff in front of Greenville High School
*(Courtesy of William Alexander Percy Memorial Library)*

Foote (right) with close friends, Walker Percy (center) and LeRoy
Percy (left) *(Courtesy of William Alexander Percy Memorial Library)*

Yearbook picture
for the University
of North Carolina
*(Courtesy of the University of
North Carolina Libraries)*

With his boxer,
Bo, in the 1950s
*(Courtesy of Jim
Shackleford,* The
Commercial Appeal,
*Special Collections
Department, University of
Memphis Libraries)*

Shelby and his son,
Huger, in the late
1960s
*(Courtesy of Jim McKnight,* The
Commercial Appeal, *Special
Collections Department, University of
Memphis Libraries)*

Ben Wasson and Foote in Greenville
*(Courtesy of William Alexander Memorial Library)*

Celebrating the completion of *The Civil War: A Narrative* trilogy, (left to right) Justine Smith, wife Gwyn, Foote, and Dayton Smith at the Memphis restaurant Justine's, 1974 *(Courtesy of Jack Cantrell,* Memphis Press-Scimitar, *Special Collections Department, University of Memphis Libraries)*

Foote and Ken Burns *(Courtesy of Al Levine, General Motors, Florentine Films)*

Jimmy and Roslyn Carter and Foote at Gettysburg, July 6, 1978

*(Courtesy of Gettysburg NMP Archives, photograph 29V-1053)*

Foote and Walker Percy on a 1980s trip to Vicksburg
*(Courtesy of Haydee Ellis)*

Shelby and Huger, celebrating the 1992 return to the University of
North Carolina *(Courtesy of Dan Crawford)*

Shelby Foote *(© Huger Foote)*

highlife magazines." From this twisted perspective, the Carruthers are able to avoid investing in the community in which they live, and they can live out their life guiltlessly. Accordingly, "they sailed for the old world, after the honored custom, and it was flamboyant enough for the most avid reader of the slick-stock magazines whose photographs gave an impression that their subjects' wardrobes were limited to riding clothes, evening wear, and abbreviated swimsuits."

The Carruthers' indecorous actions echo their denial of their supposed societal responsibilities. Their sexual relationship is weird and twisted, beginning with Jeff "studying" Amy's encounters with other men, while he "masturbates in the bushes": "It seemed to him that at such times he could enjoy his pleasure with a greater clarity, his mind being less clouded by emotion." As they grow older, their relationship grows even less conjugal, and ultimately the novel equates their indecorousness with their self-destruction. In its most literal form, that destruction comes through Jeff's blindness, which has resulted from a car wreck, the product of Jeff's crazed driving after Amy allows another man to place "his knee between her knees and she was enjoying it, answering the pressure." After Jeff goes blind, the couple lives in a sexual and alcoholic haze, ultimately leading to Jeff shooting Amy after he has caught her with Drew. Their debauchery would lead V. P. Hass to comment in his review of the book, "One wonders when [Foote] will lift his head from the maggots."

If the Carruthers' actions speak of having too little appreciation for their status, then Barcroft represents the opposite pole: Being so obsessive about the family name, he actually brings about a demise of the Barcrofts. The major's desire to have his lineage passed on led to the deaths of his wife and son, making demands of them that he deemed appropriate for a family of their status, and his lack of willingness to leave any money for his daughter ensures, even from the grave, that no suitors visit Amanda. Barcroft ensures, in other words, that if his lack of a male heir presages the end of the Barcroft line, no one else will corrupt it before its demise.

The selfish actions of the Carruthers and Barcroft do, ironically, serve the public good in one regard. The destruction with which they carry out their private lives demonstrates that the privilege that

Southern aristocrats claim for themselves is not naturally bestowed upon them by some divine blessing, but is purely a product of their wealth. At one point, Drew inquires about the prospects of joining the town's country club, something that he assumes will be "expensive" because it was "so desirable." Instead he learns that, assuming that one has the right social connections, membership is inexpensive and can be arranged by having someone else serve as collateral. After first being amazed, Drew was "somewhat disappointed . . . as a result of finding that one of his great desires was cheap after all."

"The Arms You Bear" brilliantly extended the false naturalness of divisions to the supposed fixity of racial—and particularly gender— boundaries that dictated the survival of Southern culture. Although the novel would feature no significant black characters, Jeff Carruthers's interest in jazz and blues represents a blurring of racial prescriptions. Jeff's rooms "pulse with the thump and throb of drums, the wail of clarinets, the moan of saxophones, the scream of trumpets." Instead, it was within the gender issues that had traditionally structured Southern plantocracy that Foote unleashes his greatest challenges. Traditionally, Southern culture had relied on a strong male image. According to Richard King, the Southern family romance organized its ethos around the male paternalist, "the 'presiding presence' in the myth," who was "gracious, courteous, but tough." By contrast, white women were "shadowy figure[s]," weak and servile. Foote's novel questions the roles that women are expected to play, challenging in the process Foote's own previous assumptions that women could only be virgins or whores.

On the surface, Amanda and Amy seem to represent both poles. Because she was never chosen by any man, Amanda is seemingly destined to become a stereotypical old maid. But even after being spurned by Drew and victimized by her father, in the novel's final pages Amanda grows more active in the town's activities: "Sometimes she had little exchanges, almost conversations, with transients who asked for advice about restaurants and picture shows and what there was to 'do.'" Amy's blurring of these categories is even more dramatic. Her sexual proclivities do not paralyze her or transform her into a whore; ironically, Amy's promiscuity actually paralyzes the begetter of the categories: men. For Drew, "Where Amy was concerned he never relaxed." Assuming that wives are either "satisfied" with their husbands or "frigid," Drew becomes puzzled by the fact that "since Amy was obviously neither 'satisfied' nor 'frigid,' it was inconceivable that she did not desire him." But no scarlet A would adorn her breast. Instead, Drew finds that Amy's actions are a "refutation of all he had learned and lived by." Her unwillingness to play by the rules he has learned frustrates him: "Man, you cant tell about women, no way in the world." Foote's novel succeeded because it dared to question whether Southern aristocracy was rooted in fictions about class, race, and gender that became naturalized by the ruling class.

After a quick trip to show Percy the manuscript in early 1951, Foote returned home to make the necessary corrections before submitting it to Dial in April. Joel and Hoffman were "very happy" with Foote's work. They did have one major suggestion, though; they wanted to change the title. However metaphorical Housman's poem was, they may have been afraid of the title's military associations. At the very least, Joel and Hoffman wanted a title more reflective of the aridness of the novel's 1930s setting. Foote racked his brain for a new title. Thinking of a line from Virgil's "First Georgic" ("Linseed and fruitful poppy bury warm, / In a dry season, and prevent the storm. / Sow beans and clover in a rotten soil"), Foote first suggested "The Dry Season," which he thought "expresses the sterility of people as well as the 30s." Continuing to tinker with the title, Foote also thought of "Thoughts in a Dry Season," and then he suggested "Love in a Dry Season." Of all the titles, Joel "went crazy" over the last, "bombarding" Foote to use it. There was one more change to be made. Someone at Dial had realized that Charley Drew was the name of a contemporary singer, so Foote scrambled for a new name for his villain, ultimately changing the name to Harley Drew. As he wrote Percy two days after the decision to change Drew's name, "I damn well wasnt going to change his last name: not after spending eight months of avoiding using the past tense of the verb 'to draw.'"

Once the changes were made, Foote settled in to await the novel's publication in September 1951, anxious to see if what he had believed to be his best book yet was considered a success by the critics. He was not disappointed. When *Love in a Dry Season* came out, it was met with the best reviews that Foote had yet seen. Much of the praise was centered on his ability to finally draw three-dimensional characters. The *Kirkus* reviewer found that "while you loathe practically every character in the book, you believe in them." On a broader basis, the reviewer found the novel "shrewdly contrived and skillfully executed." Even Hass, who had questioned when Foote would "lift his head from the maggots," claimed that Foote was "markedly gifted" and "has told his story with great skill." The best review came from Frances Gaither. Writing in *The New York Times,* Gaither claimed, "Shelby Foote ably fashions a drama as modern as today's newspaper, as old as the Mosaic law." Claiming that Foote's "narrative is stripped and summary," Gaither also claimed that Foote had achieved his objective in terms of character development. She wrote, "Character is revealed almost entirely through behavior with relatively little talk and less introspection."

Although Foote was happy with the reviews, he felt that they fell short of fully capturing the dynamics of his best novel to date. Still convinced that the reviewers did not understand what he was doing, Foote told Percy that he wanted to reside "above the conflict. . . . It's much better up here."

Foote had no questions about what he was going to do after he finished *Love in a Dry Season*. Looking back through his projects in the hopper, Foote knew that he wanted to complete some unfinished business—he wanted to return to *Shiloh*. Still echoing in his head were the earlier rejections of the novel by Random House and Dial. But 1951 was not 1947. With the Korean War now a year deep, war was back in the American collective consciousness. The war's action not only stirred the latent nationalism that he harbored, but it offered, at least theoretically, another opportunity to fight—and thereby redeem himself. Foote had become like *Love in a Dry Season*'s Major Barcroft, anxious to enter any war available. "Much as Ive sworn I'd never anything more to do with the military," Foote wrote Percy, "I'm perfectly willing to go right now." General Douglas MacArthur, in particular, had inspired Foote: "MacArthur is the damndest creature I ever heard of, quite a combination of actor and hero; I'm glad we've got him."

The emergence of the fighting in Korea was not the only event that now made publishing a book on war palatable. Another war was suddenly coming back into vogue: the Civil War. With its centennial less than a decade away, publishing houses were already gearing up to feed what they hoped would be the public's desire for works on the bloody exercise in nation-building. Allan Nevins was writing a Civil War series for Scribner, and Bruce Catton was midway through his Doubleday Civil War trilogy. A work on Shiloh would have even more immediate marketing possibilities, however. Because the battle had been fought in 1862, the ninetieth anniversary lay just over the horizon in April 1952. And when Foote met with the Dial editors in May 1951, he pitched these items as reason to exhume *Shiloh*. Contrary to their reception of his novel in 1947, Joel and Hoffman were now so excited about its prospects that they agreed to publish the novel as soon as Foote could revise it. They also began urging *Life* to run a story on the battle, which would, of course, mention Foote's new novel. Ecstatic about his editors' approval, Foote told Percy that the acceptance "gives me everything I want." With all four of his novels published or bound for the press, he told his friend, "If I felt any better I'd bust."

While Foote sang paeans of joy, his friend struggled to finish his second novel, "The Charterhouse." The first, "The Gramercy Winner," had now been committed to the fire, and in an effort to boost Percy's confidence during the development of "The Charterhouse," Foote repeatedly provided his friend suggestions about composition. Although Foote, in the words of Tolson, "sometimes took his role as taskmaster to rather Prussian extremes," his prodding was instrumental in getting Percy to finish the manuscript. Even so, Percy's efforts to have the manuscript published sputtered. After enlisting Caroline Gordon to provide an editorial review of his novel, he incorporated her suggestions into the manuscript. Still, Percy could interest no publishing house in the book.

Even if he himself had scored no literary successes, Percy had a hand in Foote's literary projects. During these years, Percy repeatedly subsidized his friend, who conveniently forgot his earlier claims that money corrupted writers. After receiving one of Percy's checks in December 1950, Percy wrote his friend, "I accept it gladly; there's no such thing as tainted money—it's all just money; the taint is in the mind." Although Foote himself could live on virtually nothing, the demands of running a household on a minimal income cut channels in his pride. When he had written Percy in April 1951, he indicated how miserable his present financial situation was. Foote told Percy that he was "broke," and in a sign that he felt awkward about asking for the money, he emphasized that his upcoming New York trip was being made "to talk finances" with his publisher. (Foote would dedicate *Shiloh* to Walker Percy because "for one thing, you financed me through it.")

While Percy struggled, Foote's efforts continued unabated. After the May trip to New York, he returned home to revise *Shiloh* through one of the hottest, driest summers on record; the farmers were "screaming blue murder." As always, Foote relished the warm weather, but presumably he would have liked any weather because the revision of *Shiloh* was going so well, as he was making so few changes in the original version. During one week in May, Foote rewrote seventy-two pages of the manuscript. Indeed, whole pages went by with hardly more than the change of a single word or punctuation mark. "In some ways," he wrote Percy, "it's the best thing Ive done." On one occasion, his praise for his work even bordered on arrogant boastfulness: "I'll swear thats a good piece of work. It's a miracle to me how I did it."

By early fall he had finished a revised draft, and he returned immediately to the manuscript. By October 10 he had "finished the final fine-tooth combing of Shiloh." But before he sent the finished revision back to New York, he drove to the battlefield to meet with the park historian, who verified that the facts of Foote's novel were accurate. Meanwhile, Foote's editors were still attempting to create a public relations blitz for Foote and his novel. Now, Joel and Hoffman were contacting book clubs to ask them to include *Shiloh* in their offerings. Moreover, Joel continued to lobby *Life* to write a piece, even having Foote go by their offices and talk to the editors when he delivered the manuscript in October 1951.

Although the *Life* article did not pan out, Joel had also arranged for Foote to speak to a Columbia University creative writing class. The fit was an odd one because Foote, in theory, detested college campuses. "You would be better off riding freight trains than being on a college campus during formative years," he once said. But anxious to get his name out and excited about being appreciated, Foote had no qualms about speaking at the Ivy League school. The showman Foote spent almost an hour talking nonstop to the class "and could have gone on for two more." He felt obligated, he boasted to Percy, "to refute much that had been told them by the previous week's speaker, Norman Mailer."

Returning to Greenville, Foote waited confidently to hear news of the publication. Dial "believes that SHILOH is going to go like a house afire." In late October Foote wrote Percy, "Big hopes for SHILOH, they say— both as regards the critics and sales. Hope so." Every rock seemed to spring forth water. Foote soon learned that the London publisher Hamish Hamilton would be bringing out a British edition of *Follow Me Down* early in the summer of 1952 and Signet would be issuing a paperback edition of *Follow Me Down* in late June. On the heels of this news, Foote preached to Percy, "If you're going to be a great writer, you must be dedicated." Foote knew, apparently, about great writers because *Shiloh* would make him "among the American writers of all time—got there on the fourth book, which surely is soon enough." Nor was America large enough for Foote's ego at this point. However comical it was, Foote grouped himself with those on the highest rungs of Western art:

HIC JACET

SHELBY FOOTE

OF ALL WHO EVER LIVED UPON THIS EARTH

HE LOVED THREE:

SHAKESPEARE, MOZART, AND HIMSELF

ALTHOUGH NOT NECESSARILY IN THAT ORDER

Unfortunately, not enough people believed what Foote believed about himself. The prepublicity for *Shiloh* helped, leading to a sale of more than six thousand copies in its first few months, far and away the largest sale of a Foote book to date. But Foote and Dial considered these numbers hardly the astronomical sales they were looking for. Foote blamed the slow sales in part on Dial's decision to sell the book at $3 instead of the $2 figure he had campaigned for.

He did find satisfaction, however, in the fact that for the first time, the reviewers, almost unanimously, praised the novel. However, there were some criticisms. The anonymous *Saturday Review* critic wrote, "Mr. Foote writes a clear, unaffected, and telling prose and he has kept his eye on his main purpose: to recreate the battle for us. In this he has succeeded admirably. He has not, however, succeeded in investing his material with novelistic purpose or any larger significance." Similarly, George McMillan in *The New York Times* wrote, "Shelby Foote handles the facts well. But they are almost too interesting to him. He has allowed Shiloh, the real Shiloh, to dominate his fancy."

Most critics, however, found the book's marriage of facts and figures compelling. As R. P. Basler wrote in *The Chicago Sunday Tribune, Shiloh* was "a rattling good story of one of the bloodiest battles in history." According to *The New York Herald Tribune*'s Avery Craven, "This is an original and interesting way to write history and fiction." Even McMillan admitted that *Shiloh* was a "refreshingly modest historical novel, written with honest and unaffected craftsmanship." Faulkner too hailed the book. Although Foote would not learn of his mentor's view of the book for years, Faulkner told his stepson Malcolm Franklin, "It's the damndest book I have ever read and one of the best." Later, Faulkner told Franklin, *Shiloh* is "twice the book that *The Red Badge of Courage* is." Recalling Faulkner's command, after reading *Follow Me Down,* to "do better next time," Foote had definitely accomplished that with *Shiloh.*

# First Failures

## 1952–1954

### "Two Gates to the City" and *Jordan County*

The writer is the Faust of modern society, the only surviving individualist in a mass age. To his orthodox contemporaries he seems a semi-madman.

—Boris Pasternak

HIS WORK DONE FOR the day, Foote sat down on the afternoon
of December 31, 1951 to write Walker Percy a letter. Given the
fact that this was New Year's Eve, it was easy for the letter to turn into
a retrospective surveying the work he had done for the previous year.
He had done much during a year that Tolson has called Foote's *"annum
mirabilis."* In April he had finished *Love in a Dry Season,* and in October
he completed *Shiloh.* Moreover, in the weeks since the submission of
the latter, Foote had roared into a great start on what he thought
would be his magnum opus, "Two Gates to the City." As he said later,
into his new novel he "plan[ned] to put . . . everything I ever saw or
heard down in the Delta, 1916–1946 and maybe after: planters, niggers, flappers, sheiks, the works." Given this enormous output and
success, not surprisingly, Foote trembled with excitement in his
December letter. In a statement as optimistic as any he would ever
write, Foote told his friend, "Life is a wonderful thing, believe me . . .

a Godgiven wonderful thing." Too much of a good thing, however, apparently scared the cynical Foote. His novels had never sold in the numbers he dreamed of, nor had the literary establishment deemed him to be its hero. Just one line after preaching about the riches of existence, Foote qualified his exuberance: "Or so I say now. Next month I'll be tearing my hair, messing up reams of paper with unsightly inkblots and cursing God for having put me on this clod of a planet." Summarizing such a potential, Foote wrote, "Ooooo!—[I'll be] like a dog baying the moon."

For the present, however, he thought of his existence as "a Godgiven wonderful thing," mainly because he had made progress on the "big book." For years, he had batted "Two Gates" around in his head, but he only had begun outlining the novel after submitting *Love in a Dry Season* in April 1951. So pregnant had he been with ideas that one week into "working at the plan" for the novel, Foote had an excellent idea about its "subject, the characters, and the form." At a projected 250,000 words, the novel "will run about the length of my first three books all put together." Because the book was to be so large, Foote knew that it "wont be finished for at least two years, if my past rate of composition is any guide. I should be at it seriously by early summer God willing." Although Foote would soon have to push back his timetable to revise *Shiloh,* he continued to prepare for the writing: "I'm still making jottings in the big ledger, notions for the background of the book," Foote wrote Percy on August 22, 1951.

By October 1951, with all of the proofing of *Shiloh* out of the way, Foote brimmed with confidence about the coming book: "It's going to be very good I think, experimental in both context & form, but valid in the best sense. . . . I feel very sure of it as far as *form* goes. . . . The emphasis will be on character. Action will be for the sake of delineating character; there will be no 'fine' writing for its own sake; the whole thing will be inexorable, unavoidable, unrelenting—always with that precision which I hope has become characteristic of my style, my 'quality of vision.'" Foote had even put together an outline:

TWO GATES TO THE CITY
A Landscape With Figures
(200,000 words or 150,000)

ONE: THE RETURN: EARLY SPRING

  1. a. Paul arrives on Cannonball; also Alice.

     b. Met by Ben and Wiley, drives to house.

     c. Katy meets them, goes to the hospital.

  2. a. Lundy and Katy; he asks for the pistol.

     b. Grandfather's biography: the last-born.

     c. Katy returning home meets Wiley, Alice.

  3. a. Wiley the young businessman, his plans.

     b. Interviews: Ben & Alice, Paul & Alice.

     c. Funeral; Katy to hospital with pistol.

TWO: RIDE OUT: 1910–1939

  4. a. Prolog. Boyhood, reform school, home.

     b. Mansion House, showboat, NO, NY—TB.

     c. Chance & Julia: the shooting. Epilog.

THREE: THE VORTEX: LATE SUMMER

  5. a. Gfather unsuicide; Katy acts as nurse.

     b. Wiley after legacy—Wiley & Alice.

     c. Ben's problem as to Alice; her reaction.

  6. a. Paul and his work—the two gates.

     b. G'grandfather's biography: Lieut Lundy.

     c. Paul & Wiley: statement of the problem.

  7. a. Events leading up to the club dance.

     b. Dance at country club: Walpurgis night.

     c. Climax of dance; death of grandfather.

FOUR: CHILD BY FEVER: 1878–1911

  8. a. Prolog. The Wingates: birth of Hector.

     b. His boyhood; a sketch of early Bristol.

     c. Youth—the death of the grandmother.

  9. a. Marriage to Ella—sketch of background.

     b. Death of son; infidelity; he forms plot.

     c. Ella and drummer: a hotel asphyxiation.

 10. a. Her funeral; Bristol as it was in 1910.

     b. The "biography"; return of the dead wife.

     c. Ghost leads Hector to the attic. Epilog.

FIVE: THE ENVOY: FALL & WINTER

 11. a. Grandfather's funeral; then transition.

b. Ben & Alice; Wiley; rivalry to a head.

c. Rivalry resolution; Paul on Cannonball.

As he had explained in shorthand the contrapuntal structure several months earlier,

> I, III, and V are a continuous story, 90% dialog and without flash-backs, except as they occur in conversation. . . . II and IV are excursions into Bristol's (or Jordan County's) past. . . . The conversations will sparkle about nothing; there will be furious entrances and exits amounting to nothing—a sense of constant motion and excitement without progress. If I do it well enough, the reader will know each character just by the pitch of his voice, the individualities of his syntax.

The outline signaled that Foote's effort to "put . . . everything I ever saw or heard down in the Delta" would involve all of its stories. It was going to be, as White and Sugg claim, "comprehensive and massive, on the grand theme of fathers and children under the Delta dispensation." In the novel's main plot, Foote would feature the meeting of three cousins at the Delta funeral of their younger uncle. One of the cousins was a businessman and another a planter with "literary appreciations." The primary focus, however, would be on the third cousin, Paul, a Memphis businessman whose journey back into his family's past left him struggling to decide whether he wanted to remain in the business world or return to the Delta agrarian life. Paralleling the Nashville Agrarians' division between Southern agrarianism and Northern industrialism, Foote explained that Paul "has a choice . . . industrialism or agrarianism, spiritualism or materialism." Thinking in such either-or terms also led to Foote's title, taken from *The Odyssey*'s Book XIX. In that chapter, Penelope tells her disguised husband that "Twin are the gates to the impalpable land of dreams, these made from horn and those of ivory. Dreams that pass by the pale carven ivory are irony, cheats with a burden of vain hope: but every dream which comes to man through the gate of horn forecasts the future truth."

Although Paul's decision represented the main story, Foote also wanted his decision to be set against the alternating stories of Duff Conway and Hector Sturgis, which featured repercussions of the liberties available to wealthy white Southerners. "Ride Out," the latest edition of "Tell Them Good-by" would depict the efforts of a black man to get out of the Delta, whereas "Child by Fever" would show the potential self-destruction of the very class that Foote would relay in the main plot. Echoing the kaleidoscopic possibilities of the dynamics of plantation-owning families and plantation laborers, Foote predicted that the book would "read like a disassembled jigsaw puzzle until the reading has been completed; then everything falls into place as clearly as if I'd told it chronologically, but with ten times the effectiveness because (as in fact) the past is always strained through the present."

After all of the preparation, at the end of October 1951, Foote chiseled out the opening sentence:

> Three years ago they took it off; but up till then, since back beyond the memory of any man now living, there was a midnight train out of Memphis, south one hundred and fifty miles to Bristol; the Cannonball they called it, in inverse ratio to the compliment implied, for the trip was scheduled at just under seven hours and even so the thing was always late, stopping at every station along the line, backing up onto spur-tracks to reach others, and panting on sidings—not so much from impatience as from age—while faster trains ran past without even a hoot.

Pursuing Paul's journey back to the Delta where he had grown up, Foote, unlike the Cannonball, roared at a pace uncharacteristic for him. A month into his work, he wrote, "I'll vow and declare it's going mighty good! The manuscript is stacking up apace, solid good thick analytical stuff which I'll pick up as I come to it in the start-to-finish writing of the book." Two months later, he exuded excitement: "It's going to be a great book; I feel ten inches taller than Shakespeare." A week later, Foote reported, "Terrific burst of creativeness! To date . . . I have 9/22nds of TWO GATES in first draft, 260-odd pages." Into the Christmas season, Foote bored ahead at a breakneck pace: "I'm still on the crest of a manic wave. The work is all that really matters. I think I could smile at the clap if my work was going good." That same week, he wrote his friend again, "This is the ticket, as they say, I'm riding the Glory road." By February 1952 he was so sure of the composition of

"Two Gates to the City" that he called the book "the most stupendous book since The Brothers [Karamasov]."

The comparison to Dostoyevsky represented the high-water mark for his novel. The book that had been a labor of love soon became a boulder that, in spite of his greatest efforts to push it up the hill, flattened him on his back in its downward slide. His extreme engrossment in "Two Gates" and the speed with which he was working signaled that his novel had become sanctuary, refuge, and escape from a personal world threatening to collapse around him. Foote was walking into a torture chamber, one that would have him beset with divorce and near suicide. In short, he was, as he had predicted, "tearing my hair, messing up reams of paper with unsightly inkblots and cursing God for having put me on this clod of a planet."

His relationship with Peggy had foundered. Just days into 1952 Foote brought himself to tell his friend what his dark allusions had only cryptically suggested earlier. On January 5, Foote reported to Percy that he was at the end of a two-week "holiday devoted to drinking, dancing and staying out late." He had not been partying with his wife, but having an affair with a married woman. Although he refused to tell his friend who the married woman was, he did say that the experience was "wonderful." At the same time, Foote felt "like hell and I'm confused and God knows what will come of all this." His confusion was actually worse than he could bring himself to say. Thoughts of death crept into his mind, almost as something that would extricate him from his present dilemma. At the end of January, before a flight to New York, Foote scribbled out an uncharacteristically short note to Percy, "For the past two days Ive been having the damndest presentiment of death; I think I'm going to be killed somewhere along the line. . . . I havent told anyone and of course wont tell anyone but you (who wont get this till after I have left and am safe or dead)." The atheist Foote manifested none of the sarcasm with which he frequently taunted the Catholic Percy: "If I knew a Hail Mary I'd surely say one." Foote implored his friend, "Pray *for* me."

Foote did not receive an easy out, however, and he soon found himself in trouble with Peggy. Once his wife learned of Foote's affair, she began divorce proceedings, a resolution Foote agreed to. When he told Percy of their breakup, Foote said, "There has been no real outgoing love in a long time, no tenderness or concern; it was merely an 'adjustment'—which will work only so long as there are no problems, and of course there have been problems from the beginning." His only regret about the impending divorce involved the fact that Peggy would take Margaret. Even so, he "couldnt live like this any longer, not even for [Margaret's] sake." In addition to paying monthly alimony to Peggy, as well as a percentage of "all my future earnings," Foote also agreed to pay child support. In return, he would receive "reasonable visitation."

Not coincidentally, at the same time that he was experiencing these marital problems, his work on "Two Gates" ran into a roadblock. Robert Phillips has suggested that the problems with Peggy directly led to the writing problems: "Foote's creative gates were slammed shut with Peggy's leaving." Such an interpretation does not take into account how troubling the relationship had been all along, during which time Foote had worked with great success. Phillips's assertion also fails to consider how Foote's final marital problems with Peggy may have actually *resulted* from work on a book that was to land him, at least in his eyes, among the giants of American literature.

Over the course of his life, Foote would reveal little about the content of "Two Gates to the City," but what does seem clear is that the protagonist's two choices paralleled Foote's own struggles to balance the way that he had structured his sense of Southern culture. Like Foote, Paul had to choose between remaining in a modern, commercial culture, which had its own problems, as Foote had repeatedly chronicled, or returning to an ethos Foote increasingly saw as entangled with not merely injustices but also a self-destructive impulse. Reaching this impasse, Foote could only stare at the two paths, and his response to this dilemma was to retard his progress, thus avoiding having to choose either gate. In the same January letter where he referred to his marital infidelities, Foote wrote, "I'm scared to death at just the prospect [of finishing "Two Gates"]; it could be one of the worst books ever written, and it's going to take two years to whip into shape. So far I have exactly 19/44ths of it written in first draft. But thats nothing: even when I have 44/44ths of it in first draft I'll only just be ready to start work, because itll have to be re-written and put together and re-written. A monster of a thing."

As late as January 5, 1952 Foote reasserted his belief that "the writing is all right; the writing's fine," but his work had turned tail on him. What happened next was nothing short of monumentally catastrophic for a writer who preached and practiced steady industriousness. Foote's writing first slowed and then stopped. The normally sedentary—even stationary—Foote began traveling. From Harrisburg, Pennsylvania, on March 3, Foote telegrammed Percy, "HAVE RUN OFF INTO THE NIGHT." Eleven days later, Foote wrote from Hagerstown, Maryland, "I have a tale to unfold whose smallest word would harrow-up your blood, make each particular hair to stand on end like quills upon the fretful porpentine." Back at home a week later and with "a mountain of woe upon my head," Foote tried to use a steady diet of reading to rev up his engine. All of his efforts sputtered, and by April he acknowledged that he had stopped his work: "I havent written one line in more than a month, and for all I know, I'm utterly through, both as a person and a writer." Foote had fallen into despair so deep that he entertained previously unthinkable thoughts: "For the first time in my life writing is not the most important thing in the world, not even when I lean above a sheet of paper; and if I cant feel that when I write, I just wont write—it's that simple."

At times during these months, the deeply romantic Foote seemed to induce the struggles, making himself believe that such trials were a necessary ingredient for his art. "The thing you dont understand," Foote told Percy, "is the artist's terrific affinity for the difficult, the thing he *cannot* do." Encapsulating the virtues of suffering, Foote wrote, "Loneliness is an artist's strength; thats where everything comes from and he knows it even though he hates it; thats why he wont surrender it." If Foote could, at moments, advocate the virtues of suffering, he withered under its oppression: "I cant seem to learn to live with it." From New York in March Foote wrote, "I'm being dragged through hell by the heels but I hope I'll win through in the end. I know what suffering means at any rate, and now I dont want any more of it." A month later, he wrote Percy, "I'm like a man flayed alive. Dont talk to me about 'peace.'" His body registered his mental agony. Already slim, Foote had lost fifteen pounds. His hair ripened toward gray. In hollowed-out sockets, his eyes bulged. "I doubt if youd even know me on the street," he told Percy.

Foote hoped the publication of *Shiloh* in early April to pull him out of his funk: "The coming success of SHILOH is going to be a great help, I hope." On April 6, the date of the novel's release and the ninetieth anniversary of the battle, Foote drove up to Shiloh, picking up Faulkner in Oxford. On the way, they stopped in Corinth, Mississippi, a dry county just south of Shiloh, to see if they could find some whiskey. Seeing a well-dressed man around the courthouse, Faulkner told Foote that he thought that "anybody getting his shoes shined on Sunday morning would know where [whiskey] was." The man did, and Foote and Faulkner, brown bag in hand, resumed their trip. Wonderful day though it was, that trip proved no antidote for Foote's maladies. Nor could the fact that *Shiloh* had gone into a third printing within a couple of weeks. "I dont care," Foote told Percy. He only wanted to "get through [my dilemma] somehow."

As May rotted into June, Foote tried to gear himself up again for "Two Gates." Making notes, Foote wrote his friend, "I'm back at it and it goes slow, painful; but it goes and I'll be in the vein again before long." A week later, he began "writing brief first-drafts of scenes already quite clear in my mind," but, in general, "it doesnt go well & I take no pleasure in it." In fact, the experience was torture: "I spend a good deal of time right here at my desk holding my head in my hands," as he found that he could not "possibly hold my mind on the paper long enough for anything but the briefest periods of time, the very thought of trying to sustain an illusion over a series of paragraphs, let alone chapters, seems utterly repulsive to me, false & deadly." One month later Foote told his friend that his writing felt like "sweating blood, like having the words tatto'd on my skin."

Although their divorce had gone through in March, Peggy and Foote continued talking. At one point, he suggested to Percy that they might be remarried in the fall, even though during that summer Foote bounced from one woman to another. He had "turned into a sort of sex fiend. Seems like I cant get enough." Foote was "draining [his] vital energies for the sake of these unappreciative little wide-eyed Southern girls who have nothing to offer but the resilience and rosiness of flesh." What he needed was an "intellectual type, real egghead understanding . . . the ass wouldnt be as good, but ass isnt everything; at least between while we could talk—Bergson, Huxley, Santayana, all that." Foote was not able to work, and by the end of July he began traveling again. After staying a few days in Myrtle Beach, South Carolina, he moved north to Washington, D.C., and New York. Finally settling back in at home, by the end of September he admitted, "I should have stayed drunk these past six months; theyd have been more profitable."

Because he could not get going on his novel, Foote took a $2000 offer from *Holiday* to write a piece on Memphis for the magazine's Cities of America series. He set out to write the article, but was interrupted by James Jones, the author of *From Here to Eternity*, who stopped over in Greenville with a "milelong aluminum trailer [and] with three blackclad motorcyclists for outriders, like a Nazi general." After surviving a hangover that saddled him for several days afterward, Foote sat down to hammer out the article. "I got interested in the Memphis thing and did a good job," he told his friend. He had been particularly intrigued by the "early early history—Andy Jackson, Davy Crockett, and all those, including my g-g-g-great-grandfather Isaac Shelby." But *Holiday* was not interested in Foote's approach. After sitting on the article for six months, they rejected it. They wanted, the magazine told Foote, a "travel personality with a warm, human slant." Angry about not being paid, Foote told his friend, "If God wanted to give the world an enema, Memphis is where he would insert the nozzle."

Near the beginning of 1953 Foote's horrible 1952 was beginning to set, leaving in its wake a divorce, a daughter 200 miles away in Memphis, and an unwritten novel on which he had staked his career and existence. But as the new year approached, his earlier confidence and contentedness began to rise again. "Dostoyevsky was absolutely right about suffering," Foote told Percy. "I always knew it, but this was the first real suffering of my life. . . . I touched absolute bottom; then I came back up. Man, it's dark down there!" Looking forward to the new year, Foote wrote, "I'm done with it for now, all right. 1952 was pure nightmare, and here comes 1953. Peace be with us."

Trying to piece his life together, Foote salvaged part of the "Two Gates" project by combining "Ride Out" and "Child by Fever" with the collection that he had started in 1951. As before, the collection would run backward from the present to "The Sacred Mound," depicting the Catholic conversion of a Choctaw Indian, Edward Postoak. Postoak had been sent to the Spanish rulers of the Mississippi Territory because the tribe felt a need to atone for the murder of two white trappers, men who had been burned at the stake because they had infected the Choctaws with smallpox. With "Child by Fever," "Ride Out," and "The Sacred Mound" already written, all Foote had to do was to write another long story, "Pillar of Fire," which featured the burning of an antebellum home by Northern soldiers during the Civil War, and three vignettes, "Rain Down Home," "A Marriage Portion," and "The Freedom Kick." "Rain Down Home" would feature the return of an unstable World War II veteran, Pauly Green, who goes on a shooting spree at a local restaurant; "A Marriage Portion" would feature the monologue of a bitter woman who has married a drunken, abusive husband; and "The Freedom Kick" would center on the celebration of a former slave's freedom in the face of continued oppression.

Starting afresh with his work, Foote also felt that he needed an additional move to complete his transformation. For the first time in his adult life, he wanted to leave his beloved Delta, and with Margaret now living in Memphis with her mother, he thought that he should look there for a new place, even if the city did have its drawbacks. After asking around, Foote learned of a vacant three-room shotgun apartment at the corner of Arkansas and Carolina Streets, deep in the heart of a riverside black neighborhood. Visiting the 697 Arkansas Street apartment, Foote found that he liked the duplex's privacy. Although he could see the citadel of downtown Memphis buildings a mile north of him, the only sounds he would have to contend with were regular neighborhood noises and the sound of trains crossing the series of Mississippi River bridges below him. Lodged in "niggertown," as he called the neighborhood, he realized that he would also enjoy insulation from his Memphis friends. Living on the Mississippi would also ensure his continued connection to the exiled region that had cir-cumscribed and constituted his life. Lying 200 miles south of him and

butting up next to the river stood Greenville, his home, and by extension, the Delta. The same water running around this Memphis bend
of the Mississippi would, in less than a day, touch the shores of
Greenville.

Charmed by the apartment and its location, Foote approached the
downtown cotton broker who owned the property. The owner could
not understand why Foote was even interested in living there. No
white person had lived in the neighborhood since the yellow fever
epidemics of 1878 and 1893 ran whites into the Memphis interior.
Although William Gorgas had discovered that mosquitoes—and not
"noxious vapors" from the low-lying river areas—carried yellow fever,
whites had not moved back into the neighborhood. And with racial
problems cresting again in the 1950s South, no one, save Foote, was
moving now.

Although he welcomed the solitude, Foote found his new life
strange. Having always lived with his mother, a wife, or both, Foote
was for the first time in his life a bachelor: "It's strange," he wrote
Percy, "I dont like the cooking & the loneliness, but I'll learn." If it was
an unfamiliar experience, his new life also offered the peace and quiet
that he longed for, and with that solitude he could finish what he was
now calling *Jordan County: A Landscape in Narrative.*

In several ways the new work explored issues he intended to address
in his failed novel. Like Paul's plunge backward through his family's
history, *Jordan County*'s retro-chronological progression conveyed
Foote's foundational belief that any understanding of the present has
"all the past . . . behind it." Similarly, Foote's use of "landscape" in the
title extended his view that place was a continuum through which
historical development could be gauged. According to Foote, *Jordan
County* has "place for its hero and time for its plot . . . [Jordan County]
is the main character in the novel—the land itself. And you go back-
wards through time to find out what made it what it is." More than
just bearing the same orientation toward the past, like "Two Gates,"
*Jordan County* was to be an exhaustive exploration of all elements of
Southern culture. If "Two Gates" represented an effort to get "planters,
niggers, flappers, sheiks, the works" into it, then *Jordan County* represented the realization of that impulse. Not merely with "Ride Out" and

"Child by Fever," but with its new stories, the collection would extend the sullying of the pure, white, patriarchal ethos to the dilemmas of post-Reconstructionist blacks, and, in "A Marriage Portion," to the trials and tribulations of women in Southern patriarchy.

As much as the new work carried out many of the themes of "Two Gates," it differed from the failed novel in one crucial aspect. Whereas "Two Gates" proposed the possibility of reconciling the two poles of Southern aristocracy—its glamour and its injustices—Foote had now fallen back on a notion that the only means of reconciling these contradictions lay in some imaginary or aestheticized view of the South. In *Jordan County,* Foote would not longer try to resolve the South's struggles with one answer that would render everything coherently, symbolized by Foote's earlier notion that one gate had to be taken. The new collection would repeatedly invoke artistic responses as the means to reconcile these dilemmas. Not coincidentally, the only three artists that Foote ever featured would appear in *Jordan County.*

The novel, "if it is a novel," Foote once said, begins with Green's return to Bristol from World War II. There, Green finds a dead culture where residents "wont . . . be happy. Not cant: *wont*." As *Saturday Review*'s Jerome Stone would write of the work, Foote's "emotionless prose style" echoes this societal situation, providing an ironic counterpoint, a "whiplash effect to the unexpected turns of events with which its stories bristle." Tired of the inability of the townspeople to live outside of their immediate sphere, Green erupts with a rage that has him spraying bullets, killing a restaurant's patrons while he laughs hilariously.

Given the fact that "Rain Down Home" itself attributes Green's outburst to the town's loss of "love," it is easy to see why Phillips connects Jordan County's problems with the frustrations of the "modern" world. According to Phillips, "Modern Bristol is the child parented by feverish economic developments, and it is a child that has abandoned its formative aesthetic and religious traditions." What Phillips misses is that this deadness reflects not an abandonment from formative aesthetic and religious traditions, but a reflection of the vicious land- and slave-owning practices that drove Southern injustices. That sense of Faulknerian original sin comes out most clearly in the last story,

"The Sacred Mound," in which the rapacious whites demand of the Indians, "Sell us the land, they said: Sell us the land. And we told them, disguising our horror: No man owns the land; take and live on it; it is lent your for your lifetime; are we not brothers?" The Spanish act satisfied with the Choctaws' statements, but then the whites apply principles of ownership to the ownerless land, "put[ting] up houses of plank and iron" until "they were many; the bear and the deer were gone."

At the end of "The Sacred Mound," the governor frees Postoak. That repudiation is not so much a benefit for the Spanish—it actually represents an effort to purge all the actions that have already occurred in the decades following this original cross-cultural experience, actions represented throughout the course of *Jordan County*'s stories. In other words, that emancipation serves as both an imaginary desire for the troubled present—as if to say that things could have been different—and a counterpoint to the history that the stories represent.

In "A Marriage Portion," the unnamed female narrator marries the son of a plantation owner, but the husband turns out to be a drunk, underscored by his passing out on their wedding night. Furthermore, the woman finds that he is a philanderer. The wife withstands their relationship for several years, enough time to see him sent to "Keeley several times," but leaves him finally after she returns home one day to find him destroying—" 'killing flies,' he said"—her silver with a hammer.

If *Jordan County* suggests that patriarchal guidelines have suppressed women, Foote also understands that Southern patriarchy has suppressed other marginalized voices in Southern culture. In what was an evolution for him, Foote understands that blacks were the victims of the greatest injustices of the culture. Significantly, Foote sets the collection's story of black oppression, "The Freedom Kick," during Reconstruction, a period when blacks had been emancipated. That period, however, does not represent some glorious promised land but marks the presence of "Kluxers, smut ballots, whipping-bees, all that." The story depicts the narrator's mother being beaten by Bristol's sheriff after she demands an apology for her husband being beaten and imprisoned. The man had dared to exclaim, upon seeing a black policeman, "Captain, what was that? . . . Was that a colored *policeman?*" At the jail, the wife yells at the top of her voice "about freedom and justice and the vote," producing a response that even her accommodationist son "cant justify." The sheriff "kicked her full in the mouth, twice, cut both her lips and knocked several of her teeth right down her throat."

Along with this airing of the injustices of the Southern ethos, Foote's collection repeatedly tries to imagine a figure who could provide deliverance from these societal problems. Several potential heroes are paraded out. One of these, Clive Jameson of "Pillar of Fire," represents a *Shiloh*-like hero whose potential is based not merely on his well-to-do background, but on his military skill. Jameson's brilliant tactics and strong leadership make him "one of the sainted names of the Confederacy," someone about whom "poetesses laureate in a hundred backwoods counties submitted verse in which they told how he had streamed down to earth like a meteor to save the South."

As a hero, what Jameson lacks, apparently, is the willingness to air these injustices. But another figure in *Jordan County* has that potential. As the son of an Irishman and a figure from the Delta elite, Hector Sturgis represents the actual heterogeneity of the Delta, something frequently suppressed in favor of the myth of nobility begot by those with money. In fact, as Foote makes clear in his biographical comments on Mrs. Wingate, the "Mother of Bristol," in spite of her "New Orleans style" dress, her father had been the son of an "Ohio merchant," an impoverished immigrant to the Delta. Mrs. Wingate's insistence on playing the Southern aristocrat requires transforming her mongrel grandson into a gentleman planter, sending him to a Maryland prep school and then the University of Virginia. Foote visits upon the family a punishment that he reserves for similar, pushy Old South families—trying to force a person into the mold of a gentleman planter, paradoxically, turns him into an effeminate fop. Hector returns from school to drive about the streets of Bristol, "always in a hurry but going no place, an outlander, rakish and modern, sitting ramrod straight with his elbows up, wearing hard bright yellow dogskin gloves to match the hard bright yellow spokes of the surrey."

The story suggests that Sturgis promises to go the way of Barcroft's son in *Love in a Dry Season,* with one crucial difference. Sturgis has a creative side that enables him to compensate for his failures at playing the gentleman planter: his elaborate maps. Starting with "small-scale drawing[s]" for a new subdivision, Hector finds himself soon rushing to represent "new ideas [that] came crowding fast." Suddenly, he found himself "gridding the sheets into sections . . . reproduc[ing] those sections a sheet at a time, on a scale of one to one hundred." In time, Hector gives himself over to "the crowded, multicolored sheets that had begun as maps . . . wound up resembling work done by a latter-day amateur Breugel or Bosch looking down from a seat in the clouds." Hector's drawings, in other words, began to replace the demands that his grandmother has for him.

The theme of art as liberator appears throughout *Jordan County*. Not only was "Ride Out" revised to focus squarely on Conway and his efforts at creating his unique "blare" as his personal and social passport, but the theme appeared even more prominently in "Pillar of Fire." There, Foote suggests that it is only the imaginative process of fiction that can alleviate cold reality. Significantly, Isaac Jameson, father of the soldier Clive, cannot respond to the burning of his Solitaire because of his motor aphasia, but as the son-in-law of a professor of Greek, and by extension the Homeric epics of *The Iliad* and *The Odyssey*, he is symbolically connected to the possibility of turning this horrible tragedy into narrative.

But it is Sturgis for whom Foote reserves his most resounding post–"Two Gates" statement. Sturgis's cartographic renderings act as a substitute for the personal realities, as well as the political and social realities, around him. As "Child by Fever" indicates, Hector's "total absorption" in drawing the maps for the development of Bristol coincides with his "troubled years." Hector's drawings provide an individual satisfaction that enables him to displace all other external concerns. He finds "the neat geometrical simplicity in which a single line, drawn clear and sharp, was as mind-filling as the most complicated theory any philosopher ever contemplated and evolved." His drawings enable him to forget that he had sullied the "highborn Wingate tradition." Hector "would see a thing while out for a stroll, for instance a group of boys running after the ice wagon," and then he would rush home "to get out his instruments and put it on the map, crowding them in one after another, colors and details overlapping, until at last the sheets resembled a futuristic painting." The drawing completely engulfs him: "In the end it became compulsive, obsessive."

Hector's work does not represent a complete displacement of these anxieties, however. In fact, what is striking about his work is that, to some extent, it has a functional and utilitarian quality, an urban planning schema, as it were, for "the foundation for a future Athens, an Athens of the South." Among other things, the color-coded maps feature "green for trees and lawns, red for underground installations, mains and sewers." But his drawings are not received as potential urban planning suggestions. Instead, "bound in tooled morocco with watered silk end-sheets," they come to serve as museum artifacts, as they are "placed on display in the foyer of the city hall for all the people to see." As the years pass, they even become the grounds for declaring him "crazy as a betsy bug."

Regardless of how they are received and however much he is sniggered at, Hector's drawings do represent an ability to deal with the South's dilemmas through a transmutation of the culture's anxieties into artistic projects. This transformation would be a key ingredient for Foote's next work, the *Civil War* trilogy, and it advanced a notion that the new heroes for the troubled Southern society are not its wealthy or even its politicians, but its artists. The artist may not be able to resolve all of the political and social dilemmas, as Foote himself had found out, but Foote had provided a way of life that could exist side by side with, and effectively displace, these political and social dilemmas.

Particularly after the tortured efforts to write "Two Gates," the completion of *Jordan County* at the end of 1953 was enormously satisfying. After sharing in Foote's struggles over the previous two years, Joel and Hoffman were extraordinarily pleased to receive something from their writer. Although they were not sure at first whether to market it as a collection of short stories or a novel, they did want to get the book out quickly, deeming it important to keep Foote's name before the book-buying public. Rushing through the process of editing and typesetting the novel, they had the book published in late April 1954.

The genre issue of short-story collection versus novel was something on which critics seized. As Coleman Rosenberger wrote in his *New York Herald Tribune* review of the book, "To call the collection a novel, as the publishers do, is to miss something of the book's particular excellence, which lacks in Mr. Foote's mastery of the shorter form—the complete and self-contained narrative more complex than the short story and more compressed than the novel." Edmund Fuller went further, not even entertaining Dial's designation. As Fuller wrote in *The New York Times*, "The present volume is a collection of four short stories and three short novels, having a Faulknerian unity of locale and mood, but otherwise unrelated and sharply varying in quality."

Although they could debate the issue of whether it was a series of stories or a novel, most critics did not have sympathy for Foote's writing. As *The New Yorker* reviewer wrote, "Mr. Foote's angry, muffled tone seems to promise a great deal, but the unfortunate thing about these stories is not that they lack it, but that the life in them is stale." Even Fuller, who praised "Pillar of Fire" and "Ride Out," found the other stories dead and lifeless. "Child by Fever," for instance, read "like a grotesque parody of a Southern-decay school. It has family hate, seduction, insanity, infidelity, death, gloom, contemplated axe-murders, dreams of mutilation and blue babies. But of merit I think it has none."

Foote's prose came under similar scrutiny. Although Stone championed Foote's book, other critics were not so sympathetic. "'Jordan County' is perhaps a literary gem," *The Southern Observer* reviewer wrote, "but it is a most depressing book. Nowhere is there any happiness and only occasionally is there a rather grim humor." Foote's happiness would fully emerge only with the publication of his next work, one whose grim humor would become many Americans' introduction into a war that had little comic about it but had enormous possibilities for becoming the greatest American story ever told.

# CHAPTER SEVEN

# The Civil War

## VOLUME I

## 1954–1958

> The further I go in my studies, the more amazed I am. What
> a war! Everything we are or will be goes right back to that
> period. It decided for once and for all which way we were
> going, and we've gone.
> —Shelby Foote to Walker Percy, November 29, 1956

TWO EVENTS OCCURRED IN 1954 that would forever alter Foote and the region that constituted him. During that year, Random House approached Foote about writing a short history of the Civil War, a project that rerouted his fiction project and tied up his creative energies for two decades. The year 1954 also marked the handing down of *Brown v. Board of Education,* which ushered in a political struggle that tore asunder his region and, indirectly, Foote himself.

Even with these events on the horizon, that milestone year began as ignobly as one could imagine. The personal crisis that "Two Gates to the City" had precipitated seemed to come back for a repeat performance. During these months, Foote told Percy that he had begun outlining "a torturous novel, absolutely black and savage, with all the horrors of a nightmare." That work would never even be started, but it corresponded to a slide that seemed to echo the earlier degeneracy. "For the past two months," Foote wrote Percy in late February, "Ive done a great deal of drinking good whiskey and fucking beautiful women." As much as he enjoyed these bacchanalian flights, Foote realized that they brought only temporary relief: "The one is about as unsatisfactory as the other, except at the time."

While Foote seemed to be going nowhere with his work, an unexpected offer landed on his doorstep. With the Civil War centennial fast approaching, Random House wanted a work on the Civil War to anchor its new history series. According to Bunt Percy, Walker had contacted Random House about getting Foote under contract for a Civil War history, a claim that contradicts Foote's assumption that Bennett Cerf, the Random House president, had contacted him based on a reading of *Shiloh.* Regardless of the impetus for this initial contact, Cerf's letter indicated that the press was looking for a "short history of the Civil War," which they envisioned would run about 200,000 words.

Cerf's offer was a godsend. Although Foote would later claim that the Civil War history gave him the "pause and assessment" that he needed from a fictional project "that if I hadn't actually exhausted . . . I had at any rate used . . . enough," these rosy retrospective accounts failed to mention how the Random House proposal had saved him from the crisis that he seemed to be plunging toward with the "dark, horrible novel." Foote gladly accepted Cerf's offer after meeting that July with Random House editors in New York. Figuring that he wrote about 100,000 words a year and assuming that he could write a history book twice as fast—"fiction is hard work; history I figured, well, there's not much to that"—Foote thought that the entire project, including revision, would take about eighteen months. Immediately, Foote put everything else aside. Not only was he rearing to get on with the project, but he also needed the $400 advance that would come with the submission of an outline. (Random House also agreed to pay Foote $300 per month for one year, meaning that he would receive $4000 total for the project.) Although he could subsist on Kelly's beef stew, cigarettes, and coffee, he needed money to pay alimony and Margaret's child support.

Working twelve hours a day, Foote spent the next few weeks fleshing out an outline for the work. As he had always done, he followed Aristotle's *Poetics'* dictum about events having an inherently intrinsic structure. "Every story has a plot: a beginning, a middle, and an end,"

Foote would say later. "You just have to determine what that plot is." By August he had found that structure, and, around his view of the war's trajectory, he had built "a frame that will take all the strain I can place upon it." That framework was "revolutionary in its simplicity," as it primarily consisted of alternating between the eastern and western theaters. (The inclusion of the latter as a chief component was itself groundbreaking. Whereas previous commentators, including Allan Nevins and Bruce Catton, had given disproportionate attention to the Virginia battles, "my history," Foote wrote Percy, "will be the first to have any true balance, east and west.") Moreover, Foote's simple framework was bound together by a beginning and ending that would focus on the same figures, Abraham Lincoln and Jefferson Davis. The first chapter would introduce the two presidents, and the last would be organized around the assassination of Lincoln and the flight of Davis south out of Richmond with the Confederacy's papers and monies.

Solid as the outline seemed, Foote realized that his plans portended a project far more detailed than the 200,000 words Random House was calling for. A book of that length would require too much summary: "Nothing about me would be happy writing a little summary of the war," he told himself. "In fact, I might as well not write it." Whipping off a letter to Robert Linscott, the Random House editor assigned to him, Foote wrote, "Instead of a short history, I think I would rather do this three-volume thing, running about say 500,000 or 600,000 words a volume." While the editors huddled in New York, Foote waited in his apartment by the Mississippi.

Ten days later, Linscott responded with the Random House verdict, ironically short and brief for a project that would require so many words and resources: "Go ahead; fine; much better that way." The publisher rewrote the contract to give Foote $5000 for each volume. At Foote's projections, they assumed that the entire trilogy would take under nine years to complete, giving him a little more than $1700 per year. Little did the editors know that the trilogy would require twenty years to complete, filling Foote's life from the ages of thirty-seven to fifty-six. "It expanded as I wrote," Foote said. Comparing this expansion to an enigmatic culinary dish, he said, "There's a French soup I've heard of. . . . It's a job of compression and, as you move your spoon through it, the soup swells, and if you don't eat fast enough it over-flows your bowl. I sometimes felt I was engaged in that during the writing of the war." In a 1978 interview Foote said, "If I had had any idea that it was going to take twenty years out of the middle . . . of my writing life, I would not have started the *War.*"

Within days of receiving Linscott's approval, Foote began adding flesh to his outline, creating a biblical-like prose. Whereas Foote's writing had always plodded with a heavy emphasis on nouns, now his parenthetical phrases containing information about a person or situation provided, without sacrificing gravity, a certain suppleness. Foote opens the book this way: "It was a Monday in Washington, January 21; Jefferson Davis rose from his seat in the Senate. South Carolina had left the Union a month before, followed by Mississippi, Florida, and Alabama, which seceded at the rate of one a day during the second week of the new year. Georgia went out eight days later; Louisiana and Texas were poised to go, and few doubted that they would, along with others."

As Foote started the first volume, he began rediscovering what had always made him happiest: writing. Three years before, he had told Percy, "Prayer may bring a man in touch with the angels; I dont know. But I do know that the closest to God I ever come is when I'm at my work." Now, with *The Civil War* underway, Foote said that his work was "enough to warrant daily prayers of thanksgiving to God that all this came your way and not some yuk in the adjoining hospital bassinet." After three of the most difficult years he had ever known, a bog of personal, professional, and financial difficulties, Foote was now delighted to write about such things as Union General Ulysses Grant's and Confederate General Albert Sidney Johnston's opening maneuvers in the West. He relished each day's work in a way that he had not since *Love in a Dry Season.* "All I want," he told Percy after a few months of working on *The Civil War,* "is to work at my book, a great wide sea of words." Foote's life quickly became the Civil War. Wanting to feel what it felt like to be a soldier, he grew a beard for the first time in his life. More broadly, he found his project—and the war itself—all-engrossing: "Dont underrate it," he told his friend, "as a thing that can claim a man's whole waking mind for years on end."

Foote's outline of individual pieces had set him up to write each chapter section—and in a few cases, an entire chapter—on a particular battle. Before he began a section, he either visited the battlefield or labored over maps of it, absorbing all of the details before weaving together his own account. That visual exercise was "teaching me to love my country—especially the South, but all the rest as well. I'm learning so many things: geography, for instance. I never saw this country before now—the rivers and mountains, the watersheds and valleys." Foote also pored through diaries, journals, and autobiographies of the participants, making notes or pinning quotations above his desk that he wanted to use. In particular, he relied on the 128-volume *War of the Rebellion: A Compilation of the Official Records of the Union and Confederate Armies* and the 30-volume *Official Records of the Union and Confederate Navies in the War of the Rebellion*, which recorded the day-to-day reports from military leaders. "What I have to do is learn everything possible from all possible sources about a certain phase or campaign, then digest it so that it's clear in my own mind, then reproduce it even clearer than it has been to me."

In an extension of the showing-versus-telling development that he trumpeted during the writing of *Love in a Dry Season*, Foote wanted to "re-create [that world], by their separate methods, and make it live again in the world around them." Because the armies' outdated tactics had not kept pace with technological breakthroughs of the mid-nineteenth century, the Civil War was ripe for poignant stories of individuals, and Foote planned to capitalize on that opportunity by making his account "wonderfully human." Writing to Percy just several months after he had begun, Foote asserted that in the "furnace" of the war, the soldiers "were shown up, every one, for what they were."

Foote's efforts to humanize the Civil War chipped away at many of the myths that had calcified around figures in the aftermath of the war. By January 1955 Foote indicated that he had developed a real sympathy for Union General Ambrose Burnside, whom he had known previously as an incapable leader. Foote now found him a "poor damned forked-radish man, subject to all the skyey influences." More than Burnside and other Union generals, however, it was the Southern icons whom he had grown up revering who received fresh consideration. Foote loved discovering how wonderfully human the "Marble Man," Robert E. Lee, was. "So far," Foote excitedly wrote Percy in 1955, he had created a new Lee: "R E Lee is a failure: failed in W Va, failed again on the South Atlantic coast." Referring to Lee's inclination to build trenches, a defensive move that irritated the offensive-minded Confederate population, "Granny Lee, they call him, The King of Spades."

Although his work centered on the anecdotally driven set pieces, Foote also had to thread the accounts of the individual battles into an interlocking series of campaigns. He had to create a story with enough drive to encompass the whole of the war. It was here that he believed the possibilities of playing novelist-historian enjoyed their greatest advantage. Historians generally, Foote thought, lulled readers to sleep with analytical accounts of events. As he later told John Griffin Jones,

> It's what makes historians such poor reading, and I'm not talking about being entertaining, I'm talking about what makes you dissatisfied with a historian . . . There are great historians, I'm not talking about them. There has never been a greater novelist or writer of any kind than Tacitus, for instance, who was a great historian by any standards; Gibbon, Thucydides. It's just that a lot of modern historians are scared to death to suggest that life has a plot. They've got to take it apart and have a chapter on slavery, a chapter on "The Armies Meet," chapters on this, that, and the other.

As a novelist dealing with historical material, Foote assumed that he could avoid the dry history in favor of a vigorous narrative: "Novelists," Foote declared dogmatically, "know instinctively not to do things that historians do all the time."

Foote's focus on the battlefield theatrics, however, revealed his own ideology. While Nevins and Catton included political and economic matters, Foote did not. Those omissions meant that the causes for the war, including slavery, were barely mentioned. "As far as my 'Civil War' is concerned there are serious gaps in it," he acknowledged in 1961. "For instance, I do not go into the financial difficulties of the Confederacy. These are enormously important if you want to really understand why the South lost. I think professional historians are going to be able to point out shortcomings like this in my work." In fact, when Foote does make claims about the cause of the war, he tends to focus on the issue of whether secession represented a constitutional right: "For more than a decade," Foote suggests in the opening paragraphs of volume I, "there had been intensive discussion as to the legality of secession, but now the argument was no longer academic." Foote's initial depiction of Jefferson Davis, moreover, not coincidentally centers on his desire to stay in Washington long enough to "be arrested as a traitor, thereby gaining a chance to test the right of secession in the federal courts."

Never was the de-emphasis of the slavery issue more glaring than in a Civil War book written in the 1950s and 1960s. Capping a series of post–World War II legal victories, the April 1954 *Brown v. Board of Education* decision set off a firestorm of protest by Southern whites. In its decision, the Supreme Court overturned the 1897 *Plessy v. Ferguson* separate-but-equal criterion, demanding, in a sweeping ruling, that not only schools be integrated, but all public facilities, including railroad cars, buses, and public drinking fountains. With the stroke of a pen, the Supreme Court, under the direction of its new chief justice, Earl Warren, made the theoretical breakthrough of delivering a racial equality that had never existed between Southern whites and blacks.

Or so it thought. In actuality, what the Supreme Court had done was merely set the terms for the decades-long racial crisis that would tear asunder the country. Those wounds would be nowhere bloodier than in the South. Although it would still be more than a year before Rosa Parks refused to give up her seat at the front of a Montgomery bus, inadvertently launching the civil rights struggle, what had been a delicately woven tacit pact of racial tolerance exploded into a fast-approaching racial Armageddon. Groups for and against the *Brown* decision marshaled forces. Particularly vehement in this growth of forces were the white supremacy groups. Just two months after *Brown*, the white Citizens' Council was established in Indianola, Mississippi, and within two years, council chapters would claim 80,000 members.

From his black neighborhood in Memphis, Foote followed what was going on outside his window. As much as anyone in the social circles around him, Foote understood the dynamics of fear and anger that plagued racial relations in the South:

> Most of the fear of Negroes, which is a very real thing, is based on what you would do if you were in his place, and that will scare you to death. You think you would kill people all over the horizon. Well, you wouldn't. But you think you would. So you're afraid of him. I've seen people just frozen with fear when some Negro who had too much to drink got out of line. They think he's fixing to blow them up, because they're thinking that if they were in his place, they would blow everybody up.

Although this comment would come in the 1970s, it represented views that Foote harbored in the 1950s, when he was considered among his friends as being in the vanguard. "Shelby was way ahead of us on this issue," Richard Leatherman said. At the time, Foote was particularly interested in the novel idea of integrating the schools grade by grade, in order to have friendships across racial lines precede any racially conditioned thinking.

Yet if Foote sympathized with the blacks' plight, he also worried that integration would usher in the loss of the region's distinctiveness. Because his previous novels had challenged the ideological manipulation of Southern rulers, Foote could no longer fall back easily on Southern aristocracy. Instead, he began to rethink aristocracy, not as a concept dependent on wealth, but one specifically related to what Daniel Singal calls a "passionate concern" among many twentieth-century Southern thinkers: "upholding some measure of civilization in a society they believed woefully undercivilized." Consequently, Foote, in this moment of crisis, began attacking those undercivilized, race-baiting whites who had gained control in the South. "The Ku Klux Klan," Foote would say a few years later, "could not make any headway if it weren't for the responsible white folks who sit back in silent approval during the burnings and atrocities—ministers, businessmen, even newspaper publishers who prefer to let the redneck white trash do their work."

Yet, as one of what he called "right-thinking whites," Foote refused to get involved, exemplifying the very group that he criticized. His friend LeRoy Percy was actively involved in combating Greenville's

Citizens' Council, efforts that Foote was quick to praise, but Foote himself did almost nothing to effect change, something that he later expressed guilt about. In an interview with *The (Jackson) Clarion-Ledger* in the 1980s, Foote said that he always felt obliged to grant interviews to media from his home state because he had not helped out during the hours of the state's greatest crisis: "If I had been down home, maybe I could have said some things and made some sense to somebody."

Instead of going home, Foote buried himself in writing his trilogy on a war that was to have settled, one hundred years earlier, the very issues paralyzing his contemporary South. *The Civil War,* in other words, became his escape from a new civil war. Although Foote presumably did not fashion the work's focus on heroism expressly for this purpose, such a concentration did enable him to avoid those base actions crowding around him. As he told Percy just weeks after starting it, *The Civil War* was going to be a dramatic arena of heroism, an "American iliad." How close this avowal of his work's heroism was to its utility as a sanctuary from present political anxieties was suggested in an interview with John Carr. After telling Carr that "the Southern culture was not able to support the strain that was put on it," Foote immediately launched into the esprit de corps of the war's soldiers:

> You don't want to overlook something that they did have and that was tremendous courage. I've studied and studied hard the charge at Gettysburg, the charge at Franklin, the charge at Gaines Mill or the Northern side charging at Fredericksburg wave after wave. . . . It absolutely called for you to go out there and face certain death, practically . . . [because] the tactics . . . were fifty years behind the weapons. . . . They thought that to mass your fire, you had to mass your men, so they suffered casualties. Some battles ran as high as 30 per cent. Now thats unbelievable, because 4 or 5 per cent is very heavy casualties nowadays. You go into a battle and suffer 30 per cent . . . at Pickett's charge, they suffer and it's inconceivable to us . . . the stupidity of it.

Such acts of bravery provided sustenance for Foote. His restaging of the Trojan War in nineteenth-century America would ensure that he kept those twentieth-century issues at bay.

Whatever factors provided the raw material for *The Civil War,* Foote polished that rock into sculpture. And as he did, he grew more and more engrossed not merely in the war itself, but the writing about that war. "Forgive long silence," Foote wrote in January 1955, "Ive been working harder than ever in my life, and have 60,000 words to show for it, nearing the end of 1861." A month later he wrote that he was struggling with "the task of fitting a small brain around a large subject, and a new-found humility at having presumed to sit in judgment on an era whose worst fool was in many ways superior to the wise men of today." Foote was "pleased" with the project: "Homer himself had no better subject, and I intend to do it all the justice within reach of my talent, both as history and as a work of art." Three months later, he wrote, "My interest in the war grows more every day." He was developing, for one thing, "a growing admiration for the Westerners: Grant, Sherman, A. S. Johnston, and above all Forrest and Cleburne. . . . Modern-style war was born out here in Tennessee and Mississippi and Georgia."

Much as Foote wanted to swim in that "sea of words," his bleak financial condition dictated that he had to consider other projects. Most of the novels had gone out-of-print; only *Shiloh* registered any sales, and even those came in at only a dribble. Living week to week, by the spring of 1955 Foote needed to again be what he called "financial." While asking if Percy could "spare" $500, Foote told his friend, "All I can do is stave off [financial] collapse." He particularly needed money to travel to some Virginia battlefields about which he would soon be writing. With the backing of Random House, Foote also applied for a Guggenheim fellowship, even though, as "coterie carryings-on," he considered the application a "bit of a compromise for me." Compromise or not, he was excited to learn in April that he had been awarded a year's fellowship. "God bless Guggenheim!" Foote told his friend. With the $3800 award, he traveled to Virginia in late June, where he saw Appomattox, the Seven Days, Fredericksburg, First Manassas, Second Manassas, the Wilderness, Spotsylvania, and Cold Harbor. "Never enjoyed anything more than this trip," Foote wrote Percy on a postcard in late June. Leaving Virginia, he drove up to Antietam and then to Gettysburg for the July 4 battlefield celebration.

Back home in Memphis, work went "slow and well" during the rest of 1955, as he wrote about the minor events that would lead to the larger battles looming on the horizon. Even these "little-known events" fascinated Foote. After writing of the Union conquest of Roanoke Island, Foote wrote Percy that he could not understand the "neglect" of the Confederacy to defend Roanoke Island, "now that I know how important [it was]": "Loss of that island . . . lost the Confederacy the whole NC coast, both Pamlico and Albemarle Sounds and Norfolk [Virginia] to the north." A few weeks later and into chapter 2 now, Foote wrote of Lincoln replacing Irvin McDowell with George McClellan. Of the boy wonder, Foote wrote, "Galloping twelve hours a day or poring over paperwork by lamplight, he had in fact the Napoleonic touch. Men looking at him somehow saw themselves as they would like to be, and he could therefore draw on their best efforts."

Added to the heap of his monthly expenses, the Virginia travel had cut deep into the Guggenheim grant. Near the beginning of 1956 Foote again found himself in dire financial straits. "Ive reached my limits of debt again," he told his friend, "and if possible would like to increase the running account with you. I'm keeping books; so the day I strike it rich youll strike it, too." After receiving a check from Percy, Foote responded a few weeks later: "Forgive delay. Ive spent all this time deciphering your letter. Had no trouble at all deciphering the check: for which much thanks: it came like rain on parched grass. But when wouldn't it?" So desperate was Foote for money that he applied for another Guggenheim grant, even though he knew that they were rarely awarded twice, much less in consecutive years. In the meantime, Foote entertained projects that he previously would not have given more than a glance. With word out that Foote had a Civil War project in the works, Signet asked him to edit a collection of Civil War–related fiction.

Even before he had gathered together all of the works for what would become *The Night Before Chancellorsville and Other Civil War Stories,* a more exciting project came his way. The film producer and director Stanley Kubrick had approached Jacques Chambrun about having Foote write several filmscripts. The twenty-seven-year-old Kubrick, who had made a splash in Hollywood with such films as

*Fear and Desire,* wanted a script of a late–Civil War incident involving James Mosby, a daring Confederate cavalry leader, about whom a television show was being filmed, "The Gray Ghost of the Confederacy." Kubrick wanted a story about Mosby's retaliatory response to Union General George Custer hanging some of his own men: Mosby had his thirty Union prisoners draw straws to see who would be hanged. When he first heard of Kubrick's project, Foote expressed no interest. Although he admired Kubrick's films, Foote knew the horrors of Hollywood from Faulkner. Passing on Faulkner's sentiments, Foote told Percy, "These people are all crazy, them and their funny money." But Foote also knew that he was in no financial position to refuse any tempting offer. Begrudgingly, he sought out Faulkner for advice on what to do. The Nobel laureate told Foote, "Go if you want to. But let me give you a piece of advice. If you go, never take the work seriously, but always take the people seriously. Hollywood is the only place where you can get stabbed in the back while you're climbing a ladder." Armed with this information, Foote contacted Kubrick to tell him that he would meet with him, but only on one condition: If they went ahead with the project, Foote wanted to stay in Memphis because he "wanted no part of California."

Kubrick agreed to Foote's stipulation, and in mid-February 1956 the two met in New York. For what was being called "The Down Slope," Kubrick would pay Foote $500 upon receiving an outline and $2250 after the complete script had been accepted. If filming ensued, Foote would receive an additional $1000. At the meeting, Foote also learned that Kubrick had optioned *Love in a Dry Season.* To his surprise, Foote found that he liked Kubrick. After the meeting, he wrote Percy, "They seem like good people and apparently want to do a decent film. We'll see."

At home, Foote found a stopping place in *The Civil War.* Perhaps he would not have ventured into the film project at all if he had known that he was going to win the Guggenheim again, a $3600 windfall. But having already submitted an outline to Kubrick, Foote began writing the script in late April. By May 10, he was halfway through, and although he would "be glad to get back to my book," he enjoyed writing "The Down Slope," particularly as it offered him the opportunity jump ahead of the war's first-year circuslike aspects to its ugliest side, a horror borne of four years of wading through mud and fighting people and dysentery. The script was "a true picture of the war in its last stages, off in the [Shenandoah] Valley, after it turned bitter—hanging and retaliation, and the effect this sort of thing had on the men engaged: hangers and hangees." As he wrote his friend, "I like it: think it will be a good movie."

By June Foote had finished the script. After trading correspondence with Kubrick and now having invested time and energy into a project he felt good about, Foote sang the wunderkind's praises: Kubrick was "the only authentic genius to hit Hollywood since Orson Wells [sic], they say. I believe it. He'll do a good job if anyone will." But in spite of Foote's hopes, "The Down Slope" would never be produced. Kubrick felt that he needed to cast marquee stars in the film, so he contacted Gregory Peck and James Mason. When these actors rejected the roles, Kubrick scrubbed the project.

Although "The Down Slope" had not worked out, Foote's world was sliding comfortably in another direction. Foote was in love. Since the divorce with Peggy, his romantic life had been merely sex-driven, but when twenty-five-year-old Gwyn Rainer Shea walked into his life, Foote altered his outlook. In many ways, Gwyn bore striking similarities to both of Foote's earlier wives. Like Peggy, she came from a wealthy Memphis family, and like both Peggy and Tess, she was stunningly beautiful. In the words of one Percy biographer, she was a "Lauren Bacall-look alike." More than just beautiful and a member of a Delta planter's family, Gwyn was well-educated. She had attended Miss Porter's School in Farmington, Connecticut, where one of her classmates had been Jacqueline Bouvier. After Miss Porter's, she matriculated at Sarah Lawrence College. A voracious reader, Gwyn matched Foote's own interests. She was, in short, the "intellectual type [with] real egghead understanding" that Foote had said would be the only woman for whom he would give up his bachelorhood.

There was only one problem—she was Mrs. John Shea. After one year at Sarah Lawrence, Gwyn had married Shea. Simultaneously fascinating and dogmatic, John Shea by turns engaged or repulsed people.

After their marriage, John and Gwyn moved to Boston, where he attended Harvard Medical School and Gwyn raised their two children. When Shea graduated from Harvard, the family moved back to Memphis, where John joined Shea Clinic, his father's renowned otolaryngology clinic. In Memphis, Foote came to know them because their social circles frequently overlapped. Foote knew of Shea's excellent medical reputation—he would later create several revolutionary ear surgery techniques—and in 1955, when the Percys were looking for a teacher for their deaf daughter, Ann, Foote asked Shea for a recommendation. Shea suggested Doris Mirrielees, a St. Louis woman whom the Percys began employing.

At some point in early 1956 Foote and Gwyn began meeting. Gwyn was open to seeing Foote because she was experiencing, according to her brother, a "dissatisfaction with the marriage." She was attracted to Foote not only because of his intellectual bent, but as a "reverse snobbist," Gwyn even found Foote's life as a struggling artist, living in a forbidden part of town, appealing. "It was a big adventure for her," one of Gwyn's friends said. Under the pressure of hiding out from a Memphis society set that bordered on the incestuous, their relationship developed quickly. By summer, Foote wrote Percy that he was "thriving." Although he did not name the object of his affection, Foote told his friend, "I'm in love . . . what I call love, anyhow. . . . I went without that warmth a long time. It's scarcely living. Never again." That warmth changed his entire perspective: "Now I see beauty everywhere—a sunset or a flower, a birdsong or the pressure of a hand; I even smile instead of scowl at people, though I'm still convinced that there's no good in them."

That warm feeling could not continue long without incident. With a "hooraw" brewing, as Foote later described the situation, Gwyn knew that she had to make a decision. Expecting the vindictive Shea to unleash a full legal attack on her, Gwyn knew that she would not be able to leave her husband in any methodical way. She would, literally, have to go in the middle of the night. Such a flight to freedom would involve sacrificing custody of her two children. It was an incredible concession, a "big thing," Foote said understatedly, and one that she did not take lightly.

In late August Gwyn made the break, an action that infuriated her parents. The Rainers "couldn't believe that she would leave a man who was on the verge of becoming a successful ear surgeon for a starving artist." Nevertheless, Gwyn negotiated a divorce with the livid Shea, and as she expected, Shea demanded that she give up her children, granting her only "reasonable visitation" with them. It would be 1964 before Shea extended her additional access to her children. Seeking an annulment so that he could marry the 1960 Miss America Linda Mead, Shea got Gwyn to agree to fly to Rome to testify before Pope Paul VI, but not before Gwyn demanded that she be allowed to see her children more often.

With the divorce settled, Foote and Gwyn married on September 5, 1956, afterward taking a two-week East Coast honeymoon that included a trip to the North Carolina Outer Banks, Virginia Beach, and New York City. After a regal stay, they returned to Memphis. In an action that augured well for the relationship, Foote did not immediately resume his writing, much as he had done after his two previous weddings. Instead, he and Gwyn scoured Foote's bachelor pad. Fastidiously clean by habit, Foote said that his duplex nevertheless required a "prolonged spell of housecleaning."

While they settled in together in the shotgun apartment, Foote sat down to tell Percy the news of the last few months, one of the most important and revealing letters in all of their correspondence. Because Foote had maintained what he called a "silence" through the Sheas' divorce proceedings, Percy did not even know that he was married. By way of introduction, Foote wrote on October 6, "Wife's name's Gwyn . . . she's 26 and quite handsome. Memphis girl." Foote's reluctance to tell Percy much about what had happened signified a change in not only Foote's life, but also in his relationship with his best friend. Marking a reversal from his earlier homiletic proselytizing, Foote's deferential tone suggested a fear that he had pushed his friend to the brink of permanent alienation. Whereas Percy always had a number of good friends, Foote, even though he had his own acquaintances and friends around him, invested much more emotional energy in his relationship with Percy, and he sensed that he could not afford to lose his confidant. Part of Foote's subdued tone toward Percy also had to do with the fact that, for the first time, he was beginning to see Percy as an intellectual equal. Having published "The Man on the Train: Three Existential Modes," a work that explored the importance of Kierkegaard's three modes for daily life, Percy was now a published writer, something that gave him legitimacy in Foote's eyes.

But Foote's delicacy in telling Percy about his situation with Gwyn had more to do with his fear of what Percy would say not only about Foote's third marriage, but stealing away a married woman. Hardly a man joyously announcing his marriage, Foote's letter reverberates with a nervous cautiousness. Notwithstanding his claim that the issue "cant very well be told of in a letter anyhow," Foote nevertheless preemptively defended his action: "Youd have to know her, and us together, before you could very well do anything but suspect and disapprove." The Percys did know who John Shea was, or at least they would recognize him as the doctor who had recommended Mirrielees, but Foote did not dare broach that issue, only opaquely identifying Gwyn's former husband as a "young doctor."

Settled now into his new living situation, Foote returned to his work. "I'm back at work and liking it," he reported to Percy in November. It was never easy, though. "All thats happened to me is I have been engaged in the hardest, or at least the most tedious, occupation of my writing life." Foote had been following a group of renegade Texans attempting to make the Southwest Confederate territory. Lacking the green grass of most other battlefields, Glorieta Pass, where the Texans fought a group of Union soldiers, was "a sandy, miserable country for fighting, with thirst as much an enemy as anything, maybe more-so." After their defeat, the Confederate band struggled home across barren country on "one of the great marches of all time, and one of the great nightmares ever after for the men who survived it."

In December 1956 Foote and Gwyn traveled to New Orleans, where they feasted at good restaurants and, one night, made a tour of local strip joints, where "the girls sort of took us into the family," Foote wrote his friend. Back at home, Foote returned his effort of "trying to bail out the Mississippi with a teacup," as he once called his daily regimen of writing *The Civil War.* After completing his writing in midafternoon,

he would rework the day's five hundred words on his manual typewriter. Once done, the completed pages would be added to the growing stack sequestered in a box in his study. By the end of March 1957
Foote had returned from the Southwestern desert waste to the more
familiar Mississippi, "back in the mainstream of the war," where the
Confederate soldiers had been told by General P. T. Beauregard that
the island batteries were to be "held at all costs," instructions that "in
soldier language meant that those guns were worth their weight in
blood and must be served accordingly." With the Island 10 victory, the
North had gained control of the Mississippi down to middle Tennessee.
On the horizon was Shiloh, "which I can write with one hand tied
behind me," Foote told Percy.

As he got deeper into volume I, he believed more and more in his
"method": "I'm plugging along at the War; it grows bigger the longer
I examine it, and more complex in every way." Part of the complexity
involved the different sources and points of view commanding his
attention: "Everyone saw it differently; it's up to me to combine their
views and yet avoid bedlam." By his own admission, "the only way
to keep it simple" was to "face its complexity," reading the various
accounts and then "translat[ing] it by selection and cutting-through."
As he translated each section, Foote attempted to have the reader
vicariously feel the soldier's experiences: "The idea is to strike fire," he
said in one of his most eloquent comments about his methodology,
"prodding the reader much as combat quickened the pulses of people
at the time." As he repeatedly told himself, "Dramatize! Dramatize!
But don't goose it up!"

Foote had also found another literary model for his efforts: Richard
Lattimore's translation of *The Iliad*, which he found to be a "miracle of
a book." He wrote Percy, "This is writing as it should be." In November
1956 Foote filled almost all of a short letter to Percy with one of
Lattimore's Book XVII passages:

> The Trojans came down on them in a pack, and Hektor let them. As
> when at the outpouring place of a rain-glutted river the huge surf of the
> sea roars against the current, outjutting beaches thunder aloud to the
> backwash of the salt water, with such a bellow the Trojans came on, but
> now the Achaians stood fast about the son of Menoitios, in a single

courage and fenced beneath their bronze-armoured shields, while the
son of Kronos drifted across the glitter of their helmets a deepening mist.

With its marriage of rich, descriptive language and individual heroism,
Lattimore's translation legitimized his own project: "I never knew how
really good war-writing could be until I read this translation," Foote
exclaimed to his friend. (In an effort to influence James Jones's writing
of battle scenes in *The Thin Red Line*, Foote sent him Lattimore's *Iliad*.)

Rich as such writing was, Foote had to remind himself that his method
included not sacrificing "facts," not "goos[ing] it up." After an interview,
Lydel Sims summarized Foote's approach as bearing "not one syllable of
historic intervention. Nobody says so much as 'Yes, sir, General,' unless
it's a matter of record." Although it was always a question of whose facts
he took, Foote insisted on the benchmark of factual information. After
Percy wrote "The American War" for *Commonweal* in 1957, Foote kidded
his friend about some mistakes that he had made: "Ive been in a state of
shock over your retention of the first-draft exclamation-point after
SHILOH. Also the misspelling of Brice's Crossroads. We buffs cant stand
little things like that; sets our teeth on edge. Facts, man; facts!"

Foote's war of bravery continued, and he increasingly found himself
in demand as word leaked out about what he had been doing. One of
the places that contacted him about speaking was the University of
Alabama. In January 1956 the university had made national news due
to a failed attempt by Autherine Lucy, a black woman, to enroll. During
her first day on campus Lucy was pelted with rocks and jeered by
students and faculty alike. Perhaps because he felt compelled to play
his part in this racial crisis, Foote agreed to speak at the university in
March 1957. His appearance there—and his recounting of those
days—reflected again his deep frustration about the South's racial crisis.
As he told Percy in a letter immediately after his appearance, Foote
had told the students that "a writer learning his craft was better off in
jail than in an academic atmosphere, that any 'help' in learning to
write was really a hindrance, an interference." In making this claim,
he essentially was targeting the faculty, who "arent scholars, not in any
sense of the word." They seem to me to be pitifully inadequate human

beings," Foote claimed. "It's not that theyre sealed off from life. It's that they see it through the screen of a curriculum, a theory of education."

Showing his confusion about the situation, Foote immediately doubled back, saying that his assessment about the faculty was unfair because he had not properly taken into account how the Lucy affair had affected the university. "Morale was shattered," Foote reported to Percy. "It had a much worse effect than you might think." According to Foote, "The faculty was feeble and confused, repudiated by its own board of regents and smothered under guilt through knowing its inadequacy."

All in all, his experience at the University of Alabama had been "incredible: incredibly bad." He hated what had happened there, but he did not know whom to blame. Foote hated the "rocks and eggs" of the "mob" that had driven Lucy from the campus, but he also despised the "ruthless Madison Avenue methods of the NAACP."

The visit to the University of Alabama marked yet again Foote's struggle to reconcile an unjust South and a South he considered governed justly. His only escape was to descend back a century to the Civil War. Now, he readied himself to finish the last 250 pages of volume I. Although he was confident of his work thus far, Foote still felt unsettled about it because no one, not even Robert Linscott, had yet seen the fruit of his previous three years. Wanting Percy to see it, Foote began arranging a time to go to Covington, Louisiana. Six months before, he had suggested a "longrange" plan, during which, as he dictated to Percy, he and Gwyn would stay in the Percys' cottage: "We could work all day and talk all night. . . . That way we could make up in part for much of the being apart." But only now was that trip materializing. Although he still had some work to complete volume I, by May 1957 he wanted to see his friends. Warning Percy to "sharpen up your reading eye," Gwyn and Foote, armed with the hundreds of pages that he had written, drove down to Covington for a week's stay.

Pleased to find that his friend shared his opinion about the merits of the book, the reenergized Foote returned and immediately set out to wrap up volume I. Moving through the Seven Days and then Antietam, Foote pushed on toward the end of 1862, a high-water mark for the Confederacy's control of territory. While he labored through these last campaigns, the Little Rock integration crisis occurred in September 1957, a charged month during which Arkansas Governor Orval Faubus attempted to prevent nine black students from entering Little Rock's Central High School by using the Arkansas National Guard. President Dwight Eisenhower's subsequent federalizing of the Arkansas Guard meant that the guardsmen had to protect the very students whom, days earlier, they had resisted.

A few months later, Foote had his own crisis to deal with—hardly the crisis of conscience occurring in Little Rock, but one that affected him deeply. In January his beloved boxer, Bo, disappeared. Even though he was closing in on the last few pages of volume I, writing about Lincoln's efforts to make the Civil War a "holy war," Foote found himself unable to work, devastated by his dog's absence. After he contacted the *Memphis Press-Scimitar,* the newspaper ran a story on Bo's disappearance, along with a picture of the dog and a t-shirted Foote. The exposure paid dividends, as Foote soon received a phone call from a nameless "negro man," according to a second *Memphis Press-Scimitar* story, who had chained Bo up after finding the dog "killing his chickens and fighting his dogs." Foote retrieved Bo and was relieved to find that though he was "a little thin," he had been "treated all right." Foote shelled out $10 for the dead chickens, a figure that Foote pronounced "sure worth it," because "I haven't been able to do any writing since he left."

With Bo at home again, Foote hurtled toward the book's conclusion, which would feature Lincoln's December 1862 message to Congress. Although that 50,000-word message "covered a host of subjects," Foote characterized "all of them [as] connected directly or indirectly with the war." Growing ever fonder of Lincoln and his stylistic flourishes, Foote quoted the last lines of the president's address:

> We say we are for the Union. The world will not forget that we say this. We know how to save the Union. The world knows we do know how to save it. We—even we here—hold the power and bear the responsibility. In giving freedom to the slave, we assure freedom to the free—honorable alike in what we give and what we preserve. We shall nobly save or meanly lose the last, best hope of earth. Other means may succeed; this

could not fail. The way is plain, peaceful, generous, just—a way which, if followed, the world will forever applaud, and God must forever bless.

As Foote described these lines, "through the droning voice of the clerk, the Lincoln music sounded in what would someday be known as its full glory." After spending several months preparing the index, Foote traveled to New York in late May 1958 to meet with Linscott, Cerf, and other Random House editors. Anxious to get the book out, Random House set November 10 as the publication date for the $10 book—no small price at the time. At home that summer, Foote spent his time proofreading galleys. On the evening of August 13, the day on which he had finished reading the last page of galleys, Gwyn threw a small party with champagne and a cake adorned with Union and Confederate flags.

With two more volumes to write and fearful of laboring through them under the oppressive memory of a poor reception, Foote was particularly anxious to see the reviews for volume I. Indeed, many reviewers did have reservations about Foote's work. Several critics questioned his relationship to his sources, including, most particularly, Foote's unwillingness to use footnotes. Foote had dismissed this subject in his bibliographical note by asserting that they would "detract from the book's narrative quality." As John Cournos wrote in *Commonweal*, "Footnotes are the very thing the careful reader may want. He may want to know on what authority the author has made this or that statement and has drawn certain conclusions therefrom." Some critics also questioned Foote's relationship to the sources that the footnotes would have signified. Frank Vandiver, in *The New York Times Book Review*, wondered whether Foote needed to rely less on the *Official Records* and more on "original sources." Along similar lines, R. N. Current suggested that Foote was frequently unwilling to challenge declarations made by military leaders: Foote often "relates as accepted truth a number of things that historians question or dispute."

In what was a more serious criticism, several reviewers questioned Foote's disproportionately military focus. It was, as Jonathan Daniels wrote in *Saturday Review*, "largely a battlefield book." According to the *Kirkus* reviewer, "This bids fair to be a definitive history within the limitations Shelby Foote has apparently set himself." Vandiver even wondered whether the "very breadth and scope of the task" compromised his ability to delve into depth on certain issues: Foote had to "touch lightly on some topics and to omit others. Economic history, for example, so important in the war period, receives almost no attention."

But if there was cause for criticism, there was also enormous praise. Even though he criticized the book's military focus, Daniels also found it "significant and satisfying." In *The Christian Science Monitor,* Francis Russell praised Foote's work even more favorably: The book was "vivid and readable, and above all [it was] a true book. When the latter two volumes are completed the whole may well turn out to be the most encompassing general work on the war." According to Vandiver, "Mr. Foote is a stylist, able in description, deft in characterization and shrewd in analysis. He blends these talents well. . . . Foote has achieved much, by bringing together the results of so many secondary studies he has produced a book that refreshes the memory of the old Civil War hand and makes a veteran of the beginner." Perhaps the greatest compliment of Foote's efforts came from Current: "Any one who wants to relive the Civil War, as thousands of Americans apparently do, will go through this volume with pleasure and then await the next one with impatience. And, years from now, when the centennial ephemera have been forgotten, Foote's monumental narrative most likely will continue to be read and remembered as a classic of its kind." Current's words echoed almost exactly what Foote had told Percy just weeks before the publication, "I think Ive got a really good book, one that will stand down the years. Youre going to be amazed at how much can be got between one pair of covers—all as *narrative.*"

# The Civil War

## VOLUME II

## 1958–1963

It's a long war, but enormously rewarding.
—Shelby Foote to Walker Percy, December 30, 1957

FOOTE HARDLY STOPPED TO take a breath before beginning volume II of *The Civil War*. After finishing reading the galleys for the first volume on August 13, 1958, Foote woke up the next morning and began work on chapter 1, "The Longest Journey." Following Jefferson Davis's morale-boosting trip westward through the Deep South, as well as the Battle of Fredericksburg in the Virginia that Davis had left behind, that chapter would complete 1862 and move into 1863. Davis's trip was intended to rally not only the troops but the general population, where "the spirit of enlistment is thrice dead," as Confederate Senator James Phelan wrote his fellow Mississippian. "Enthusiasm has expired to a cold pile of damp ashes. Defeats, retreats, sufferings, dangers, magnified by spiritless helplessness and an unchangeable conviction that our army is in the hands of ignorant and feeble commanders, are rapidly producing a sense of settled despair." As Foote quoted Davis's address to the Mississippi legislature, "After an absence of nearly two years, I again find myself among those who, from the days of my childhood, have ever been the trusted objects of my affection, those for whose good I have ever striven and whose interests I have sometimes hoped I may have contributed to subserve."

Into his own new year of 1959, Foote proceeded with volume II, spirited by the enthusiastic reception of volume I. "Work goes good, guns booming," Foote wrote Percy that spring. When the history book awards were being handed out in early 1959, Foote smarted a little after winning none of them: "No prize-winner I," he told his friend. But he also knew that, in all likelihood, any consideration of *The Civil War* would have to wait until the completion of the trilogy. He did win one award, however, the Guggenheim, marking the third time that he had received the award, an unprecedented honor.

The Footes would avail themselves of the $4500 almost immediately because they unexpectedly found themselves having to look for a house. In the name of urban renewal, the Memphis city government planned to raze Foote's riverside neighborhood to construct a high-rise housing project. "We're about to be bulldozed off the bluff—quite literally," Foote wrote Percy a little melodramatically in April. Scrambling around for a home, Shelby and Gwyn ultimately found a ranch house at 507 South Yates Road, which, in 1959, was about as far removed from the Mississippi River as they could be and still be in Memphis. Even though they were buying their own house, the move was a sad one, as they would have to sacrifice the isolation and the gorgeous river view for a suburban homogeneity. Some of Foote's neighbors refused to leave; Annie Plunkett, who lived across Arkansas Street, steadfastly refused all of the city's offers until almost under the shadow of the wrecking ball, she took the city's offer, sold her chickens, and moved out.

Interrupted already by the search for the new house, Foote extended the layoff to take a short vacation. In May, the Footes traveled down to New Orleans with Southwestern at Memphis Professor Ross Pritchard and his wife. That month they also picked out a new dog from the pound to replace Bo, who had died after almost fifteen years with Foote. Rattler, a "sort of hound, part Labrador but long-eared and very deep voiced," settled in with the couple. Foote liked having another dog, but he found him "very funny": he "sounds like he's ten feet tall, but bolts like a shot the minute anything starts his way in anything resembling a threatening manner."

Foote was visited with a "tragedy" of another kind in early June. During a visit, Margaret jumped on her father in a swimming pool, tearing a tendon in his ankle. Although the doctor constructed a cast around his ankle, the foot continued to swell to the point that the cast had to be cut off, leaving Foote bedridden, where he did "no work, no nothing." Even when the pain diminished, he lacked the mobility necessary to move around his study. "I just lie here . . . mean-miserable," he told Percy. Foote particularly regretted missing what were for him "the best work-weeks of the year—the advent of hot weather."

Toward the end of his stabling, Foote began chomping at the bit. Hastily arranging another New Orleans trip to see the Percys, whom they had seen but for an hour on the May trip, the Footes headed southward again in early July. For the most part, the trip was for leisure— because he was not writing, it was a good time to go calling on others. But the trip also had a study component: Once Foote was ambulatory again, he would be writing about Vicksburg, and he needed another "look at the field," even if it meant traipsing on crutches through fields and over monuments. Foote needed to "unravel" what he once called "one of the most confusing pieces of real estate in the world," a place where "sometimes I point [a compass] north and it turns out south."

After the July trip, Foote settled in to write about Fredericksburg, a battle that would center on Burnside's repeated attempts to storm straight up the town's Confederate-held heights. With ironic understatedness, Foote reported that Burnside's "unsupported, heavily outnumbered" troops "paid dearly for their daring; more than a third of the men who had gone in did not come out again." Surveying the remains, Lee responded, "It is well that war is so terrible. We should grow too fond of it." From Fredericksburg, Foote turned his attention again to the western theater to write of the December 31, 1862 to January 2, 1863 Battle of Murfeesboro (or Stones River), a "tremendous battle," as he told Percy, "fought about the time of Fredericksburg but much bloodier: Bragg vs. Rosecrans, with Pat Cleburne and Phil Sheridan whooping it up."

Foote felt confident of his work's progress: "The work goes well. . . . The overall thing grows mightily. If I can last it out I'll have created one of the big American things." As much as he was conscious of writing for others, he also received enormous personal pleasure from writing about the war. As he told Percy,

> There's a satisfaction to be got from surrounding a historical event, assimilating it so to speak, and making it your own. It belongs to you thereafter, and when you go and stand on the ground, you feel and hear it all around you. I have been where Davis and Lincoln were, sat in the same chairs and felt what they felt—at least to my own satisfaction. I have stood on ground that was fought for and bled on, and sometimes I have almost thought I heard them yelling. Best of all, though, I have shared their decisions in the off-hours, so to speak, on matters that concern the general public very little. In some ways, thats the best of all. I can understand those dusty scholars who get so much satisfaction from minute things.

Other than a two-day trip on his forty-third birthday to clean up his Rosenstock ancestors' Delta burying ground and several weeks spent moving to their East Memphis home, Foote worked hard through the fall and winter. Foote finished chapter 1 on January 18, 1960. Boxing that away, the very next morning he began "Unhappy New Year," the story of Grant's herculean effort to take Vicksburg. Chapter 2 marked the first time that he had begun dating his daily *Civil War* work, as if he recognized that he was writing "one of the big American things" and needed to record his activities for posterity's sake. Through the first half of 1960 Foote wrote as steadily as he had ever written. He was working so well that he even allowed himself an interruption in April to give a reading at Nashville's Vanderbilt University. Foote appreciated the opportunity to speak to the gathering of 150 people. Using the occasion to return to his fiction, Foote read "The Freedom Kick" and "A Marriage Portion" from *Jordan County.* Perhaps because of its germaneness to the civil rights movement, "The Freedom Kick" enabled him to have the "fantastic experience of seeing their hearts wrung." As he told Percy, "There wasnt a dry seat in the house when I got through." Immediately after this cathartic experience, Foote read "A Marriage Portion," which "convulsed them in laughter and embarrassment." All in all, Foote told his friend, "It was quite a thing."

Returning from Nashville, Foote sealed off his study door to descend again into the Civil War. His return landed him back at the war's pivotal season, the summer months of 1863 that would see, in the West, the Confederate surrender of Vicksburg after a month-long siege, and in the East, the epic battle over three July days that would sear the name of a small Pennsylvania town into the consciousness of all Americans.

Before he could get to Gettysburg, though, he focused on Grant's multiheaded approach to take Vicksburg, the fortress, without which the Confederacy could not maintain control of the Mississippi River. Foote launched himself into Grant's chess match, a series of eight maneuvers that the general employed to try to take the heavily guarded bluff town. Mapping and writing the various stratagems, ranging from trying to create an alternative pass to the Mississippi River to storming the town, thrilled Foote. "It makes a wonderfully dramatic story," he wrote Percy in May, "and I'm giving it all I have."

Finding a stopping point in his campaign on Vicksburg, Foote snuck away in June to Louisiana's Cajun country. He would soon be writing about the ascent of Union General Nathaniel Banks, a former Speaker of the House and Massachusetts governor, up the Bayou Teche region in southern Louisiana, and he did not want to interrupt his momentum by having to make an unpropitious halt. Although Foote had no idea what this outpost of regress held, what he found was a gold mine among the primordial "liveoaks and moss, the strange flat lazy land with the salt deposits forcing up like mushrooms miles across." Foote also relished their food. Arriving in the middle of crawfish season, Foote ate "12 dozen [crawfish] in less than 24 hours." In between crawdads, he feasted on étouffée ("Jesus, what a thing"), redfish courtbouillon ("'koo-beyon,' they call it"), bisque, crawfish stew, and gumbo. "Was I you," Foote told the Catholic Percy, "I'd live there and look forward to Fridays."

More than just delicious food, Foote found in the Bayou Teche "a part of what Ive been looking for all my life," a selfless version of Southern hospitality that in his more civilized realm was not necessarily dead and gone, but dying and disappearing. "I know now," Foote wrote Percy, "there's at least one corner of earth where money doesnt count for everything. Every time anyone did something extra for me, like fix the car or take me boatriding, by reflex I would ask them how much." In response to his question, Foote "always . . . got the same kind of hurt expression, the same wince, as if I hadnt been worth the courtesy."

Back at home in June, Foote delved again into Vicksburg, but along with his work, that summer brought another special pleasure. Percy had finished his third novel, and finally publishing houses showed interest. *Carnival in Gentilly or Confessions of a Moviegoer* was seriously being considered for publication. Over the previous few years, Percy had written several philosophical essays, usually related to the nature of symbolization in language, and he had made a name for himself in certain circles. (The French philosopher Jacques Maritain had written him, saying how much he liked Percy's work.) But in the arena of fiction, he had little to show for his efforts, something that Foote too often reminded him of.

Scarred by his previous failures and his friend's pushiness, Percy parried questions that Foote plagued him with about the work-in-progress. As Foote had asked him in late 1959, "Tell me something of how things are shaping up for . . . your work. Does it move? Is it combining, making a whole, moving toward some consolidated future?" Percy did not respond to Foote's entreaties; indeed, he became evasive. In what is the earliest surviving letter from Percy (until the 1970s Foote threw away most of Percy's letters), he reported to Foote in mid-May 1960 that he was continuing to be, in the eyes of his neighbors, the "deliberate egghead who writes unreadable things." His writing, as he characterized it, was "all pissing in the wind or rather peeing into the abyss."

But encouraged by comments from a New York agent and a Knopf editor, Percy had dared to send Foote the first twelve pages of the new novel. Foote liked what he read: "It has a fine tone and . . . carries right along. . . . In spots it came home to me harder than anything Ive read in a long time." Much to Percy's pleasure, Foote "wished hard for more." Emboldened by his friend's praise, Percy sent the entire manuscript, which was already circulating in New York, to Foote in early August. After finishing writing about the siege of Suffolk, Virginia, Foote sat down late one morning to begin reading Percy's novel. That late morning burned into afternoon and then into evening, as Foote sped on, mesmerized by the strength of his friend's work. At the end of his reading, Foote whipped off a quick letter to his friend. Calling Percy's novel a "breakthrough of the spirit," Foote said, "I take it, now, you are ready for whatever it is you want to do. And I dont think for a minute you are anything like ready to give up fiction, as you said. This is more in the nature of a beginning. . . . All I can say is I like it fine and I hope you keep on working in this very vein. I enjoyed it from start to finish and always with a sense of wonder. I congratulate you." According to Patrick Samway, Foote's approval "pleased Walker greatly." Percy's pleasure only grew greater when he learned, on the last day of August, that Knopf had accepted what would finally be called *The Moviegoer*. (Later that year, Percy's novel would win the coveted National Book Award, triumphing over Joseph Heller's *Catch-22* and J. D. Salinger's *Franny and Zooey*.)

Foote would soon have the opportunity to congratulate his friend in person. On October 7, 1960 the Footes and Percys met in Vicksburg for a weekend that combined a reunion with Foote's exploration of the battlefield. The friends talked about the upcoming presidential election, which particularly excited Foote. Not only did Gwyn have a personal connection to Jacqueline Kennedy, but Foote thought that Kennedy could deliver the country from Eisenhower and its crisis of "moral fiber." Foote hated Eisenhower's hands-off approach to the South, choosing to swing golf clubs while Southerners had swung at each other. He thought that Kennedy's vigorous leadership, however couched in a thick Boston accent, could signal sweet relief for the region.

Given Foote's idealism, suppressed though it was under his cynicism, it was not surprising that he would have been a Kennedy supporter. What *was* surprising was that Percy too was, according to Tolson, "completely behind Kennedy." Although Kennedy was Catholic and a figure who combined "intelligence and wit with patriotism and political vision," Foote's friend had a history of voting for patrician Republicans. Also, there were more personal reasons why he would oppose Kennedy. Percy's brother, Phin had served with Kennedy in the central Pacific and had a less-than-favorable view of the candidate.

On election night, Foote stayed up until the wee hours of the morning, when Kennedy was declared the winner over Vice-President

Richard Nixon in what had been the closest presidential election in U.S. history. The next day, Foote put aside his work to celebrate Kennedy's victory, as he and his friend Ed Giobbi, a local artist and food critic, spent the day drinking. For weeks, his good feeling about Kennedy persisted. Calling Kennedy a "golden boy," Foote told Percy, "I'm delighted with Kennedy. . . . I cant tell you how much those eight Eisenhower years depressed me. I saw everything I prized most about this country going down the drain. Now I feel reborn; I honestly feel the country is about to experience a rebirth. . . . Jesus, what a delivery!"

Born again in the woods of Camelot, Foote considered tackling a project that he had contemplated for years, but never acted on. In what he called a "return of the native," Foote wanted to purchase and relocate to the seat of the Footes' erstwhile prominence and fame: Mount Holly. For several weeks, Foote and Gwyn visited the site in south Washington County, wondering what they would have to do to repair the ancestral house. But after meeting with bankers and realizing how expensive the mortgage payments would be, Foote nixed the project. However romantic the relocation would be, he did not think that he could afford to write under such pressure.

Although they ultimately did not relive the rich past through the purchase of Mount Holly, Foote was in the midst of reliving the high-water mark of the Confederacy. Finishing the 56,000-word "The Beleaguered City" in late April, Foote began "Stars in their Courses" on May 1, a 140,000-word account of the Gettysburg campaign—what David Herbert Donald would later call a "substantial monography" in itself. In Foote's military pageantry, Gettysburg became, in many ways, the climax. Discussing the proposal for this "second invasion of the North," Foote said that Lee considered that "something drastic had to be done to reverse the blue flood of conquest." As Foote characterized Lee's plans to Davis, Lee

> would march without delay into Pennsylvania, deep in Washington's rear, where a victory might well prove decisive, not only in his year-long contest with the Army of the Potomac, in which he had never lost a major battle, but also in the war. It might or might not cause the withdrawal of Grant from in front of Vicksburg, but at least it would remove

the invaders from the soil of Virginia during the vital harvest season, while at best it would accomplish the fall of the northern capital.

Foote worked diligently not only because of the white-hot intensity of the battle, but because Gwyn steadily grew larger with their first child. In October, he honored a commitment that he had made to speak at Louisiana State University. While there, he could not even make the short trip to Covington, Louisiana, to see the Percys because he had to be ready to return, as he told Percy in a letter before he left, "in case she drops the baby while my back is turned." Gwyn did not deliver the baby while Foote was gone, but on November 13—just four days before Foote's forty-fifth birthday—she did, giving birth to Huger Foote (who would come to be called "Huggy"). Upon the arrival of his son, Foote immediately put aside his work, even though he had reached a point just thirty minutes before Confederate General George Pickett led his troops up Cemetery Ridge on that fateful July 3, 1863 day, sealing, in effect, the fall of the Confederacy. While Pickett stood poised for the charge, Foote, for the next three months, played doting father. He had done "no writing whatsoever: not even a letter."

By the beginning of February 1962 Foote returned to his work, resuming with Pickett and leading him toward Cemetery Ridge. In what was a brilliant tour de force, Foote chronicled the various movements of the mile-long charge as if he were creating a cyclorama. Showing both sides poised for the Confederate charge, Foote then followed Pickett's men marching across the wide plain until the Union soldiers opened fire. Suddenly, everything became, as Foote quoted a Confederate colonel, "a wild kaleidoscopic whirl." A nearby lieutenant "waved his sword and exulted as if he saw the end of the war at hand. 'Home, boys, home!' he cried. 'Remember, home is over beyond those hills!'"

That third day at Gettysburg served as prelude to a period of intensive work. Finishing "Stars in their Courses" in March, throughout the summer, Foote was leading Sherman from Atlanta toward Savannah on his "March to the Sea." So well was Foote working that he did not plan to remove himself until he finished volume II, but news of Faulkner's death on July 6, 1962 caused an interruption. (After checking into a Byhalia, Mississippi, clinic, where he had been admitted after a drinking binge, Faulkner suffered a fatal heart attack.) Faulkner had been a literary god to Foote, a beacon who had always lived no more than a hundred miles away from wherever Foote had lain his head. More than just a literary mentor, Faulkner had been a friend. Although the number of times that he said he had spent with Faulkner would grow over the years anywhere from "maybe five, six times," as he told John Griffin Jones in 1979 to, "eight or nine times in all," as Foote told Luke Lampton in 1990, he had developed a friendship with Faulkner. The feelings were returned. As Faulkner biographer Frederick Karl wrote, Faulkner "had particularly liked and admired" Foote.

Wanting to pay his last respects to his literary hero, Foote drove down to Oxford with *Memphis Press-Scimitar* reporter Edwin Howard for Faulkner's funeral. In a published discussion with Joan Williams, Foote said, "A lot of us have been influenced by Faulkner, but nobody has ever come anywhere near him yet." The Nobel laureate's talent was "a great one because it was so varied, so many-faceted. One time you would say, what he could really do was tell a story. Another time you would say, no, what he could do best was capture the texture of things. Then you would say the thing that made him great was the way he could create characters. And you could say all these things, at different times, with justice, because they were all things he did best."

Faulkner had died at a good time, for an increasingly difficult racial situation was emerging, a situation that, as one of the South's most prominent figures, Faulkner would have been asked to address. Over the last years of Faulkner's life, Foote thought that his mentor had embarrassed himself repeatedly when asked to comment on racial issues. Earlier, Faulkner had urged integration, but increasingly throughout the 1950s he began to resent outside interference. As Faulkner biographer Joseph Blotner claimed, Faulkner may have been against "compulsory segregation," but he was also against "compulsory integration." In perhaps his most glaring misstep, Faulkner told a *London Sunday Times* reporter in 1956, "If it came to fighting I'd fight for Mississippi against the United States even if it meant going out into the street and shooting Negroes." (Faulkner would later excuse the statement by claiming that he was drunk during the interview.) As Foote had written a few years earlier, "I blush for him every time he opens his mouth."

In the months after Faulkner's death, the civil rights crisis came home to roost, square on the doorstep of Faulkner's and Foote's beloved Mississippi. That fall, Oxford took the nation's center stage as James Meredith's matriculation at the University of Mississippi set off riots on the campus. President Kennedy called in the National Guard to escort Meredith to the university and restore order, but before they arrived, two students were killed. The Oxford riots were only one aspect of the unrest, as a wave of white segregationist governors swept into office, topped off that November by the election of George Wallace as governor of Alabama. Arkansas and Mississippi had already elected segregationist governors in Orval Faubus and Ross Barnett, but the election of Wallace upped the ante. After losing the 1958 gubernatorial election, Wallace had declared that he never would be "out-niggered" again. Perhaps the ugliest campaign in modern American political history, his 1962 campaign bore out that promise.

These matters haunted Foote as he moved toward the completion of volume II. For the first time in his life, he considered permanently leaving his beloved South. As he would write Percy in the coming months,

> I feel death all in the air in Memphis, and I'm beginning to hate the one thing I really ever loved—the South. No, thats wrong: not hate—despise. Mostly I despise the leaders, the pussy-faced politicians, soft-talking instruments of real evil; killers of the dream, that woman [Lillian Smith] called them, and she's right. Good Lord, when I think what we could have been, the heritage that was perverted!—the misspent courage, the hardcore independence, the way a rich man always had to call a poor man Mister, the niggers who stood up for a century under what would have crumpled the rest of us in a month. . . . All that; and now we trust it to the keeping of Ross Barnett!

As always, Foote blinded himself to the contemporary situation by opening his eyes wide to a past century's war. On August 13, 1962 he began chapter 8, "The Center Gives," an account primarily of the battle for Chattanooga, Tennessee. Foote would write that chapter as fast as any in volume II, a clip all the faster because that period included a seven-week layoff brought on by the Russian missile crisis. By February 24, 1963 Foote had begun the final chapter, "Spring Came on Forever," which spelled out the establishment in early 1864 of the Union's two-pronged attack of Grant moving South into Virginia and Sherman cutting a swath through Georgia. Now, with the end of volume II in sight, Foote told Random House that he would be finished by summer. Subsequently, they set November 18 as the tentative publication date. With the deadline hanging before him, Foote settled in to knock everything out. In the mornings and early afternoons, he worked on the last chapter; later in the day, when he was too tired to do anything fresh, Foote corrected the proofs of the earlier chapters and prepared an index for the volume. When Martin Luther King gave his "I Have a Dream" speech at the August 28 march on Washington, Foote was hours away from finishing. Two days later, at precisely 10:10 A.M., he lifted his pen from the page. Depicting Sherman's return visit to Cincinnati twenty-five years after the war, Foote quoted the Union general remembering the March 17, 1864 meeting between Grant and himself: "Yonder began the campaign," Sherman said, pointing to a hotel. "He was to go for Lee and I was to go for Joe Johnston. That was his plan."

Foote only had to finish the volume's bibliographical note, which he would write, after a breather, over the next few weeks. But during those weeks, one of the stranger events of his life occurred, an event that would once again reproduce all of the ambivalent love and hatred that he felt about his region. On September 15, a day after the bombing of Birmingham's Sixteenth Street Baptist Church killed four young black girls, Foote pulled up to a Prentiss, Mississippi, diner to buy a newspaper to learn the latest news about the bombing. As Foote later remembered the scene with the owner and a Mississippi highway patrolman who was there, "I went up to the proprietor and said, 'Do you have a morning paper?' and he said, 'We're all sold out.' I said, 'I wanted to find out something if I could about this Birmingham explosion, a bombing or something in a church over there.' He said, 'Yeah, that was all in the paper this morning. I guess those niggers will learn sooner or later.' I said, 'Well, I must not have heard it right on the radio. It said three little girls were killed.' He said, 'That's right.'"

The owner's response sent chills up Foote's spine. He was disgusted with the man's racism, but Foote also sensed that were he in trouble, this man would help him without question. "There's a lot of ugliness down here," he admitted in the same interview in which he told of the encounter, "yet I know from my experiences in the North and in the South that that same man, if I had been broken down on the side of the road with car trouble or something, he would stop, get the jack out of his car and help me, get all greasy and dirty, and would not have expected anything more than a 'thank you' for doing it." In this "curious mixup of traits," Foote saw again the contradictions of Southern life that made it both damn appealing and damn detestable.

Dumbfounded by this "curious mixup of traits," Foote ultimately lighted on the knowledge of their heritage to attack the people at the diner. Remembering that the owner had claimed, "We've got to preserve our heritage," Foote challenged his use of the term: "I turned back to him and the patrolman and I said, 'This town is called Prentiss; is it named for Sergeant S. Prentiss [a Civil War general]?' He said, 'I don't know,' and I said, 'It seems likely.' . . . He said to the waitress, 'You know how Prentiss got its name?' She said, 'No, I don't know,' and the highway patrolman said he did not have any idea. That showed you how much their heritage meant to them." A slippery term, heritage would nevertheless be something that Foote explicitly invoked over the next few years, as he found himself struggling to reconcile his region's contradictions.

At home in Memphis, Foote sat down to write the bibliographical note for volume II. In part a response to critics' concern about the lack of documentation in the first volume, Foote had intended the note to provide a full list of the sources that he had used. Although he did give his basic sources, Foote deferred providing a detailed list, instead promising "a complete bibliography at the end of the third volume." While this postponement suggested laziness, it also signified that his attention lay elsewhere, with events such as the Prentiss diner tableau. With trenchant irony, Foote thanked the race-baiting governors for their contribution to his understanding of the Confederate leaders:

> I am obligated also to the governors of my native state and the adjoining states of Arkansas and Alabama for helping to lessen my sectional bias by reproducing, in their actions during several of the years that went into the writing of this volume, much that was least admirable

in the position my forebears occupied when they stood up to Lincoln. I suppose, or in any case fervently hope, it is true that history never repeats itself, but I know from watching these three gentlemen that it can be terrifying in its approximations, even when the reproduction—deriving, as it does, its scale from the performers—is in miniature.

Never had the connection between civil rights and *The Civil War* been so clear.

When Random House released the book in November, at a price of $12.50, critics were even more receptive to Foote's work than they had been to volume I. As Richard Harwell wrote in *The Chicago Tribune,* "The second volume maintains the breadth of coverage, the depth of understanding, the unflagging interest, the skillful writing that made the first a major achievement among Civil War books." In *Atlantic Monthly,* Phoebe Adams praised the volume's research and level of detail,

> If there is anything about the Civil War that Mr. Foote has not discovered, from the price of flour in Richmond to the origin of the nail with which General Hancock was shot, it must be undiscoverable. . . . He quotes continually from the letters and diaries of soldiers on both sides, so that the large-scale description of events is peppered with the small, sharp recollections of men who heard the mockingbirds sing around a midnight ambush, or gawked over the fortifications on Cemetery Ridge while the Confederates dressed their line under fire.

In spite of the general appreciation of Foote's work, some critics continued to rail at its lack of documentation. In *Bookweek,* T. Harry Williams wrote, "It is on the question of sources that the academic historian may wish to quarrel again with Mr. Foote." Williams noted that the work contained neither footnotes nor a "formal bibliography," but he did defend the author, saying that "Foote has drawn his material from published documents and secondary accounts." Less sympathetic to these bibliographical issues was David Herbert Donald. In *The New York Times Book Review,* Donald wrote,

> Unlike both his distinguished rivals, Mr. Foote is more concerned with telling a good story than with settling disputed historical points. His book is undocumented—and, while there is no reason to question his statement, "Nothing is included here, either within or outside quotation

marks, without the authority of documentary evidence which I consider sound," he nowhere makes his criteria for soundness clear. Where the evidence conflicts, he lets the reader choose. Did General Grant go on a spree before the battle of Vicksburg? He paraphrases for four pages the belated recollections of Sylvanus Cadwallader relating this memorable bender—only to conclude anticlimactically that some historians question the authenticity of Cadwallader's account and to add that "No harm had resulted from the army commander's two-day absence from headquarters, drunk or sober." Was much damage done in the New York draft riots? Mr. Foote repeats without evaluation the usual horror stories of the affair—and then adds, also without evaluation, that "some Democrats later protested that the figures [on casualties] had been enlarged by Republican propagandists."

Donald's review did not just question Foote's willingness to sacrifice historical issues for the sake of novelistic drive; it also suggested again Foote's disproportionate focus on military affairs—what James Nelson Gaddell in *The St. Louis Post-Dispatch* called Foote's "story of the fortunes of the armies and the battles." Donald bored into the Faustean pact that Foote had struck:

> To give unity to his narrative, he has minimized everything but the military aspects of the Civil War. Probably not more than one-tenth of the present book is devoted to politics, diplomacy or public opinion, North or South. Almost no attention is given to economic, social or intellectual developments. While Mr. Nevins clearly regards battles as a troublesome interruption and Mr. Catton is concerned with the broad outlines of strategy, Mr. Foote takes great delight in the tactical details of major engagements—and even more pleasure in the minutiae of smaller, less famous military episodes.

More sympathetic to Foote's standing in this trinity, *The Dallas News*'s reviewer wrote,

> We now have three multivolume histories of the Civil War in process of publication, [and] each of the three performs a distinct public function. Bruce Catton's centennial history might be termed a "popular" work, for it undoubtedly will have the widest appeal, from Catton's fluency of language, perceptive analyses and incisive treatment. The

massive 10-volume study by Allan Nevins, embracing the prewar and Reconstruction periods, must be regarded as well-nigh definitive in scope and thoroughness. But even in such distinguished company, Foote's work stands erect on its own merits as a masterful work, splendidly conceived and splendidly written.

That assessment pointed to the way that, in spite of such criticisms as Donald's, Foote's Civil War study had forged its own niche: "One closes this 960-page narrative of the military and naval operations of 1863 with the sense of having," Louis Rubin wrote, "never before, been told what it was all about, authoritatively and interestingly. Battles and campaigns have been clearly explained; the characters of the major participants have been convincingly drawn; the degradation, the horror of a most bloody civil war have been dramatically depicted. The skills of the novelist and the historian have been combined to produce a masterly military narrative." As *The Dallas News*'s reviewer wrote, "The freshness of the Shelby Foote approach, and the striking incidents with which he enlivens the central account of holocaust are the unexpected . . . new profits. As much as has been written of the last battle and death of Stonewall Jackson, Foote has still contrived to even make that well-covered tragedy new in aspect. Decidedly the man has a way about him." Even Donald, for all of his criticism, called it "immensely readable." In what was a perfect summation of Foote's herculean efforts, Frances Russell claimed, "Compared with Civil War II, Civil War I was a simple operation."

# The Civil War

## VOLUME III

## 1963–1974

It was on the night of June 27, 1787, between the hours of
eleven and twelve, that I wrote the last lines of the last
page, in a Summerhouse in my garden. . . . I will not dis-
semble the first emotions of joy on the recovery of my freedom, and perhaps, the establishment of my fame. But my
pride was soon humbled, and a sober melancholy was
spread over my mind, by the idea that I had taken an ever-
lasting leave of an old and agreeable companion, and that
whatsoever might be the future date of my History, the life
of the historian must be short and precarious.

—Edward Gibbon, on the completion
of *The Decline and Fall of the Roman Empire*

IN A 1961 INTERVIEW with Charles Edmundson, Foote told the
Memphis reporter that he had but "four years" more to finish the
entire trilogy. Implicit in that forecast was that Foote's work on volume III would be steady and unrelenting. With the light at the end of
the tunnel peering inward, Foote assumed that in spite of any fatigue
developed from writing two thousand-page tomes over the last
decade, sheer momentum would bear him onward. That quest did not
begin too promptly. In fact, for the first time since he had started *The
Civil War*, Foote began accepting honoraria, offers that had heretofore

sprouted all around, but now, tired and unexcited about putting pen to paper, ones that he gathered gladly. With those positions would come demands and obligations that would necessarily delay the completion—and even the beginning—of volume III.

The first came from the University of Virginia, which asked Foote to serve as its 1963–1964 writer-in-residence. Conveniently forgetting his anti-university sentiment, Foote readily accepted the position, justifying the post because of its personal significance. Not only did he consider Thomas Jefferson's masterpiece a "beautiful campus," but as UVA's writer-in-residence Foote would be following in the footsteps of a series of great writers, including Katherine Anne Porter, John Dos Passos, Stephen Spender, and, most notably, William Faulkner. It was at Jefferson's university where Faulkner, in 1957, singled out Foote as a promising young writer, telling a class that he "shows promise, if he'll just stop trying to write Faulkner, and will write some Shelby Foote." Just two weeks before volume II was released, Foote drove to Charlottesville, and from November 4 to 8, he fulfilled his duties as writer-in-residence. During that week, Foote spoke to several English classes, and in the centerpiece of the week, he gave a lecture on historical narrative "as I practice it," an address that included readings of several sections from volume II.

When Friday arrived, instead of heading westward back to Memphis and the Mississippi, he drove eastward toward Washington, D.C., and the Potomac. Mr. Foote was going to Washington, where he had accepted another position. Several months earlier, the Ford Foundation had come calling, armed with an offer for a residency at a theater either in Houston, Washington, or San Francisco. As he told Edwin Howard, in a *Memphis Press-Scimitar* article, the Ford Foundation wanted to know "why more writers today aren't gravitating toward the theater. Their notion is to make it possible for some novelists and poets to spend a year watching the theater tick from the inside in the hope that when we see the problems of the theater some of us may respond to them." At first, Foote hesitated to take the offer. He never wrote well away from home, and having built up a head of steam in finishing volume II, he did not want to lose that drive. Moreover, the possibility of relocating to Houston did not excite the Footes, but Washington particularly appealed to them. Still inebriated with the Kennedys, the Footes wanted to be party to the Kennedy mania. "I'm very pro-Kennedy, you know," Foote said. "I may not be after coming in contact with all that vigah, tho. I'm very opposed to vigah." Gwyn also believed that if her husband landed the Arena Theater position in Washington, she could cash in on her former friendship with Jackie Kennedy, a relationship that the Footes hoped to parlay into White House visits. "They thought they were going to go up there and there were going to be state dinners and all that," said Lila Saunders, a friend of the Footes. At the very least, they could orbit around political stars, no small thing for two news fanatics. As Foote told Howard, it would be "interesting to see what makes the government tick."

Foote pursued the fellowship on the condition that he would be assigned to the Arena Theater. He got what he wanted, and within weeks, the Footes found a Georgetown apartment to rent. But what was given with one hand could also be taken away with the other. Just two weeks after they had settled in, the intoxicating Camelot they had come to drink in disappeared, as President Kennedy was assassinated on November 22. The Footes were stunned—not so much because their pass to Washington's inner political circles had been lost, but, more deeply, Foote felt that the country had lost the one man who could restore the nation to its erstwhile prominence and could bring, if not harmony, at least peace to the beleaguered South. As Foote told an interviewer years later, "I don't think history will ever get any true view of John Kennedy and what he meant to us at the time he was alive, because the facts don't support what we felt. What we felt about Kennedy cannot be expressed with facts."

As hard as Foote took the loss, Percy took Kennedy's death even more painfully. The assassination waylaid Percy. According to Tolson, Percy burned with "anger . . . at the loss of the one president he had ever believed in." Interrupting the direction of his new novel, Percy spent countless hours over the next year attempting to incorporate Kennedy into his work. Finally, after writing almost three hundred pages of Kennedy material, Percy's agent convinced him to condense all of his sound and fury into a mere eight lines. In *The Last Gentleman,* Will Barrett finds one of Sutter Vaught's reveries:

> Kennedy. With all the hogwash, no one has said what he was. The reason he was a great man was that his derisiveness kept pace with his brilliance and his beauty and his love of country. He is the only public man I have ever believed. This is because no man now is believable unless he is derisive. In him I saw the old eagle beauty of the United States of America. I loved him. They, the (unreadable: bourgeois? Burghers/ bastards?), wanted him dead. Very well, it will serve them right.

Although Foote did not share Percy's need to elegize Kennedy, the president's death partially contributed to a writing malaise that would last an entire year. Before he left for Washington, Foote envisioned himself borrowing books from the Library of Congress for his work on volume III. Fifteen years later, he would claim that he had pushed himself to "do some research and take some notes and things like that." Just four years after his Washington stay, Foote would claim that he was at the Arena Theater "all the time. I went in the morning, or . . . what they called morning which was about eleven o'clock. . . . I stayed right on through the afternoon or went home to dinner and came back and saw the performance that night."

In spite of these later claims, Foote's daily existence in Washington consisted of little more than mustering the energy necessary to get himself poolside. He did not write anything—not even letters to Percy. Nor did he make it often to the Arena. An administrator there remembers that Foote was "never around." In more candid moments, he could admit to this laziness. As Foote told John Griffin Jones, the Ford Fellowship soon became a respite, a "sort of vacation, a way of resting up for starting the third volume." During that year, Foote boasted, "We spent Mr. Ford's money right and left."

Being away from his work and away from Memphis did give Foote an exile's perspective on the proceedings in the Deep South. As he would later invoke one of his literary heroes, "Proust said somewhere, 'Noah never saw the earth so clearly than when he was on the ark.'" Free from the confusion and indifference of his wealthy white Memphis friends, Foote seemed to grow more bitter. One friend, Meg Turner, remembers a dinner with the Footes around this time where Foote questioned Turner's family's membership in the Memphis Polo Club, an exclusive gathering place for wealthy Memphis socialites. Foote questioned how detrimental the exposure to the country club setting would be for Turner's children. Such an opinion was not new for Foote. Normally, though, he backed down quietly after expressing his views. But in this instance, the debate grew louder and louder, until Foote's and Turner's shouts reverberated through the restaurant.

In terms of writing, that embitterment equated to an indifference about doing even the work he had agreed to do for the Arena. As the spring came on and with the fellowship year coming to an end, Foote had done nothing other than write a one-page introduction for a production of *The Taming of the Shrew.* Rousing himself enough to fulfill what he considered his obligations, Foote nevertheless did the bare minimum, dramatizing the three shortest stories from *Jordan County.* In its acts 1 and 3, *Jordan County: A Three-Part Landscape in the Round* featured the monologues of "A Marriage Portion" and "The Freedom Kick" with minimal staging. The most work that Foote did for the production involved, in act 2, making decisions about omitting certain narrated sections of Pauly Green's shooting spree in "Rain Down Home."

Once he finished the script, Foote passed it off to Mel Shapiro, who directed a cast that included Ned Beatty and Joan Van Ark as the narrator of and waitress in "Rain Down Home." In its only staging, on June 15, 1964 the Washington Drama Society produced Foote's play. From his seat in the audience, Foote watched it with mixed emotions. As he would tell a group later at Memphis State University, "The play was rather successful. These people [actors] were out there saying these things some of which were fairly funny. And the audience would laugh." But what he did not care for about drama was the audience's integral role: They "would keep on laughing and not hear the next funny line. And I did not like that at all."

After the production of *Jordan County,* the Footes returned home to a South that, if in turmoil when they left in 1963, had now descended into outright chaos. On June 21, 1964 Andrew Goodman and Michael Schwerner, two whites from New York, and James Chaney, a black Mississippian, disappeared in Philadelphia, Mississippi. The three were college students working for a civil rights organization during their summer break. (Their bodies would be discovered in an earthen dam outside the town on August 4.) Although Southern blacks, such as Medgar Evers, had already been killed, the death of whites—Northern whites—ensured that the region's civil rights struggle could not be contained within the South's boundaries. President Lyndon Johnson's subsequent Civil Rights Act sailed through both houses of Congress and on July 2, 1964 was signed into law. Johnson's actions infuriated white Southerners, smacking as it did of Reconstructionist carpetbagging. Worse yet, as a Southerner, Johnson had turned, in the minds of these Southerners, scalawag.

Leery about diving into this cauldron, the Footes particularly did not want to go back to Memphis. With its huge black population and the corresponding siege mentality of its whites, the city had become a powder keg in search of a match. But Memphis was home, and, at least at first, they had few other real options. Within weeks of their return, however, they began developing plans for building a house on the Gulf of Mexico, something that had been on their mind for almost a year. Foote harbored a romantic fascination with the ocean: "The sea's edge appeals to me as a notion, the glassy expanse opening out and the salt wind coming off of it in the winter." Furthermore, as a coastal area, Gulf Shores, Alabama, would also presumably provide sanctuary from the racial and political issues electrifying the South.

At Gulf Shores, they moved forward on what was to be a monstrosity of a house. "I wanted something based on the old plantation style [house] plus the idea of a steamboat," Foote said. Foote, who fancied himself as something of an amateur architect, also wanted a gallery around the house that would overlook the Gulf of Mexico. After hiring Memphis architect Gus Adalotte, who was considered "very hot," Foote presented his ideas. What Adalotte came up with was essentially two houses side-by-side, with a runway connecting both of them. Around the two top stories of the three-story house, Adalotte ran a gallery that had sliding glass doors that opened onto the Gulf and a lagoon behind the house.

While the house was being constructed, the Footes rented a house. It was a curious year spent on the Alabama coast—hardly the paradise that they had hoped for. Although it was there that he finished "Novelist's View of History" for *Mississippi Quarterly*'s fall 1964 issue, a nine-page rehashing of his formula of "accepting the historian's standards without his paraphernalia [and] employ[ing] the novelist's methods without his license," Foote found himself with time on his hands. To break the monotony, he started playing a name-that-musical-phrase game with Greenville friend Kenneth Haxton. Foote and Haxton would write down anonymous musical phrases from various classical works on white postcards and send them to each other. As they passed phrases back and forth, neither could stump the other. Finally, Foote, devilishly, sent a passage from a violin solo so generic that it was virtually unidentifiable. Realizing that he had been duped, Haxton then sent back a musical passage that Laurence Sterne had created for his eighteenth-century novel *Tristram Shandy*. According to Haxton, Foote responded, "Well, it could be so-and-so, but it's definitely not so-and-so, but I'm not sure who it is." *"Tristram Shandy,"* Haxton remarked gleefully on his return postcard. The game had ended.

His epistolary exchange with Haxton signaled how lonely Foote and Gwyn felt while living at Gulf Shores, a solitude exacerbated by Foote's growing disfavor with area residents. Foote had gotten himself into about the worst kind of trouble he could find in Alabama in 1964. He got, as he later put it, "crossways with the Ku Klux Klan." As if intent on instigating trouble, Foote proudly sported a pro-Johnson bumper sticker on his car. At gas stations and in local stores, Foote found himself "embroiled in name-calling arguments with fiery-eyed racists." He remembers being in a service station when a mechanic started cursing blacks. Foote took him on: "Man, you're wrong as hell," a claim that started, as Foote remembered it, "trouble."

Mixed up with Foote's disgust for their racial prejudices was his abhorrence of residents' claims to kinship with the Confederacy. In Foote's words, they "translated themselves into terms of being modern-day Confederates, which is what they were not." In a statement that suggests Foote's fashioning of the Confederacy not as an institution defending slavery and plantocracy but as an entity rooted in challenging the constitutionality of secession, Foote claimed that the Confederacy "believed in law and order above all things." By comparison, Klan members "were cussing the courts and wanting not to have anything to do with them and wanting to disobey the orders of the courts."

The sight of a Confederate flag in the hands of the Klan sympathizers particularly galled him. With its multiple significations of rebelliousness and white supremacy, something even codified in Georgia's incorporation of the Confederate battle flag into its own state standard, the Confederate flag was a contentious issue throughout the 1950s and 1960s. Yet, even with these political connections moiling about, Foote narrowly fixated on the flag as only the emblem under which brave soldiers had fought. Relying on this belief, Foote was quick to point out the dissimilarities between the Klan members' use of the flag and the appropriate understanding of it: "I told them every time I had any kind of confrontation with one of them or saw them with a Confederate flag; I told them they were a disgrace to the flag, that everything they stood for was almost exactly the opposite of everything the Confederacy had stood for." Because of his outspokenness, Foote "created . . . resentment" against himself. The Alabamians viewed him as "that liberal writer" and an "agitator," and for the first time in his life, Foote considered carrying a pistol.

There were limits to his protests, however. In March 1965 the Footes watched television footage of six hundred black marchers beaten bloody as they crossed the Edmund Pettus Bridge in Selma, Alabama. Visiting during the next week, Percy suggested that they join the protesters who were going to retry the crossing on the following Sunday. Foote recognized what his friend's suggestion signified. "It was an about-face for Walker to want to do something like that, but it did not surprise me," Foote later said. Since the 1950s, Percy had been rethinking the views of Southern paternalism inculcated him by his adopted father, until, by the 1960s, he had moved to the political left of his friend at least in terms of civil rights issues. Even though he theoretically concurred with Percy's sentiment, Foote balked at the suggestion. Apparently, he would challenge the Klan, but when he came to publicly advocating for Southern blacks, his sense of social conscience withered up.

While they struggled through the trials of living amid the unconverted, the Footes joyfully watched their three-story house go up.

Foote took particular pride in what he considered a "beautiful house." "It was the most remarkable thing you've ever seen," echoed their friend Lila Saunders, a Memphis realtor. "It was very chic." But just as Gulf Shores had disappointed them, so did the house. Problems plagued its construction. The gulf's salt air ate away at the house's paint, so that expensive epoxy had to be used. Furthermore, because the salt weakened the steel, the Footes discovered, with a jocularity only made possible by a distance of thirty years, that "in a fifty-mile-an-hour wind the gallery would fly." Because of these needed construction changes, cost estimates for the house "tripled."

The delays frustrated Foote, who, two full years after the completion of volume II, felt an obligation to begin volume III. His new editor at Random House, Bob Loomis (Linscott had died), had been pushing him to begin, and with the beach house going nowhere but up in the air, the Footes decided to abandon the project in the summer of 1965. Even though they continued to fear Memphis, they returned, finding a rental house at 3020 Homewood in Raleigh, a suburb just north of Memphis.

Settled again, by early fall, he prepared to write. On October 1 he put down on paper the first sentence of volume III: "Late afternoon of a raw, gusty day in early spring—March 8, a Tuesday, 1864—the desk clerk at Willard's Hotel, two blocks down Pennsylvania Avenue from the White House, glanced up to find an officer accompanied by a boy of thirteen facing him across the polished oak of the registration counter and inquiring whether he could get a room." That officer was Grant, a man whom the desk clerk saw as bearing "rather a scrubby look withal . . . as if he was out of office and on half pay, with nothing to do but hang round the entry of Willard's, cigar in mouth." With the emergence of Grant as one of volume III's central figures, Foote was off, a journey that by the beginning of the new year had him writing about the "Kafkaesque" efforts of Banks to move up Louisiana's Red River. Banks's campaign involved a protracted effort to reach Shreveport, which failed, followed by an even more prolonged retreat as Banks waited for the low water to inch up to levels navigable for his ships.

While he ran Banks through the gauntlet, Foote began reading the carbon of Percy's new novel, *The Last Gentleman*. Featuring the wanderings of a displaced Southerner in New York City, Will Barrett, Percy's new novel was a picaresque odyssey from New York to the South and then to the West, from heroic romanticism to satisfied everydayness. Seeking answers for the existential void that he feels, Barrett struggles not only with his father's romantic conceptualization of the South, organized around the mantra of honor, but with the self-destructiveness Percy associated with that ethos. Foote admired *The Last Gentleman* more than he had *The Moviegoer,* perhaps because the novel brought him face to face with his own nostalgia for an earlier South. After reading the manuscript, Foote sat down to write Percy a note. As always, his analysis referred only to the novel's mechanics: "God bless us all, it's very very good; much better I think than Moviegoer, especially the plotting and the writing itself. It gets seriouser as it goes, tightens up just fine, and doesnt break at all in two."

Perhaps Percy's novel was a little too good for Foote. Whereas his own novels had elicited small splashes, Percy's novel, Foote knew, would be well-received. Although Foote had published five novels before Percy could even get one accepted, Percy had now leapfrogged him—by miles. Not surprisingly, Percy's work made Foote want to write fiction again. "I feel wonderfully encouraged on all kinds of counts," Foote told Percy about *The Last Gentleman,* "For one thing, it makes me want to get back to novels; something not many nowadays do."

He was a long way away from writing fiction; in fact, mired still in chapter 1, Foote struggled in early 1965 to write history. Requiring almost twenty months to complete, "Another Grand Design" would not only represent the most time taken to write any of the other *Civil War* chapters, but it would almost equal the time required to write half of the earlier volumes. Almost any diversion during this period became great enough to distract him.

In the spring of 1966 one of those detours was house-hunting. The Footes had grown tired of constantly moving around. As Foote would tell a *Commercial Appeal* reporter just a few months later, "I've moved four times in the last three years, more than in all the rest of my life. I don't plan to move again." Although that statement disregarded his frequent childhood moves, it did reflect Foote's desire to settle somewhere permanently. For weeks, the couple searched for houses in

midtown Memphis, an area that, in spite of white flight, had maintained its cachet. On East Parkway South, they found a modest but
comfortable house, a 1930 Tudor-style brick with large, cathedral-
ceilinged rooms, including a spacious back room that Foote would use
for a study. Even though it fronted the busy East Parkway, the house
offered the sort of privacy that Foote relished. With several large,
sprawling magnolia trees in the front yard and a side-yard brick wall,
the noisy traffic outside went virtually unheard. Interrupting his work,
as he indicated in a margin note of his manuscript ("moved from
Raleigh to East Parkway about 3/4ths DOWN this page"), the Footes
moved on September 13.

Saddled by the debt incurred with the purchase of the house,
Foote soon arranged to be the first writer-in-residence at Memphis
State University. Dr. William Osborne, the chairman of MSU's English
Department, had pursued Foote for more than a year, but it was only
after the purchase of the house that Foote agreed to take the post.
Osborne told a local journalist that a "novelist of Mr. Foote's caliber
will undoubtedly bring insights to literature that the rest of us have
not had." Foote was motivated by an effort to educate students: "I felt
that it would be a good thing if I could somehow participate in [edu-
cation]." Foote felt called to do his duty after seeing a recent report
on the poor academic performance of MSU freshmen: "I'm really concerned with this great difficulty the students seem to be having with
basic grammar and composition." Privately, though, he told Percy
that he had taken the position for the purpose of "earning a little
living-money."

The writer-in-residence position entailed several responsibilities.
Foote refused to teach the creative writing classes that Osborne had
suggested: "I don't believe creative writing can be taught. I won't be an
instructor of creative writing." However, he met several times with history classes to "discuss my notion on the Civil War." Teaching aside, the
primary obligation of the position involved a series of twenty weekly
lectures. Beginning with "The Short Stories of Ernest Hemingway," and
running through "William Faulkner," Foote pontificated on subjects
ranging from "Journalism" to "*Jane Austen.*" At first, Foote spent a
great deal of time putting together the lectures, an uncharacteristic

investment for him, but one that he was making because, surprisingly, he was enjoying the experience. "Truth to tell," he wrote Percy, "there is the delusion of doing good, of being to them what such things (few as they were) were to me; of tipping the scale, however little, in the direction in which they are encouraged very little."

But by February, with eight lectures left to deliver, Foote was investing less and less energy. Feeling guilty about the two-month layoff from his work, Foote focused again on the "only thing that really matters," his writing. Beginning chapter 2, "The Forty Days," Foote followed Grant southward to and through the labyrinth of the Wilderness and Sherman southeastward toward Atlanta. His progress gained apace until June, when Gwyn, who had been carrying another son, suffered a miscarriage. The event stunned Foote. Unable to talk to even his closest friends about the event, he could only note in the manuscript's margin, on July 5, that he was returning to work after a "four-week layoff following birth & death of son on June 9."

If the death of his son led to a break from his writing, other, lengthier interruptions loomed in the offing, including another related to parental responsibilities. In the fall of 1968 Margaret matriculated at Hollins College in Roanoke, Virginia. During the previous decade, Foote's role in Margaret's life had diminished. Until the late 1950s Margaret had lived in Memphis, where Foote saw her frequently. Then, accompanying Lucy Fischer, Peggy and Margaret moved to Ireland's County Sligo. The mistress of Lucius Burch, Fischer had agreed to live at Dromehaire, a manor house that Burch owned. Several years later, when Peggy married Peter Hall, a British officer, Margaret returned to live with her grandmother Foote in Greenville, where she lived through her high school years. When Margaret began considering colleges, Mrs. Foote impressed upon her an interest in going to one of the schools where she or her sisters had attended. Margaret subsequently enrolled at Hollins, which after many years of being an all-women's school had recently gone coed. To pay for her tuition, Foote contacted Hollins officials; by the fall of 1967 he had arranged to teach a modern novel class during the 1968 spring quarter. Foote told the English Department that he would teach four novels: George Eliot's *Middlemarch*, Ernest Hemingway's *In Our Time*, Scott Fitzgerald's *Tender Is the Night*, and Faulkner's

*The Hamlet,* all high modernist novels except for Eliot's, which he once called his "favorite novel."

In March 1968 Foote, accompanied by Rattler, arrived at Hollins with great trepidation. He had viewed anti–Vietnam War demonstrations nightly on television, exhibitions that stung Foote's latent patriotism, and he feared that he would find himself placed in compromising and contentious positions. In spite of their liberation rhetoric, the students were, Foote thought, actually refreshing. As he wrote Percy, "I was about to despair but now I feel better." In fact, he found the Hollins students, "hippie or no," no more menacing than his own contemporaries at the University of North Carolina: "They arent nearly as bad as they look and sound, only about as bad as you and I were thirty years ago."

In spite of these happy discoveries, that spring marked a difficult time in Foote's life. While he was in Virginia, Martin Luther King Jr. was assassinated in Memphis on April 4, 1968. Just a week before in the Memphis airport, Foote had walked past King, who had arrived to participate in a black sanitation workers' strike. Foote wanted to say something to King, but nothing came out of his mouth. A few weeks later, Foote was still stewing about the murder. As he told Bob Mottley of the *Roanoke World News,* "The main problem facing the white, upper-class South is to decide whether or not the Negro is a man. If he is a man, as of course he is, then the Negro is entitled to the respect an honorable man will automatically feel to an equal." Foote told Mottley that because he had been willing to defend blacks while he lived at Gulf Shores, "they thought I was a nut. But they knew deep inside what was right. Just admitting it is the white Southerner's biggest hangup."

King's murder was not the only tragedy playing itself out in Foote's life in the late spring of 1968. His mother was dying. In her first medical examination since 1933, doctors at Memphis' Baptist Hospital had discovered a tumor that was "the size of half a grapefruit." A series of fifteen weekly radium treatments began immediately, after which the tumor would be removed. Although Gwyn became his mother's daily caretaker, Foote and Rattler returned home from Virginia almost every weekend. His mother's illness gave the reserved Foote the opportunity to express his love for his mother, whose indulging of him had often gone unthanked. "It's a strange thing," he wrote Percy, "being in close touch with a Saint. . . . She was a widow at 28 and paid her way, and mine too way past the norm. At last I dont care how much she sees how much I care about her. She takes a lot of satisfaction in that—and so do I, at last." After the surgery in mid-May, Mrs. Foote suffered from what Foote called a "depression of spirit": she wanted to die, Foote said, and "now she has to get ready to live with a piss bag strapped to her thigh." For six more months she fought, all the while passing on her Social Security checks to her granddaughter, but with the recurrence of her cancer, she died on January 12, 1969.

During the next three months, Foote mourned. By April, though, he returned to *The Civil War* with a fury and momentum that he had not previously displayed, perhaps seeking to channel his grief. While he had been at Hollins, he had eked out only four and a half pages, and his pace during his mother's illness had not increased appreciably. But now he worked at his old rate, producing two pages per day. Late in April, he finished "The Forty Days," and he immediately launched into chapter 3, "Red Clay Minuet," a chapter that would feature both Sherman's winding effort to take Atlanta and Admiral David Farragut's bold move against Mobile.

Farragut's challenge against Confederate Admiral Ralph Semmes came first, and Foote loved writing about the Battle of Mobile Bay. With all of the excitement of a little kid, Foote wrote Percy, in a statement that suggested again that writing history could serve as a substitution for actually experiencing the event: "This week I sank the *Alabama*. . . . [W]rote me a lovely little cadenza on her final going-down. Did you know Semmes threw his sword into the sea? He did— to keep it, like the *Alabama*, he said, from 'the polluting touch of the hated Yankee.'" Several months later, Foote led Sherman up to and through Atlanta's gates, a military win that would ensure Lincoln's victory in a bruising 1864 presidential campaign against Democrat George McClellan, who had risen from his military ashes to run against his former leader. Foote was, as he told Percy, "crossing the Chattoochee [River] with Sherman and getting ready to send a bullet straight up James Birdseye McPherson's ass. A good lodgement."

Even with these advances, interruptions from unexpected quarters continued to dog him. Late in the summer of 1969, only a month after Foote had been at Hollins to participate in a literary conference, Margaret was involved in a terrible automobile wreck on a Roanoke road, an accident that would land her in plaster and traction for the next year. Foote immediately flew up to Roanoke to be with her, and after she was transferred to a Memphis hospital, he spent long hours at her bedside.

His patience with her roguish ways, however, was growing thin. For several years he had worried about her drug use. As early as her first semester at Hollins, her father had begun to note her habit, and after the accident, Foote told Percy that Margaret's bed-ridden depression could be easily alleviated by a "few pills and shots . . . as soon as she gets the chance to pop or shoot them." Perhaps seeing his own former rebelliousness in her, Foote continued to provide emotional and financial support, but she was also playing out her hand with her father. After her recovery and return to Hollins, in late 1970, Margaret called Foote to tell him that she was flying home unexpectedly. Begrudgingly, Foote drove to the Memphis airport to meet her. The plane arrived, but Margaret was not on board. Disgusted, Foote told her that he was cutting her off, a decision cemented no doubt by Margaret's subsequent ventures, which included traveling with the Jimi Hendrix entourage on a European concert tour and dancing for several years at New Orleans' Big Daddy's strip club. (Foote's erasure of his daughter was so complete that in 1994, when asked by C-Span's Brian Lamb if he had children, he answered, "One child, a son.")

While Margaret was certainly responsible for drawing Foote's patience to the breaking point, he could not get out of his head that Margaret's actions reflected some chaotic new world—"the freaked-out young . . . and the stultified old. . . . A nation of halfmad teenagers." That sense of disorientation was nowhere more apparent than on a November 1969 visit to Greenville. Going home usually meant slipping back in time to something more familiar, but this trip did not return such comforts. When he visited LeRoy Percy's Trail Lake Plantation, Foote found himself stunned to find that the "air" there was, as he reported to Walker, "full of efficiency and money." Imagining and hoping for a period of several decades before, when "Negroes gathering at store and drinking pop and guying each other; or even working in the fields," Foote only witnessed modern agribusiness. Trail Lake was "strangely like one of those oversized factories that covers 20-odd acres and employs about twelve people." Foote felt like an "outsider" who "couldn't hook it up."

Even Greenville had changed. Foote lamented the way that the developers of a new apartment building had gutted the Percy house at 601 Percy Street. The house was a "skeleton. You can look right through the walls and see where we used to sleep and read, and the fireplaces where the fires were and where Mr Will used to light his matches, padding around in fuzzy slippers and robe that he couldn't keep the belt tied to." Two months after having his images of his native Mississippi challenged, Foote still shook. "Ive been haunted lately," he told Percy, "by the ride down to Trail Lake and back. It gave me the willies, seeing the changes and not comprehending them. I didnt know what to think; still dont." Even worse, Foote sensed that his incomprehension singled him out: "It seemed to make sense, though, to everyone but me."

While Foote struggled to hold on to the past as a stabilizing presence for the present, Percy more willingly moved forward—even though such progress came at a price. After testifying in a New Orleans federal court as an "expert witness (an observer of the culture)" in a dispute over the presence of the Confederate flag at St. Tammany's High School, Percy received several death threats. The danger was exacerbated when Percy told some Covington residents that the local St. Paul's Catholic High School was nothing more than "a seg school with holy water thrown on it." As a result of the second comment, the local Catholics blew up at him, "And I do believe," Percy told Foote, "they're more unpleasant than the Klan." Fearful of a fire-bombing of their house, the Percys slept in their attic for two weeks.

Percy's actions apparently made Foote feel guilty about his inactivity, triggering a series of angry, ambivalent responses. On June 15, 1970 he wrote his friend, "You always did care a good deal more for the decent regard of your fellow citizens than I did (partly I guess because youve always had a better claim to it)." The letter continued, wavering confusingly between defense and accusation. After praising his friend's actions, Foote then defended the region that had brought on the racism. Foote declared that it was the South "that catches it; gets left out." Moving back on the attack, Foote understood the region's complicity in making itself a scapegoat: "The South certainly cooperates in the estrangement." Claiming that he always "wince[d] at southern accents on TV," Foote reminded Percy that Hemingway had once warned his brother, "Dont ever trust a man with a southern accent unless he's black." So bad was the situation that Foote could claim that the region had in the previous decades produced only one admirable white man: "Lyndon Johnson is the only decent public man we've produced in a generation. . . . White, that is."

As always, his escape from these issues involved sinking back into his work. As Percy jokingly would tell his friend in 1971, "You're going to end like William Ellery Leonard who lived within a shrinking circle, first not being able to leave Wisconsin, then Milwaukee, then his house, then his bedroom. You're going to end up in that turret with Rattler and the Magic Mandarin and As the World Whirls."

During these years, even his work could not sufficiently divert Foote from the contemporary societal conflicts, and those struggles increasingly spilled over into his view of the Civil War, which he characterized on one occasion as "a bloody mess from start to finish, unredeemable even by Lee or Lincoln, and all the 'glory' aura isnt worth the death of single soldier. The cause was bad on both sides, and the worst cause won." Maybe the worst sin, according to Foote, was the presumption that after the war, the country's racial problems were resolved:

> We freed the Negro into indignity and serfdom, and turned promptly to every golden calf on the horizon. Jim Fisk won the peace, along with Harriman and Carnegie, while kidnappers were trying to steal Lincoln's body from his tomb in Springfield and Belknap (Grant's Secretary of War) was selling PX franchises for $50 each, cash on line. . . . This is not a nation, it's a grabbag, an arena where you pay for any trace of decency with your life or by going bankrupt.

Referring to the Red Mountain statue overlooking Alabama's largest city, Foote exclaimed, "Our God isnt Christ, it's that iron Vulcan over in Birmingham."

With the exception of a quick October trip to New York for some living, Foote worked throughout 1971. When the work went well, his spirits soared. Reporting in October 1971 that "my stretch of good hard work continues," Foote wrote Percy, "I tell you, that R. E. Lee is a *bear*. He wanted Grant's ass so bad he stayed in a tremble all through the last year of the war. I'm with Ben Butler now; got a plan for blowing up Fort Fisher (near Wilmington) with a steamer packed to the gunwales with 350 tons of black powder. He tried it. Nothing. Next day a Confederate cannoneer wrote home: 'It was awful! It woke up everyone in the fort.'"

Foote's spirits also soared after he saw the *Mississippi Quarterly*'s fall 1971 issue, an edition devoted exclusively to him. The issue included two interviews with Foote and two critical essays on Foote's work, as well as a bibliography of Foote's writing by University of Georgia Professor James Kibler. Foote appreciated the interest in his work, something that Percy, who was finishing *Love in the Ruins,* was not slow to pound into his head. Percy liked the essays ("The Miss. Quarterly on Foote is a delight, mostly first-class and long overdue"), but more importantly, he was pleased that his friend was seemingly becoming accepted in the academic realm. Percy told him, "You ought to be proud. I am for you, despite what you used to say about not caring what the bloody scholars say about you."

From the beginning of *The Civil War,* Foote had aged dramatically. When, in 1954, he wrote that "it was a Monday in Washington, January 21," he had been a youthful thirty-seven. A jet black mop of hair crowned his unlined face. But in 1972, he was fifty-five, and despite his continued good looks, channels began to cut into his face. An avuncular distinguishedness had settled in. Paralleling his aging mien, his body began to show consequences of ripening age for the first time. As a result of a tumble during his "annual goat dance" in April, Foote's knee swelled up. After "a weekend spent lying up in bed like a Turkish whore," Foote visited a local doctor, who found that Foote had "pinched" the cartilage in his knee. For ten days, he wore a knee brace and took cortisone. The injury reminded Foote of his gathering years, a belief reinforced by a nurse's acceptance, without question, of Foote's age as "Fifty-five." As he recounted the scene to Percy,

"I said [it] with some surprise, though I detected none in her." Forced to get a stronger prescription for his glasses about this time, Foote felt that he was "old, indeed." Although scared by his aging, Foote could still find something humorous in the process. Mapping the knee injury and the need for glasses onto the extremes of his body, Foote claimed that "it occurs to me I'm failing simultaneously at the top and bottom. Someday my ailments will meet in the middle and that will be it. A scrotum-tightening thought if ever there was one."

Stumbling toward Valhalla, Foote nevertheless sped toward the end of volume III. He was enjoying the hot summer of 1972 and planned "to stay here and work right on through Appomattox and Durham Station, Citronelle and Galveston." A few weeks later, Foote wrote,

> I'm truly excited about this stage of the book, a gray twilight shot through with lightning flashes, and the poor goddam ragged Confederates fighting on parched corn and Nassau bacon, and Sherman ripping up Georgia and the Carolinas with nothing but old men and boys in his path, and Jefferson Davis mumbling, "We'll whip them yet" and almost believing it, and Sheridan (that bastard) going around grinding one fist in the other palm and hissing "Smash em up!" It's much of it highly unreal.

So involved was Foote in his writing that summer that twice he reneged on plans to meet up with the Percys, plans that he himself had initiated. Early in the summer, Foote wondered whether the couples "could get together some time this summer." Percy wrote back immediately, accepting Foote's invitation, but it was two weeks before Foote responded. Excusing his silence as a by-product of his recent concentration: "I got into a stretch of work I couldnt look up from." In the same letter, Foote backed out of the summer vacation, saying that, instead, they would come down to New Orleans later in the summer.

The mention of yet another trip to see the Percys set off a usually suppressed belief that it was he and Gwyn who always traveled to see the Percys: "I wish you could get up here for a week of leisurely talk and lounging around doing nothing. I think in all fairness you ought to admit it's time. How many times have we been to Covington? Fifteen? Twenty? Not to mention my numerous excursions in my far-away bachelor existence. Do it." The directive was as pointed as any that Foote ever leveled on his friend, but almost immediately, he toned down his language, knowing that he could ill afford losing Percy. "Stand fast," he wrote at the end of the letter. "I want very much to see and talk with you as soon as can be. We'll get down there sooner or later."

As the time for the Footes' planned visit to New Orleans neared, Percy wrote his friend; but five months passed before Foote wrote back. "Sorry to have been so wobbly about getting down there to see you," Foote finally wrote on the afternoon of January 26, 1973, just after finishing page 1400 of the volume III manuscript. Foote had been "deep into a Lincoln thing—the two weeks down at City Point, winding up with Grant's breaking of Lee's line and his taking off after the old gray fox en route to Appomattox. I got him back to Washington yesterday (Lincoln I mean) with five days left between Sunday and his Good Friday appointment with Booth's der-ringer. . . . Now I go back to Lee and tell of that assbreaking march from Richmond to Appomattox—the real chapter ending." Foote told his friend, "Working tail off," with "some of [the] best writing Ive ever done; all I'd hoped for when the end loomed. . . . If this part isnt copacetic, all the rest wont matter. But it is, man, it is!" Apologizing for his lack of communication on the trip to Louisiana, Foote wrote, "You know how much I want to come, and would have come if possible."

Two months later, Foote still bored ahead. "All well here," he reported to Percy. "War winding down fast, loose ends knotting up nicely, just as I planned from the outset. . . . 1,500,000-plus words, of which I have only about 50,000 to go: a mere bag of shells. . . . Thank God I was always aware of the dangers that lurk in iotas. It's beautiful—like the 20th act in a 20-act play." Foote was conscious what it meant to be nearing the end of a project to which he had dedicated the best years of his writing life. After penning the trilogy's last words, he jokingly planned to "blow my brains out by way of a finale." With hardly less bravado, Foote counted himself among the West's literary giants: "Me and Gibbon. Me and Proust. Me and the Complete Shakespeare."

The war continued, and as it did, Foote's excitement about and relief at finishing the book was almost palpable. "Evacuated Richmond yesterday: Jeff Davis on the road," he wrote Percy. "Lee strung out. Grant yelling, 'Git em.' And Sheridan doing it. And Lincoln about to get shot. First was Old John Brown; now there's J. W. Booth—two madmen, one to start it, another to wind it up." Two months later, and just three days before the Footes would finally meet the Percys at Gulf Shores, Foote reported, "I'm working like a fiend, cooking Bobby Lee's goose but good. He sure looks good in those last scenes. Grant in some ways looks even better—for the first time in his life." Of the former Galena, Illinois, store clerk, for whom he had no particular fondness, Foote wrote, "Got overawed into goodness I expect."

After their quick trip to Gulf Shores, Foote returned home to finish the book. Suddenly ambushed by a "vicious head cold," Foote found himself absorbed by the end of the Watergate hearings. Although he detested Nixon and his colleagues, a "sorry bunch of coves," the ever ceremonially driven Foote was, like some viewer at the execution of Charles I or Louis XVI, fascinated. For Foote, the whole event replayed David Halberstam's claims about the machinations behind the Kennedy and Johnson administrations in *The Best and the Brightest.* Foote considered the book "an amazing revelation of what went on between 1960 & 1971 to rip this country apart—from the top. Power doesnt so much corrupt; that's too simple. It fragments, closes options, mesmerizes." After watching Nixon's August 15, 1973 television address, during which the president attempted to rebuff criticism against him, Foote claimed that Nixon was "not even pitiful: just clonk. He *deserves* paralysis."

In the wake of the Watergate hearings, Foote, like Lee's Army of Northern Virginia in the face of Grant's juggernaut, hunkered down for a bittersweet end. "There's a strange sort of twilight over all this part of the book, a murkiness as if the rebels were slogging along the floor of hell, stomachs all knotted with hunger and knees about unjointed from fatigue." Sympathizing with the defeated in a way that no doubt touched his regional loyalties, Foote told Percy, "There was never an army so thoroughly whipped, short of annihilation." Exemplifying his point, Foote wrote, "Yanks threw down one scarecrow retreater, yelling, 'Surrender! We got you!' He dropped his rifle, raised his hands, 'Yes,' he said, 'and a hell of a git you got.'"

During the next three months, Percy did not hear from his friend. Then, out of the blue, on December 11 Foote emerged to announce, "I killed Lincoln last week—Saturday, at noon." For Foote, the moment had been high drama, operatic enough to even endure "some halfassed doctor [who] came to the door with vols I and II under his arm, wanting me to autograph them for his son for Xmas." Once Foote got rid of his neighbor, he returned to his work where he found the prostrate Lincoln with "his chest arched up, holding his breath to let it out. . . . Then I killed him and had [U.S. Secretary of State Edward] Stanton say, 'Now he belongs to the ages.'"

Foote's study of Lincoln had trumped the doggerel that had filled his childhood. "Christ, what a man," Foote told Percy. "It's been a great thing getting to know him as he was, rather than as he has come to be." With Lincoln gone, Foote feared that the last seventy Lincolnless pages would be "strange, . . . like *Hamlet* with Hamlet left out." But even without this support, Foote was writing at a rate of 10,000 words per month, double the speed at which he normally wrote. One month later, Foote was midway through "Lucifer in Starlight," which followed Jefferson Davis and the Confederate cabinet racing their wagons, teeming with the Confederate archives and monies, through North Carolina and Georgia. On January 22, Foote reported that he "captured Jeff Davis yesterday, locked him up in Ft Monroe today. Now on to Andy Johnson, who looks to me as if he's headed for impeachment." Three months later, he was "into the final ten-page stretch": "will wind it up, God willing, by the end of this week or early next."

Finishing his mammoth project elicited both positive and negative feelings from Foote. On the one hand, he had trouble imagining exactly what could serve as an encore to the herculean task he had just finished: "I'm feeling as if I'm about to be orphaned or left childless; cant tell which." Alluding to St. Matthew's passage about the blind leading the blind into a ditch, Foote asked himself, "Who's leading whom?" The sense of wonderment both at what he had done and the uneasiness about what he would possibly do in the future continued to escalate. In the last letter that he wrote to Percy before the completion of the book, Foote wondered aloud, "Twenty years! What could there be left worth writing about? Whats a rape or a lynching or a kidnapping compared to

Chancellorsville or Booth coming busting out of the smoke in Lincoln's box? Where am I going to find me another hero to put alongside R. E. Lee or Bedford Forrest? My life slips onto the down slope."

It would be some time before Foote began thinking about a novel. With the completion of volume III on May 1, 1974, there was a party to plan, a celebration that Foote had contemplated for years. On a 1961 New York trip, Foote had bought a "very special bottle of wine," an imperial of 1959 Mouton Rothschild, which at the time cost $60. Time had ripened the wine, and by the early 1970s its value had appreciated to almost $300. In an interview with William Thomas, Foote laughed, "It's so damn high it's almost a shame to drink it."

Although he appreciated its value, Foote of all people considered ceremony and ritual priceless, and there was no question that he would drink the wine at the May 10 dinner party. He wanted his closest friends there, including, of course, the Percys. When Foote summoned the Percys to Memphis in a letter of late April, he said, "I hope tis doesnt clash with any plans or commitments you and Bunt may have made." Foote was not going to take no for an answer: "If so," he added, "tell whatever it is youre sorry. . . . Get here that day or anytime earlier. The guest room will be ready and I hope youll stay as long as can be."

After the party, Foote spent the summer reading proofs for volume III, which was scheduled to be released on November 26, a task in itself, because this longest of the three volumes "has something of the look and heft of the Manhattan Telephone Directory." It was a delightful period for Foote, much as it allowed him to contemplate what he had done, and he loved noting that his *Civil War* was longer than Proust's *Remembrance of Things Past* and Gibbon's *Decline and Fall of the Roman Empire*. With no work on his hands, he luxuriously spent the time "drifting, waiting." Such free time led him, in early November, to watch an episode of "The World at War" on the Jewish concentration camps. Watching the television program, Foote found himself "sobbing." He realized that members of his Rosenstock family could have been victims of the Holocaust:

> somewhere among them, for all I knew, some kinsman of mine from
> Old Vienna, with his long gray beard and the old old faces on some of

the children in the camps and the women stripping naked in the cold before they stepped into the shower rooms, already knowing what was going to happen to them inside, and then, later, the bodies, all crowded into a sort of pyramid from having huddled together and then clawed their way to the top for air, the strongest of them. For me, it started with tears. I didnt even know I was crying until the sobs came.

Whatever agony persisted from the television episode was soon doused as the reviews for volume III began to trickle in, critiques that heaped on the sort of credit he believed his twenty-year effort deserved. That praise would not come without the by-now-expected criticism of the work being, in C. Vann Woodward's words, a "purely military history." As Woodward wrote in *The New York Review of Books,*

> While he is willing to admit that there is "a good deal more to war than killing and maiming," Foote has little space for the other aspects. We are admitted to a few of Lincoln's cabinet meetings and some of the president's public speeches and private conversations. We are taken backstage occasionally in the Richmond theater of politics. We are permitted a passing glance at an election, diplomatic exchanges, and (particularly in the South) an economic crisis that had immediate military consequences. The politics of command in both armies—personal rivalries, political animosities, and power plays among the brass—are adequately kept before the reader. But always the main matter before us is the "killing and maiming."

In *The New Republic,* Louis Rubin echoed Woodward's comments. Describing what he called "old-style history," Rubin wrote, "What [Foote] has written is . . . a disenthralled narrative of just how the war was fought out. . . . He has sought to show what happened, to describe the way that the commanders on both sides planned their campaigns and fought their battles."

But now, for the first time, that military focus seemed less of a detriment—and even the work's special strength. Phoebe Adams may have called it "too dense with facts and too intricately organized to pass off as 'narrative,'" but other reviewers were enormously impressed with Foote's achievement. According to Rubin, "Written with flowing style and unfolding narrative art, drawing upon massive research but with all material thoroughly incorporated and placed in the service of his narrative, he has told the story of the war." "The result is not only monumental in size," Peter Prescott claimed in *Newsweek*, "but a truly impressive achievement." In *The New York Times*, Nash Burger added, "To the complaint that it has taken him five times as long to complete his account of the war as it did the participants to fight it . . . [o]ne might also add that the author . . . knows more about the details of the fighting than any of those who were there." In an assessment that echoed Foote's inherent structure, Prescott particularly praised Foote's ability to write about the denouement of the war: "Not by accident . . . but for cathartic effect is so much space given to the war's unwinding, its final shudders and convulsions."

In what was an especially prescient claim, Rubin even suggested that the delay in finishing volume III only added to its appreciation. "When novelist Shelby Foote first began work on his narrative history of the American Civil War," Rubin wrote, "there were still six years to go before the centennial observance of the war was scheduled. . . . In publishing circles the boom market was on for Civil War books." But by being published in the 1970s, Foote's volume III avoided the hoopla of the centennial celebrations:

> It is Shelby Foote's good fortune . . . that his narrative of the fighting of the American Civil War was not finished and published during or immediately following the years of the centennial, but comes to completion only now, when it can be read for the majestic work of history that it is. For essentially it is different from most of the other Civil War books—and perhaps the circumstance that the first two volumes were published in 1958 and 1963, respectively, may account for the fact that, however they were well received and widely praised, the originality was not properly recognized.

"All three volumes," Rubin wrote, were "the finest writing to have come out of the centennial. . . . In range, in mastery of detail, in beauty of the language and feeling for the people involved, this work surpasses anything else on the subject. Written in the tradition of the great historian-artists—Gibbon, Prescott, Napier, Freeman—it stands alongside the work of the best of them." In what was perhaps even higher praise than Rubin's encomium, Prescott claimed, "To read [this] chronicle is an awesome and moving experience. History and literature are rarely so thoroughly combined as here; one finishes this volume convinced that no one need undertake this particular enterprise again." The war that had begun two decades earlier had finally ended. Now, Foote could once again write the fiction that had been his raison d'être.

# After the Deluge

## 1975–1978

*September September*

> I wrote it slowly, taking pleasure in the pains, with the
> notion of getting my hand back in after twenty years of
> writing history.
>
> —Shelby Foote to Walker Percy, June 29, 1977

O N MONDAY, MAY 5, 1975, in a meeting room a thousand miles
north of the Memphis study where Foote puttered about, a committee of three people mulled over the nominations for the 1975
Pulitzer Prize for American history. Among those works being considered was Foote's *The Civil War: A Narrative*. Foote's earlier volumes had
been talked about as candidates for the prize, but it was only after the
third volume was completed that his trilogy was being given full consideration. Although Foote felt pleased that his work was nominated,
he also believed that it deserved to *receive* the Pulitzer, a prize that he
had been "lusting after." One award committee after another had considered *The Civil War*, yet silent afternoons had filled his spring. As a
historical narrative, Foote's *The Civil War* seemed ideally suited for the
Parkman, an award for the year's best historical work; but the granting
of the Parkman had come and gone, and Foote had yet to don a tuxedo.
Just weeks before this Pulitzer day, Foote had waited anxiously by
the phone to hear news that he had won the National Book Award,

an award that he thought "I had . . . more or less in my pocket." The phone had never rung. Although he did win "something called the Fletcher Pratt Award," which he considered "small potatoes," he turned his attention to the Pulitzer after the National Book Award disappointment. Receiving it would restore his belief in the importance of his work; without it, he felt certain that he would not receive the recognition he deserved.

Filled with anxiety, he "fribbled" around that Monday, waiting to hear word. Hour after hour passed as the morning wore into the afternoon. After lunch, he settled back into his study, ostensibly to read; but the tension had grown so great that he could do little else other than shuffle through various papers. Around two o'clock and still trying to keep his mind off the imminent decision, Foote sat down at his typewriter to peck out a letter to Percy. After three pages of spelling out to Percy the best translations of Homer's *Odyssey* (T. E. Shaw's translation) and Dante's *The Divine Comedy* (Thomas Bergin's translation)—part of his lifelong attempt to get Percy to read these works—Foote revealed the anxiety consuming him: "So much for litry matters. Today's the first Monday in May—Pulitzer Day. It's 3.20 in the afternoon; which presumably means I didn't win it, since I havent received a wire or a phonecall. I really thought I had it sewed up—the Pulitzer at least." In his anger, Foote displayed bitterness:

> Actually, I'm coming to understand it a lot better. If merit was the basis for selection, the confusion would make decision impossible. Far better to let politics decide. Then at least the judges have something concrete to go on. Anything else would be anarchy, a bruhaha; blood would flow at every meeting and theyd never arrive at any decision at all. Besides, if some professor gets it, he gets so much more than someone like me would get. He gets promotion, marvelous offers from rival faculties, even tenure. All I would get is sales and a salving of pride; both of which he would get anyhow.

Foote admitted that his logic was dictated by "sour grapes . . . but I don't think that invalidates the reasoning." Wrapping up the letter by suggesting some New York restaurants, stores, and barber shops for the Percys to visit when they went up North in a few weeks, Foote then signed the letter, "Rgds, Shelby." The letter was apparently ready to be sent off. But when Percy received it several days later, he saw that news had come down from Gotham. Inserted in ink below the body of the letter trembled a postscript, whose understated quality spoke volumes about his friend's dejection: "(Dumas Malone won the Pulitzer for history, I just learned. So be it. I consider myself chastened for my presumption & unworldliness.)"

In the days following the Pulitzer announcement, Foote did as he had done with the previous rejections: He feigned indifference. Underneath his mask of pleasantness, though, scars showed through. Several friends remember these days as the darkest of all of the time that they knew him. Lila Saunders claimed that during this period, Foote was unwilling to socialize with any friends, while Richard Leatherman sensed that "it was probably the angriest I ever saw him." Although he hardly waded in the depths of depression that had marked his entrance into Memphis two decades earlier, he felt, as he euphemistically acknowledged later, "bitter and angry."

Marshalling his fury, Foote began channeling that rage into plans for a novel. Two years before he had conceived its narrative motor: "Three Mississippi gangsters come up to Memphis and kidnap a rich Negro's child for ransom." But as would become clear in the coming weeks and months, that novel would also serve as a tool of revenge against a national literary industry that had overlooked him. At this point in his life, Foote did not need money. Now that it could be sold as a set, *The Civil War* sold briskly, and he had already "piled up" almost $100,000 in royalties. What he wanted now was fame, signified, he believed, by great sales; if he could not achieve that fame and money, he wanted notoriety because garnering attention would be his way of avenging those award committees who had overlooked him. Consequently, he planned to make *September September* a sensational potboiler.

Foote did not have to look far to find a model for the new book. After he had published three financially unsuccessful books, works that quickly went out of print, Faulkner warped his next novel, *Sanctuary* (1932), into a story that featured Memphis brothels and gangs, enough corn whiskey to soak the prohibitionist South, and the corncob rape of a University of Mississippi coed. Not coincidentally, *September September* mentions *Sanctuary.* One of the kidnappers, Rufus Hutton, calls Faulkner's novel not "all that dirty—or all that understandable either."

Even before he began work on the new novel, Foote put in motion a process that, hopefully, would have him logging headline-splashing sums. "I figure," he had written Percy some months earlier, "it's good for, say, $72,000 from paperbacks. Maybe more." Now, though, he wanted to make good on that forecast. On the advice of his longtime friend, the writer Calder Willingham, Foote talked with Bob Rosen, an agent whom Willingham said would have Foote bathing in money. Rosen told Foote that not only would he place his novels with publishing houses, but he would find buyers for the books' movie and television rights. Rosen told Foote that *The Civil War* would translate easily into public television filmscripts, and his novels would be good fare for the big screen. Rosen's rosy forecast had Foote dreaming of dollars. "You can't tell," Foote wrote Percy in April 1975, "I might end up rich."

Although he initially failed to deliver any movie deals, Rosen had "flown into an frenzy of activity" on finding a publisher for *September September.* With yet the first word to be penned, Foote had received "flaming offers" from Simon and Schuster and, abroad, from London-based Athenaeum. Both firms, Foote reported to Percy, "say there's nothing they wouldn't give to have me." Going with Simon and Schuster meant turning his back on Random House, whose Bennett Cerf had bent over backward in 1954 to grant him the time, space, and resources he needed for *The Civil War.* But in Foote's current mindset, dough, not devotion, was of paramount importance: "under the double influence of flattery and money—especially money . . . loyalty melts as fast as snow at midday."

In the end, loyalty did not melt so fast—Foote signed a contract with Random House after the firm agreed to publish a novel that would follow *September September.* Random House gave Foote a $15,000 advance, plus $10,000 when he turned in a 90,000-word manuscript on or before March 1, 1977. In addition to the standard 15 percent in royalties from the sales of the novel, Foote would also receive $25,000 one year after the acceptance of the work plus one dollar for every hardcover trade edition sold after the book had reached $30,000 in sales.

With the money matters in place, it was time for Foote to start writing. By July 26, 1975 he had settled on the chronological and geographical parameters of the narrative. Foote's choice of setting was brilliant—building on his earlier claim about the novel being about the Mississippi gangsters' kidnapping of the young Memphis black child, Foote decided to combine that with the Little Rock 1957 school integration crisis. He would have his kidnappers time their abduction to take advantage of the white-hot situation. "They were waiting," states the narrator, early in the story, "for the time to be right; waiting, that is, for a maximum of disturbance across the way in Arkansas, and in Memphis as well, to provide a background of fear and discord, a heightening of tension and apprehension." By integrating the novel's thriller plot with this racial crisis, Foote planned to look his region's dynamics square in the face—much as he had planned to do with "Two Gates to the City."

Always a stickler for accuracy, never more so than in a work following *The Civil War,* Foote set out to conjure up that period now as thoroughly as possible—in fact, authenticity would become a modus operandi for *September September,* as well as a noose. Much like James Joyce preparing to write *Ulysses,* Foote immersed himself in the newspapers of the period. At the Memphis-Shelby County Public Library, Foote sought out *The Commercial Appeal*'s and *The Memphis Press-Scimitar*'s September 1957 editions. When librarians directed him toward the microfilm on which the newspapers had been recorded, Foote demanded to see the original hard copy. Day after day Foote soaked in the print of the yellowed, faded newspapers to recall the details of the actual events that would surround his fictional kidnapping. "The papers brought it all back to my mind," Foote said. "They triggered my memory." In a small accounting ledger, Foote made copious notes about the events of that month, to the point that he "knew what time the sun came up, what time it set, how much it rained and when the autumnal equinox occurred." Given his absorption in these newspapers, not surprisingly, newspaper headlines and news stories would flood the pages of his new novel, from captions ("President Eisenhower escorts

Mrs. Eisenhower from the car at National Airport in Washington as they prepare to leave for a vacation at Newport, R.I.") to headlines ("FAUBUS TO GIVE SCHOOL STAND / IN DRAMATIC TALK WITH IKE").

Paralleling his demand for historical accuracy, Foote insisted that his novel be faithful to Memphis' downtown geography and topography. Working from old maps of the city, he reproduced in his ledger the neighborhoods that he was going to write about, down to the streets and intersections. Where the maps lacked specifics, Foote relied on his memory to reconstruct the black neighborhood where he himself had lived. As if to recover imaginatively that neighborhood, Foote located the house rented by Hutton, Reeny Perdew, and Podjo Harris in the same "all-Negro section . . . until three years ago [when] a writer moved into one side of the raw brick duplex, down the way." Recalling his fondest memories of the neighborhood, Foote would have the kidnappers' back door look out onto the river, where they could see "the three mile-long bridges, amazingly close, striding westward across the river and the Arkansas flats beyond."

Everything was ready now, except one thing: Foote. Even though he seemed fully prepared to sink himself into his new work, he told Percy that he was not ready to "disappear into the dark abyss of labor." Instead, he continued to "noodle around with . . . [the novel's] diagram." Foote could not write because he feared representing Southern blacks, an issue that he had repeatedly skirted. The issue of race was never far from his consciousness during these years, a preoccupation apparent in his assessment of William Styron's *The Confessions of Nat Turner.* Years before, Foote had criticized the novel's historical liberties. Now, though, he zeroed in on Styron's writing on race. In a letter to Percy, he claimed that Styron had relied on "discussions with a Harlemite, James Baldwin" for his views on Southern blacks. In *his* new novel, Foote told Percy, he wanted to show that he knew Southern blacks better than Styron and Baldwin: "I told some interviewer that I knew a hell of a lot more about Negroes than Baldwin even began to know—mainly, I said, becauseI was Southern," a claim that not only overlooked the fact that Styron was a Virginian, but also that Styron filtered any claims that the "Harlemite" made.

Yet, when Foote began to contemplate representing the consciousness of black characters for his novel, he realized how difficult

Styron's task had been. Writing black characters "scared [the] hell out of me," he admitted later. Part of the problem lay in his outdated assumptions about Southern blacks. Eight years before, on the trip to the Percys' Trail Lake Plantation, what Foote had missed was having no "Negroes gathering at the store and drinking pop and guying each other; or even working in the fields." Given the fact that Foote harbored this view of Southern blacks as servile sharecroppers, he not surprisingly struggled to describe and articulate a situation in which blacks, by 1957, the setting of the novel, had fanned out into a motley crew of entrepreneurs and businessmen, particularly in an urban setting such as Memphis. Foote struggled to understand and depict the consciousness of people, such as the novel's black patriarch, Theo Wiggins, whose insurance business had made him not merely one of the richest black Memphians, but one of the wealthiest Memphians period. Wiggins was, as Foote told Percy, one of those "bourgeois Negroes, and I never really knew a single bourgeois nigger in my life."

Frustrated and scared to write about these "bourgeois Negroes," Foote turned away from beginning his novel to sink himself into reading projects that were at the furthest distance from the South's social fabric. For days, he disappeared into a deep exploration of the work of Percy Bysshe Shelley, a task that followed hard on the heels of a reading of Aileen Ward's new biography on his favorite Romantic, John Keats. After reading Ward's book and "then romp[ing] happily through the [Keats] poems and letters," Foote had turned to a new Shelley biography, Richard Holmes's *Shelley: A Pursuit.* Now "tuned in to the inner workings that tie [Shelley's] work to the life, the forces that brought the poems to the surface of his thought," Foote tackled Shelley. Percy found Foote's obsession with Shelley incomprehensible. "What type of a fellow are you?" Percy asked his friend, barely able to contain his laughter about Foote's fixation. "Are you telling me you can sit there in your castle in Memphis happily reading Shelley 5 hours a day?" Foote wrote back immediately: "Dont underrate Shelley. He's a kind of a sort of a shithead in an ideological way, but he sure as hell burned with a gemlike flame. He could light up a poem with a line that would burn like a searchlight down into all kinds of shadowy corners of your brain."

If Foote needed more reasons to delay starting *September September,* he found plenty in a packed fall schedule. Among the events that fall was Foote's participation in a Mississippi Educational Television documentary on Faulkner, an event that would take up Foote's time throughout the next two years. Were it any other project, he would have begged off, but for his literary hero, no sacrifice was too great. That concession brought its own rewards; while there, he learned of some soon-to-be-published Faulkner compliments about Foote's work in *Bitterweeds,* the memories of Malcolm Franklin, Faulkner's stepson, about the Nobel laureate. Almost upon walking into his Memphis home, Foote recounted them to Percy,

> During one of these discussions Pappy [Faulkner] turned to me and said, "Buddy [Franklin's nickname], have you read Shelby Foote's *Shiloh*?" I said no, and he told me, "Well, Buddy, you should read it. It's the damndest book I have ever read and one of the best." One day a few weeks later Pappy said, "I have something for you, Buddy," and he handed me a copy of *Shiloh.* He must have gone by or written to the Three Musketeers bookshop in Memphis (across from the Peabody Hotel) where he preferred to get such books. "This is twice the book that *The Red Badge of Courage* is," he told me, adding that Shelby wrote as if he had been there himself—"he knows what he's talking about."

Faulkner's praise continued. Telling Franklin that "Shelby was writing several volumes on the War," Faulkner indicated that "he was going to present me with them as they were published." Beside himself with excitement at Faulkner's high praise, Foote nevertheless felt surprised. During his lifetime, the tight-lipped Faulkner had indicated only that Foote had real potential. Now, though, Foote learned that underneath all of his prodding, Faulkner had great admiration for his work. Foote beamed, "You can imagine how set-up I felt when I saw that." Although he expressed fear that after these words, all praise henceforth would pale by comparison, he basked in Faulkner's praise: "What compliment will I ever receive that will compare with it?"

By January 1976 Foote found himself "trembling on the verge of the plunge." The "long synopsis-outline" of his novel was finished, an outline that indicated that the novel would be seven chapters, units that alternated between a focus on the kidnappers and on the Wiggins and Kinship families. January came and went, though, and six months later, as the nation's bicentennial celebration rolled around, Foote still was only doodling thoughts about how to begin. Finally, shortly after all of the fireworks had sputtered out, Foote began dipping his fountain pen into his ink well, dirtying the ledger sheets when he scrawled, "It was a bad time in many ways, some of them comprehensible, others not. We had a great big kewpie doll in the White House, commander-in-chief of all the cold-war warriors on our side, and the Russians were up to something they would fling skyward from the dusty steppes of Kazakhstan just one month later." Writing slowly, but steadily, his goal, he soon decided, was a chapter every two months, and the box that Foote set aside for his manuscript filled up steadily throughout the late summer and early fall. So focused was Foote that not even a drinking-and-driving accident on September 12 fazed him. On September 25, Foote wrote Percy, "Things are going well here I do believe. I'm into the middle chapter (fourth of seven) of the novel-in-progress, SEPTEMBER SEPTEMBER, and enjoying it a lot; dreadful and funny, both at once." Work was going so well that he reneged on travel plans with the Percys so that he could finish the novel: "I intend to hang on tight here . . . down to the wire, and finish the novel by late spring." Although several weeks later he pushed back the date of completion to summer 1977, he expressed an unleashed excitement that had never appeared in all the anxiety about starting the new novel: "Mine's a boomer. I'm past the midpoint now and going great guns: SEPTEMBER SEPTEMBER—whole flocks of incredibly believable people, black and white, cruel and gentle, and all absurd. I like it very much, so far."

By February, he had completed "What Went Down," a chapter that fully spelled out the thriller elements that had driven his novel. In it, Foote detailed the arrangement that the kidnappers used to get the money from Teddy Kinship's family, even having Rufus and Podjo go through a dry run on the day before the pickup. In a stunning panoramic scene looking over downtown Memphis, Rufus and Podjo, perched high up in a Hotel Tennessee room, watch to make sure that Teddy's family follows their directions about avoiding any police interference. Coinciding with the buildup of the novel's detective-thriller elements,

Foote ramped up the sexual dynamics between the kidnappers. Following up on her swap of partners in the previous chapter—Rufus to Podjo—Reeny allies herself with Podjo, a trade that has repercussions for the novel's final outcome two chapters later. Out of this switch emerged Rufus's anger, which would ultimately lead him to steal the majority of Reeny's and Podjo's share of the ransom money. With that money, Rufus buys a "shiny white Thunderbird," the means by which he speeds off from Memphis—at least until his car crashes into the framework of one of the bridges that the kidnappers' rented home had overlooked. "Well, that's one piece of luck that came our way if nothing else did," Podjo tells Reeny. "They'll get no prints off our friend there, even off his toes."

If the book was driven by the thriller elements, which were tied up in Foote's desire to create a moneymaker, for the first time, he had also explored fully the racial dynamics governing Southern life. Although he still fixated on the novel exclusively as a process of form and structure, Foote revealed something of this breakthrough when he said, "Whatever else I did or didn't do, I sure as hell got my hand back in, and now I'm ready to go on." Internalizing the lesson of Kirwan's *Revolt of the Rednecks,* Foote had come to realize that racial difference was an empty fiction that could be easily manipulated, a tool trotted out conveniently by powerful whites when they feared that their society was changing.

On the surface, the Little Rock crisis and the kidnapping it spawns invite a restatement of the South's historical division of power along strict racial lines. As Foote's novel makes clear, race serves as a familiar and convenient divider, a well-worn rhetoric that Foote's Faubus, who is in the midst of a gubernatorial campaign, falls back on in his defense of Southern whiteness. Faubus tells the media that he is "apprehensive of violence" that may erupt if "those black scamps tried again to get in Central High when the bell rung next morning." That white-black dichotomy conveniently manipulates Southerners of both stripes. The fear radiating from the Little Rock situation leads the Wiggins and Kinships to heed the kidnappers' request not to call the police about the kidnapping. Based on their understanding of the way that Southern whites could be rallied around politicians' race baiting,

Teddy's family realized that Faubus's words and inaction offer a "blanket invitation" for the "yahoos to take over," a potential vigilante force that lies somewhere between "the double threat of the amateur and professional . . . [the] Klansmen and the Mafia."

Such a racial division also, as Foote's novel suggests, denies the diverse stratification occurring within both the white and black communities. Foote's black community features Snooker Martin, whom Martha Kinship has earlier been in love with. Theo Wiggins, by virtue of his wealth, is one of the most powerful men in the Memphis black community, a position that engenders fear among other blacks, including, most notably, his son-in-law, Eben Kinship. As Theo constantly reminds him, it's "my money" that Eben worked for, an assertion that Eben deeply resents.

Foote shows how Faubus's racial rhetoric glosses over differences within the black society, but he also suggests that such a dichotomy reduces the stratification within the white community as well. In fact, the novel suggests that the kidnappers' actions and motivation are not due to any inherent criminality, but, like the barn-burning habit of Faulkner's Ab Snopes, the result of the economic oppression of white elites. Foote's kidnappers are from families that he identifies as manipulable simply because they do not have the money that would translate into power.

Reeny's flexibility in attaching herself first to Rufus and then to Podjo is not due to any inherent promiscuity; the victim of a number of empty promises from men, this floater seeks "a chance at something real—the money, of course, which would bring us lots of things, once we had it." Furthermore, Podjo comes from a Missouri logger's family, and the murder that earlier lands him in Parchman Prison to serve an eight-year manslaughter term results from a desire to gain something more than the hand-to-mouth existence he lived as a child. In the pursuit of an easier life, he had had a sexual relationship with a "society type, a Buick dealer's wife" whose husband discovers the tryst and, in the fight that follows, Podjo slides a knife into his gut.

Even more explicitly, Rufus's grandfather, a former bank clerk in Jordan County's Planters Trust Bank, who has "never touched so much as a dime, one thin dime," displays a bitterness as he nears death because he realizes how much he, a poor dutiful white, has been manipulated by the town's wealthier whites. As Rufus explains his last words, "He was talking about the bank, those that owned it, those that ran it, those that used it and him with it—a fixture, with his eyeshade and sleeve garters, like one of the machines now junked and chunked aside." Raising himself up for a last breath, he tells his grandson, "You take um, Rufus, hear me? Take um. It's the only way youll get justice. Steal 'um blind."

In spite of its brilliant insights, Foote's novel was still riddled with the authorial heavy-handedness that had plagued his earlier novels, a problem especially acute because of all of the historical research that he had done and felt obligated to include—to the point of ramming a square peg into a round hole. His "inexcusable auctorial voice-over," as Walter Clemons called it, often creates awkwardness and, when put in the mouths of characters, implausibility. Not only does the poorly-educated Podjo think about John Webster's seventeenth-century play *The Duchess of Malfi*, but Rufus, who is ultimately kicked out of the University of Mississippi for "cheating and petty theft" is, improbably, a student of the Finnish composer Jean Sibelius: "I thought of all the hours I spent over in the Music Department, when I should have been in class—mostly math—listening to that crashing, spooky music he wrote, with the icy wastes of Finland in it and the loneliness of all men everywhere." Once he introduced this material, Foote felt the need to reassert this connection. Accordingly, as he drives out of town, under the pursuit of the police, Rufus hears in his head "the clarinet solo at the start of the E Minor [Symphony]." It is not that Rufus had ever been to Finland, a trip that could have engendered such a passion, but Sibelius had died in September 1957; given the novel's time period, Foote felt obligated to include that information.

These incongruities are not limited to the kidnappers. When Theo Wiggins goes to hand off the $60,000 ransom, a personally devastating time since he assumes that the money will never be returned, Foote has him, upon seeing a statue of W. C. Handy, think about the Memphis musician: "Blind now and crowding eighty-five, the Professor, as they called him, had left for New York nearly forty years ago, even before Mr Crump closed down the sporting life in response to having

Prudential Life declare Memphis the murder capital of the nation. . . .
He would die in the spring—March 28, just six months from today."
Wiggins's thoughts about Handy conveniently serve as an occasion
to mention the "other forgotten heroes in the Memphis pantheon:
Ed Crump . . . Machine Gun Kelly: Casey Jones . . . Bedford Forrest:
Davy Crockett . . . Andrew Jackson."

In spite of this constant reminder of the author's presence, *September
September* represented his best novel ever, a dramatic story intertwined
with the complexities of the 1950s historical context. Soon after finishing his novel in June, Foote sent Percy a photocopy of the manuscript. A few weeks later, Percy wrote back, "*September September* is real
good. Read it straight through." Percy enumerated what he liked about
the novel:

> (1) the handling of the details, the plan of the kidnap, the cash, the
> notes, the attention to places and streets etc., (2) the transformation of
> a cliché—thieves fall out over women and money—into a believable
> action. I see *how* thieves fall out over women, (3) Rufus getting wiped
> out, erased, fingerprints, and all at the end. The clean getaway of Podjo
> and Reeny is very satisfying. (4) The handling of the children—Teddy
> is very real (and funny)—maybe the first real black child I ever read
> of. . . . An 8 yr old child—that's hard.

"I think," Percy ended his letter, "you got a winner."

In spite of Percy's praise, Foote still felt anxiety about the novel's
representation of blacks, and he sought out local lawyer D'Army Bailey
to make sure that he "represented blacks properly." Foote had never
met Bailey, but he had read his vitriolic weekly *Commercial Appeal*
columns. When Bailey received the manuscript, he "didn't know who
[Foote] was," and in the letter that accompanied the manuscript, Foote,
according to Bailey, was "almost apologetic about the imposition he
was making on me."

Having Bailey's approval, Foote then sent the manuscript to Random
House. As he waited for the book to come out, he continued to deal
with his agent, Rosen, who had already tallied more than one success.
Rosen got the Book-of-the-Month Club to choose the novel as its first
alternate, and had successfully lobbied Random House to reissue all of

Foote's earlier novels except *Tournament,* which Foote did not want released because he considered it juvenalia. Several movie deals were also "pending," though "nothing really heavy had come down" by early December. Foote himself was staying out of the negotiations, letting his agent "take the heat and ten percent." Even with his anticipation of financial success, Foote again struck an aloof pose that would buffer future possible rejections: "I cant really imagine anything of mine raking in big money; it's far too well worked-out for that, and the boys who have the heavy money know it. Any book of mine wont stand a glib superfluous look; it comes apart under such treatment and theyre left with a handful of chaff. Result: they take options and then a good hard look at the work itself; whereupon they decide not to do it after all."

If Foote had been counting on favorable book reviews of *September September* to catapult his novel and him into the limelight, he was sorely disappointed. Several reviewers did claim that Foote had done an impressive job of capturing the political and racial landscape of the 1950s South. As Richard Freedman wrote in *The New York Times Book Review,* "Shelby Foote moves with equal dexterity between white and black minds, between private and public racial attitudes, and he admirably maintains suspense about the fates of both kidnappers and their victim." Freedman went on to say that Foote "gives the novel that rich impasto of alluvial Mississippi mud that so distinguishes the best Southern writing from its barer, sparer Northern counterparts." In *Newsweek,* Walter Clemons wrote that, with *September September,* Foote "returned to fiction with the best novel of his unusual career." Although the novel, according to Clemons, was "a slow starter," it "becomes tenaciously readable": "*September September* combines the historian's viewpoint with the Southern storyteller's sure grasp of speech, character, and locale." It was, finally, "a humane, solidly satisfying novel."

At the same time that these critics praised Foote's work, they were also quick to point out the novel's flaws. Freedman claimed, "He is rather less assured in shifting between conventional third-person-omniscient narrative and first-person accounts by the main characters, a device more fancy than effective." Echoing Clemons's criticism of Foote's "inexcusable auctorial voice-over," Freedman pointed out the irony of Rufus's "knowledge of Sibelius, Kafka and Faulkner" not "prevent[ing] him from pronouncing 'yes' as 'yair' in the best Good Ol' Boy manner." As Clemons claimed, Foote was "not a perfect artist." Perhaps the most damning review of all was Phoebe Adams's short review in *Atlantic Monthly* because it attacked Foote's execution of the thriller concept, the original motivation for *September September:* "Mr. Foote has sacrificed suspense in this novel about the kidnapping of a black child by white extortionists."

On the heels of these lukewarm reviews, sales stumbled forward. After publication, Foote indicated that the "book is crippling along, 7/800 a week on reorders." In spite of these weak numbers, Foote suggested that the novel was "more or less marking time till it takes off." But never one to be too optimistic for too long, Foote added, "Which it might do [take off] any week now; or else it wont and that is that." As for the movie rights, no one showed immediate interest: "Rosen says one reason is theyre scared to death of kidnapping stories out there this year, alas. They'll come round, though, in time. God willing." (In 1990, Turner Broadcasting Service did turn *September September* into *Memphis,* a film starring Cybil Shepherd.) By early April, the first printing of 15,000 copies had been sold, and the novel had gone into a second printing. Even so, Foote realized that sales had been disappointingly slow. The novel that was going to make him millions was now "selling at a trickle, nothing great." Pronouncing himself "snakebit," Foote considered the slow sales another rejection of his novel-writing skills, and another period of dejection set in.

By September 1978, though, Foote received word that his novel would provide something of the riches that he had counted on. Rosen had negotiated a contract with Ballantine Books to bring out the novel in paperback: Ballantine would publish 600,000 copies of the novel, a generous run given the relative lack of success of the hardcover. Foote calculated that even with Rosen deducting 10 percent of his royalties for his agent fee, Foote could still earn as much as $203,125. With the promised movie deal not yet coming to fruition, this agreement was something to celebrate. "This will put me in clover, and that aint hay," Foote told Percy.

Money did not necessarily equate to fame, the philosopher's stone that had driven Foote's work on the novel, and his infallible formula seemed plagued by faults. No American award committees would come calling that spring. Although he did not receive great kudos from the American reading public, however, French readers and critics had "gone ape" over his work. Although French intellectuals had forged a special appreciation for Southern writers, Foote felt that their interest in his work was still surprising. Other than the fact that "most of my favorite writers have been French," Foote had almost no connection with the French: "Isnt it strange that it should work this way. What are the French to me or I to the French?" Nevertheless, Foote appreciated becoming a darling of the French critics, an association Foote found all the more pleasing because Faulkner had been embraced by the French establishment long before being welcomed at home. "My sun is rising in the east," Foote reported to Percy in March 1978, "and the hope is that some rays will be shed in this direction."

In 1973 Maurice Edgar Coindreau, Faulkner's French translator, had begun collaborating on translations of Foote's work with Gallimard—Proust's publisher, as Foote liked to note. After Gallimard published *L'Enfant de Fièvre* ("Child by Fever") in 1975, along with *Le même ouvrage (Follow Me Down)*, Coindreau began translating *Tournament*, which would appears as *Tourbillon* in 1978. Although Coindreau finished the translation of *Follow Me Down* in 1976, Gallimard held the novel until he could translate *Love in a Dry Season*, so that, published together, they would make a bigger splash. The publisher calculated correctly. In 1977 a special edition of *Delta*, a literary review of American literature published by Université Paul Valéry at Montpelier, France, was dedicated to Foote's work. Although only one of the twelve articles was in English, Foote found himself treading through the other articles, finding them so "fascinating," as he told Percy, that "I even studied up on my Chapel Hill French."

Although the fame had not yet carried back to the country where he lay his head, he had, if not fame, then money from his most recent enterprise. Well-buffeted, Foote nevertheless felt unsatisfied, and his ambivalence toward money made the whole process of writing and publishing *September September* one of the oddest experiences of Foote's life. Although the paperback printing of the novel should have marked one of the high points of his work, at the very same time that he told

Percy of his success, he admitted that he had few material needs in life—other than the periodic trip to New York. "Fortunately," he admitted, "I really don't know of one damned thing in this world I really want—that money can buy I mean, except maybe servants to bring me things on trays in my old age and make me comfortable by the fire."

Foote forged an alliance with Percy around the issue that artists should bond together against the materialists of the world. Percy himself, however, could easily be construed as the unverbalized target of Foote's anger. While Foote had repeatedly been eking out an existence, Percy swam in royalties. Predicting that he would receive "250 Gs" from *Lancelot,* Percy could not wait to see Book-of-the-Month Club subscribers' responses: "The beauty of B.O.M. which I never until now appreciated: 100,000 subscribers will have to address and stamp and mail a letter with instructions in order *not* to receive Lancelot. . . . Now ain't that something, two Mississippi boys turning their backs on high finance to court the muse and getting their pockets stuffed with simoleons!" While Percy's *Lancelot* did not turn out to be the full gusher that he had hoped for, the novel sold and, by most standards, sold well.

By contrast, the *September September* project had fallen short of Foote's expectations. Like Percy, he now had money, but, unlike his friend, he had not garnered the fame that he assumed would accompany that money. No literary awards would be forthcoming. Foote *had* found an audience, but it was in another country.

# Turning Home
## 1978–1990

So the people shouted when the priests blew with the trumpets: and it came to pass, when the people heard the sound of the trumpet, and the people shouted with a great shout, that the wall fell down flat, so that the people went up into the city, every man straight before him, and they took the city.

—Joshua 6:20

It all ties in to my TWO GATES TO THE CITY—if I can ever get off my 71-year-old ass to write it. Even if I don't, I've got it here in my head, a glowing coal of a book, right up there with Conrad['s *Nostromo*]: that is, so long as it remains a notion.

—Shelby Foote to Walker Percy, December 17, 1987

IN 1976, WHEN ROSEN negotiated with publishing houses for the rights to *September September*, Foote demanded that any contract would also have to include a novel that was to follow. Eager to publish another of Foote's books, Random House had no problem swallowing that stipulation. For the next project, Foote proposed a 250,000-word novel, three times as long as any of his previous novels. When Foote "commenced writing" the book, he would receive $12,500, and upon its "delivery and acceptance," slated for "January 15, 1980," he would receive another $12,500. Foote's next project was not a bold venture into something fresh that had crossed Foote's mind during the *Civil War* odyssey. Instead, it was nothing other than the infamous "Two Gates to the City," the angel with which Foote had wrestled in the early 1950s. Haunted by the fact that he had not finished "Two Gates," his only failure at writing a book in his entire career, Foote felt the need to grapple again with that magnetic burden. As before, it would be about the three cousins, but now Paul was a war veteran, wounded in the Ploesti raids, where Louie Nicholson had been killed. More significantly, this time "Two Gates" would not have "Ride Out" and "Child by Fever" to serve as contrapuntal stories for the main plot.

As early as 1976 Foote indicated to Percy that he had decided to have another go at "Two Gates to the City." The novel would be "a sort of Civil War all its own, outdostoyevskying Dostoyevsky." As he finished *September September* a year later, Foote reported that he had continued to amass ideas for the forthcoming novel. In 1978, seemingly on the brink of beginning the novel, Foote wrote his friend, "I propose to examine the Delta for what made it what it is and us what we are; a tall order." With "Big Sixty . . . looming," Foote felt the need to jump straight into the middle of things. But for all of his efforts to jumpstart the project, all Foote could continue doing was "plotting and counterplotting."

If he was struggling with "Two Gates," Foote had no problem getting his dander up for other issues. In what was supposed to be a reading of *September September* on April 2, 1978, at the Memphis-Shelby County Library and Information Center, Foote launched into an attack on Tennessee legislator Larry Parrish, who had just authored an anti-pornography bill in the Tennessee state assembly. Ever the First Amendment absolutist, Foote opined that Parrish "should be cut down and cut down fast." Foote told the audience of seventy-five people, "I have never met Mr. Parrish, but I know the type. . . . They are what are called true believers. . . . Look out for these people. True believers are dangerous people." The Memphis newspapers quickly picked up Foote's comments, and in response, Parrish told a reporter that he was saddened by the author's comments, particularly because he was a fan of Foote: "I have a great deal of respect of him . . . and it is disheartening for me to know that he has taken that kind of superficial view of the problem." According to Parrish, Foote "obviously is not fully aware of the ramifications and the effects of this issue."

A debate with Parrish never materialized, but Foote had plenty of other things on his plate. A series of lucrative offers came his way, including an offer to write a book on the Revolutionary War. Anxious to return to "Two Gates," however, Foote turned down almost all of the requests. As he told William Thomas, "It is not true that there is no discharge from . . . war. I got my discharge." However, there *was* one war offer that he did not refuse: *National Geographic* wanted a piece on Shiloh. Perhaps he saw it as a vindication of the futile efforts of Joel and Hoffman twenty-five years earlier to get *Life* to write a Shiloh story, but at the very least, he reacted to the $3000 the magazine was offering: "How in God's name am I going to turn down a chance to be paid $2 a word at least once in my life? Answer: I'm not."

After a June trip to reacquaint himself with the battlefield, his first visit in more than a decade, Foote settled down to write "Echoes of Shiloh," an unusually dramatic piece for the magazine's customary anthropologically driven format. Throughout the summer of 1978 Foote chiseled away at the article. Unable to let go of that little scrap of unremarkable Tennessee land that had been so central to his career, Foote found the article growing well beyond *National Geographic*'s 1500-word limit to 2200 words. Except for honoring a request to guide President Jimmy Carter around Antietam, Gettysburg, and Harpers Ferry during the first week of July, Foote refused to be interrupted. Although the story was largely about the battle, Foote did not hesitate to reassert his belief that certain places, once written about, serve as psychic landmarks: "One of the great satisfactions a historian, professional or amateur, derives from his work . . . comes after he has put the work behind him. Once he has studied and written of an event in relation to the ground on which it happened, that scrap of earth belongs to him forever. To some extent, he even feels he owns it."

Before Foote could return to "Two Gates to the City," he had one more debt to pay. In response to his grumbling about the disproportionate number of awards being given to academics, the National Book Award organizers offered Foote the opportunity to judge the 1979 history prize. Foote knew they had him "boxed": "I'd been claiming," he told Percy, "that nothing but academics were sitting judgment on historians, so when they asked me I had no valid way of saying no." Foote agreed to serve on the three-member committee, but he resigned himself to the fact that the two academics would reward their fellow brethren: "You just wait and see what gets the prize . . . it will be some badly written drivel that will get its author tenure." After an initial meeting in New York in mid-February 1979 with the two other judges, Foote returned to Memphis to study the nominated books. In New York again in late April, the committee chose the academic Richard Beale Davis's *Intellectual Life in the Colonial South* as the winner, after "plots and elbows and late-night discussions about nothing whatever." Tired as he was of all of the "foolishness," Foote nevertheless "was pleased . . . to find those various Harvard-Yale professor types genuinely respectful of my *Narrative*." Even so, Foote sneered at the belated appreciation: "Damned white of them now that it's safely in the past."

With the deck now clear, Foote felt that it was time to start cutting a path to "Two Gates." The deadline for submitting the book to Random House loomed, but Foote had not put down word one. In fact, he was still mired in preparatory sallies. He continued studying literary models to hone the technical skills he considered necessary for the novel's juggling of plots and subplots: "I'm just winding up my fifth or sixth rereading of Dostoyevsky's BROTHERS, by way of seeing whether I can bring off one of my own," Foote wrote Percy, "that galloping drive, that bigness; a drive so furious that it has to be bridled with filler stuff . . . to keep the writer and reader from being run off with."

More than just sharpening his technical skills, Foote spent time reacquainting himself with his childhood and home region by burrowing through his mind's archives. Not only were the letters to Percy during these months filled with Foote's reveries of their schoolmates, but after old friend Harold Mosby dropped by unexpectedly one January afternoon in 1979, Foote found himself bathing in a flood of memories: "I suddenly remembered things I'd long since forgotten—corn whiskey, dances, a girl named Jean Kent Early, hosts of things." Foote also attempted to build context for these items by getting himself down to Greenville and the Delta. A January 30 speech at Greenville's Percy Library was not enough; he needed to "spend a week or ten days down in Greenville . . . getting reacquainted with the thirty years I spent there, then come back to the quiet of Memphis and put all thirty of them into TWO GATES." Two months later, Foote was still sputtering: "I cant start till I get down home and somehow manage to quit shaking in my boots."

The shaking signaled that Foote was remembering too well how horribly he had failed in his first attempt at writing the novel. He had worked up the steam necessary to get over the hurdle, but now the effects of obsessing over the hurdle meant that he had lost sight of the rest of the track. By May 1979 desperation had crept into his letters to Percy. Although he had "all my people worked out, birth dates, highlights, etc. Even got the Goddam thing organized as to length and method," Foote found himself staring catastrophe in the face, "TWO GATES is so huge, so all-inclusive, I'm as terrified to start it as I would be when contemplating a leap into the Atlantic off a cliff." Scared to venture out, Foote was even looking for an escape. "I keep telling myself," he wrote, "what I ought to do is another short one—something I'll be pretty sure of having time to finish."

Part of the reason for the requiem involved Foote's growing belief that the region into which he had invested all of his energy had changed beyond any measure of recognition. As he revealed to Percy, "Ive long had a growing feeling that there's very little down there much worth writing about; especially the people." Because Foote had staked his fiction on the South, that acknowledgment, he intuited, would essentially end his writing career. Wary about making this connection, a sentence later, Foote immediately rushed in to say, "which of course isnt true." Even then, he admitted, "But it seems true from time to time."

For a year Foote fumbled with the project. Getting nowhere, panic had set in by September 1980. "I'm still blocked and blocking on TWO GATES," Foote said.

> The Goddamn thing is going to be so all-inclusive I'm terrified to really buckle down to it. My hope is to catch, to freeze in motion, the whole

bloody Mississippi delta—as of 1948, with analeptic reaches back to 1868 and proleptic jumps to the 1960's. A real son of a bitch to tackle, and for the first time in my life I'm scared pissless at the prospect, not because I'm afraid I cant do it, but because I damned well know I can. It's going to be murder, everything working on three levels to bring a whole region and way of life to task for the evils woven into its fabric from the outset.

Knowing what the failure of "Two Gates" had done decades earlier, Percy feared for his friend's well-being. In a letter uncharacteristically long for him, Percy wrote back immediately, "The only thing to do with Two Gates is get going and let 'er rip. Where I'd be hung up in a book like that is the very beginning." After moving on to several other issues, Percy returned at the end of his letter to rally his friend: "Get on with Two Gates. Being blocked, I am convinced, means that you're blocking yourself which is a dirty trick to play on yourself since the one thing we need above all else is the perfect freedom to get hold of the beast, which is hard enough without grappling with yourself like Dr. Strangelove." Throughout the next year, Percy would continue to encourage his friend. "Hope you're forging ahead with Two Gates," Percy wrote in November 1981, "Get it on the road."

But by 1981 Percy's encouragements had fallen on deaf ears: Foote had given up. Talking about the book later, he said, "I was trying to do things that were not clear enough for me. The outline was firm enough, but I wasn't clear." Although he would tell reporters throughout the 1980s that he was writing "Two Gates," in truth, he had done nothing. In fact, it became a project that he did not want to even begin, lest he incur another failure. He needed to freeze his concept of the South, and any attempt to articulate it would challenge that conception. As he had said several years earlier, "I cant imagine anything better than collapsing in the shafts." Echoing that claim, in 1987 Foote would finally bring himself to admit that "actually written, it might not be nearly as good as I envision it."

As opposed to his failure in the 1950s to write "Two Gates to the City," the early 1980s provided more of a cushioned fall. Notwithstanding his earlier claim that he had been "discharged" from the Civil War, Foote increasingly allowed himself to fall back on the role of Civil War historian. The war was enjoying a "resurgent nostalgia," as evidenced by the fact that almost 40,000 Americans had become part of the reenactment industry. That revival was not merely rooted in an interest in the past, but in a displacement of the racial anxieties and fears of the loss of organic, agrarian society in multinational capitalism: As Tony Horowitz put it, "Remembrance of the War had become a talisman against modernity, an emotional lever for their reactionary politics." Not coincidentally, it was during this period that fights began brewing over Southern state flags that incorporated the Confederate battle insignia: those of Alabama, Georgia, Mississippi, and South Carolina.

Although Foote was reluctant at this point to get involved in any of the emerging battles associated with the Confederate totems, he certainly became the beneficiary of the growing interest in the war. Civil War Roundtable groups and Sons of Confederate Veterans chapters peppered him with requests, which Foote, now with time on his hands, gladly obliged. How easily he was adapting to this new role is suggested by his making a tape of himself on July 30, 1982 reading sections of *The Civil War*'s volume III. On that Wednesday morning, Foote sat in his study and read into a tape recorder his accounts of Appomattox, Lincoln's assassination, and the pursuit of Jefferson Davis's runaway train. Falling back on his Civil War qualifications also meant playing honoree for a number of occasions. In June 1982 he accepted an honorary degree from Southwestern at Memphis (later renamed Rhodes College), and two months later, on Shelby Foote Day, Mississippi Governor William Winter hosted a dinner in his honor, after which Foote spent the night at the governor's mansion, sleeping in the bed of former governor and racist extraordinaire Theodoro Bilbo.

Foote also began thinking about his literary legacy. His preoccupation with dating each day's work suggests that, almost from the outset, he assumed that scholars would someday view his manuscripts. But in the early 1980s Foote began scouting about for a proper home for those manuscripts. At the urging of Louis Rubin, a University of North Carolina professor, he had sent his *Civil War* manuscripts to the school's Southern Historical Collection in 1975. Now, though, he wanted to send all of his material, including his correspondence with Walker Percy.

There were several places that Foote could logically send his papers, including Memphis State, Greenville's Percy Library, and UNC. Because of *September September*'s Memphis focus, he would send the novel's galleys to Memphis State, but the rest of the material was sent to the Southern Historical Collection, beginning in 1983.

UNC had been much on his mind over the previous years because it was one of the colleges to which Huggy applied, a list that included Pomona College, Sarah Lawrence College, and Tulane University. Living vicariously through his son, Foote had advocated strongly for UNC. "God forbid [that Huggy go to] Pomona and S. Lawrence," Foote wrote Percy. Instead, Foote wanted his son to grace the campus that he himself attended: "It pleases me greatly to think of him up there, much as we were fifty years ago, a poor damned lost soul in search of his bearings." With admission to UNC extremely difficult for out-of-state students and with Huggy's expulsion for marijuana offenses from Memphis University School and Connecticut's Pomfret School, his acceptance bordered on the impossible. Nevertheless, Foote lobbied Percy and Rubin to write recommendations on his son's behalf. (Huggy was ultimately wait-listed at UNC, but he opted to go to Sarah Lawrence.)

Not working, Foote began reaching out to people in a way that he had rarely ever done. One of these outlets for Foote was a book group of six Memphians, including Fred Deans, Bob Johnson, Mike McDonnell, Charlie Newman, Bill Pearson, and Bill Reed. Although the group had begun meeting in 1973, Foote joined their monthly meetings at the downtown Wolf River Club beginning in the early 1980s. After Foote found himself almost subject to a carjacking in front of the club, the group began meeting at Paulette's, a French restaurant in Overton Square. In what became something of an uncomfortable situation for the group, Foote repeatedly submitted his own books for the group's monthly reading assignments. During these years Foote also joined the Memphis Polo Club, the same group about which he had lambasted his friend Meg Turner two decades earlier. Almost as if replaying Faulkner's late transformation into a fox-hunting Virginian, Foote would sit out on the Polo Club's patio, drink in hand, playing the perfect socialite. "I think that he really enjoyed being there," Turner said.

Foote even began allowing himself to travel, not just on the short trips to New Orleans or to the Alabama coast, where he had previously gone to decompress after intense periods of writing, or even to New York, for meetings with agents or publishing houses, but on longer, transcontinental trips. When the Percys proposed a cross-country train trip in September 1982, Shelby and Gwyn excitedly agreed to go. The four planned to ride the Amtrak Flyer cross-country to San Francisco. As they boarded, however, they walked into a labor dispute. All was well as they crossed the Great Plains, until their train rolled into Utah around midnight on the night the strike was to begin. At Ogden, the train stopped, and passengers were ordered into the rainy night to board a bus that would take them to an airport. Foote, Gwyn, and Bunt got off the train—Foote said that he needed to claim his recently purchased luggage—but Percy refused to deboard. When Foote tried to coax his friend out of his cabin, Percy yelled, "You take your expensive piece of luggage outside. I'm going to sleep." In what would become a comic refrain for the two couples, Foote responded, "Walker, I think there's a man with a gray sombrero who's hanging around my expensive piece of luggage." After much coercion, Percy agreed to deboard, and from Ogden the couples caught a plane to San Francisco.

Foote's good feeling took a hairpin turn several months later. During his periodic checkup at New Orleans' Oschner Clinic in April 1983, Foote found himself carted away to the hospital's cardiac care unit after doctors noted something suspicious on his electrocardiogram. An angiogram determined that Foote's left anterior descending artery showed 75 percent stenosis. On the following day, Foote underwent an angioplasty, which removed the blockage. Needing to wait three months to see whether the artery remained clear, the doctors sent Foote home.

Back in Memphis and scared for his life, Foote adhered faithfully to the strict regimen that the Oschner physicians demanded. He previously had declared that he was "violently opposed to exercise of any kind," but now he laced up his walking shoes twice daily for a two-mile walk. Foote found it more difficult to give up smoking, which he had done since his youth and which he had come to regard as much of his reading and writing regimen as his books. As he later said in an interview, "I wrote every page that I ever wrote with a cigarette in my left hand." Although he reported to Percy that he had survived two weeks, he feared that the elimination of tobacco verged on a sacrifice of self: "I'll stay with all that for a reasonable length of time, but not so long that I will no longer be *me*."

During the months that Foote waited to see if, in his layman's terms, the "plaque . . . stayed stuck to the wall," death preoccupied him. When Percy sent him a copy of his high school graduation program, Foote viewed the list in terms of how many people were still alive: "But, my God, that list of the dead and missing! I had not thought that death had undone so many. We heard the chimes at midnight and now theyre gone. Incredible."

In the weeks before his return visit to Oschner, feeling the need to leave something for posterity, Foote prepared a list of what he considered to be the greatest ninety-nine books of all time, based on "literary worth or influence." Not surprisingly, the list mirrored Foote's own lifetime of reading. Anchoring the list were fourteen Greek and Roman works, including Lucretius's *De Reum Natura,* Herotodus's *History,* and Plato's "Dialogues." The rest of the works were more modern, but only to a point. Surprisingly, only eight twentieth-century works made the list, including Joyce's *Ulysses* and *Finnegans Wake,* Gabriel Garcia Marquez's *100 Years of Solitude,* and Proust's *Remembrance of Things Past.* Even his hero Faulkner only merited one selection, *The Hamlet.* Revealing Foote's Victorian sensibilities, the vast majority were nineteenth-century works. Of these, a handful were American, including Melville's *Moby Dick* and Twain's *Huckleberry Finn* and *Life on the Mississippi,* but most were British, among them Dickens's *David Copperfield, Bleak House,* and *Little Dorrit;* Thackeray's *Vanity Fair;* Meredith's *The Egoist;* and Trollope's *The Way We Live Now.*

As the July 23 appointment neared, Foote's anxiety came through. He feared that "they would have to split my chest for a bypass," which would lead to the "ultimate indignity": "a fall into the machine—life supports, tubes in, tubes out, all that nightmare subjugation modern medicine visits on us at the drop of a hat." The night before the exam

at dinner with the Percys, which would have normally been a boisterous affair, Foote felt "gloom." The next day at Oschner, his doctor put
him on the treadmill, where he "walked till I was puffed." Foote
returned two hours later to hear great news—his artery remained
unclogged. The results were "excellent, in fact spectacular." Although
he was told to be "prudent," Foote considered himself "the healthy
animal I had thought I was before I found out otherwise and made the
changes that made my mistaken notion true." Foote did realize that
"I'm an odds-on favorite to die of this goddam thing one of these
(I hope faroff) days," but now he felt "home free." He acknowledged
afterward to Percy, "I had been prepared to tell you not to be alarmed
at the loss of a friend."

Although Foote would soon return to his tobacco, albeit in the form
of a pipe, the walking grew into a regular routine. Employing a favorite
malapropism heard by Bunt Percy, Foote often said that each afternoon
he would "lace up [his] Nickeys and put on [his] Parkman." On his
two-mile circuit, Foote ambled to his favorite classical music. "I listen
to Beethoven, Mozart, and the rest of them," he told William Thomas.
"When you're walking you play music you already know. If you're too
intent listening to certain themes, you can step off into traffic."

Although the walking routine got Foote out of the house, he soon
began to develop an itch to go much further than just around the
neighborhood. No doubt spurred on by his recent death scare, Foote
began to set out for places that had always been in his mind's eye.
Understandably, Paris was his first destination. Not only had Foote's
works been received well in France, but Paris was Proust's home.
In December 1983 the Footes set out on the three-week pilgrimage.
Staying at the Hotel Pont-Royal, in the Left Bank's Fauborg–St. Germain
neighborhood, Foote found that he was perfectly positioned. Gallimard
was a block away, and just across the Seine stood the house and the
cork-buffered room where Proust had written *Remembrance of Things
Past*. Day after day, the couple made their way about Paris. Foote com-
prehensively saw a world that he had only imagined through his reading or seen, disconnectedly, through isolated photographs. In particular,
he loved the Louvre. Although he had come to avoid museums, tired
of fighting crowds to see paintings, he found himself spending hours

within the ancient castle. Mesmerized by the entire city, a place where a "real sense of peace descends on me," Foote could not even bring himself to get out to nearby Versailles or Chartres.

With the blocks of Paris now firmly fixed in his mind and its sounds ringing in his ears, Foote opened up Proust again when he returned home. For yet another time, he tried to get Percy interested in Proust. This time, however, after so many futile attempts, the suggestion took. In a move that stunned Foote, Percy asked his friend,

> Does this sound familiar?—how to choose, any more than between individual persons who are not interchangeable, between Bayeux, so lofty in its noble coronet of russet lacework, whose pinnacle was illumined by the old gold of its second syllable; Vitre, whose acute accent barred its ancient glass with wooden lozenges; gentle Lamballe, whose whiteness ranged from egg-shell yellow to pearl gray; Coutances, a Norman cathedral which its final consonants, rich and yellowing, crowned with a tower of butter.

Percy found himself "excited" by *Swann's Way*, the first of seven novels in the *Remembrance of Things Past* collection. He saw in Proust's account a dramatization of what he had been advancing in his theory of language: the integration of symbol and things symbolized. Although Percy had previously focused on the "transformation of common nouns and verbs," he realized that Proust was "interested in proper names." "If this passage excited me," Percy wrote, "imagine what it would have done to a French me what with all the resonances and connotations which these names must have for a Frenchman."

In addition to the linguistic connection, Percy found himself experiencing a "mixture of awe and irritation" about Proust's genius and his social position. Percy was disgusted by the author's "flat-out toadying up to that crew of lower-case aristocrats just as the upper- and middle-bourgeoisie were doing." Even so, Percy saluted Proust's genius: "What one is most aware of is a genius going at that very thing which his genius is about, so totally absorbed that one can imagine that it's all the same whether he's holed up alone or not."

By return mail came Foote's response: "The best news by far is that youve sailed into Proust." Foote's excitement was tangible. He included an extensive outline that he had made of *Into the Budding Grove,* *Remembrance*'s second book, as a crib sheet intended to help Percy get through the novel. In what was not only his clearest statement of Proust's aesthetic, but maybe the clearest statement of his own formalist artistic philosophy, Foote closed the letter, "For these and other reasons it does what all the great books do, and does it superbly; that is, enlarges life. . . . Dont be put off by any foolish notion that it seems 'loose' or undisciplined. It's altogether the tightest, best-constructed and most disciplined novel I ever read."

Foote frittered the rest of 1984 away, but by early 1985 he and Gwyn were bound for Paris again, where Huggy, having graduated from college, was now attempting to establish himself as a professional photographer. Trying to entice the Percys to travel with them, Foote wrote, "We'd have a great time in the City of Light, especially with Hugs as cicerone; he knows all the cheap low places." On the verge of finishing *The Thanatos Syndrome,* Percy said that he could not make the trip, leading Foote to declare it a "blooming outrage that you and Bunt arent coming along." While there, Foote sent Percy a postcard imitating Dostoyevsky:

> I'm not sure I approve of all these West-European carryings-on, but the city itself presents occasional vistas not unlike some in my beloved Petersburg, which I badly miss while resting between spurts of work on my novel; *L'Idiot* I'll call it.
>
> > Homesickly,
> > Fyodor D.

Later that year, on his annual visit to Oschner for a checkup, problems were found not with Foote's heart, but with his prostate—he had cancer. Because the cancer had not spread to the lymph nodes, however, Foote's prognosis was good, and he had several options: surgery or radiation treatments. Opting for the latter, Foote was put under the care of a Memphis urologist, Dr. Mark Soloway, who soon began administering a series of radiation treatments that lasted into 1986. Confident that the cancer had been caught early enough, Foote assumed that he would "live out my normal span, at any rate until something comes along that they dont have a cure for. By that time I'll be glad to hit the road to glory anyhow."

He had survived two close calls, and in March 1986 Foote suffered another medical setback—although this was far less severe than the heart and prostate problems. His foot had been "trucked-over," and with it throbbing, Foote lay in bed for several weeks: "Doctor tells me the only treatment is to keep it elevated so that the bad blood will run down out of it. My prayers are all to Gravity." Still hopping around in April, Foote nevertheless welcomed Ken and Ric Burns, filmmakers who were working on a PBS Civil War television series, which would ultimately air in the fall of 1990.

In September, Percy sent Foote a copy of *The Thanatos Syndrome*, Percy's darkest novel. With plenty of time on his hands, Foote read the manuscript carefully. After a few days, he sent back two pages of comments and corrections, not the least of which involved Dr. Tom More's use of "Shelby Foote" as the source for dating Benjamin Butler's arrival in New Orleans as 1863. "Since you quote me as Dr Tom's source," Foote wrote, "I damned well want him to get such matters right. The goddam buffs will land all over both of us—not you, who simply passed the word along: just Tom and me." Percy welcomed Foote's suggestions: "I deeply appreciate your taking time with that peculiar novel— and pinpointing what's wrong. Well, you're right. Every time Fr. Smith opens his mouth he, I, is in trouble. What I do is cut, cut, cut. You can't get away with a Fr. Zossima these days and probably shouldn't." Percy was particularly relieved to find that Foote believed that the "humor and irony comes across. . . . I worried about the heaviness of the idea— the warning about the Nazi and the pre-Nazi 'humanist' scientists. Since you did not object too much to Fr. S's 'confessions,' I reckon you didn't mind. Some folks will."

Although Foote was not doing any writing, he learned in late 1986 that Summa Publications, a small publisher in Birmingham, Alabama, wanted to reissue *Tournament*. Although Foote had asked Random House not to issue his first novel when the press reissued his other works, now he okayed the deal. Foote even agreed to write a foreword, which would precede Louis Rubin's introduction. Foote's eight-page account of the creation of *Tournament* was, on the whole, a factual recording of his early life and the context for the production of his first novel. But his account also had significant omissions. Perhaps because of the public's increasing association of Foote with war, albeit the Civil War, Foote expertly chronicled in detail Germany's evolving war machine, an effort that would lead him to join the National Guard. But when he reached the point of writing about his own wartime activities, Foote reduced them to the "five years that intervened," a significant reduction in an account that had heretofore been so specific. By not detailing his wartime activities—or lack thereof—Foote had presented a biography that dodged troubling elements from his past.

Over the next year, with Percy struggling to write *Contra Gentiles*, a book that was to be his definitive statement on semiotics, or as Percy humorously characterized it, "a somewhat smart-ass collection of occasional pieces," and with Foote doing nothing more than biding time, their correspondence became an exercise in playfulness. While reading soap opera summaries in one Sunday's newspaper, Foote saw a synopsis of *One Life to Live* that made him think that "maybe we've watching the wrong soaps all these years": "Gabrielle and Tina argued over the fact that Tina never intended to marry Max, who is Al's real father. Gabrielle kidnapped Al, Jonathan accosted a detective, Bradshaw, who said Sandra's husband, Frank, hired him to tail Sandra. At the prison in Africa, Kate was reunited with Patrick, then surrounded by guards. Pamela agreed to sell Vernon Inn to Max, then told Asa she's returning to Malakeva." Foote ended the postcard with "Heavy, man." Watching the summaries fly by in the Sunday papers, Foote soon found that the story had progressed: "Tina split the scene after fighting with Maria, who accidentally spilled a vial of lethal poison on herself and then died. Tom confronted Lee, who finally confessed that she's his former wife, Carole. Rick left for Austria without Mari Lynn. Max insisted to Gabrielle that they should continue the search for the money Dante left behind." "I hadnt thought this plot could thicken," Foote wrote Percy, "Man, was I ever wrong!—as you can plainly see. But how in the world did *Dante* get himself involved with scum like this?"

During the summer of 1987 Percy sent pictures of the still-extant tea house that he and Foote had built at Brinkwood during a summer stay in 1938. The Percys had been up to Monteagle in July and visited Uncle Will's old house. When Foote saw the pictures, he fell into a pool of memories: "My God, my God: fifty years come next July 4. We ought to meet there for a decent observance—rededicate ourselves and perhaps construct an annex." Near the end of the August 8 letter, Foote repeated again the suggestion of the anniversary meeting: "If we meet for the fiftieth anniversary, I suggest we toast it with Two Naturals—knocking it back Russian-style past our taste buds to avoid cauterization."

Whether Foote was serious about a meeting became a moot point, for 1988 brought a devastating blow to Percy. In late 1987 Percy had complained about feeling run down. An exam at Oschner turned up nothing, but the problems persisted into early 1988. In early March, after a visit to a Tulane doctor, Percy learned that he had prostate cancer, which, unlike Foote's, had spread to his testicles. Surgery was performed almost immediately, and the doctors believed that the cancer was localized and non-life-threatening. Through the summer, Percy kept a busy schedule, but by the end of the year, doctors discovered that the cancer had actually spread beyond his testicles. Throughout 1989 Percy underwent a series of treatments at Minnesota's Mayo Clinic with an experimental combination of interferon and 5-fluorouracil.

Because the friends were calling each other more, their letters grew increasingly fewer during Percy's illness. In fact, for the first time in their correspondence, Percy's letters, however short, outnumbered Foote's. Because he had been seriously ill himself, Foote presumably knew what Percy was going through, but perhaps he could not fathom why his friend, someone who had always lived a holier life than he, was dying, while he was relatively hale and fit—the survivor of two serious illnesses. Foote even struggled with what to say to his dying friend, and as always, denial was his better form of valor. Even though Percy had little problem talking about his illness, Foote's letters continued to focus on artistic issues, even while his friend grew sicker.

Pondering the successes of Anton Chekov, for example, Foote wrote his friend, "My God, my God, what a writer! How he does it is a mystery you cant solve by analyzing it—he just does it; does it out of being

Chekov . . . he landed running and never looked back, a highly individual man with his own particular fond absurdity that enabled him to
see it in others when he wrote about them." Almost insensitively,
Foote droned on, talking about a number of Chekov stories; but by the
end of the letter, it became clear that contained within his monologue
on Chekov's talent lay his cryptic efforts to reach out to his friend.
About Chekov's "The Bishop," Foote told his friend, "He was researching
dying while he wrote it; that is, he was dying himself, and Lord, Lord,
what a job he did. It takes the mystery out of dying, makes it almost
an ordinary occurrence, and in the course of doing it, makes dying
more of a mystery than ever." Foote sent Percy the story, and Percy
apparently appreciated what his friend was trying to convey, however
indirect it came. "It's all you say," Percy wrote Foote, after reading the
story. "Nothing short of miraculous." Seeing himself as a later mani-
festation of the Bishop, Percy added, "The Bishop is in poor shape,
dying in fact." Perhaps even trying to nourish his friend's soul as he
approached his own end, Percy finished the note by saying, "What's so
good about it is that it doesn't matter in the least that Chekhov was,
apparently, an unbeliever."

Percy was indeed dying. "Not such good news here," he had written Foote in June. "I've been having some abdominal and back pain
for past few weeks. Thought it was my periodic diverticulitis." As a
result of the pain, Percy had gone for an exam, which showed that his
colon was normal but that "there were masses around the aorta and
along spine. Don't yet know what it is, but presumably it's metastases
from prostate carcinoma or pancreatic CA[ncer]. Will keep you
informed. Due for bone scan and more endoscopy next few days."

By early 1990 the end was near. With Percy's strength too drained
to permit correspondence, Foote called him frequently. Even when the
pain worsened for Percy, to the point that he was sure that he was
about to die, Foote continued to keep in touch with Percy and the
family through phone calls. On April 28, just a day after Walker had
received last rites, Foote called and talked to LeRoy; somewhat deliri-
ous from all of the valium he had been taking, Walker nonetheless
asked for the phone. "I've got an hour, maybe an hour and twenty
minutes," Percy told his friend. "Goodbye." Fearful that this was the

last time that he would ever talk to Percy, Foote cried out, "My God, Walker, I'm an only child, and you're the closest thing to a brother I ever had." All Percy could muster was another "Goodbye."

In spite of Percy's claim, he held on for a few more weeks. Wanting to stay out of the way of family members, Foote planned to remain in Memphis until Percy's death. But by May 3, he could no longer sit still, and he and Gwyn drove down to Covington. Over the next week, Foote took turns sitting with his dying friend, holding his hand at times. "Sad time, but a good time, too," Foote wrote in a diary. Finally, on May 10, 1990, Walker Percy died.

For all of the comfort he provided for his friend during that last week, Foote had also irritated several family members. Foote was not in the room when Percy expired. Nevertheless, when a *Jackson Clarion-Ledger* reporter called, Foote asserted that, as Percy's best friend, he had been in the room when Percy died. As one angry family member said, Foote could not have been in the room because he was in the next room, "holding court with stories about the Civil War."

When Percy was buried at St. Joseph's Abbey two days later, Foote served as one of the pallbearers. But there was one more final tribute to his friend. In a November memorial service held at a packed St. Ignatius Church in New York City, Foote gave the next-to-last speech. In keeping with the ceremony, his words were brief:

> The English essayist E. H. Carr said at the close of his early-thirties critical biography of Dostoyevsky: "A hundred years hence, when Dostoyevsky's psychology will seem as much of a historical curiosity as his theology seems to us now, the true proportions of his work will emerge; and posterity, removed from the controversies of the early twentieth century, will once more be able to regard it as an artistic whole."
>
> Similarly, I would state my hope that Walker Percy will be seen in time for what he was in simple and solemn fact—a novelist, not merely an explicator of various philosophers and divines, existentialist or otherwise. He was no more indebted to them or even influenced by them, than was Proust, say, to or by Schopenhauer and Bergson. Proust absorbed them, and so did Walker absorb his preceptors. Like Flannery O'Connor, he found William Faulkner what Henry James

called Maupassant, "a lion in the path." He solved his leonine problem much as Dante did on the outskirts of hell: he took a different path, around him. Their subject, his and Faulkner's—and all the rest of ours, for that matter—was the same: "the human heart in conflict with itself."

Foote's words signaled a desire that his friend be remembered not as "an explicator of various philosophers and divines, existentialist or otherwise," but as a "novelist." The speech also suggested that Percy had been fixated on Faulkner. In both instances, those issues were only of relatively small concern to Percy. They were, however, issues of paramount interest to Foote.

# A Star Is Born

## 1990–

[Shelby Foote is] the last of the Southern gentlemen. In the
best sense of the word, he's a man of grace and courtesy.

—Reynolds Price

A T THE BEGINNING OF September 1990 Shelby Foote's work was
known by a relatively small number of people. Civil War buffs
certainly knew of his narrative, and Mississippians and Memphians
considered him a local hero. If his townspeople had read his work at all,
they had read *The Civil War,* for beyond the limits of a handful of scholars, almost no one knew his novels. Aging, Foote was destined to be
a footnote in American literary history, known for his trilogy and for
his relationship with Walker Percy. That September, however, would
forever change the public's view of Foote and Foote's view of himself.
Instead of seeking to insinuate himself into the public eye, Foote would
soon seek cover from the hordes of media and fans who descended
upon him.

That transformation resulted from the airing of Ken Burns's *The
Civil War,* a blockbuster hit for PBS, a network more accustomed to
gracing the bottom of the Nielsen ratings. As the series' most frequently
seen commentator, with his mellifluous voice, anecdotal storytelling,
and exhaustive knowledge of the war's events, Foote mesmerized

a nation. Just four months after his friend had died, Foote now vaulted beyond the fame that even the award-winning Percy had enjoyed. As Bunt Percy said, "It's too bad Walker wasn't here to see all of [Foote's] success. It would be really nice if Walker could see all of this." Without lifting his dip pen, the industrious writer achieved fame in a way that he never could have imagined. This old-fashioned Southerner had achieved stardom, ironically, through "the power of television." He became, as *People* characterized him in the week after the series aired, "a kind of video folk hero."

Weeks before the series aired, expectations had been building, not merely because of the country's growing interest in the Civil War but because of Burns's reputation. Thanks to films such as *Brooklyn Bridge* (1981) and *Huey Long* (1985), Burns had made a name for himself in the field of television documentaries. His trademark combination of old photographs, music, and present-day talking heads enlivened dead history by capitalizing on television's unique characteristics. As one television critic wrote, he could present "drama the networks could [only] invent." In Burns's able hands, the Civil War hopefully would translate into good television.

Historically, the medium's relationship with the war had been woeful. The last major television series on the Civil War, CBS's *The Blue and the Gray* (1982), had exemplified this struggle. Although *The Blue and the Gray* had used Bruce Catton's Civil War books for its historical background, the series had descended into a "soap opera," as Foote himself said at the time: "They took the historical background from Catton, but they perverted it and soaped it up. . . . Soap in its place is just fine. I'm a 25-year veteran of watching *As the World Turns*. But I think that soap should be clearly marked as such. . . . They made a piece of junk." All in all, Foote found it "much worse than I thought it would be."

Burns had started work on his new series soon after the completion of *Huey Long*. In preparation for the new film, he assembled a group of prominent Civil War historians, including C. Vann Woodward, Eric Foner, and Barbara Fields. Foote was not among the group; at this point, in fact, Ken Burns knew Foote's name as "just one among many who had written on the Civil War." Robert Penn Warren changed all of that with a phone call one night in early 1986. As Ken Burns remembers the call, "In that great Southern voice of his, Warren said, 'Thinking about the Civil War, Ken. If you're going to do it right, you need to contact Shelby Foote.'" Warren was not a great friend of Foote's; they had met several times at official functions, and they were both founding members of The Fellowship of Southern Writers, a group established in 1987. (Walker Percy was also a charter member.) But Warren and Foote had never had a conversation of any length, and Foote even disliked Warren's philosophically driven novels, claiming that they "stink too much of the lamp." But Warren knew and admired Foote's trilogy, and his appreciation of *The Civil War: A Narrative* led him to place the call to Burns. Still not having read Foote at the time, all Burns knew was that "when Red Warren tells you what to do, you do it."

Quickly reading through Foote's books, Burns decided that Warren was right, and the filmmaker induced Foote to sit for an interview in his Memphis home and travel with the film crew to Shiloh. Burns offered Foote a modest fee to work as a consultant on the project. At first, Foote had been reluctant to take their offer. As he told Percy at the time, "I don't much go for that stuff but in this case they persuaded me with money, a powerful persuader indeed in my current financial state." Foote said that he needed to have his house painted as well as help Huggy pay rent.

With Foote under contract, Ken Burns and his brother Ric, the series co-producer, and cameraman Buddy Squires traveled to Memphis in late April 1986 to interview Foote. Setting up shop in the small, book-lined anteroom outside the study, Burns began the three-hour interview, only to discover that Foote had a habit of not answering questions directly. Burns realized that he need only bring up a topic and Foote would springboard into seemingly incidental anecdotes about the war. When Ken Burns later wondered aloud how successful the interview had been, the cameraman responded lukewarmly, saying that he had not been too impressed.

But when the Burns team returned to New Hampshire, the memories of the interview still lingered. When the film rolls were developed and Ken Burns saw them, he became certain that Foote and his anecdotal accounts could, in fact, be used in an integral way for the series. Because he believed that "story is a central part of the word 'history,'"

Burns found Foote's storytelling particularly attractive. Unlike many of the academics that he was working with, whose comments implicitly assumed that the war was a past event, Foote "didn't give away the story." Instead he "put people in the moment."

At a November 1986 meeting in Washington, D.C., two dozen consultants hired for the project critiqued the draft of a script for the series, a process that would separate potential commentators into, in Burns's words, "showhorses and workhorses." Foote emerged there as a leading voice for the project. While most of the consultants "pontificated" about some battle or issue with which they had specifically dealt, Foote alone among the consultants knew "everything cold." "Shelby could, without notes, tell you everything about a particular situation, where everybody was, who was there, and who was sitting where on the fence [as during a counsel of war]." As a result of Foote's display, Burns found himself taking "copious notes of what [Foote] said" for a second interview that he would later conduct.

Foote's performance at the Washington meeting made an indelible impression. Although the series would feature a number of academic figures, Burns envisioned a film driven by narrative and centered on battlefield events. Thus, the voices telling the stories would play as significant role in the production as the expert historians offering commentary. Among others, Jason Robards would provide the voice for Ulysses Grant, Jody Powell for Stonewall Jackson, Sam Waterston for Abraham Lincoln, playwright Horton Foote (no relation to Shelby Foote) for Jefferson Davis, Morgan Freeman for Frederick Douglass, and Garrison Keillor for Walt Whitman.

Burns realized that Foote would be a central figure, and he made arrangements to go to Memphis to interview Foote again and then to have him accompany the film crew to Vicksburg. In 1987 they returned to Foote's house, where, in the same book-lined room, Foote sat for another seventy-minute interview. Fully aware of Foote's propensity for storytelling, Burns just got him started and let him talk. The next day, Foote and the crew traveled down to Vicksburg, where they filmed scenes around the battlefield. During the course of driving around the eighteen-mile circuit of the Vicksburg Military National Park, Burns found Foote's narration of the events of the battle so compelling that he had the crew pull over to a cul-de-sac, where they set up an impromptu interview session, filming another three rolls.

It would be several years before the series was ready to air, and during those years, Foote and Ken Burns stayed in frequent contact. On one occasion, when Burns expressed concern about how he was going to fit everything together, Foote shared with him his Aristotelian belief that a narrative pattern already exists within an event, one that merely needed to be discovered. Foote encapsulated his beliefs to Burns by saying, "God is the greatest dramatist."

More than Foote's directive, the author's interview sessions resonated with Burns. As he completed *The Civil War* he repeatedly inserted more and more of Foote and his stories. By the time the series was ready to air in September 1990, Foote would appear in nearly ninety spots, much more often than any of the other experts. Foote's appearances represented, according to Burns, "one of the greatest shooting ratios that I've ever had": "Normally, after shooting six rolls of someone, we'll use maybe three sound bites." Three forty-second bites, approximately two minutes of television time, equated to approximately a 30:1 shooting ratio. But with Foote, the shooting ratio climbed to 3:1, "an incredible rate." In all, Foote's appearances added up to approximately one hour of the eleven-and-a-half-hour series. Indeed, Burns's use of Foote would become a standard for his later productions. When Burns interviewed people for future series, such as *Baseball* (1994) and *Jazz* (2001), they would wonder "whether they're going to be the next Shelby Foote."

When the series aired over the week of September 23–27, 1990, it was seen by more than 39 million viewers, making it the most-watched PBS series ever. On the heels of its success, the series continued to reap enormous publicity during the following weeks. As *The Washington Post*'s television critic, Tom Shales, claimed a week after the series, "We are living in the aftermath of *The Civil War*." According to Shales, the series had "blazed new trails of glory for public television." In *The Commercial Appeal*, Tom Walter wrote that "viewers whose only connection to history is an involuntary shudder when they recall the deadening way it was taught in high school [found] this film irresistible." Even *People*, which normally steered clear of any PBS fare, featured a story declaring *The Civil War* a "masterly" production.

Spellbinding as the production was, Foote's role in that series proved equally enchanting. In the stories on the Burns series, writers discovered the man whose work had always been before them. *The Washington Post*'s Charles Trueheart praised the work of all of the series' speakers, but among those luminaries, "none had quite the presence of Foote. Sitting against the backdrop of his book-lined study in Memphis, or the horizon of the Shiloh battlefield in Tennessee, the native Mississippian managed to convey the subliminal authority of an eyewitness." Up close, Trueheart found Foote equal to his television persona: "the punctuations of light in his eyes, the easy mental retrieval of datum, anecdote and utterance: In person, these are no different than they were on camera. Burns could not have anguished long over the decision to let Foote tell so much of 'The Civil War.'" Trueheart labeled Foote the "Toast of Public Television," while *USA Today*'s Craig Wilson called him "the media's newest darling." Even more grandly, *Newsweek* deemed him "Prime Time's New Star."

While these stories explicitly pointed to Foote's storytelling abilities as the source of his appeal, they also adumbrated the nation's continued fascination with all things Southern—particularly the region's supposed gentility. As Richard King has argued, the rest of the nation often combats its democratic homogeneity by invoking, at least imaginatively, the aristocratic tradition of Southern culture. Capturing this elitism, *USA Today*'s Craig Wilson wrote that Foote was a "pipe-smoker who admires Mozart and is proud to be a yellow-dog Democrat, he drinks bourbon outdoors, Scotch indoors." Appealing even more to the stereotype of the Southerner, many reporters found Foote's accent a source of fascination. Although for Burns, Foote's accent "didn't matter," according to Michelle Green and David Hutchings, Foote combined "a drawling delivery and erudite insights in an anecdotal style perfectly suited to the task of putting a fresh spin on a familiar story." Underscoring this point, Trueheart's *Washington Post* story even transliterated Foote's speech into dialect. Reporting Foote's account of the television makeup artists who had worked on him before going on

CBS's *Nightwatch*, Trueheart wrote that Foote said, "They just blotted out the circles under my eyes. I worked hard for those circles." Trueheart then Southernized this innocuous comment: "Ah weuhked hahd fuh those seuhkles." For these writers, Foote's drawl was connected to his patrician gentility. *People* called him "courtly," while Wilson quoted Reynolds Price, a fellow Southern novelist, who claimed that Foote was "the last of the Southern gentlemen. In the best sense of the word, he's a man of grace and courtesy."

Foote was eager to play along with the myth being shaped about him. The reason that he preferred drinking bourbon outdoors, Foote told Wilson, was because it reminded him of drinking the sweet whiskey "in cool weather when I used to be out huntin' and all," a statement that completely misrepresented the fact that he had always deplored hunting. As one friend suggested, for the media, Foote "played the part of being a Southern gentleman—he gave them what they wanted." It was an easy role for him to play. Being a media-created Southern gentleman enabled Foote to enjoy the status that his grandfathers had without being freighted with the injustices inherent in being an actual Southern planter.

Southern aristocrat or just smooth-talking Civil War expert, Foote had been pushed into the national limelight. His *Civil War* had always sold fairly well, but in the days after the series, it suddenly "went off the register." During one week at the end of September, each volume of the paperback edition of *The Civil War* sold a thousand copies per day, a figure that included neither the sale of hardback copies of the trilogy nor his novels. Random House rushed to reissue its Foote works, but they could not publish them fast enough. Through the middle of 1991, Random House sold 400,000 volumes of *The Civil War*, netting Foote $800,000. "Ken," Foote told Burns in a call a year after the series, "you've made me a millionaire."

More than just his books, Foote himself became a hot commodity. No longer invited to appear only before Civil War groups, he was now besieged by requests for appearances. In 1991 Foote appeared on NBC's *The Tonight Show*. At the same time, speaking requests poured in from literary conferences and groups of all types. Whereas just years before, Foote had jumped at any offer made, he now became very selective: "I'll go to places for several reasons, either I feel some obligation to the group or it's a place that I've never been to before." Another reason that he accepted speaking engagements was that, at $25,000 a speech, he could "build a nest egg" for Gwyn and Huggy. These speeches came easy to him, as they were nothing more than extemporaneous talks consisting of loosely connected anecdotes—usually about the Civil War. It did not matter—that was exactly what they wanted, and Foote spoke to overflow crowds wherever he went.

Almost as if to spite academics' resistance to his work, Foote seemed especially willing to accept universities' requests to bestow him with honorary doctorates. Foote accepted virtually all of their offers. Indeed, over the next few years, the honorary degree that he received from Southwestern at Memphis in 1982 would pale amid the twenty degrees that he received from schools across the country. None was sweeter than from the University of North Carolina, however. In 1975 Foote had received the university's Distinguished Alumnus Award, but in 1992 he was given an honorary doctorate. Several years before *The Civil War* series, Foote had been nominated by Louis Rubin to receive the degree. But only after the PBS series aired and the nomination of Dr. George Sheldon, head of surgery at UNC's Medical School, did the university agree to give the former dropout its highest degree. UNC's belated acceptance of its famous alumnus echoed another belated honor that would come when the American Academy of Arts and Letters endowed Foote with membership in 1994. During the 1970s and 1980s Walker Percy and Eudora Welty, both members, had lobbied for his inclusion. Now, though, Foote's ship had come in. When he received the call from the academy, Foote asked, "Where have you all been? I've been waiting twenty years for this call."

All of these public appearances fed a connection that many people felt they had developed with the avuncular Foote through *The Civil War*. Letters poured in from people, including "opportunists and star-chasers." Women wrote to propose marriage. As Foote told William Thomas, "A woman named Baer wrote to say she'd propose marriage, but she didn't want to be called Mrs. Baer-Foote." Mrs. Baer was not alone in finding Foote sexy. A California newspaper identified Foote as one of the three sexiest men alive—an honor he shared with Sean Connery and Robert Duvall.

The letters he could disregard, but phone calls presented more of a problem. Refusing to be "different from everybody else," Foote did not want to have an unlisted phone number: "I want people to be able to call me, but I want them not to do it." But people did call, and his phone often seemed to be some hotline. During the day, radio talk-show hosts often called. At night, drunks called to ask Foote to play mediator for their arguments on whether Lee or Grant was the better general. However much he did not like the interruptions, he carried them out with civility. When Rhodes College student Trent Scofield called one afternoon to ask about possible sources for a term paper on the role of religion in the Confederacy, Foote was very "friendly and informative." According to Scofield, "He quoted two or three paragraphs verbatim from the preface of another historian's work and then shared his insights for approximately ten minutes. I could not write my notes fast enough."

Appearing everywhere, Foote became a national celebrity. "Everywhere I go," said Fred Smith of his travels for his Memphis-based Federal Express, "people want to know if I know Shelby Foote." In response to the demand, Federal Express began including Foote's three *Civil War* volumes in the gift packages they provided potential clients. When U.S. Senators George Mitchell and Fritz Hollings visited Memphis for a Democratic fundraiser, Smith arranged to have his friend Foote eat lunch with them at Owen Brennan's, a local Cajun restaurant. For most of the afternoon, Mitchell and Hollings, who were already quite knowledgeable about the Civil War, sat spellbound listening to Foote's stories. "They were getting ready for dinner," Smith remembered, "before we finally left."

Foote had the ear of other senators, too, including Ted Kennedy and Al Gore. On several occasions, Kennedy asked Foote to visit his family, including one trip to the Kennedy compound in Hyannis Port, Massachusetts. Closer to home, Foote and Gore occasionally talked. The two had met through mutual friends, and before Gore began his 1988 presidential campaign, Foote suggested that he begin at Thomas Jefferson's Monticello, for its symbolism. Although Gore had not taken his suggestion in 1988, Foote's idea was used at the beginning of Bill Clinton's 1992 presidential campaign. Side by side with Gore, his vice-presidential candidate, Clinton began his campaign from the steps of Jefferson's home. (When Gore began his 2000 presidential campaign, he called Foote and asked, "Do you have any more ideas for me?")

These high-level contacts certainly had their advantages. In May 1994 Foote agreed to join Protect Historic America, a group of historians who were against a proposed Disney history theme park slated for construction in Manassas, Virginia, the site of two Civil War battles. Over the next month, as the issue intensified, Foote became a de facto spokesman for the group, making himself available for newspaper and radio reporters, who eagerly lined up to see what he had to say about the project. On one occasion, Foote asserted, "Disney people will do to American history what they have already done to the animal kingdom—sentimentalize it out of recognition." The participation of Foote, the country's ranking Civil War expert, was a public relations coup that soon paid dividends. A month after Foote became involved in the project, twenty U.S. senators and representatives introduced a congressional resolution objecting to the project, no small stand because Disney ranked as one of the country's largest corporate political contributors. Three months later, Disney found itself scrapping the project in what *USA Today* called a "huge surprise": "Community opposition" had "derail[ed] the Disney entertainment express."

The Disney project was not the only public issue that Foote was asked about during the 1990s. As Faulkner, following his 1950 Nobel Prize, had become the expert on the South, now Foote had ascended to the position. Not surprisingly, one of the issues that Foote was repeatedly asked to comment on was the appropriateness of the Confederate flag within state flags and, more specifically, the Confederate flag itself. Foote understood that because of the recent debates the Confederate flag had become something of "a banner of shame and disgrace and hate." Still, his view was essentially the same one that he had espoused in the 1960s. Now, as then, he saw the banner not as a badge for slavery, but a battlefield standard. What had changed from his earlier claims was the vehemence with which he asserted his belief that the flag controversy did not involve other associations, either now or during the Civil War. The Confederate flag, Foote insisted to Tony Horowitz, "stood for law, honor, love of country."

With his popularity, Foote also found himself asked to comment about the role of blacks in Southern life. As had been true throughout his life, Foote's views were deeply divided and strewn with contradictions. Even a few years after his son Huggy had been shot in the downtown area where Foote had lived in the 1950s and 1960s, Foote could still say that he thought "a lot of what's happening, especially the rapes and muggings [by blacks] is a kind of celebration. . . . They've been held down for so long that when they're let up they celebrate by doing all kinds of things including raping women and everything else." Foote believed that blacks "enjoy the muggings and rapings with the idea of the racial thing, getting the balance."

But if he could sympathize with black violence, increasingly, Foote began to grow weary of the extension of this "celebration." And with this impatience seeped in the old stereotypes that had filled his youth. "What has dismayed me so much is the behavior of blacks," Foote told Horowitz. "They are fulfilling every dire prophecy the Ku Klux Klan made." Perhaps remembering Huggy's shooting, Foote said, "It's no longer safe to be on the streets in black neighborhoods. They are acting as if the utter lie about blacks being somewhere between ape and man were true." Upon hearing these words from the Southern gentleman, Horowitz claimed, "This was a side of Shelby Foote that hadn't come through in Burns's documentary."

In spite of his willingness to be a public man, Foote still wanted time for a few private projects. At first, he had relished the attention, but slowly all of the demands on his energy and time had made him feel, as he told a friend, "like a cat on a hot tin roof." "I'll be glad when Andy Warhol's 15 minutes of fame are up for me," he told a reporter. For a time, he began to turn down requests that he would have earlier accepted. When his longtime friend Clarke Reed invited Foote to speak at a Delta Council meeting, Foote declined. Foote told Reed, "I don't want to show up right now. I'm going to stay out of all of this for a while."

As the decade progressed, Foote began invoking his need for privacy more and more because he wanted to write. Not only was he well into his seventies, but perhaps as a response to all of his fame, he felt the need to show that he was not content resting on his laurels. Moreover, he had grown afraid that the focus on his Civil War expertise would lead people to forget that he identified himself, first and foremost, as a novelist. Anxious to right this wrong and now a member of Random House's Modern Library editorial board, Foote asked about the possibility of writing introductions for several Modern Library releases. The publishing house leapt at the offer, knowing that anything with Foote's name on it would sell.

Foote's first choice, Crane's *Red Badge of Courage,* was not surprising, given the novel's importance as an influence for *Shiloh* and *The Civil War.* Foote's heavily biographical forty-four-page introduction spelled out the influences that had led to Crane's novel. Devoting a few pages to a consideration of the novel itself, Foote praised Crane's ability to be "highly evocative in communicating sensation, the sight and sound and feel of an action or an object." In particular, Foote fell back on intuition for determining the merit of a novel: Crane's novel, Foote claimed, was "true." Quoting Crane, Foote wrote, a man "is merely responsible for his quality of personal honesty. To keep close to this honesty is my supreme ambition." For Foote, such truth was only obtainable through literature, but even then it was true only because it was unarticulable.

After writing another Modern Library introduction—for *Anton Chekhov: Longer Stories from the Last Decade,* which would appear in 2000— Foote turned back to something more substantial, his old demon, "Two Gates to the City." As it had done twice before, the book presented another bout of wrestling. Only now, with the options of playing literary critic available, he did not feel the need to stake his whole existence on the completion of the book. In the late 1990s, Foote spent his free days scratching out the story, then typing the day's work onto the large 11 × 17-inch yellow sheets that he had used for *The Civil War.* He struggled to work up enough steam, but he could never figure out exactly what he wanted to write. By the fall of 2000, all that survived were sixty pages—the last efforts of what was once to have been his magnum opus. "I'm not going to continue," he said. "I'm a different person. I can't go back twenty years and pick up where I left off. It'd be a different book." Perhaps mindful of sullying the fame that he had gained not through writing, but speaking, Foote would not write: "I don't intend to write any books imitating myself." The novel that had plagued much of his life would forever remain a "notion."

Foote's failure to complete "Two Gates to the City" stands as a testament to his ongoing quarrel with his beloved South. Earlier in his life, his novels had introduced him to the complex racial, class, and gender dynamics governing his culture. Each new work moved this boy, who had been "given . . . to understand as a child that I was a Southern aristocrat," further away from his instinctive defense of plantocracy to a realization of the injustices underpinning that order, as he had suggested in *Love in a Dry Season* (1951) and *Jordan County* (1954). Those insights, however, had to incorporate a new challenge with the onset of the civil rights crisis of the 1950s and 1960s. Although to his friends he vehemently argued for the integration of public facilities, Foote also fell victim to a belief that the interventionist forces brought about by the crisis potentially compromised his region. Seeking sanctuary from his deeply ambivalent feelings, Foote enlisted himself in the project of writing a history of the Civil War, which, although brilliant, was also admittedly apolitical and removed by a century from the events racking his homeland. In other words, Foote had used his Civil War to escape the civil rights era.

Foote's *Civil War* was not merely a work that took twenty years of his writing life, but one that determined the events of the rest of his life. The military focus of *The Civil War* dovetailed neatly with the emergence of the Civil War reenactment industry in the 1980s and 1990s, and Foote's name grew among the faithful. With Ken Burns's *Civil War* series, his popularity mushroomed, a fame often constructed in terms of his Southern gentlemanliness. Foote gladly played the professional Southerner for the journalists who came calling, enjoying the fact that being this Southern gentleman enabled him to reconnect with the status of his grandfather planters—without the burdens of their ethos.

It was this combination of Civil War expert and Southern gentleman that appealed to the Sons of Confederates veterans celebrating Nathan Bedford Forrest's birthday in 1996. Revealing the military focus that had enabled him to avoid the political struggles of his culture, Foote said of this slave-trader and Civil War veteran, "I have enormous respect for him. He would be a study in any command school." By making Forrest simply a military hero, free from all of the other contaminating aspects of his life, Foote had ensured that he himself would be viewed as a Southern gentleman.

# N O T E S

Abbreviations used in the notes:

FMD   *Follow Me Down*
  JC   *Jordan County*
LIDS   *Love in a Dry Season*
   S   *Shiloh*
  SF   Shelby Foote
 SHC   Southern Historical Collection, University of North Carolina, Chapel Hill
  SS   *September September*
   T   *Tournament*
Vol. I   *The Civil War, Fort Sumter to Perryville*
Vol. II   *The Civil War, Fredericksburg to Meridian*
Vol. III   *The Civil War, Red River to Appomattox*
  WP   Walker Percy

PAGE

**xiii**  Information on the reenactment industry: See Tony Horowitz, *Confederates in the Attic: Dispatches from the Unfinished Civil War* (New York: Pantheon, 1998).

**xiv**  "head of the KKK": Christina Connor, "Symbol of Reverence or Racism? Dozens Honor Forrest; One Says He 'Stood for Hatred,'" *The (Memphis) Commercial Appeal*, 17 July 1995: B1.

**xiv**  "Native White Protestant Supremacy": Connor B1.

**xiv**  Agrarians' interest in Forrest: Among other works, the wife of Agrarian Allan Tate, Caroline Gordon, wrote novel, *None Shall Look Back* (New York: Charles Scribner's Sons, 1937), in which Forrest emerges as one of the central figures.

**xv**  Apparel at Forrest celebration: Interview with Allen Doyle.

**xvii**  SF's royalties: Interview with Bill Reed.

**xviii**  "Slavery is a huge stain": Brian Lamb, "Interview with Shelby Foote," *Booknotes*, 11 September 1994. Available via http://www.booknotes.org/transcripts/10141.html. 25 pages. (13 November 1997) 10.

**xviii**  "There was not a morsel": John Branston, "The True Pulse of Life," *Memphis*, April 1996: 44.

**xviii**  "The poor, deluded negroes": Quoted in SF, Vol. III (New York: Random House, 1974) 112.

**xviii**  "crossways": John Griffin Jones, "Shelby Foote," *Conversations with Shelby Foote*, Ed. William C. Carter (Jackson: University Press of Mississippi, 1989) 181.

**xix** "civilization": Daniel Singal, *The War Within: From Victorian to Modernist Thought in the South, 1919–1945* (Chapel Hill: University of North Carolina Press, 1982) 27.

**xix** "religion": Harvey Breit, "Talk with Shelby Foote," *Conversations with Shelby Foote* 6.

**xx** "reproducing, in their actions": SF, Vol. II (New York: Random House, 1963) 971.

**xx** "He would be a study": Lela Garlington, "Honoring a Legend: Civil War Buffs Pay Tribute to Forrest," *The (Memphis) Commercial Appeal*, 15 July 1996: B1.

**xx** "The Klan of the 19th Century": Gene Ingram, "Letter to the Editor," *The (Memphis) Commercial Appeal*, 23 July 1995: B7.

**xxi** "I have enormous respect": Garlington: B1 (my emphasis).

**xxi** "they agreed that they disagreed": Interview with Lela Garlington.

**xxi** "last of a dying breed": Interview with D'Army Bailey.

**3** "major crisis": Edward Foote, *Chotankers: A Family History* (Florence, Ala.: Thornwood, 1982) 108.

**4** "social whirl": Edward Foote 59. One of George II's cousins married Washington's sister, and another cousin married Lund Washington, Washington's cousin and manager of his Mount Vernon estate. Edward Foote 70.

**4** George I's birthdate: Edward Foote 74.

**5** "unjustly ... proposed": Edward Foote 108.

**5** Settlement of suit: Edward Foote 108.

**6** Although the 1813 date is consistent with a number of sources, including his gravestone, Henry Foote's daughter by his fourth wife cites 1810 as Henry Foote's year of birth. John Anderson Tyson, *Historical Notes of Noxubee County, Mississippi* (Macon, Miss.: privately published, 1928) 283.

**6** "reading law": Tyson 279.

**6** "From 1815 to 1850": James M. McPherson, *Battle Cry of Freedom: The Civil War Era* (New York: Oxford University Press, 1988) 42.

**7** Creation of Macon: Henry Broox Sledge, *Dancing Rabbit: A Book About People, Places, and Things in Noxubee County* (Macon, Miss.: Noxubee County Historical Society, 1986) 18.

**7** Henry Foote's first years in Macon: Sledge 18, 55, 145.

**7** "discharge[d] the trust": Tyson 279.

**7** Henry Foote's salary: Tyson 278.

**8** "very lucrative": *Biographical and Historical Memoirs of Mississippi*, Vol. 1 (Chicago: Goodspeed, 1891) 748.

**8** "brilliant intellect": Tyson 280.

**8** "special pride": Tyson 280.

**8** "contracted": Tyson 280.

**8** Mary Foote's relation to Henry Foote: Edward Foote 244.

**8** Death of Mary Foote: Noxubee County Public Library, Foote family file.

**8** The *Macon Intelligencer:* "Newspapers of Noxubee County," *Noxubee County Historical Society Bulletin,* September 1977: 3.

**9** "Old Gentleman's Party": McPherson 221.

**9** "unquestionably the most prosperous people on earth": McPherson 808.

**9** "to recognize no political principle": McPherson 221.

**10** "opposed secession": Tyson 278.

**10** "composed of many of the best citizens": Tyson 278.

**11** Shiloh casualties: SF, Vol. I (New York: Random House, 1958) 350.

**11** Henry Foote's Shiloh experience: Jones 152.

**11** "ubiquitous blue column": SF, Vol. II 338. See also Vol. II 334–41.

**11** "He was probably shaking": SF to Stuart Chapman, 12 February 1995, SHC.

**12** Henry Foote's marriage to Messinger: Tyson 281.

**12** Henry Foote's judicial election: Tyson 279.

**12** "administered justice": Tyson 279.

**13** Henry Foote's election to the Mississippi Senate: Tyson 279.

**13** "Whatever the delta": Robert L. Brandon, *Cotton Kingdom of the New South: A History of the Yazoo Mississippi Delta from Reconstruction to the Twentieth Century* (Cambridge, Mass.: Harvard University Press, 1967) 29.

**13** "practically roadless": SF, Vol. II 190.

**13** Deltans' wealth: James C. Cobb, *The Most Southern Place on Earth: The Mississippi Delta and the Roots of Regional Identity* (Oxford: Oxford University Press, 1992) 31.

**13** "reverted back": Cobb 79.

**14** "Every year my capital": Cobb 76.

**14** "soon produced enough": Cobb 74–77. By 1880, 25 percent of Delta land came under rental agreements. Another 17.2 percent was farmed under some form of a sharecropping agreement. Cobb 74–77.

**14** Size of plantations: Tyson 280. Cobb claims that by 1880 only "293 farms exceeded a thousand acres." Cobb 77.

**14** Hugh Foote's education: Helen White and Redding Sugg, "A Colloquium with Shelby Foote," *Conversations with Shelby Foote* 202. See also Jones 152. By his own admission, SF realized that his earlier stated claims about his grandfather attending Chillicothe Business College were wrong. SF to Stuart Chapman, 12 February 1995.

**15** "first rode into town": Faulkner, *Absalom, Absalom!* (New York: Vintage, 1986) 7.

**15** "cotton merchandising": *Biographical and Historical Memoirs of Mississippi* 751.

**15** "These Jews": Mike Gold, *Jews without Money* (New York: Carroll and Graf, 1930) 83.

**15** "grandfather Rosenstock": Jones 155.

**16** Immigrants in Delta: As Cobb argues, "The river counties of Tunica, Coahoma, Bolivar, and Washington [were] most readily accessible by water to migrants from Kentucky and Tennessee." Cobb 9.

**16** "old southern gentleman": *Copies of Newspaper Articles, Marriage and Death Notices from Greenville Times, 1878–1906,* copied and indexed by Eunice Stockwell, Vol. II (Greenville, Miss.: privately published) 38. At the time of his death, Peters owned Avon, Granicus, Linden, and Ashland Plantations. *Copies of Newspaper Articles,* Vol. 1 25.

**16** "How a Jew bookkeeper": Jones 155.

**16** Rosenstocks' wedding date: *Copies of Newspaper Articles,* Vol. 1 25.

16 Births and deaths: Jo Cille Hafter, "Peters-Pettit Cemetery," *Genealogical Sources: Mississippi–Mostly Washington County, Mississippi,* notebook, ts., William Alexander Percy Library, Greenville, 2.

16 Sunnyside: John Barry, *Rising Tide: The Great Mississippi Flood of 1927 and How It Changed America* (New York: Simon and Schuster, 1997) 111.

17 "debt peonage": Barry 107–11, 194–95.

17 "experiment": John Carr, "It's Worth a Grown Man's Time: An Interview with Shelby Foote," *Conversations with Shelby Foote* 44.

17 Hugh Foote's marriage: *Biographical and Historical Memoirs of Mississippi* 751.

17 "clearing the land": Cobb 78.

18 "swapped for livestock": Cobb 78.

18 Land prices increasing: According to Cobb, "The rise in land values accompanying the breakthrough in levee construction and rail expansion and the stabilization of cotton prices in the 1880s had enhanced the attractiveness of land as collateral." Cobb 82.

18 Size of cotton crops: Cobb 82.

18 Architects: Clinton I. Bagley, "National Register Properties in Washington County," *Washington County Historical Society Bulletin,* July 1977: 36–40; Mount Holly layout: Robert Long, "Historic Mansion Greets Foote Visitors," *Delta Democrat Times,* 3 April 1989: A1 ff.

18 Marriage date: *Copies of Short Newspaper Articles of Interest (Including Marriage and Death Notices) from Greenville Times and Democrat Times (1906–1920),* copied and indexed by Eunice Stockwell (Greenville, Miss.: privately published) 114.

18 Payment for Mount Holly: White and Sugg, "A Colloquium" 202.

19 "no solicitation on his part": Tyson 282.

19 "close to a million dollars": SF, "Faulkner's Depiction of the Planter Aristocracy," *The South and Faulkner's Yoknapatawpha: The Actual and the Apocryphal,* Ed. Evans Harrington and Ann Abadie (Jackson: University Press of Mississippi, 1977) 49.

19 "most spectacular style": Interview with SF.

20 "he came out farther ahead": SF, *T,* 2d ed. (Birmingham, Ala.: Summa Publications, 1987) 204.

20 Hugh Foote's card playing: Jones 153.

20 Hugh Foote's cancer: Jones 153.

20 Date of Hugh Foote's death: *Copies of Short Newspaper Articles of Interest* 109.

20 "where the credit is easy": Carr 38.

21 "He had every reason to expect": Interview with SF.

21 "didn't do anything": Jones 152.

22 "exceedingly popular": "In Society," *The Daily Democrat,* 2 July 1915: 5.

22 Anti-Semitism: See Barry 211–58 and 337–60 for a suggestion of just how rampant anti-Semitism was in New Orleans at this time.

22 "I remember being amazed": Richard Tillinghast, "An Interview with Shelby Foote," *Conversations with Shelby Foote* 221.

22 Wedding information: "In Society," *The Daily Democrat,* 2 July 1915: 5.

**23** "mad as hell": Interview with SF.

**23** Cotton crops: U.S. Department of Commerce and Labor, Bureau of the Census, *Cotton Production and Distribution, 1915–1916,* Bulletin no. 134 (Washington, D.C.: U.S. Department of Commerce and Labor, 1916). See also Cobb 99.

**24** "nice boy": "In Society," *The Delta Democrat,* 18 November 1916: 5.

**24** "suddenly caught fire": Jones 152.

**25** "Your father": Quoted in Robert Phillips, *Shelby Foote: Novelist and Historian* (Jackson: University Press of Mississippi, 1992) 4–5.

**25** "Who will get": Quoted in Phillips 4–5.

**25** "most important event": Interview with SF.

**26** Lillian's sale of goods: Interview with Margaret Foote.

**26** Preparation for new job: Interview with SF.

**26** "simply diverted": Cobb 179.

**27** Ratio of students to expenditures: Cobb 179.

**27** "reams of obscene doggerel": Horowitz 148.

**27** "the South": William Thomas, "Shelby Foote's Love Affair with Civil War Began in '54," *The (Memphis) Commercial Appeal,* 15 July 1973.

**27** "perished because of the oppression": Thomas, "Shelby Foote's Love Affair."

**27** "I was given": Horowitz 149.

**27** Standoffishness of SF: Anonymous interview.

**27** pencil lead in arm: Interview with SF.

**27** "We were very close": Interview with SF.

**28** "almost everyone boasted": Hortense Powdermaker, *After Freedom: A Cultural Study in the Deep South* (New York: Russell and Russell, 1966) 30.

**28** "she used": Interview with Betty Carter. Also confirmed by Peggy Hall.

**28** "She had the idea": Interview with Peggy Hall.

**28** "A lot of bad things": Jones 155.

**29** "Though they were both": Carr 38.

**30** "the greatest disaster": SF, *The Mississippi River and Her People,* Belle McWilliams Lecture, University of Memphis, 15 March 1996.

**30** "three-quarters of a mile across": Barry 203.

**30** "triple the volume": Barry 203.

**30** "Of all the counties": Barry 330.

**30** Number of deaths: Barry 330–31.

**30** Flood aid: Barry 331–34.

**31** "chocolate bands": SF, "Tell Them Good-by," *Saturday Evening Post,* 15 February 1947: 50.

**31** Reception to flood: SF, *The Mississippi River and Her People.*

**31** "Mama Maude": Interview with SF. See also Jones 155.

**31** "was a great place": SF, *The Mississippi River and Her People.*

**31** "would tease him": Anonymous interview.

**32** "Shelby was the only boy": Interview with LeRoy Percy.

**32** "dreadful golfer": Jones 157.

**32**  "giants": Barry 45.

**32**  "led both the South and the nation": Barry 45.

**32**  Percys' suicidal tendencies: See Bertram Wyatt-Brown, *The House of Percy: Honor, Melancholy, and Imagination in a Southern Family* (New York: Oxford University Press, 1994).

**32**  "Some kinsmen of mine": Jones 157.

**32**  "under his wing": Interview with LeRoy Percy.

**33**  "It had nothing to do": Interview with LeRoy Percy.

**33**  "He was the first boy": Interview with LeRoy Percy.

**33**  "Shelby spent": Interview with LeRoy Percy.

**33**  "Shelby and I": Interview with LeRoy Percy.

**33**  "Shelby liked to": Interview with LeRoy Percy.

**34**  "stir things up": Interviews with LeRoy Percy and Joe Reilly. Curiously, both Percy and Reilly used the same "stir things up" phrase to characterize SF's antics.

**34**  "most ungrateful people": Interview with LeRoy Percy.

**34**  "he was the wrong kind": Interview with Joe Reilly.

**34**  "those yappy little dogs": Phillips 9.

**35**  "serious": Anonymous interview.

**35**  SF's fight as a "woman": Interview with Margaret Foote. Also confirmed by Hugh Payne.

**35**  Fighting: Horowitz 146.

**35**  "that there was a world": Jones 156.

**35**  "He liked to fool": Interview with LeRoy Percy.

**35**  "shell": Jay Tolson, *Pilgrim in the Ruins: A Life of Walker Percy* (New York: Simon and Schuster, 1992) 91, 85.

**36**  Model airplanes: WP, "Uncle Will's House," *Architectural Digest,* 1 October 1984: 44.

**36**  Significance of SF's and WP's different plane-building exercises: Tolson 85.

**36**  "That was amazing": Interview with SF, William Alexander Percy Memorial Library, Greenville Writers Room, Shelby Foote file.

**36**  "a great melting pot": Carr 36.

**36**  "The Delta has been": Carr 36–37.

**37**  Klan encounters: Tillinghast 220.

**37**  "Will Percy was regarded": WP, introduction to *Lanterns on the Levee: Recollection of a Planter's Son* (New York: Knopf, 1973) xiii.

**37**  "thought Mr. Will": Jones 166.

**37**  "a magnificent composite": Tolson 86.

**38**  Percy's hospitality: Patrick H. Samway, *Walker Percy: A Life* (New York: Farrar, Straus and Giroux, 1997) 43.

**38**  "resembled a hotel": Samway 43.

**38**  "a salon": Barry 46.

**38**  "risen above race": Barry 419.

**38**  "the most ideologically aggressive poetry": Barry 419.

**39**  "communist speech": Jones 166.

**39** "he was furious": Jones 166.

**39** "The stability of Delta society": Cobb 184.

**39** "He could read": White and Sugg, "A Colloquium" 205.

**39** "Uncle Will wasn't much for": WP, "Uncle Will's House" 44.

**40** "shake his head about it": Jones 164.

**40** "Whether distracted": WP, "Uncle Will's House" 50.

**40** "made a fool": Jones 164.

**40** "Faulkner never had": Jones 164.

**41** "the greatest conversationalist": Interview with Bern Keating.

**41** "quite literally almost everything": Evans Harrington, "Interview with Shelby Foote," *Conversations with Shelby Foote* 79–80.

**41** "many books that I had never heard of": Harrington 80.

**41** "big summer": John Graham, "Talking with Shelby Foote," *Conversations with Shelby Foote* 72.

**41** "I have reread": Graham 72.

**41** "what, if anything": Jones 156–57.

**41** "Shakespeare of our time": see, for example, SF to WP, 5 August 1970, SHC.

**41** "like a colt": Jones 156.

**41** "two separate Quentins": Faulkner, *Absalom, Absalom!* 5.

**42** "The grandeur of real art": Marcel Proust, *The Past Recaptured* in *Remembrance of Things Past*, 2 vols., Trans. Frederick A. Blossom (New York: Random House, 1932) 1013.

**42** "prize": William Thomas, "Appomattox for Shelby Foote," *Mid-South Commercial Appeal Magazine*, 19 March 1978: 24.

**42** "different": White and Sugg, "A Colloquium" 204.

**42** "was showing me": White and Sugg, "A Colloquium" 204.

**43** "miracle worker": Anonymous interview.

**43** "Shelby Foote, you would argue": Interview with LeRoy Percy.

**43** "walked with a stiff": SF, *JC* (New York: Vintage, 1992) 117.

**44** "Mr. Leuckenbach, this novel": Interview with LeRoy Percy.

**44** SF's suspension: Interview with LeRoy Percy.

**44** WP's poetry: WP to SF, 7 February 1972, SHC.

**45** "Death took my love": SF, "Death Took My Love," *The Pica*, 27 February 1934: 2.

**45** "all the grass": SF, "Five Images," *The Pica*, 23 January 1934: 3.

**45** "most of the best writers": Phillips 21.

**45** "Pick some writer": Phillips 21.

**46** "Jeremiah Jones was a man": SF, "Jeremiah Jones," *The Pica*, 27 February 1934: 2.

**46** "If I loved you": SF, "Madrigal (Almost)," *The Pica*, 27 October 1933: 2.

**47** "The Man Who Played God": *The Pica*, 23 February 1935.

**47** "Shelby is still running around": *The Pica*, 23 February 1935.

**47** "Everybody turned on Shelby": Tolson 106.

**47** "It's amazing": Anonymous interview.

**47** "I don't know what": Bland Simpson, "His Way from the Start," *Carolina Alumni Review,* Summer 1994: 37.

**47** SF's desk: Interview with Phillip Carter.

**48** "You *must* see": SF, "Reading and You," *The Pica,* 28 February 1935: 2.

**48** Deaths of Mic and Maude Moyse: Interview with Roy Hanf.

**48** "untoward advances": Interview with LeRoy Percy.

**48** "Leuckenbach Hangs at Dawn": *The Peek-Ah,* 5 May 1934: 1.

**48** "unfair and ridiculous": Samway 79.

**49** Howard Odum: Singal 115–52.

**49** "By no means": W. Hampton Sides, "Conversations with Shelby Foote," *Conversations with Shelby Foote* 237.

**49** "We are sorry": Sides 237.

**49** "salt pills": SF, *T* (Birmingham, Ala.: Summa Publications, 1987) preface.

**50** Greenville hit hard by the Depression: Interview with SF.

**51** "drift[ed]": Tolson 123.

**51** "He would have loved": Interview with Bunt Percy.

**52** "We knew he was coming": Interview with LeRoy Percy.

**52** "We told you not to come": Sides 237.

**52** "I know that you have classes": Interview with SF. See also Tolson 126.

**52** "special student": "Graduate Flashes," *The Pica,* 9 October 1935: 2.

**52** Size of SF's freshman class: Samway 81.

**53** UNC speakers: Simpson 39.

**53** "You can't be a Communist": Interview with SF.

**53** "all over the campus": Interview with SF.

**54** "I was absolutely amazed": Samway 80.

**54** UNC weekend dances: Simpson 38.

**54** "a genteel repressed Southern Presbyterian sexuality": Samway 83. Also quoted in Simpson 39.

**54** "Every city of any size": Joel Williamson, *William Faulkner and Southern History* (New York: Oxford University Press, 1993) 386.

**54** Katy Mae's: Samway 82.

**55** "straight to the whorehouse": Interview with SF.

**55** "Women I'm no good with": SF to WP, 19 February 1954, SHC.

**55** "earthworm": Interview with SF.

**55** SF's synagogue attendance: Horowitz 148.

**55** Attendance at St. James Episcopal Church: Interview with Margaret Kirk Virden.

**55** "a decision": Samway 81.

**56** *Carolina Magazine*'s national reputation: Tolson 119. Two years before SF arrived at UNC, *The New York Times'* education editor had singled out the magazine for its excellence. Tolson 119.

**56** "soon became": Singal 270.

**57** "a way": Interview with SF.

**57** "malarial valetudinarian": SF, "This Primrose Hill," *Carolina Magazine*, April 1936: 10.

**57** "some obvious connections": Phillips 43.

**57** "would restore health": Phillips 45.

**57** "the only two people": SF, "The Old Man That Sold Peanuts in New Orleans," *Carolina Magazine*, January 1936: 6.

**57** "can bring the nine cents": SF, "The Old Man That Sold Peanuts" 8.

**58** "like a fool": SF, "The Old Man That Sold Peanuts" 9.

**58** "It came furiously": SF, "The Good Pilgrim: A Fury Is Calmed," *Carolina Magazine*, November 1935: 6.

**58** "He knew": SF, "The Good Pilgrim" 6.

**58** "conditions of love": Phillips 43.

**58** "the harsh unpainted cabins": SF, "The Good Pilgrim" 5–6.

**58** "Sitting there": SF, "The Good Pilgrim" 6.

**59** "louder and stronger": SF, "The Good Pilgrim" 6.

**59** "Francis felt": SF, "The Village Killers," *Carolina Magazine*, February 1936: 32.

**60** "accumulated over a period": SF, "This Primrose Hill" 9.

**60** "acquired something": SF, "This Primrose Hill" 9.

**60** "On our way back": SF, "This Primrose Hill" 9.

**60** "If that's blueblood": SF, "This Primrose Hill" 10.

**60** "not so much a hard drinker": SF, "This Primrose Hill" 10.

**60** "clinger-on of the upper stratum": SF, "This Primrose Hill" 10.

**60** "was filled with": SF, "This Primrose Hill" 10.

**61** "Nobody hates me": SF, "This Primrose Hill" 11.

**61** "He picked his way": SF, "This Primrose Hill" 11.

**61** "way back then": Interview with SF.

**61** Percy's grades: Samway 84.

**61** UNC drop-out rate: Interview with Donald Wetherbee.

**62** "I don't think": Interview with SF.

**62** Trip to New York: Interview with SF.

**62** "raise them up": Interview with SF.

**62** "Do you call yourself": Interview with SF.

**63** "I had no use for it": Interview with SF.

**63** "he had heard": Interview with SF.

**63** "We don't want you": Interview with SF.

**63** "I hadn't been on the campus": Harrington 80.

**64** "I have very small smatterings": James Newcomb, "WKNO Presents a Conversation with Shelby Foote," *Conversations with Shelby Foote* 113.

**64** "particular hell on earth": Tolson 157, 161.

**64** "You mustn't laugh": Jones 164–65.

**64** Memphis visit: Samway 85. See also Tolson 188.

**64** "perhaps the most racist society": Interview with SF.

**65** "experiences about race": Interview with SF.

**65**  "canvas of war and peace": SF, review of *None Shall Look Back* by Caroline Gordon, *Carolina Magazine*, May 1937: 28.

**66**  "The heroes are all dead now": SF, review of *None Shall Look Back* 28.

**66**  "The contrasting word": SF, "The Literature of Fury," *Carolina Magazine*, November 1936: 30.

**66**  "to look deep into the bowels": SF, "The Literature of Fury" 30.

**67**  "the vacuous mandacity [sic]": SF, "Bristol's Gargoyle," *Carolina Magazine*, February 1937: 8.

**67**  "the soul leaving me": SF, "And the Gay and the Blue," *Carolina Magazine*, April 1937: 14.

**68**  "them pale-eyed": SF, "And the Gay and the Blue" 15.

**68**  "funny experience": Graham 73.

**68**  "One of the reasons": Jones 161–62.

**69**  "I read . . . Civil War things": Newcomb 121.

**69**  Information on joining the Spanish Civil War: Interview with Peggy Hall.

**69**  "indirectly": Newcomb 114.

**69**  "That's the real reason": Simpson 41.

**70**  The 1937 flood: Material taken from *The New York Times*, 1–15 February 1937.

**71**  "know [my homeland] better": SF, *T* preface.

**71**  "at least as valuable": Simpson 42.

**71**  SF's Greenville work: SF, *T* preface.

**71**  Work at a cotton gin: Simpson 42.

**71**  "It was Hodding himself": Jones 162.

**71**  "He was a terrible worker": Interview with Betty Carter.

**71**  "I wouldn't bet my last dollar": Interview with Donald Wetherbee.

**72**  "partly cloudy with shitty winds": Tolson 146.

**72**  "white lice": SF, *FMD* (New York: Vintage, 1993) 22.

**72**  SF's newspaper coup: Interview with Betty Carter.

**72**  "I wanted to learn": Interview with SF.

**72**  "a young man's attempt": White and Sugg, "A Colloquium" 197.

**73**  "I don't know that man": Dick Cavett, "Interview with Shelby Foote," *Conversations with Shelby Foote* 135.

**73**  "waded": Cavett 148.

**74**  "For Shelby": Samway 99.

**74**  Attendance at *Birth of a Nation:* Samway 100.

**74**  "Jordan County was laid down": Newcomb 115.

**74**  "rage for symmetry": Newcomb 115.

**74**  SF's *Tournament* synopsis: Shelby Foote file, SHC, no. 4038, folder 52.

**74**  "It was in": SF, *T* xxx.

**75**  "When all the facts": SF, *T* xxx.

**75**  "He kept saying": Interview with LeRoy Percy.

**75**  "*Tournament* was a sort of thrashing around": Harrington 99.

**75**  "Its dusty brick rainstreaked": Shelby Foote file, SHC, no. 4038, folder 56.

**75**   "whitewashed walls": Shelby Foote file, SHC, no. 4038, folder 56.

**75**   "all that remained": Shelby Foote file, SHC, no. 4038, folder 56.

**76**   "had been the region's": SF, *T* 12.

**76**   "historical unrest": SF, *T* 182–83.

**76**   "four-block business section": SF, *T* 181.

**76**   "represented one of the leading families": SF, *T* 161.

**76**   "I'm so tired": SF, *T* 164.

**76**   "It was coming soon": SF, *T* 162.

**76**   "would all be burnt to cinders": SF, *T* 162.

**76**   "banks and saloons": SF, *T* 181.

**77**   "Whites and blacks": Grace Elizabeth Hale, *Making Whiteness: The Culture of Segregation in the South, 1890–1940* (New York: Pantheon, 1998) 195.

**77**   "facades … slashed with banners": SF, *T* 181.

**77**   "baited mainly for Negroes": SF, *T* 181.

**77**   "Metaphors of natural disaster": Michael Denning, *The Cultural Front: The Laboring of American Culture in the Twentieth-Century* (New York: Verso, 1996) 265.

**77**   "There was a strange new countryside": SF, *T* 112.

**77**   "Captain, I aint lying": SF, *T* 113.

**77**   "Youre going to do it": SF, *T* 113.

**77**   "He took out": SF, *T* 114.

**78**   Attitudes toward Roosevelt: Bruce Schulman, *From Cotton Belt to Sunbelt: Federal Policy, Economic Development, and the Transformation of the South, 1938–1980* (New York: Oxford University Press, 1991) 54–62.

**78**   "conservative revolution": Pete Daniel, *Standing at the Crossroads: Southern Life since 1900* (New York: Hill and Wang, 1986) 120.

**78**   "We of my generation": William Alexander Percy, *Lanterns on the Levee* 313. Although *Lanterns on the Levee* was "almost completed" (Wyatt-Brown 280) by the time that SF began *Tournament* in 1939, SF had been privy to Percy's beliefs throughout the 1930s.

**78**   "In time": William Alexander Percy 60.

**78**   "I didn't develop": White and Sugg, "A Colloquium" 206–7.

**78**   "The roof": William Alexander Percy 270.

**78**   "The four walls": SF, *T* xxxiv.

**78**   "look … at my homeland": Harrington 99.

**79**   "Solitaire": SF, *T* 183.

**79**   "Ernest": SF, *T* 65, 64.

**79**   "Get off this place": SF, *T* 65.

**79**   "strategy in dealing": Cobb 103.

**79**   "too hard a worker": SF, *T* 67.

**79**   "offer[ed] as humane": SF, *T* 280.

**80**   "began to know": SF, *T* 67.

**80**   "having women trouble": SF, *T* 141.

**80**   "pattern": SF, *T* 66.

**80** "the best-looking books in America": SF, *T* preface.

**80** "too experimental in nature": SF, *T* preface.

**80** "surely [were] the longest two": SF, *T* preface.

**81** "cold storage": White and Sugg, "A Colloquium" 198.

**81** Burning the *Tournament* manuscript: SF, *T* preface.

**81** "I don't regret": SF to WP, 31 December 1951, SHC.

**81** "peace for our time": Bergen Evans, *Dictionary of Quotations* (New York: Delacorte, 1968) 515.

**81** "That was something that we felt": Interview with Roy Hanf.

**82** "I felt very strongly": Newcomb 114.

**82** Isaac Shelby connection: John Carr, "Interview with Lillian Foote," 7 February 1963, Shelby Foote file, William Alexander Percy Library.

**82** World War II books: Lamb 9.

**82** "Sgt. Foote": Susie James, "Shelby Foote Visits Buddies at Barber Shop," *The Oxford Eagle*, 6 August 1976: 6.

**83** "outstanding soldier": Interview with Roy Hanf.

**83** "first and only time": Interview with Roy Hanf.

**83** Ferrying soldiers home: James 6.

**83** "some reference": Interview with Roy Hanf.

**83** "He lived": Interview with SF.

**84** "God Almighty, Louie": Interview with SF.

**84** "cried for days": Interview with SF.

**84** "a natural born officer": Interview with Roy Hanf.

**84** "he had the oldest-looking body": Tolson 161.

**84** "coat": Tolson 161.

**85** Visits to William Alexander Percy's deathbed: Samway 119.

**85** "gone to hell": Tolson 166.

**86** "worse than irregular": Interview with Margaret Kirk Virden.

**86** "I had to make a decision": Interview with SF.

**86** "matter of convenience": Interview with SF.

**87** SF's first visit to Saranac Lake: Tolson claims that Percy's first visit to Saranac Lake was in the fall of 1942 (167), whereas Samway claims that the initial meeting took place in July 1943 (131). Because Samway provides more details and the trip seems to coincide with SF's appearance in New York, I am following Samway in the dating of this first visit.

**87** WP's contraction of tuberculosis: Samway 122.

**87** "went rapidly downhill": WP to SF, 29 July 1989, SHC.

**87** "He put aside": Samway 126.

**88** "cure cottage": Tolson 167.

**88** "immediately struck by": Tolson 167.

**88** "a fast train ride away": Interview with SF.

**88** "too busy drinking": Interview with SF.

**89** "He was keeping books": Quoted in Tolson 178.

**89**  "alibis": Interview with SF.

**90**  "other than honorable": Samway 133.

**90**  "I couldn't go home": Breit 5.

**90**  "That was the story": Interview with Eddie LaFoe.

**91**  Associated Press work: Samway 133.

**91**  WP and SF in New York: Tolson 180.

**92**  "I have never seen": Interview with Bunt Percy. See also Tolson 180 and Samway 134.

**92**  "You used to be": Jones 169.

**92**  Training for Pacific fighting: Samway 134.

**93**  "missed the great trauma": Horowitz 149.

**93**  "Rejected, dejected": SF, *LIDS* (New York: Vintage, 1979) 16.

**94**  "afforded the unfamiliar triple luxury": SF, *T* preface.

**94**  Acronym for WJPR: Interview with LeRoy Percy.

**95**  "Out of boredom and desperation": SF, *T* preface.

**95**  "Some of it": White and Sugg, "A Colloquium" 198.

**95**  "Major Dubose": SF, "Flood Burial," *Life,* 6 September 1946: 17.

**95**  "microscopic characters": SF, "Flood Burial" 17.

**95**  "Then I reckon he's through Shiloh": SF, "Flood Burial" 17.

**95**  "Man you sep": SF, "Flood Burial" 161.

**96**  Truman's concerns: David McCullough, *Truman* (New York: Simon and Schuster, 1992) 589.

**96**  "screw his ass": Interview with Bill Reed.

**96**  "The dog would": Interview with Kenneth Haxton.

**96**  "that mean old man": Quoted in interview with Roy Hanf.

**96**  "He hasn't paid": Interview with Bill Reed.

**96**  "quickly went from bad to worse": Tolson 188.

**96**  "galled": SF to WP, 6 October 1956, SHC.

**97**  "Read this one, Bud": Ben Wasson, *Count No 'Count: Flashbacks to Faulkner* (Jackson: University Press of Mississippi, 1983) 89.

**97**  "I re-typed it": Thomas, "Shelby Foote's Love Affair."

**97**  Cutting of manuscript: Shelby Foote file, SHC, no. 4038, folder 76.

**98**  "taking": Interview with Kenneth Haxton.

**98**  Shopping spree: Carr 52.

**98**  Rents a study: Phillips 13.

**98**  Office features: William Thomas, "Best Foote Forward," *The (Memphis) Commercial Appeal,* 17 September 1978.

**98**  "pull any more out": Quoted in Phillips 13.

**98**  "develop[s] his final tone": SF, "Tell Them Good-by" 54.

**98**  *"Something is happening":* SF, "Tell Them Good-by" 46 (emphasis in original).

**99**  "deep, pulsing hum": SF, "Tell Them Good-by" 64.

**99**  "Yair!": SF, "Tell Them Good-by" 64.

**99**  "to take some of the blare": SF, "Tell Them Good-by" 54.

99 "two hundred and fifty dollars a week": SF, "Tell Them Good-by" 54.

99 "my horn don't suit": SF, "Tell Them Good-by" 54.

100 "Rex put a mute": SF, "Tell Them Good-by" 54.

100 "so long": Allen Tate, "The Profession of Letters in the South," *Collected Essays* (Denver: Alan Swallow, 1959) 280–81.

100 "county in general": Newcomb 135.

100 "the years which made him": SF, "Tell Them Good-by" 54.

100 Length of "Tell Them Good-by": As he explained in a 1967 lecture, "The one I had sold them ['Flood Burial'] was twenty-two pages long. And I said, 'The correct way to approach this thing is to write one forty-four pages long.'" Phillips 13.

101 "We do not know": Quoted in Phillips 13.

101 "A complete novelette": *Saturday Evening Post,* cover, 15 February 1947.

101 "The most heart-breaking thing": SF to WP, 1 May 1948, SHC.

101 "His experiments with other women": Tolson 190.

101 "the locus of pure possibility": WP, *The Last Gentleman* (New York: Farrar, Straus and Giroux, 1982) 356.

102 "I seriously think": SF to WP, 19 November 1949, SHC.

102 "If you take the claims": Quoted in Tolson 190.

102 "Yours is a mind": Quoted in Tolson 191.

102 "who was always with us": Interview with Bunt Percy.

103 "informing": SF, *T* preface.

103 "kind of hurt feelings": Phillips 13.

103 "terrible day": Interview with SF.

103 "I settled down": Phillips 14.

104 "A lot of people think": Jimmie Covington, "Trouble with Klan Helped to Bring Foote Back to Memphis," *The (Memphis) Commercial Appeal,* 21 August 1966: 15.

104 "little sonnet": Thomas, "Shelby Foote's Love Affair."

104 Sentence rhythms: Interview with Carol Leatherman.

104 "provided the precise rhythm": SF to WP, 29 November 1956, SHC.

104 "strange Oriental": "Shelby Foote's 'Civil War,'" *The (Memphis) Commercial Appeal,* 16 November 1958.

104 "cheated": Horowitz 149.

104 Future books: SF to WP, 19 November 1949, SHC.

104 "For me": Horowitz 154.

105 "the finest": SF, "The Merchant of Bristol," (Greenville, Miss.: The Levee Press, 1947) 14.

105 "Ive lost my honor": SF, "The Merchant of Bristol" 14.

105 SF's involvement with the Levee Press: James Robertshaw Jr., "The Levee Press," *Washington County Historical Society Bulletin,* January 1980: 1–10.

106 "In the first": SF, "Bone to Pick with South Biases Author of Civil War History," review of *Ordeal by Fire: An Informal History of the Civil War* by Fletcher Pratt, *Delta-Democrat Times,* 2 January 1949.

**106**  "When he turns novelist": SF, "Confederate Ship Saga Soundly Told," review of *Gallant Rebel* by Stanley F. Horn, *Delta-Democrat Times,* 12 October 1947.

**106**  "Mr. Pratt is apt to": SF, "Bone to Pick with South."

**106**  "Accepting the historian's standards": SF, Vol. I 815.

**106**  Sleeping at Shiloh: Carr, "Interview with Lillian Foote."

**106**  "diptychs": Helen White and Redding Sugg, *Shelby Foote* (Boston: Twayne, 1982) 77.

**107**  "oyster itch": SF, *S* (New York: Barnes and Noble, 1992) 65.

**107**  "wishing like Jesus": SF, *S* 115.

**107**  "the first cavalryman": SF, *S* 150.

**107**  "Historical characters": SF, *S* 205.

**107**  "a book about war": SF, *S* 164.

**108**  "Seen that way": SF, *S* 4–5.

**108**  "neither pro nor anti": SF, *S* 51.

**108**  "plantation": SF, *S* 26.

**109**  Allusions to Shakespeare: SF, *S* 13.

**109**  Napoleonic battle order: SF, *S* 13–14.

**109**  "suspicion of insanity": SF, *S* 39.

**109**  "changed our minds": SF, *S* 40.

**109**  "I have nothing to do": SF, *S* 51.

**109**  "The soldiers never put much stock": SF, *S* 52.

**109**  "an uncle in a livery stable": SF, *S* 145.

**109**  "who did not fight": SF, *S* 218.

**110**  "the rebels": SF, *S* 192.

**110**  "wanted the same things": SF, *S* 192.

**110**  Clean draft of *Shiloh:* Shelby Foote file, SHC, no. 4038, folder 63.

**110**  Date of completing *Shiloh:* Shelby Foote file, SHC, no. 4038, folder 63.

**110**  "He was a disciplinarian": Interview with LeRoy Percy.

**111**  "People came from the Delta": Sides 237–38.

**111**  "the Mississippi Delta": David Cohn, *God Shakes Creation* (New York: Harper and Brothers, 1935).

**111**  "When I was a boy": Sides 237–38.

**111**  "It was the place to go": Interview with Fred Smith.

**111**  Stinson's medical accomplishments: "Dr. William D. Stinson Dies of Heart Attack," *The (Memphis) Commercial Appeal,* 19 October 1953: 8.

**112**  Peggy threatened with being cut off: Interview with Margaret Foote.

**112**  Mrs. Stinson's drug dependency: Interview with SF.

**112**  "William Shelby Foote": "Foote and Stinson to Wed Today," *The (Memphis) Commercial Appeal,* 30 August 1947.

**112**  Party at Feliciana: Interview with Betty Carter.

**113**  "twitches and jumps": SF to WP, 1 May 1948, SHC.

**113**  Working on "Vortex": SF to WP, 1 May 1948, SHC.

**113**  "peddling it all over New York": SF to WP, 2 July 1948, SHC.

**113**  *Blue Book* buys *Shiloh* excerpt: SF to WP, 6 July 1948, SHC.

**113**  "women readers": SF to WP, 8 November 1951, SHC.

**113**  "in mind": White and Sugg, "A Colloquium" 198.

**113**  "It sounded like a good subject": SF to WP, 2 July 1948, SHC.

**114**  "my first written novel": SF, *T* preface.

**114**  "hot as blazes": SF to WP, 30 July 1948, SHC.

**114**  "Essentially it's what you read": SF to WP, 30 July 1948, SHC.

**114**  "I revised as I went along": SF, *T* preface.

**114**  "gutted, despoiled, vacant now for two years": Shelby Foote file, SHC, no. 4038, folder 56.

**114**  "then apparently without reason": Shelby Foote file, SHC, no. 4038, folder 56.

**115**  "oh oh": Shelby Foote file, SHC, no. 4038, folder 56.

**115**  "after all": Michael Ravenna, "Mississippi Delta," *The New York Times Book Review*, 25 September 1949: 30.

**115**  "need[ed] a dictionary": Harrington 99.

**115**  Carter's review: Hodding Carter, "Local Novelist, Shelby Foote, Writes Brilliant Delta Story," *Delta Democrat-Times*, 11 September 1949.

**115**  "moving, many-sided narrative": Ravenna 30.

**115**  "it cannot be said": Ravenna 30.

**115**  "This is a felicitous insight": Frederick Rutledge Smith Jr., "Fiction Notes," *Saturday Review of Literature*, 19 November 1949: 44.

**115**  "vividness, more intense": F. Cudworth Flint, "Nine First Novels," *Sewanee Review*, 9 October 1949: 142.

**115**  "Hugh Bart": "Raw, Violent," *New York Herald Tribune Weekly Book Review*, 9 October 1949: 8.

**116**  "The book gives no clear": Flint 143.

**116**  "episodes [that] seem to be included": Flint 142.

**116**  "belongs in the class": Flint 143.

**116**  "young man's novel": SF, *T* preface.

**116**  "They say it's about his grandfather": SF, *T* preface.

**116**  "quite respectable for a first novel": SF, *T* preface.

**116**  "it's not going to make us rich": SF to WP, 7 October 1949, SHC.

**117**  "Love ... entered the picture": SF to WP, 19 February 1954, SHC.

**117**  SF spoils Margaret: Interview with Bunt Percy.

**117**  Myers murder: See *Delta-Democrat Times*, 14–25 July 1941.

**118**  "bream and minnows": SF, *FMD* 6.

**118**  "a sad world": Graham 61.

**118**  "taken on implications": SF to WP, 1 May 1948, SHC.

**118**  "a brick- and glass-walled canyon": SF, *FMD* 218.

**118**  Print culture and magazine industry: Lawrence Schwartz, *Creating Faulkner's Reputation: The Politics of Modern Literary Criticism* (Knoxville: University of Tennessee Press, 1988) 4–5.

**119**  Detective stories about Myers case: Phillips 89.

**119**    Outline: SF to WP, 1 May 1948, SHC.

**120**    "get deeper and deeper": Graham 59.

**120**    "the angles": SF, *FMD* 32.

**120**    "jerk them back": SF, *FMD* 33.

**120**    "to make it sound": SF, *FMD* 27.

**120**    "beautiful blonde": SF, *FMD* 39.

**120**    "They all are": SF, *FMD* 39.

**120**    "collar of white lice": SF, *FMD* 37–38.

**120**    "ten sweet bucks": SF, *FMD* 56.

**120**    "one of those with a babe": SF, *FMD* 49.

**120**    "a good fifty": SF, *FMD* 55.

**121**    Source of title: White and Sugg, *Shelby Foote* 26.

**121**    "farm page": SF, *FMD* 40.

**121**    "rigs together": SF, *FMD* 40.

**121**    "I'm an expert farmer": SF, *FMD* 40.

**121**    "I have a desire": SF, *FMD* 209.

**121**    "low-bosomed": SF, *FMD* 225.

**122**    "rise up": SF, *FMD* 84.

**122**    "Solitaire Plantation": SF, *FMD* 62.

**122**    "I believed that what had drawn me": SF, *FMD* 94.

**122**    "dedicat[ing] his penis": Phillips 103.

**122**    "betrayed him": SF, *FMD* 252.

**122**    "yearly spree[s]": SF, *FMD* 96.

**122**    "demijohn": SF, *FMD* 95.

**122**    "all the veterans were officers by then": SF, *FMD* 95.

**122**    "provost guard lieutenant": SF, *FMD* 96.

**123**    "a promised land": SF, *FMD* 97.

**123**    "On the whole": J. J. Maloney, *The New York Herald Tribune Book Review,* 16 July 1950: 6.

**123**    "Very few young writers": Seymour Krim, "Faulkner Country," *The New York Times Book Review,* 9 July 1950: 17.

**123**    "Shelby Foote brings": *Chicago Sun,* 18 July 1950: 5.

**123**    "does have the irritating habit": Maloney 6.

**124**    "Presenting a story": R. L. Blakesley, *Chicago Sunday Tribune,* 2 July 1950: 5.

**124**    "All that keeps him": "Crime of Passion," *Time,* 3 July 1950: 80.

**124**    "good book": SF to WP, Tuesday January 1951, SHC.

**124**    "I should have told": SF to WP, Tuesday January 1951, SHC.

**124**    "perhaps": SF to WP, 19 May 1949, SHC.

**124**    "If you could read": SF to WP, Tuesday August 1950, SHC.

**124**    Dating of short story collection: SF to WP, 19 May 1950, SHC.

**124**    "my CHILD BY FEVER": SF to WP, 19 May 1950, SHC.

**125**    "smoke": SF to WP, 19 May 1950, SHC.

**125**    "I am happy to report myself": SF to WP, 6 July 1950, SHC.

**125**   "And mind you": SF, *LIDS* 60.

**126**   "This time the hero": SF to WP, 6 July 1950, SHC.

**127**   "a man of learning": SF, *LIDS* 114.

**127**   "characters who live in their own right": SF to WP, 10 October 1950, SHC.

**127**   "barely remembered": SF, *LIDS* 58.

**127**   "Yankee 'carpetbagger'": Phillips 12.

**127**   "had fallen in love": SF, *LIDS* 68.

**128**   "steel-mill labor gang": SF, *LIDS* 55.

**128**   "feeling good": SF to WP, Thursday 1950, SHC.

**128**   "hellacious": SF to WP, 10 October 1950, SHC.

**128**   "problems from the beginning": SF to WP, 29 February 1952, SHC.

**128**   Peggy's behavior: Interview with Margaret Foote.

**128**   Peggy's dress: Interview with Bunt Percy.

**128**   "What she really wanted": SF to WP, 10 October 1950, SHC.

**128**   "three weeks": SF to WP, 30 July 1948, SHC.

**129**   "Peg and Margaret": SF to WP, 10 October 1950, SHC.

**129**   "I'm baching": SF to WP, 30 July 1948, SHC.

**129**   "I approached work sluggishly": SF to WP, 22 December 1950, SHC.

**129**   "I'm past the midpoint": SF to WP, 25 November 1950, SHC.

**129**   "pit ... the rednecks against": SF to WP, 19 March 1951, SHC.

**129**   "the ones we have been raised": SF to WP, 19 March 1951, SHC.

**129**   "the son of a bitch": Jones 194.

**129**   "sincerely honorable men": SF to WP, 19 March 1951, SHC.

**130**   "three or four millions": SF, *LIDS* 231.

**130**   "For Amanda... This is All": SF, *LIDS* 231.

**130**   "donation": SF, *LIDS* 231.

**130**   "was sent to endow a library": SF, *LIDS* 231.

**130**   "translated as an obligation": SF, *LIDS* 114.

**131**   "they sailed for the old world": SF, *LIDS* 114.

**131**   "studying": SF, *LIDS* 36–37.

**131**   "his knee": SF, *LIDS* 43.

**131**   "One wonders when": V. P. Hass, *New York Herald Tribune Book Review*, 21 October 1951: 13.

**132**   "expensive": SF, *LIDS* 108.

**132**   "Somewhat disappointed": SF, *LIDS* 204.

**132**   "pulse with the thump": SF, *LIDS* 115.

**132**   "the 'presiding presence'": Richard King, *A Southern Renaissance: The Cultural Awakening of the American South, 1930–1955* (New York: Oxford University Press, 1980) 34.

**132**   "shadowy figure[s]": King 36.

**132**   "Sometimes she had": SF, *LIDS* 248.

**133**   "Where Amy was concerned": SF, *LIDS* 134.

**133**   "satisfied": SF, *LIDS* 134.

**133** "since Amy was obviously": SF, *LIDS* 134.

**133** "refutation of all": SF, *LIDS* 134.

**133** "Man, you cant tell" SF, *LIDS* 134.

**133** "very happy": SF to WP, 11 May 1951, SHC.

**133** "Linseed and fruitful poppy": quoted in White and Sugg, *Shelby Foote* xvi–xvii.

**133** "expresses the sterility": SF to WP, 11 May 1951, SHC.

**133** "went crazy": SF to WP, 11 May 1951, SHC.

**133** "I damn well": SF to WP, 22 May 1951, SHC.

**134** "while you loathe": *Kirkus*, 15 September 1951: 541.

**134** "shrewdly contrived": *Kirkus* 541.

**134** "markedly gifted": Hass 13.

**134** "Shelby Foote ably": Frances Gaither, "Dry-Rot in Dixie," *The New York Times Book Review*, 23 September 1951: 26.

**134** "narrative is stripped": Gaither 26.

**134** "Character is revealed": Gaither 26.

**134** "above the conflict": SF to WP, 28 October 1951, SHC.

**134** "Much as Ive sworn": SF to WP, 6 July 1950, SHC.

**134** "MacArthur is": SF to WP, 6 July 1950, SHC.

**135** "gives me everything": SF to WP, 26 April 1951, SHC.

**135** "If I felt any better": SF to WP, 26 April 1951, SHC.

**135** "sometimes took his role": Tolson 217.

**136** "I accept it gladly": SF to WP, 22 December 1950, SHC.

**136** "broke": SF to WP, 26 April 1951, SHC.

**136** "for one thing": SF to WP, 12 February 1952, SHC.

**136** "screaming blue murder": SF to WP, 22 May 1951, SHC.

**136** Rewriting *Shiloh:* SF to WP, 22 May 1951, SHC.

**136** Few *Shiloh* changes: Shelby Foote file, SHC, no. 4038, folder 64.

**136** "In some ways": SF to WP, 22 May 1951, SHC.

**136** "I'll swear thats a good piece": SF to WP, 16 May 1951, SHC.

**136** "finished the final fine-tooth": SF to WP, December 1951, SHC.

**136** Promotion of *Shiloh:* SF to WP, 16 May 1951, SHC.

**137** "You would be better off": "Foote to Appear on WREC," *The (Memphis) Commercial Appeal*, 5 June 1964.

**137** "and could have gone on": SF to WP, 28 October 1951, SHC.

**137** "believes that SHILOH": SF to WP, 24 May 1951, SHC.

**137** "Big hopes": SF to WP, 28 October 1951, SHC.

**137** "If you're going to be": SF to WP, 31 December 1951, SHC.

**137** "HIC JACET": SF to WP, 6 December 1951, SHC.

**137** Price of *Shiloh:* SF to WP, 31 October 1951, SHC.

**138** "Mr. Foote writes": "Fiction Notes," *Saturday Review of Literature*, 26 April 1952: 33.

**138** "Shelby Foote handles": George McMillan, "The Hero Is a Battle," *The New York Times Book Review*, 6 April 1952: 6.

**138** "a rattling good story": R. P. Basler, *The Chicago Sunday Tribune*, 6 April 1952: 5.

**138** "This is an original": Avery Craven, *New York Herald Tribune Book Review*, 6 April 1952: 4.

**138** "refreshingly modest": McMillan: 6.

**138** "Its the damndest book": Malcolm Franklin, *Bitterweeds: Life with William Faulkner at Rowan Oak* (Irving, Tex.: The Society for the Study of Traditional Culture, 1977) 59.

**139** *"annum mirabilis":* Tolson 223.

**139** "plan[ned] to put": SF to WP, 12 September 1978, SHC.

**139** "Life is a wonderful thing": SF to WP, 31 December 1951, SHC.

**140** "Or I say now.": SF to WP, 31 December 1951, SHC.

**140** "big book": SF to WP, 10 October 1951, SHC.

**140** "working at the plan": SF to WP, 22 April 1951, SHC.

**140** "I'm still making": SF to WP, 22 August 1951, SHC.

**140** "It's going to be very good": SF to WP, 10 October 1951, SHC.

**140** Outline: SF to WP, 12 February 1952, SHC.

**142** "I, III and V are": SF to WP, 5 July 1951, SHC.

**142** "comprehensive and massive" White and Sugg, *Shelby Foote* 131.

**142** "literary appreciations": Interview with SF.

**142** "has a choice": SF to WP, 22 August 1951, SHC.

**142** "Twin are the gates": Quoted in SF to WP, 22 August 1951, SHC.

**143** "read like": SF to WP, 29 November 1951, SHC.

**143** "Three years ago": SF to WP, 10 November 1951, SHC.

**143** "I'll vow and declare": SF to WP, 29 November 1951, SHC.

**143** "It's going to be a great book": SF to WP, 31 October 1951, SHC.

**143** "Terrific burst": SF to WP, 6 December 1951, SHC.

**143** "I'm still on the crest": SF to WP, 30 November 1951, SHC.

**143** "This is the ticket": SF to WP, 25 November 1951, SHC.

**144** "the most stupendous book": SF to WP, 12 February 1952, SHC.

**144** "holiday devoted": SF to WP, 5 January 1952, SHC.

**144** "wonderful": SF to WP, 5 January 1952, SHC.

**144** "For the past two days": SF to WP, 24 January 1952, SHC (emphasis in original).

**144** "If I knew a Hail Mary": SF to WP, 24 January 1952, SHC.

**145** "There has been": SF to WP, 29 February 1952, SHC.

**145** "saddest things": SF to WP, 29 February 1952, SHC.

**145** "couldnt live like this": SF to WP, 29 February 1952, SHC.

**145** "reasonable visitation": SF to WP, 29 February 1952, SHC.

**145** "Foote's creative gates": Phillips 135.

**145** "I'm scared to death": SF to WP, 5 January 1952, SHC.

**146** "the writing is all right": SF to WP, 5 January 1952, SHC.

**146** "HAVE RUN OFF": SF to WP, 3 March 1952, SHC.

**146** "I have a tale to unfold": SF to WP, 14 March 1952, SHC.

**146** "a mountain of woe": SF to WP, 23 March 1952, SHC.

**146** "I havent written one line": SF to WP, 9 April 1952, SHC.

**146** "For the first time": SF to WP, 9 April 1952, SHC.

**146** "The thing you dont understand": SF to WP, 16 February 1952, SHC.

**146** "Loneliness": SF to WP, Monday 1953, SHC.

**146** "I cant seem to learn": SF to WP, 9 April 1952, SHC.

**146** "I'm being dragged": SF to WP, March 1952, SHC.

**146** "I'm like a man": SF to WP, 9 April 1952, SHC.

**147** "I doubt": SF to WP, March 1952, SHC.

**147** "The coming success": SF to WP, March 1952, SHC.

**147** "anybody getting his shoes": Tillinghast 225.

**147** "I dont care": SF to WP, 7 May 1952, SHC.

**147** "I'm back at it": SF to WP, 2 June 1952, SHC.

**147** "writing brief": SF to WP, 2 June 1952, SHC.

**147** "possibly hold my mind": SF to WP, 2 June 1952, SHC.

**147** "sweating blood": SF to WP, 4 July 1952, SHC.

**147** "turned into a sort of sex fiend": SF to WP, 21 November 1952, SHC.

**147** "draining [his] vital energies": SF to WP, 21 November 1952, SHC.

**148** "intellectual type": SF to WP, 21 November 1952, SHC.

**148** "I should have stayed": SF to WP, 24 September 1952, SHC.

**148** Jones visit: SF to WP, 21 November 1952, SHC. Also interview with Clarke Reid.

**148** "I got interested": SF to WP, 12 December 1952, SHC.

**148** "early early history": SF to WP, 12 December 1952, SHC.

**148** "travel personality": SF to WP, 19 June 1953, SHC.

**148** "If God": SF to WP, 15 March 1953, SHC.

**148** "Dostoyevsky was absolutely right": SF to WP, Monday 1953, SHC.

**148** "I'm done with it": SF to WP, Monday 1953, SHC.

**149** "niggertown": SF to WP, 10 December 1953, SHC.

**149** Information on neighborhood: William Thomas, "Living on Bluff Had Special Quality, Recalls Author," *The (Memphis) Commercial Appeal,* 4 April 1973.

**150** "It's strange": SF to WP, 31 December 1951, SHC.

**150** "place for its hero": White and Sugg, *Shelby Foote* 49.

**151** "if it is a novel": Carr 35.

**151** "wont ... be happy": SF, *JC* 13.

**151** "emotionless prose style": Jerome Stone, "Jordan County, Miss.," *Saturday Review of Literature,* 5 June 1954: 34.

**151** "love": SF, *JC* 8.

**151** "Modern Bristol": Phillips 136.

**152** "Sell us the land": SF, *JC* 287.

**152** "put[ting] up houses": SF, *JC* 287.

**152** "Keeley several times": SF, *JC* 74.

**152** "killing flies": SF, *JC* 74.

**152** "Kluxers, smut ballots": SF, *JC* 225.

**153** "Captain, what was that?": SF, *JC* 227.

**153** "about freedom and justice": SF, *JC* 228.

**153** "cant justify": SF, *JC* 228.

**153** "one of the sainted names": SF, *JC* 260.

**153** "poetesses laureate": SF, *JC* 261.

**153** "Mother of Bristol": SF, *JC* 76.

**153** "New Orleans style": SF, *JC* 77.

**153** "Ohio merchant": SF, *JC* 78.

**153** "always in a hurry": SF, *JC* 127.

**154** "small-scale drawing[s]": SF, *JC* 146.

**154** "new ideas": SF, *JC* 146.

**154** "gridding the sheets": SF, *JC* 146.

**154** "the crowded, multicolored sheets": SF, *JC* 147.

**154** Homeric epics: Phillips 155.

**154** "total absorption": SF, *JC* 146.

**154** "troubled years": SF, *JC* 146.

**154** "the neat geometrical simplicity": SF, *JC* 146.

**154** "highborn Wingate tradition": SF, *JC* 146.

**154** "would see a thing": SF, *JC* 147.

**155** "In the end": SF, *JC* 147.

**155** "the foundation for a future Athens": SF, *JC* 145.

**155** "green for trees and lawns": SF, *JC* 146.

**155** "bound in tooled morocco": SF, *JC* 147.

**155** "placed on display": SF, *JC* 147.

**155** "crazy as a betsy bug": SF, *JC* 147.

**156** "To call": Coleman Rosenberger, "Fine Tales of Delta Country," *New York Herald Tribune*, 2 May 1954: 8.

**156** "The present volume": Edmund Fuller, "Deep South Vignettes," *The New York Times*, 25 April 1954: 29.

**156** "Mr. Foote's angry": "Briefly Noted," *The New Yorker*, 1 May 1954: 119.

**156** "like a grotesque parody": Fuller 29.

**156** " 'Jordan County' is perhaps": *Southern Observer*, June 1954.

**157** "a torturous novel": SF to WP, 19 February 1954, SHC.

**157** "For the past two months": SF to WP, 19 February 1954, SHC.

**158** "The one": SF to WP, 19 February 1954, SHC.

**158** Random House's history series: Newcomb 119.

**158** WP contacts Cerf: Interview with Bunt Percy.

**158** SF believes that Cerf had read *Shiloh:* Interview with SF.

**158** "short history": White and Sugg, "A Colloquium" 201.

**158** "pause and assessment": White and Sugg, "A Colloquium" 201.

**158** "that if I hadn't": Newcomb 129.

**158** "fiction is hard work": White and Sugg, "A Colloquium" 201.

**158** Money matters: SF to WP, 13 April 1955, SHC.

**158** SF's diet: Interview with Meg Turner.

**158** "Every story": Interview with SF.

**159**   "a frame": SF to WP, 9 August 1954, SHC.

**159**   "my history": SF to WP, 10 May 1955, SHC.

**159**   "Nothing about me": White and Sugg, "A Colloquium" 201.

**159**   "Instead of a short history": White and Sugg, "A Colloquium" 201.

**159**   "Go ahead; fine": White and Sugg, "A Colloquium" 201.

**159**   Advances for *The Civil War* volumes: Interview with SF.

**159**   "It expanded": White and Sugg, "A Colloquium" 201–2.

**160**   "If I had had any idea": Newcomb 121.

**160**   "It was a Monday": SF, Vol. I 3.

**160**   "Prayer may bring": SF to WP, 24 May 1951, SHC.

**160**   "enough to warrant": SF to WP, 15 December 1956, SHC.

**160**   "All I want": SF to WP, 31 January 1955, SHC.

**160**   SF's beard: Interview with Richard Leatherman.

**160**   "Dont underrate it": SF to WP, 13 April 1955, SHC.

**161**   "teaching me to love my country": SF to WP, 13 April 1955, SHC.

**161**   "What I have to do": SF to WP, 29 November 1956, SHC.

**161**   "re-create": SF, Vol. I 815.

**161**   "wonderfully human": SF to WP, 31 January 1955, SHC.

**161**   "furnace": SF to WP, 31 January 1955, SHC.

**161**   "poor damned forked-radish man": SF to WP, 31 January 1955, SHC.

**162**   "So far": SF to WP, 31 January 1955, SHC.

**162**   "It's what makes historians": Jones 171.

**162**   "Novelists know instinctively": Jones 171.

**162**   "As far as my": Charles Edmundson, "Writing Another Novel," *The (Memphis) Commercial Appeal*, 27 November 1961.

**163**   "For more than a decade": SF, Vol. I 3.

**163**   "be arrested as a traitor": SF, Vol. I 3–4.

**163**   Citizens' Councils membership: Charles Marsh, *The Last Days: A Son's Story of Sin and Segregation at the Dawn of a New South* (New York: Basic, 2001) 21.

**164**   "Most of the fear of Negroes": Carr 45.

**164**   "Shelby was way ahead of us": Interview with Richard Leatherman.

**164**   SF's ideas on integration: Interview with SF.

**164**   "passionate concern": Singal 23.

**164**   "The Ku Klux Klan": Bob Mottley, "Writer Critical of 'Tokenism' in South," *Conversations with Shelby Foote* 18.

**164**   LeRoy Percy's work against the Citizens' Council: SF to WP, 10 May 1956, SHC. SF misdates this letter. Originally, it was given only a "May 10" date, and when he submitted Percy's letters to the SHC in 1982, SF scrawled in "1955," although the subject matter of the letter clearly suggests that the letter was written in 1956.

**165**   Obligation to Mississippi reporters: Raad Cawthon, "Of text, Time and a Writer," *Jackson Clarion-Ledger*, 6 July 1982: 1D.

**165**   "If I had been down home": Interview with SF.

**165**   "American Iliad": SF to WP, 9 August 1954, SHC.

**165** "the Southern culture": Carr 29–30.

**166** "Forgive long silence": SF to WP, 12 January 1955, SHC.

**166** "the task of fitting a small brain": SF to WP, 19 February 1955, SHC.

**166** "My interest": SF to WP, 10 May 1955, SHC.

**166** "financial": SF to WP, 13 April 1955, SHC.

**166** "spare": SF to WP, 9 August 1954, SHC.

**166** "coterie carryings-on": SF to WP, 12 September 1954, SHC.

**166** "God bless Guggenheim!": SF to WP, 10 May 1955, SHC.

**166** "Never enjoyed anything more": SF to WP, Tuesday 1955, SHC.

**166** Trip to Antietam and Gettysburg: SF to WP, 10 May 1955, SHC.

**167** "little-known events": SF to WP, 31 January 1956, SHC.

**167** "Galloping twelve hours": SF, Vol. I 101.

**167** "Ive reached my limits": SF to WP, 1955, SHC.

**167** "Forgive delay": SF to WP, 31 January 1956, SHC.

**167** Applying for second Guggenheim: SF to WP, 13 April 1955, SHC.

**167** Filmscript details: Edwin Howard, "Hollywood's New 'Boy Wonder' Buys Two Stories from Memphis's Shelby Foote." *Memphis Press-Scimitar,* 13 June 1956.

**168** "These people": SF to WP, 31 January 1955, SHC.

**168** "Go if you want to": Edwin Howard, "Foote-Note on Faulkner," *Conversations with Shelby Foote* 14.

**168** "wanted no part of California": SF to WP, 31 January 1955, SHC.

**168** Meeting in New York: SF to WP, 31 January 1955, SHC.

**168** "They seem like good people": SF to WP, 18 February 1955, SHC.

**168** Wins second Guggenheim: SF to WP, 10 May 1956, SHC.

**168** "be glad to get back to my book": SF to WP, 30 June 1956, SHC.

**169** "a true picture": SF to WP, 30 June 1956, SHC.

**169** "I like it": SF to WP, 10 May 1956, SHC.

**169** "the only authentic genius": SF to WP, 30 June 1956, SHC.

**169** Peck and Mason refuse roles: Phillips 26.

**169** "Lauren Bacall-look alike": Samway 181.

**169** Shea's characteristics: Interviews with Mary Ann Eagle and Meg Turner.

**170** Ida Clements, "Ear Operation Developed by Young Memphis Doctor Alleviates Some Deafness," *The (Memphis) Commercial Appeal,* 27 March 1960.

**170** Shea's recommendation of Doris Mirrielees: SF to WP, Saturday 1955, SHC.

**170** "dissatisfaction with the marriage": Interview with Jim Rainer.

**170** "reverse snobbist": Interview with Mary Ann Eagle.

**170** "It was a big adventure for her": Interview with Mary Ann Eagle.

**170** "I'm in love": SF to WP, 8 August 1956, SHC.

**170** "Now I see beauty everywhere": SF to WP, 8 August 1956, SHC.

**170** "hooraw": SF to WP, 6 October 1956, SHC.

**170** "big thing": SF to WP, 6 October 1956, SHC. Also interview with Mary Ann Eagle.

**171** "couldn't believe that she would leave": Interview with Jim Rainer.

**171** John Shea's reaction: Interview with Meg Turner.

**171** "reasonable visitation": SF to WP, 6 October 1956, SHC.

**171** Gwyn's visit to Rome: Interview with Meg Turner.

**171** "prolonged spell of housecleaning": SF to WP, 6 October 1956, SHC.

**171** "Wife's name's Gwyn": SF to WP, 6 October 1956, SHC.

**172** "cant very well be told of": SF to WP, 6 October 1956, SHC.

**172** "young doctor": SF to WP, 6 October 1956, SHC.

**172** "I'm back at work": SF to WP, 6 October 1956, SHC.

**172** "All that's happened to me": SF to WP, 15 December 1956, SHC.

**172** "a sandy": SF, Vol. I 304.

**172** "the girls": SF to WP, 15 December 1956, SHC.

**172** "trying to bail out the Mississippi": SF to WP, 8 August 1956, SHC.

**173** "back in the mainstream": SF to WP, 15 December 1956, SHC.

**173** "held at all costs": SF, Vol. I 308.

**173** "which I can write": SF to WP, 23 March 1957, SHC.

**173** "I'm plugging along at the War": SF to WP, 15 December 1956, SHC.

**173** "Everyone saw it differently": SF to WP, 15 December 1956, SHC.

**173** "the only way to keep it simple": SF to WP, 15 December 1956, SHC.

**173** "The idea is to strike fire": SF to WP, 16 April 1957, SHC.

**173** "Dramatize! Dramatize!": "Volume I—By Shelby Foote," *Memphis Press-Scimitar,* 19 May 1958.

**173** "miracle of a book": SF to WP, 29 November 1956, SHC.

**173** "The Trojans came down": Quoted in SF to WP, 29 November 1956, SHC.

**174** "I never knew": SF to WP, 29 November 1956, SHC.

**174** "not one syllable of historic intervention": Lydel Sims, "Making Novel of Civil War Promises to Be 8-Year Task," *The (Memphis) Commercial Appeal,* 15 August 1958.

**174** "Ive been in a state of shock": SF to WP, 16 April 1957, SHC.

**174** "a writer learning his craft": SF to WP, 23 March 1957, SHC.

**174** "arent scholars": SF to WP, 23 March 1957, SHC.

**175** "Morale was shattered": SF to WP, 23 March 1957, SHC.

**175** "incredible: incredibly bad": SF to WP, 6 October 1956, SHC.

**175** "longrange": SF to WP, 6 October 1956, SHC.

**176** "holy war": SF, Vol. I 800.

**176** "negro man": "A Happy Ending: For Bo and the Novelist," *Memphis Press-Scimitar,* 28 January 1957.

**176** "covered a host of subjects": SF, Vol. I 806.

**176** "We say": SF, Vol. I 810.

**177** "through the droning voice": SF, Vol. I 810.

**177** Information on publication of Vol. I: "Volume I—By Shelby Foote," *Memphis Press-Scimitar,* 19 May 1958.

**177** "detract from": SF, Vol. I 815.

**177** "Footnotes are the very thing": John Cournos, "Bright Book of the Civil War," *Commonweal,* 9 January 1959: 393.

**177** "original sources": Frank Vandiver, "As Brothers Fought on Crimson Fields," *New York Times,* 16 November 1958: 1.

**177** "relates as accepted": Richard N. Current, *New York Herald Tribune Book Review,* 23 November 1958: 5.

**177** "largely a battlefield book": Jonathan Daniels, "Immortal Story Began at Sumter," *Saturday Review of Literature,* 13 December 1958: 18.

**177** "This bids fair": *Kirkus,* 1 October 1958: 794.

**178** "very breadth and scope": Vandiver 1.

**178** "significant and satisfying": Daniels 18.

**178** "vivid and readable": Francis Russell, "Platoon After Platoon," *The Christian Science Monitor,* 11 December 1958: 15.

**178** "Mr. Foote is a stylist": Vandiver 1.

**178** "Any one who wants": Current 5.

**178** "I think": SC to WP, 7 August 1958, SHC.

**179** "the spirit of enlistment": SF, Vol. II 5.

**179** "After an absence": SF, Vol. II 3.

**180** "Work goes good": SF to WP, 11 May 1959, SHC.

**180** "No prize-winner I": SF to WP, 11 May 1959, SHC.

**180** Wins Guggenheim: "Guggenheim for Shelby Foote," *The (Memphis) Commercial Appeal,* 20 April 1959.

**180** "We're about to be bulldozed": SF to WP, 18 April 1959, SHC.

**180** Annie Plunkett: Thomas, "Living on Bluff."

**180** "sort of hound": SF to WP, 11 May 1959, SHC.

**181** "tragedy": SF to WP, 18 June 1959, SHC.

**181** "no work": SF to WP, 18 June 1959, SHC.

**181** "I just lie here": SF to WP, 18 June 1959, SHC.

**181** "look at the field": SF to WP, 3 July 1959, SHC.

**181** "unsupported, heavily outnumbered": SF, Vol. II 37.

**181** "It is well": SF, Vol. II 37.

**181** "tremendous battle": SF to WP, 21 November 1959, SHC.

**181** "The work goes well": SF to WP, 21 November 1959, SHC.

**182** "There's a satisfaction": SF to WP, 21 November 1959, SHC.

**182** Work on Rosenstock graveyard: SF to WP, 21 November 1959, SHC.

**182** Dating of Vol. II chapters: Shelby Foote file, SHC, no. 4038, folder 36.

**182** "fantastic experience": SF to WP, 15 May 1960, SHC.

**182** "There wasnt a dry seat": SF to WP, 15 May 1960, SHC.

**182** "convulsed them": SF to WP, 15 May 1960, SHC.

**183** "It makes": SF to WP, 15 May 1960, SHC.

**183** "liveoaks and moss": SF to WP, 18 June 1960, SHC.

**183** "12 dozen": SF to WP, 18 June 1960, SHC.

**183** "a part of": SF to WP, 18 June 1960, SHC.

**183** "I know now": SF to WP, 18 June 1960, SHC.

**184** "Tell me something": SF to WP, 21 November 1959, SHC.

**184** "deliberate egghead who writes unreadable things": WP to SF, 12 May 1960, SHC.

**184** "It has a fine tone": SF to WP, 15 May 1960, SHC.

**185** "breakthrough of the spirit": SF to WP, 7 August 1960, SHC.

**185** "pleased Walker greatly": Samway 210.

**185** "moral fiber": SF to WP, 26 September 1960, SHC.

**185** "completely behind Kennedy": Tolson 289.

**185** "intelligence and wit": Tolson 289.

**185** Phin's familiarity with Kennedy: Tolson 289.

**186** Giobbi and SF celebrate Kennedy's victory: Interview with Ed Giobbi.

**186** "golden boy": SF to WP, 6 February 1961, SHC.

**186** "return of the native": SF to WP, 12 December 1960, SHC.

**186** "substantial monography": David Herbert Donald, "The Turning of the Tide," *New York Times Book Review,* 1 December 1963: 36.

**186** "second invasion": SF, Vol. II 431.

**186** "would march without delay": SF, Vol. II 431.

**187** "in case she drops": SF to WP, Wednesday October 1961, SHC.

**187** "no writing whatsoever": SF to WP, 31 January 1962, SHC.

**187** "a wild kaleidoscopic": SF, Vol. II 559.

**187** "waved his sword": SF, Vol. II 559.

**188** "maybe five, six times": Jones 167.

**188** "eight or nine times": Lucius Lampton, "Shelby Foote: A Conversation with the Prize-Winning Author Concerning the Civil War, Walker Percy, Pipe Smoking, and Bad Poetry," *Murmur* (the student newspaper of the Mississippi Medical Center, Jackson) May 1993: 9–12. A shorter version of the interview appeared in two parts in the Rhodes College student newspaper: Lucius Lampton, "Interview with Shelby Foote: Author of History and Fiction, Part 1," *The Sou'wester* 21 May 1987: 3; "Part 2," 28 May 1987: 3.

**188** "had particularly liked": Frederick Karl, *William Faulkner: American Writer* (New York: Weidenfeld and Nicolson, 1989) 1039.

**188** "A lot of us": Howard, "Foote-Note on Faulkner" 13.

**188** "compulsory segregation": Joseph Blotner, *Faulkner: A Biography,* Vol. 2 (New York: Random House, 1974) 1589.

**188** "If it came to fighting": Karl 933.

**188** "I blush": SF to WP, 6 December 1951, SHC.

**189** "I feel death in the air": SF to WP, 13 August 1963, SHC.

**190** "Yonder began": SF, Vol. II 966.

**190** "I went up": Jones 194.

**191** "curious mixup of traits": Jones 194.

**191** "We've got to preserve": Jones 194–95.

**191** "a complete bibliography": SF, Vol. II 970.

**191** "I am obligated": SF, Vol. II 971.

**192** "The second volume": Richard Harwell, "An Impartial History that Favors Dixie," *Chicago Tribune,* 17 November 1963: 4.

**192** "If there is anything": Phoebe Adams, "Reader's Choice," *Atlantic Monthly,* December 1963: 156.

**192** "It is on the question": T. Harry Williams, *Bookweek,* 15 December 1963: 5.

**192** "formal bibliography": Williams 5.

**192** "Unlike both his distinguished rivals": David Herbert Donald, "The Turning of the Tide," *The New York Times Book Review,* 1 December 1963: 36.

**193** "story of the fortunes": James Nelson Goodsell, "Crushing Assault on Confederate Citadels," *St. Louis Post Dispatch,* 29 December 1963.

**193** "To give unity": Donald 36.

**193** "We now have": *The Dallas News,* 17 November 1963.

**194** "One closes": Louis Rubin, "Finest History of Civil War," *The Baltimore Sun,* 2 December 1963.

**194** "The freshness": *The Dallas News,* 17 November 1963.

**194** "Compared with Civil War II": Francis Russell, "The Second Civil War," *Christian Science Monitor,* 4 December 1963: 13.

**195** "four years": Edmundson, "Writing Another Novel."

**196** "beautiful campus": SF to WP, 7 October 1949, SHC.

**196** "shows promise": William Faulkner, *Faulkner in the University: Class Conferences at the University of Virginia 1957–58,* Ed. Frederick L. Gwynn and Joseph L. Blotner (Charlottesville: University of Virginia Press, 1977) 50.

**196** "as I practice it": SF to James Kibler, 15 July 1971, quoted in Kibler, "Shelby Foote: A Bibliography," *Mississippi Quarterly,* Fall 1971: 459.

**196** "why more writers": Edwin Howard, "Year of Foote Lights Beginning," *Memphis Press-Scimitar,* 24 September 1963.

**197** "I'm very pro-Kennedy": Howard, "Year of Foote Lights Beginning."

**197** "They thought they": Interview with Lila Saunders.

**197** "interesting to see": Howard, "Year of Foote Lights Beginning."

**197** "I don't think": Newcomb 124–25.

**197** "anger": Tolson 313.

**198** "Kennedy": WP, *The Last Gentleman* 357.

**198** Plans to borrow books at the Library of Congress: Howard, "Year of Foote Lights Beginning."

**198** "do some research": Jones 181.

**198** "all the time": Phillips 27.

**198** "never around": Anonymous interview.

**198** "sort of vacation": Jones 181.

**198** "We spent": Jones 181.

**198** "Proust said somewhere": Interview with SF.

**199** Fight with Meg Turner: Interview with Meg Turner.

**199** "The play": Phillips 27.

**200** "The sea's edge": SF to WP, 13 August 1963, SHC.

**200** "I wanted something": Interview with SF.

**200** "very hot": Interview with SF.

**201** "Well, it could be": Interview with Kenneth Haxton.

**201** "crossways with the Ku Klux Klan": Jones 181.

**201** "embroiled in name-calling": Tolson 322.

**201** "Man, you're wrong": Tolson 322. See also Covington 15.

**201** "translated themselves": Jones 182.

**201** "believed in law and order": Jones 182.

**202** "I told them every time": Jones 182.

**202** "that liberal writer": Tolson 322.

**202** Thinking about carrying a pistol: Covington 15.

**202** "It was an about-face": Samway 237.

**203** "beautiful house": Interview with SF.

**203** "It was the most remarkable": Interview with Lila Saunders.

**203** "in a fifty-mile-an-hour wind": Interview with SF.

**203** "tripled": Interview with SF.

**203** Editor pushing SF: Covington 15.

**203** "Late afternoon": SF, Vol. III 3.

**203** "rather a scrubby look": SF, Vol. III 3.

**203** "Kafkaesque": SF to WP, 19 January 1966, SHC.

**204** "God bless us all": SF to WP, 19 January 1966, SHC.

**204** "I feel wonderfully encouraged": SF to WP, 19 January 1966, SHC.

**204** "I've moved four times": Covington 15.

**205** "moved from Raleigh": Shelby Foote file, SHC, no. 4038, folder 39.

**205** "novelist of Mr. Foote's caliber": Covington 15.

**205** "I felt": Covington 15.

**205** "I'm really concerned": Covington 15.

**205** "earning": SF to WP, 17 January 1967, SHC.

**205** "I don't believe": Covington 15.

**205** "discuss my notion": Covington 15.

**205** Lecture subjects: SF to WP, 17 January 1967, SHC.

**206** "Truth to tell": SF to WP, 17 January 1967, SHC.

**206** "only thing that really matters": SF to WP, 17 January 1967, SHC.

**206** "four-week layoff": Shelby Foote file, SHC, no. 4038, folder 50.

**206** Margaret and Peggy in Ireland: Interview with Mary Ann Eagle. Also, anonymous interview.

**207** "favorite novel": Interview with Carol Leatherman.

**207** "I was about to despair": SF to WP, 23 May 1968, SHC.

**207** "hippie or no": SF to WP, 23 May 1968, SHC.

**207** "They arent nearly": SF to WP, 19 March 1968, SHC.

**207** "The main problem": Mottley 18.

**207** "they thought I was a nut": Mottley 19.

**207** "the size of half a grapefruit": SF to WP, 19 March 1968, SHC.

**208** "It's a strange thing": SF to WP, 19 March 1968, SHC.

**208** "depression of spirit": SF to WP, 23 May 1968, SHC.

**208** "This week": SF to WP, 28 October 1969, SHC.

**208** "Rebel prisoner": SF to WP, 19 January 1970, SHC.

**209** Margaret's accident: SF to WP, 15 June 1970, SHC.

**209** "few pills": SF to WP, 15 June 1970, SHC.

**209** Margaret is not on plane: Interview with Mary Ann Eagle.

**209** Margaret dances at strip club: Interview with Phillip Carter.

**209** "One child, a son": Lamb 11.

**209** "the freaked-out young": SF to WP, 5 August 1970, SHC.

**209** "air": SF to WP, 17 November 1969, SHC.

**210** "skeleton": SF to WP, 19 January 1970, SHC.

**210** "I've been haunted lately": SF to WP, 19 January 1970, SHC.

**210** "expert witness": WP to SF, 12 June 1970, SHC. See also Tolson 352–53.

**210** "You always did care": SF to WP, 15 June 1970, SHC.

**211** "that catches it": SF to WP, 15 June 1970, SHC.

**211** "The South": SF to WP, 15 June 1970, SHC.

**211** "You're going to end like": WP to SF, 9 July 1971, SHC.

**211** "a bloody mess": SF to WP, 5 August 1970, SHC.

**211** "We freed the Negro": SF to WP, 5 August 1970, SHC.

**212** "my stretch of good work": SF to WP, 9 October 1971, SHC.

**212** "The Miss. Quarterly": SF to WP, 7 February 1972, SHC.

**212** "annual goat dance": SF to WP, 28 April 1972, SHC.

**212** "a weekend spent lying up in bed": SF to WP, 28 April 1972, SHC.

**213** "old indeed": SF to WP, 28 April 1972, SHC.

**213** "it occurs to me": SF to WP, 28 April 1972, SHC.

**213** "to stay here and work": SF to WP, 19 June 1972, SHC.

**213** "I'm truly excited": SF to WP, 6 July 1972, SHC.

**213** "could get together": SF to WP, 19 June 1972, SHC.

**213** "I got into a stretch of work": SF to WP, 6 July 1972, SHC.

**213** "I wish you could get up here": SF to WP, 6 July 1972, SHC.

**214** "Stand fast": SF to WP, 6 July 1972, SHC.

**214** "Sorry to have been so wobbly": SF to WP, 26 January 1973, SHC.

**214** "deep into a Lincoln thing": SF to WP, 26 January 1973, SHC.

**214** "Working tail off": SF to WP, 26 January 1973, SHC.

**214** "You know how much": SF to WP, 26 January 1973, SHC.

**214** "All well here": SF to WP, 17 March 1973, SHC.

**214** "blow my brains out": SF to WP, 13 May 1973, SHC.

**214** "Me and Gibbon": SF to WP, 17 March 1973, SHC.

**214** "Evacuated Richmond yesterday": SF to WP, 13 May 1973, SHC.

**215** "I'm working like a fiend": SF to WP, 10 July 1973, SHC.

**215** "vicious head cold": SF to WP, 16 August 1973, SHC.

**215** "sorry bunch of coves": SF to WP, 16 August 1973, SHC.

**215** "an amazing revelation": SF to WP, 10 December 1972, SHC.

**215** "not even pitiful": SF to WP, 16 August 1973, SHC.

**215** "There's a strange sort of twilight": SF to WP, 16 August 1973, SHC.

**215** "There was never an army": SF to WP, 16 August 1973, SHC.

**216** "I killed Lincoln last week": SF to WP, 11 December 1973, SHC.

**216** "his chest arched up": SF to WP, 11 December 1973, SHC.

**216** "captured Jeff Davis yesterday": SF to WP, 22 January 1974, SHC.

**216** "into the final": SF to WP, 22 January 1974, SHC.

**216** "I'm feeling as if I'm about to be orphaned": SF to WP, 22 January 1974, SHC.

**216** "Twenty years!": SF to WP, 22 April 1974, SHC.

**217** Completion date of Vol. III: Shelby Foote file, SHC, no. 4038, folder 51.

**217** "very special bottle of wine": Thomas, "Shelby Foote's Love Affair."

**217** "I hope tis doesn't clash": SF to WP, 22 April 1974, SHC.

**217** "has something of the look and heft": SF to WP, 16 October 1974, SHC.

**217** "drifting, waiting": SF to WP, 26 August 1974, SHC.

**217** "sobbing": SF to WP, 7 November 1974, SHC.

**218** "purely military history": C. Vann Woodward, "The Great American Butchery," *The New York Review of Books,* 6 March 1975: 12.

**218** "While he is willing to admit": Woodward 12.

**218** "old-style history": Louis Rubin, "Old-Style History," *The New Republic,* 30 November 1974: 44.

**218** "too dense with facts": Phoebe Adams, "Short Reviews: Books," *Atlantic Monthly,* December 1974: 128.

**218** "Written with flowing style": Rubin, "Old-Style History" 45.

**219** "The result is not only monumental": Peter S. Prescott, "Where the Action Was," *Newsweek,* 2 December 1974: 102.

**219** "To the complaint": Nash Burger, "The Civil War," *The New York Times Book Review,* 15 December 1974: 3.

**219** "Not by accident": Prescott 103.

**219** "When novelist Shelby Foote": Rubin, "Old-Style History" 44.

**219** "It is Shelby Foote's good fortune": Rubin, "Old-Style History" 44.

**219** "All three volumes": Rubin, "Old-Style History" 44–45.

**220** "To read [this] chronicle": Prescott 103.

**221** "lusting after": SF to WP, 4 December 1974, SHC.

**222** "I had more or less": SF to WP, 29 April 1975, SHC.

**222** "fribbled": SF to WP, 5 May 1975, SHC.

**222** "So much for litry matters": SF to WP, 5 May 1975, SHC.

**223** "Dumas Malone won": SF to WP, 5 May 1975, SHC.

**223** "it was probably": Interview with Richard Leatherman. Also interview with Lila Saunders.

**223** "bitter and angry": Interview with SF.

**223** Earliest mention of novel: SF to WP, 3 July 1974, SHC.

**223** "Three Mississippi gangsters": SF to WP, 3 July 1974, SHC.

**223** "piled up": SF to WP, 14 February 1977, SHC.

**224** "all that dirty": SF, *SS* (New York: Vintage, 1991) 163.

**224** "I figure": SF to WP, 3 July 1974, SHC.

**224** "You can't tell": SF to WP, 5 April 1975, SHC.

**224** "flown into a frenzy of activity": SF to WP, 4 October 1975, SHC.

**224** "flaming offers": SF to WP, 4 October 1975, SHC.

**224** "under the double influence": SF to WP, 4 October 1975, SHC.

**224** Contract details: Random House contract.

**225** Time parameters: SF to WP, 26 July 1975, SHC.

**225** "They were waiting": SF, *SS* 31.

**225** "The papers brought it all back": Interview with SF.

**225** "knew what time the sun came up": Thomas, "Appomattox for Shelby Foote."

**225** "President Eisenhower": SF, *SS* 8, 47.

**226** "all-Negro section": SF, *SS* 25.

**226** "the three mile-long bridges": SF, *SS* 10.

**226** "disappear into the dark abyss": SF to WP, 4 October 1975, SHC.

**226** "noodle around": SF to WP, 4 October 1975, SHC.

**226** "discussions with a Harlemite": SF to WP, 29 June 1977, SHC.

**226** "I told some interviewer": SF to WP, 29 June 1977, SHC.

**227** "scared [the] hell out of me": SF to WP, 29 June 1977, SHC.

**227** "bourgeois Negroes": SF to WP, 29 June 1977, SHC.

**227** "then romp[ing] happily": SF to WP, 4 October 1975, SHC.

**227** "tuned in to the inner workings": SF to WP, 4 October 1975, SHC.

**227** "What type of a fellow": WP to SF, 9 October 1975, SHC.

**227** "Dont underrate Shelley": SF to WP, 11 October 1975, SHC.

**228** "During one of those session": SF to WP, 25 September 1976, SHC.

**228** "Shelby was writing": SF to WP, 25 September 1976, SHC.

**228** "You can imagine": SF to WP, 25 September 1976, SHC.

**228** "What compliment": SF to WP, 25 September 1976, SHC.

**228** "trembling on the verge": SF to WP, 23 January 1976, SHC.

**228** "long synopsis-outline": SF to WP, 23 January 1976, SHC.

**229** "It was a bad time": SF, *SS* 1.

**229** Drunken driving incident: "Charges Continued in Historian's Case," *Memphis Press-Scimitar,* 14 September 1976.

**229** "Things are going well": SF to WP, 25 September 1976, SHC.

**229** "I intend to hang on tight": SF to WP, 25 September 1976, SHC.

**229** "Mine's a boomer": SF to WP, 17 November 1976, SHC.

**230** "shiny white Thunderbird": SF, *SS* 265.

**230** "Well, that's one piece of luck"; SF, *SS* 298.

**230** "Whatever else I did": SF to WP, 29 June 1977, SHC.

**230** "apprehensive of violence": SF, *SS* 81.

**231** "blanket invitation": SF, *SS* 80, 79, 78.

**231** "my money": SF, *SS* 249.

**231** "a chance at something real": SF, *SS* 140.

**231** "society type": SF, *SS* 49.

**231**  "never touched so much": SF, *SS* 74.

**232**  "He was talking about": SF, *SS* 74.

**232**  "You take um": SF, *SS* 74–75.

**232**  "inexcusable auctorial voice-over": Walter Clemons, *Newsweek*, 30 January 1978: 67.

**232**  "cheating and petty theft": SF, *SS* 45, 47, 99.

**232**  "the clarinet solo": SF, *SS* 276.

**232**  "Blind now": SF, *SS* 194–95.

**233**  "other forgotten heroes": SF, *SS* 194–95.

**233**  "*September September* is real good": WP to SF, 22 June 1977, SHC.

**233**  "(1) the handling of the details": WP to SF, 22 June 1977, SHC.

**233**  "represented blacks properly": Interview with D'Army Bailey.

**233**  "didn't know": Interview with D'Army Bailey.

**233**  "almost apologetic": Interview with D'Army Bailey.

**234**  *Tournament* as juvenalia: Interview with SF.

**234**  "pending": SF to WP, 2 December 1977, SHC.

**234**  "I cant really imagine": SF to WP, 2 December 1977, SHC.

**234**  "Shelby Foote moves": Richard Freedman, "Trouble in Memphis and Boston," *New York Times Book Review*, 5 March 1978: 15.

**234**  "gives the novel": Freedman 15.

**234**  "returned to fiction": Clemons 67.

**234**  "a slow starter": Clemons 67.

**234**  "a humane": Clemons 67.

**234**  "He is rather less assured": Freedman 15.

**234**  "knowledge of Sibelius": Freedman 15.

**235**  "not a perfect artist": Clemons 67.

**235**  "Mr. Foote has sacrificed suspense": Phoebe Adams, "PLA," *Atlantic Monthly*, March 1978: 128.

**235**  "book is crippling along": SF to WP, 1 March 1978, SHC.

**235**  "more or less marking time": SF to WP, 1 March 1978, SHC.

**235**  "Which it might do": SF to WP, 1 March 1978, SHC.

**235**  "Rosen says": SF to WP, 1 March 1978, SHC.

**235**  "selling at a trickle": SF to WP, 6 April 1978, SHC.

**235**  "snakebit": SF to WP, 6 April 1978, SHC.

**235**  "This will put me in clover": SF to WP, 12 September 1978, SHC.

**236**  "gone ape": SF to WP, 2 December 1977, SHC.

**236**  "fascinating": SF to WP, 2 December 1977, SHC.

**237**  "Fortunately, I really don't know": SF to WP, 25 January 1979, SHC.

**237**  "The beauty of B.O.M.": WP to SF, 8 February 1977, SHC.

**238**  New book: Random House contract. In possession of Stuart Chapman.

**239**  Changes in "Two Gates": Interview with SF.

**239**  "a sort of Civil War": SF to WP, 25 September 1976, SHC.

**239**  "I propose to examine": SF to WP, 4 March 1978, SHC.

**239**  "Big Sixty": SF to WP, 25 September 1976, SHC.

**239**  "plotting and counterplotting": SF to WP, 22 March 1978, SHC.

**239**  "should be cut down": Scott Ware, "Author Attacks Parish as 'A Dangerous Man,'" *Memphis Press-Scimitar,* 3 April 1978.

**239**  "I have a great deal of respect": Ware, "Author Attacks Parish."

**240**  "It is not true": Thomas, "Appomattox for Shelby Foote" 23.

**240**  "How in God's name": SF to WP, 12 June 1978, SHC.

**240**  "One of the great satisfactions": SF, "Echoes of Shiloh," *National Geographic,* July 1979: 111.

**241**  "boxed": SF to WP, 25 January 1979, SHC.

**241**  "You just wait and see": SF to WP, 25 January 1979, SHC.

**241**  "plots and elbows": SF to WP, 2 May 1979, SHC.

**241**  "foolishness": SF to WP, 2 May 1979, SHC.

**241**  "I'm just winding up": SF to WP, 29 June 1977, SHC.

**241**  "I suddenly remembered": SF to WP, 25 January 1979, SHC.

**242**  "spend a week or ten days": SF to WP, 10 March 1979, SHC.

**242**  "I cant start": SF to WP, 2 May 1979, SHC.

**242**  "all my people": SF to WP, 2 May 1979, SHC.

**242**  "I keep telling myself": SF to WP, 2 May 1979, SHC.

**242**  "Ive long had": SF to WP, 2 May 1979, SHC.

**242**  "which of course": SF to WP, 2 May 1979, SHC.

**242**  "I'm still blocked and blocking": SF to WP, 6 September 1980, SHC.

**243**  "The only thing to do": WP to SF, 10 September 1980, SHC.

**243**  "Get on with Two Gates": WP to SF, 10 September 1980, SHC.

**243**  "Hope you're forging ahead": WP to SF, 21 November 1981, SHC.

**243**  "I was trying": Interview with SF.

**243**  "I cant imagine": SF to WP, 2 May 1979, SHC.

**243**  "actually written": SF to WP, 17 December 1987, SHC.

**244**  "resurgent nostalgia": Horowitz 87.

**244**  "Remembrance of the War": Horowitz 136.

**244**  Taping Vol. III sections: Shelby Foote file, SHC, no. 4038, folder 51.

**244**  Shelby Foote Day: Charles Overby, "Mississippi's Gifted Authors Finally Get a Foote in the Door," *Jackson Clarion-Ledger,* 5 September 1982: 1.

**245**  "God forbid": SF to WP, 3 February 1980, SHC.

**245**  "It pleases me greatly": SF to WP, 3 February 1980, SHC.

**245**  Reading group: Interviews with Charlie Newman, Bill Reid, and Billy Pearson.

**245**  "I think": Interview with Meg Turner.

**246**  "You take": Interview with Bunt Percy.

**246**  "Walker, I think": Interview with Bunt Percy.

**246**  Blockage report: SF to WP, 23 July 1983, SHC.

**246**  Angioplasty success: SF to WP, 23 July 1983, SHC.

**246**  "violently opposed": William Thomas, "Shelby Foote: Getting Back to the Big Family Novel after Three Years before the Past," *The (Memphis) Commercial Appeal,* 17 March 1985: J5.

**247**   "I wrote every page": Interview with SF.

**247**   "I'll stay with all that": SF to WP, 30 April 1983, SHC.

**247**   "plaque ... stayed stuck": SF to WP, 23 July 1983, SHC.

**247**   "But, my God": SF to WP, 5 July 1983, SHC.

**247**   "literary worth or influence": SF, list of ninety-nine greatest books. In possession of Stuart Chapman.

**247**   "they would have to split my chest": SF to WP, 23 July 1983, SHC.

**248**   "gloom": SF to WP, 23 July 1983, SHC.

**248**   "walked till I was puffed": SF to WP, 23 July 1983, SHC.

**248**   "lace up [his] Nickeys": SF to WP, 24 September 1986, SHC.

**248**   "I listen to": Thomas, "Shelby Foote: Getting Back."

**248**   Paris visit: Interview with SF.

**249**   "Does this sound familiar?": WP to SF, 17 March 1984, SHC.

**249**   "transformation of common nouns": WP to SF, 17 March 1984, SHC.

**249**   "mixture of awe and irritation": WP to SF, 17 March 1984, SHC.

**249**   "What one is most aware of": WP to SF, 17 March 1984, SHC.

**249**   "The best news": SF to WP, 3 March 1984, SHC.

**250**   "For these and other reasons": SF to WP, 3 March 1984, SHC.

**250**   "We'd have a great time": SF to WP, 23 March 1985, SHC.

**250**   "blooming outrage": SF to WP, 23 March 1985, SHC.

**250**   "I'm not sure I approve": SF to WP, 23 April 1985, SHC.

**250**   "live out my normal span": SF to WP, 15 December 1985, SHC.

**251**   "Doctor tells me": SF to WP, 14 April 1986, SHC.

**251**   "Since you quote me": SF to WP, 15 September 1986, SHC.

**251**   "I deeply appreciate": WP to SF, 20 September 1986, SHC.

**251**   "humor and irony": WP to SF, 20 September 1986, SHC.

**252**   "five years that intervened": SF, *T* preface.

**252**   "a somewhat smart-ass collection": WP to SF, 29 July 1989, SHC.

**252**   "Gabrielle and Tiny argued": SF to WP, 4 July 1987, SHC.

**252**   "Tina split the scene": SF to WP, 29 August 1987, SHC.

**253**   Monteagle visit: WP to SF, 4 August 1987, SHC.

**253**   "My God, my God": SF to WP, 8 August 1987, SHC.

**253**   "If we meet": SF to WP, 8 August 1987, SHC.

**253**   Percy's drugs: WP to SF, 29 July 1989, SHC.

**253**   "My God, my God": SF to WP, 27 December 1988, SHC.

**254**   "He was researching dying": SF to WP, 27 December 1988, SHC.

**254**   "The Bishop is in poor shape": WP to SF, 12 June 1989, SHC.

**254**   "Not such good news here": WP to SF, 8 June 1989, SHC.

**254**   "I've got an hour.": Quoted in Tolson 487.

**255**   "Sad time": Quoted in Tolson 487.

**255**   "holding court": Interview with William Alexander Percy II.

**255**   "The English essayist": Quoted in Tolson 492.

**258**   "It's too bad": Interview with Bunt Percy.

**258**  "the power of television": Louis Rubin to Dr. George Sheldon, 22 March 1993, SHC.

**258**  "a kind of video folk hero": Michelle Green and David Hutchings, "The Civil War Finds a Home in Writer Shelby Foote," *People,* 15 October 1990: 61.

**258**  "drama the networks": Tom Walter, "Civil War Revisited," *The (Memphis) Commercial Appeal,* 23 September 1990: G1.

**258**  "soap opera": "Foote Pans TV's 'Soapy' Civil War," *The (Memphis) Commercial Appeal,* 18 November 1982.

**258**  "just one among many": Interview with Ken Burns.

**259**  "In that great Southern voice": Interview with Ken Burns.

**259**  "stink too much": Interview with SF.

**259**  "when Red Warren": Interview with Ken Burns.

**259**  "I dont much go for that stuff": SF to WP, 14 April 1986, SHC.

**259**  Reason for accepting consultant position: SF to WP, 14 April 1986, SHC.

**259**  Initial Burns response: Interview with Ken Burns.

**260**  "story": Interview with Ken Burns.

**260**  "didn't give away": Interview with Ken Burns.

**260**  "showhorses and workhorses": Interview with Ken Burns.

**260**  "pontificated": Interview with Ken Burns.

**260**  "Shelby could": Interview with Ken Burns.

**260**  "copious notes": Interview with Ken Burns.

**261**  "smarter": Interview with Ken Burns.

**261**  "God is the greatest dramatist": Quoted in interview with Ken Burns.

**261**  "one of the greatest shooting ratios": Interview with Ken Burns.

**261**  "whether they're going to be": Interview with Ken Burns.

**262**  "We are living": Tom Shales, "'Civil War': A Triumph on All Fronts," *The Washington Post,* 2 October 1990: E1.

**262**  "blazed new trails": Shales E1.

**262**  "viewers": Walter G2.

**262**  "masterly": Green and Hutchings 61.

**262**  "none had quite the presence": Charles Trueheart, "The Historian Storyteller," *The Washington Post,* 2 October 1990: E3.

**262**  "the punctuations of light in his eyes": Trueheart E1.

**262**  "Toast of Public Television": Trueheart E1.

**262**  "the media's newest darling": Craig Wilson, "Shelby Foote, Reflecting on His 'Civil War,'" *USA Today,* 1 October 1990: 4D.

**262**  "Prime Time's New Star": Trueheart E1.

**262**  See Richard King, *A Southern Renaissance: The Cultural Awakening of the American South, 1930–1955* (New York: Oxford University Press, 1980) 29 ff.

**262**  "pipe-smoker who admires Mozart": Wilson 4D.

**262**  "didn't matter": Interview with Ken Burns.

**263**  "a drawling delivery": Green and Hutchings 61.

**263**  "They just blotted out": Trueheart E1.

**263**  "courtly": Green and Hutchings 61.

**263** "the last of the Southern gentlemen": Quoted in Wilson 4D.

**263** "in cool weather": Wilson 4D.

**263** "played the part": Interview with Bern Keating.

**263** "went off the register": Trueheart E3.

**263** Sales of SF's books: Trueheart E3. Also interview with Bill Reid.

**263** "Ken, you've made me a millionaire": Interview with Ken Burns.

**264** "I'll go to places": Interview with SF.

**264** "build a nest egg": Interview with SF.

**264** "Where have you all been?": Interview with SF.

**265** "opportunists and star-chasers": William Thomas, "Shelby Foote's 'War,'" *AARP Bulletin*, November 1990: 16.

**265** "A woman named Baer": Thomas, "Shelby Foote's 'War.'"

**265** Three sexiest American men: Interview with Lila Saunders.

**265** "different from everybody else": Thomas, "Shelby Foote's 'War.'"

**265** Telephone calls: Thomas, "Shelby Foote's 'War.'"

**265** Radio programs: Green and Hutchings 61–62.

**265** "friendly and informative": Interview with Trent Scofield.

**265** "Everywhere I go": Interview with Fred Smith.

**265** "They were getting ready": Interview with Fred Smith.

**266** "Do you have": Interview with SF.

**266** "Disney people": Michael Posner, "Historians Join to Battle Disney over Theme Park," *Chicago Sun-Times*, 12 May 1994: 46.

**266** Congressional resolution introduced: "Rebelling Against Disney," *New York Times*, 19 June 1994: 41.

**266** "huge surprise": "Disney Becomes History": *USA Today*, 30 September 1994: 10A.

**266** "a banner of shame": Horowitz 153.

**267** "stood for law": Horowitz 153.

**267** "a lot": Branston 49–50.

**267** "enjoy the muggings": Branston 50.

**267** "What has dismayed me": Horowitz 152.

**267** "This was a side": Horowitz 152.

**267** "like a cat": Wilson 4D.

**267** "I'll be glad": Wilson 4D.

**268** "I don't want to show up": Interview with Clarke Reid.

**268** "highly evocative": SF, "Introduction," *The Red Badge of Courage* (New York: Random House, 1993) xxxii.

**268** "true": SF, "Introduction" xxxvii.

**268** "is merely responsible": SF, "Introduction" l.

**269** "I'm not going to continue": Interview with SF.

**269** "I don't intend to write": Interview with SF.

# INDEX

Adalotte, Gus, 200
Alabama, University of, 174–75
Alcorn, James L., 14
American Academy of Arts and Sciences, 264
Anderson, Sherwood, 38
Aristotle, 158–59, 261
Athenaeum, 224

Bailey, D'Army, xiv, xv, xxi, 233
Baldwin, James, 226
Ballentine Books, 235
Banks, Nathaniel, 183, 203
Barnett, Ross, xx, 189, 191–92
Barry, John, 30–31
Bayou Teche, 183–84
Beatty, Ned, 199
Beauregard, P. T., 173
Bell, Charles, 36
Bell, John C., 9–10
Belmont, Mo., 10
Benet, Stephen Vincent, 38
Bergin, Thomas, 222
Berryman, Francis (great-great-great-great grandmother), 4
Blotner, Joseph, 188
*Blue Book* magazine, 113
Booth, John Wilkes, 215, 217
Bragg, Braxton, 181
Breckinridge, John C., 10
Brent Town, Va., 3, 4
Brice's Crossroads, 104
Brooke, Turner, 65
Brown, John, 9, 215

*Brown vs. Board of Education*, 157, 163
Browning, Robert, 45–46
Burch, Lucius "Luke," 111
Burns, Ken, 251, 257–62
Burns, Ric, 251, 259
Burnside, Ambrose, 161, 181
Burton, Richard, 48
Butler, Benjamin, 212

Cabell, James Branch, 21
Carnegie, Andrew, 211
Carr, John, 165
Carson, Johnny, 264
Carter, Betty, 28, 71
Carter, Hodding, 71, 105, 115
Carter, Jimmy, 240
Catton, Bruce, 135, 159, 162, 193, 194
Cedar Grove, Va., 4
Cerf, Bennett, 158, 177
Chambrun, Jacques, 110, 113
Chekov, Anton, 253–54, 268
Chotank Plantation, 4
Citizens Councils, 163, 164–65
Clarke, Charles, 11
Cleburne, Patrick, 166, 181
Clinton, Bill, 266
Cobb, James C., 13, 14, 17, 18, 26–27, 39
Cohn, David, 38, 111
Coindreau, Maurice, 236
Collins, George, 14
Columbus, Miss., 6, 7, 13
Constitutional Union Party, 9, 10
Crane, Stephen, 105, 268

Crittenden, O. B., 16, 17

Crockett, Davy, 148, 233

Crump, Edward, 232, 233

Custer, George, 168

Dade, Frances Lucinda (first wife of Henry), 7, 8

Dante, 222

Davis, Jefferson, 159, 160, 163, 179–80, 182, 213, 215, 216

Davis, Richard Beale, 241

Deans, Fred, 245

Denning, Michael, 77

Dial Press, 113, 115, 116, 123, 133, 134, 135, 137, 156

Dickens, Charles, 247

Dos Passos, John, 65, 196

Dostoyevsky, Fyodor, 144, 148, 239, 241, 250

Doughty, C. M., 48

Douglas, Stephen, 10

Early, Jean Kent, 241

Edmundson, Charles, 195

Eisenhower, Dwight, 176, 185

Eliot, T. S., 46

*Enola Gay*, 97

Euripides, 3

Evans, William, 112

Farragut, David, 208

Faubus, Orval, 46, 176, 189, 191–92

Faulkner, William: death of, 187–88; on Hollywood, 168; and Levee Press, 105; mentioned in elegy for WP, 255–56; SF's review of *Absalom, Absalom!*, 66; on SF's works, 124, 138, 196, 228; visits from SF, 73–74, 187; at WAP party, 40; works of, 15, 42, 97, 223–34, 247

Fénelon, François de Salignac de La Mothe, 70

Fields, Barbara, 258, 260

Foner, Eric, 258

Foote, Elizabeth (great-great-great-great-great grandmother), 4

Foote, George, I (great-great-great-great grandfather), 4

Foote, George, II (great-great-great grandfather), 3, 4–6

Foote, Gilson, I (brother of George II), 4

Foote, Gilson, II (son of Gilson I), 8

Foote, Gwyn Rainer (third wife), 169–71, 172, 175, 177, 180, 185, 187, 197, 201, 213, 246, 250, 255, 264

Foote, Hezekiah William "Henry" (great grandfather): birth of, 6; children of, 8; death of, 19; plantation owner, 8, 14–15, 17–18, 19; politician, 7, 8, 9–10, 12–13, 14; soldier, 6, 10–12

Foote, Horton, 260

Foote, Huger Lee "Huggy" (son): birth of, 187; college, 245; expelled from high school, 245; in Paris, 250; wounded by gunshot, 267

Foote, Huger Lee "Hugh" (grandfather): birth of, 18; children, 18; education, 14–15; first wife dies, 17; gambling, 20; and Mount Holly, 18–19; plantation owner, 17–19; politician, 18–19; wealth of, 19

Foote, James (brother of William), 5

Foote, Lillian Rosenstock (mother), 16, 21–23, 24, 25–26, 27, 28, 29, 31–32, 41, 48, 50–51, 85, 94, 98, 206, 207–08

Foote, Margaret (first wife of George II), 5

Foote, Margaret (daughter): automobile accident, 209; birth of, 117; drug problems, 209; at Hollins College, 207; injures father, 181; in Ireland, 206

Foote, Mary Cavett (first wife of Hugh), 17

Foote, Mollie Frances (half-sister of Hugh), 8

Foote, Richard, I (great-great-great-great-great grandfather), 3–4

Foote, Richard, II (brother of George I), 4

Foote, Richard, III (son of Richard II), 4–5

Foote, Shelby Dade, Jr.: ages, 212–13; and American capitalism, 211; and Anne Hargrave, 61–62; and Ben Wasson, 97–98; born, 23–24; and *The Civil War* television series, 251, 257–63; can't write black characters, 226–27, 233; childhood of, 24–36; on Confederate flag, 202, 266–67; converts to Christianity, 86; criticism of colleges, 136–37, 174–75, 205; and D'Army Bailey, xiv, xv, xxi, 233; in D.C., 196–99; diet, 158; and dogs, 176, 180; encounters with Klan, xiv–xv, xviii, xx, 53, 164, 201; and father, 25; and Faulkner, 40, 66, 73–74, 124, 138, 168, 187–88, 196, 228, 255–56; fellowships and prizes, 166, 168, 180, 196–97, 198–200, 205–07, 264; and floods, 29–31, 70–71; and French, 235–36; and grandfathers, 27–28, 29–30; and Gwyn, 169–71, 172, 175, 177, 180, 185, 187, 197, 201, 213, 246, 250, 255, 264; and high opinion of himself, 47, 134, 137, 214; and houses, 180, 200, 202–03, 204–05; and Huggy, 187, 245, 250, 267; and illness, 246–48, 250–51; Jewish identity of, 55–56, 86, 217–18; and JFK, 185–86, 197–98; jobs, 71–72, 94, 98; and LeRoy Percy, 32–34, 35, 47, 49, 52, 55–56, 75, 85, 96, 110, 164–65; and location of manuscripts, 244–45; and Louie Nicholson, 27, 83–84, 239; and maps, 74; and Margaret, 117, 181, 207, 209; meets WP, 32; meets writers, 38; memorial service for WP, 255–56; and *Mississippi Quarterly* issue, 212; and MLK, 207; and mother, 16–23, 24, 25–26, 27, 28, 29, 31–32, 41, 48, 50–51, 85, 94, 98, 206, 207–08; and Mount Holly, 186; moves to Memphis, 148–50; and Moyses, 31, 50–51; and musical interests, 39–40, 201, 248; on Nathan Bedford Forrest, xviii–xix, xx–xxi, 107, 109; and Peggy, 111, 128–29, 144–45, 147; and Pensacola, 28–29; and *The Pica*, 44–48; and politicians, xx, 46, 176, 185, 186, 189, 191–92, 197–98, 265–66; and Project Historic America, 266; and reading interests, 35, 41, 42, 46, 48, 65–66, 68, 78–79, 82, 118, 124–30, 205, 215, 227; refuses to protest at Selma, 202; return trips to Delta, 209–10, 241–42; on 60s youth, 207; and soap operas, xvii, 252, 258; as soldier, 81–93, 134–35; as speaker, 264, 267–68; sympathizes with plight of blacks, xviii, 64–65, 99, 132, 142–43, 150–51, 152–53, 162–64, 174–75, 189, 190–91, 266–67; teenager, 39–49; and Tess, 89, 91–92, 94, 96–97; tires of fame, 267–68; at UNC, 50–69, 98–99, 102–07, 108–16, 117–30; view of women, 54–55; visits WP at Saranac Lake, 86–88, 91; and WAP, 32–33, 36–41, 48–49, 78–79, 84–85; WP subsidizes, 135–36, 166; in WP's wedding, 101–02; on WP's works, 174, 184–85, 203–04; worried about loss of South, 77–80, 145–46, 164–65, 174–75, 190–91, 266–67; writing routine, xvi–xvii, 103–04

**Works**

"And the Gay and the Blue," 67–68

"Bristol's Gargoyle," 126–27

*The Civil War, Volume I*, 281–311; bravery as displacement, xix, xx, 165; finishes, 309; methodology of, 281–83, 286–88; new agreement with Random House, 283–84; omissions in, 288; race ignored in, 289–92; Random House payments, 282; reviews for, 310–11; sources for, 286; as therapy, 285; trips to battlefields, 294; WP proofreads, 175; writing of, 284–309

*The Civil War, Volume II*, 312–32; reviews of, 332–36

*The Civil War, Volume III*, 195–220; approaching end, 365; party at end of, 217; reviews of, 371–73; starts, 348; tapes sections of, 244

"Death Took My Love," 93

"The Down Slope," 168–69

"Echoes of Shiloh," 401–02

"Flood Burial," 172–73; celebrates acceptance of, 176–77; *Post* accepts, 175–76

*Follow Me Down*, 203–12; beginning of, 202; comments about, 203; publication of, 212; reviews of, 212–14

"The Good Pilgrim: A Fury is Calmed," 57, 58–59

"Her Knight Comes Riding," 45

Introduction to *Anton Chekov: Longer Stories from the Last Decade*, 268

Introduction to *The Red Badge of Courage*, 268

*Jordan County*, 148–55; reviews of, 156

*Jordan County: A Three-Part Landscape in the Round*, 199; response to audience, 199

*Love in a Dry Season*, 124–28, 129–33; changes titles, 133; Dial editors like, 102–03; reviews of, 134

"Madrigal (Almost)," 46

"The Merchant of Bristol," 104–05

"Miss Amanda," 102–03; *Post's* rejection of, 102–03

*The Night Before Chancellorsville and Other Civil War Stories*, 167

"The Old Man That Sold Peanuts in New Orleans: A Story," 57–58

reviews: of *Absalom, Absalom!*, 66; of *Gallant Rebel*, 106; of *None Shall Look Back*, 105–06; of *Ordeal By Fire*, 106

"Sad Hiatus: A Short Short Story," 57

*September September*, 223–33; begins, 229; marketing of, 234–35; movie version of, 235; narrative for, 233; planned as potboiler, 223–25; reviews of, 234–35; sales of, 235; signs Random House contract, 224–25

*Shiloh*, 104–10; begins, 105; excerpt accepted by *Blue Book*, 113; finishes first draft, 110; first draft rejected, 113; methodology for, 105–06; reviews of, 138; rewriting of, 136–37; sales, 137; travels to Shiloh before beginning of book, 106; visits park historian, 136

"Tell Them Good–by," 98–101; acceptance of, 101; responds to 1927 flood in, 31

"This Primrose Hill: A Short Story," 57, 58–61

*Tournament*, 74–80, 113–15; advice from Knopf on putting away, 81; begins, 74; pitches to Dial, 113–14; republished, 251–52; reviews of, 115–16; rewrites, 113–15; sends to Knopf, 80–81; WAP's influence on, 78–79

*Two Gates to the City*, 139–48, 238–39, 241–43, 268–69; fear of starting, 241–43; plans for, 139–43;

Random House contract for,
238–39; struggles with writing,
143–48
"The Village Killers: A Story," 57, 59
Foote, Shelby Dade, Sr. (father): death
of, 24–25; expectations for planter life,
21; marries Lillian Rosenstock, 21–23;
rises up Armour ranks, 24; wanders
around, 21
Foote, William (great-great grandfather),
5–6
Ford Foundation, 196
Forrest, Nathan Bedford, xiv–xxi, 107,
109, 166, 217, 233, 271
Fort Pillow Massacre, xviii
Franklin, Malcolm, 228
Freeman, Morgan, 260
Frost, Robert, 46

Gallimard, 236
Garcia Marquez, Gabriel, 247
Gibbon, Edward, 162, 195, 214, 217
Giobbi, Ed, 186
Gold, Michael, 40
Gordon, Caroline, 65–66, 105
Gore, Albert, Jr., 265–66
Grant, Ulysses Simpson, 106, 107, 108,
109, 160, 166, 182, 190, 193, 203,
206, 212, 214, 215, 265
Green, Michelle, 262
Greenville, Miss. *See* Mississippi Delta
Grierson, Benjamin, 11–12
Guggenheim Fellowships, 166, 168, 180

Hale, Grace Elizabeth, 76–77
Hall, Desmond, 110, 113
Hall, Peggy (second wife), 111, 128–29,
144–45, 147
Hall, Peter, 206
Hamish Hamilton, 137
Hammond, James, 9
Handy, W. C., 232

Hanf, Roy, 81–83
Harrison, James, 6–7
Haxton, Josephine, 36, 112
Haxton, Kenneth, 53, 96, 105, 112, 201
Hayne, Robert Y., 6
Hemingway, Ernest, 211
Heller, Joseph, 185
Herndon, Z. P., 6
Herotodus, 247
Heyward, Nicholas, 4
Hiroshima, 97
Hoffman, Bert, 113, 114, 115, 123, 133,
135, 155, 240
Hollings, Fritz, 265
Hollins College, 206–07
Holmes, Richard, 227
Homer, 154, 166, 222
Horn, Stanley, 106
Horowitz, Tony, xvi, 93, 244, 267
Housman, A. E., 125
Howard, Edwin, 188, 196
Hughes, Langston, 38–39
Hutchings, David, 263

Ibsen, Henrik, 3

Jackson, Andrew, 6, 148, 233
Jefferson, Thomas, 196, 266
Joel, George, 113, 114, 115, 116, 123,
133, 135, 136, 155, 240
Johnson, Andrew, 216
Johnson, Bob, 245
Johnson, Lyndon Baines, 200, 201
Johnston, Albert Sydney, 11, 107, 160,
166
Jones, James, 148, 174
Jones, John Griffin, 162, 188,
198
Joyce, James, 41, 50, 225, 247

Karl, Frederick, 188
Keating, Bern, 112

Keating, Franke, 112
Keats, John, 39, 227
Keillor, Garrison, 260
Kennedy, Edward "Ted," 265–66
Kennedy, Jacqueline Bouvier,
    169, 185
Kennedy, John F., 185–86, 189, 197–98
Kibler, James, 212
King, Martin Luther, Jr., 190, 207
King, Richard, 132, 262
Kirwan, Albert, 118, 129–30, 230
Kreymborg, Alfred, 46
Ku Klux Klan, xiv–xv, xviii, xx, 37, 53,
    164, 201
Kubrick, Stanley, 167–69

Lamb, Brian, 209
Lampton, Lucius "Luke," 188
Lattimore, Richard, 173–74
Lavery, Tess (first wife), 89, 91–92, 94,
    96–97
Leadbelly, 121
Leatherman, Richard, 13, 164, 223, 290
Lee, Robert E., 10, 162, 186–87, 211,
    212, 214, 215, 217, 265
Leonard, William Ellery, 211
Leuckanbach, E. J., 43–44, 48–49, 53
Levee Press, 105
Library of Congress, 198
*Life*, 135, 136
Lincoln, Abraham, 27, 159, 167, 176–77,
    182, 211, 214, 215, 218
Lindsay, Vachel, 38
Linscott, Robert, 175, 177, 203
Loomis, Bob, 203
Lowe, E. N., 13
Lucretius, 247
Lucy, Autherine, 174–75
Lytle, Andrew, xv

MacArthur, Douglas, 134–35
Machiavelli, Niccoló, 94

Macon, Miss., 7
Mailer, Norman, 137
Mann, Thomas, 41
Maritain, Jacques, 184
Mason, James, 169
McClellan, George, 167
McDaniel, Nancy Sanders Rice (second
    wife of William), 6
McDonnell, Mike, 245
McDowell, Irwin, 167
McPherson, James, 6, 208
Mead, Linda, 171
Melville, Herman, 247
Memphis Polo Club, 199, 245
Memphis State, 205–06, 245
Memphis University School, 245
Memphis–Shelby County Public Library,
    225, 239
Meredith, George, 247
Meredith, James, 189
Messinger, Sybilla (third wife of Henry),
    12, 13
Mirrielees, Doris, 170
Mississippi Delta: commercial center,
    36–37; cotton acreage increases in
    1880s, 18; cotton crops in 1910s, 23;
    education system of, 26–27;
    immigration into, 36–37; Jews in, 22;
    New Deal manipulation, 122–23;
    1937 Flood, 70–71; 1921–1922 Farm
    Depression, 59; 1927 Flood, 29–31;
    promise of, 13; socioeconomic struc-
    ture of, 81; undrained areas of, 13, 14,
    17; wealth of counties, 36
Mississippi Educational Television, 228
Mitchell, George, 265
Mosby, John, 168
Mosby, Richard, 241
Mottley, Bob, 70, 207
Mount Holly, 18–19, 186
Moyse, Maude, 25, 26, 31, 50–51
Moyse, Mic, 25, 26, 50–51

Mozart, Wolfgang Amadeus, 137

Mussolini, Benito, 70

Myers, James Floyd, 117–18, 119

Nathan Bedford Forrest Park, xiii

National Book Award, 221–22, 240–41

*National Geographic*, 240

Nelms and Blum, 96

Nevins, Allan, 135, 159, 162, 193, 194

Newman, Charlie, 245

Nicholson, Louie, 27, 83–84, 239

Nixon, Richard M., 186, 215

North Carolina, University of, 245, 264

Ord, E. O. C., 12

Osborne, William, 205

Oschner Clinic, 246–47, 250, 253

Parker, Dorothy, 38

Parks, Rosa, xiv, 163

Parrish, Larry, 239–40

Pasternak, Boris, 139

Peabody Hotel, 111

Pearson, Bill, 245

Peck, Gregory, 169

Percy, Bunt Townsend, 51, 94, 101, 102, 248, 258

Percy Library, 242, 245

Percy, LeRoy (SF's friend), 32–34, 35, 47, 49, 52, 55–56, 75, 85, 96, 110, 164–65

Percy, LeRoy (father of WAP), 16–17, 37

Percy, Phinizy, 185

Percy, Walker: Amtrak travels, 246; attends SF's *Civil War* completion party, 217; cancer of, 253–56; celebrates with SF on first publication, 98; childhood relationships with SF, 32–34, 35–36, 39–40, 41, 44, 47, 49, 51; college, 51–52, 53, 54–56, 61, 62–63, 64; contacts Random about *Civil War*, 158; critiques SF's works, 212, 233, 243; interest in Kennedy, 185, 197–98;

reads Proust, 249; receives SF's letters, 96, 114, 116, 118, 124, 125, 128, 129, 133–34, 136, 137, 139–40, 143, 144, 146, 147, 148, 150, 157–58, 159, 160, 161, 165, 166, 171–72, 173, 174, 178, 180, 181, 182, 183–84, 185, 186, 187, 205–06, 207, 208, 209, 210, 213, 214, 215, 216, 221, 222–23, 226, 227, 228, 229, 236, 238, 240, 241, 247, 248; in SF's first wedding, 91–92; on SF's reclusiveness, 211; speaks out against racism, 202, 210, 211; subsidizes SF's writing projects, 135–36, 166; tuberculosis, 86–88, 91; visits Faulkner, 72–74; wedding of, 101–02; writes UNC letter for Huggy Foote, 246

**Works:** "The American War," 174; "The Charterhouse," 135; "Contra Gentiles," 252; "The Gramercy Winner," 135; *The Last Gentleman*, 101, 203–04; *Lancelot*, 237; *Love in the Ruins*, 212; *The Moviegoer*, 184–85; *The Thanatos Syndrome*, 250, 251

Percy, William Alexander: adopts Percy boys, 32–33; aphasia, 120–21; on blacks, 38–39; death of, 84–85; on Faulkner, 40; generous host, 38; *Lanterns on the Levee*, 64; musical interests, 39–40; renaissance man, 37–38

Peters, Dr., 16

Phillips, Robert, 57, 58, 122, 145, 151, 154

Pickett, George, 165, 187

Plato, 247

*Plessy vs. Ferguson*, 163

Plunkett, Annie, 180

Poe, Charles, 56–57

Polk, Leonidas, 10

Pomfret School, 245

Pope Paul VI, 171

Porter, Katherine Anne, 196

Powdermaker, Hortense, 28
Powell, Jody, 260
Pratt, Fletcher, 106
Prentiss, Benjamin, 191
Price, Reynolds, 257, 263
Pritchard, Ross, 180
Project Historic America, 266
Proust, Marcel, xix, 41–42, 198, 214,
    217, 247, 249–50
Pulitzer Prize, 221–23

Quackenbos, Mary, 17

Random House, xvii, 113, 157, 158, 159,
    166, 177, 190, 192, 224, 238, 241, 268
Reed, Bill, 245
Reid, Clarke, 267–68
Robards, Jason, 260
Robinson, Edward Arlington, 46
Rolo, Charles, 137
Rose, Stuart, 97
Rosecrans, William, 181
Rosen, Bob, 224, 245
Rosenstock, Morris (grandfather):
    children, 16; death of, 29; deaths of
    children, 16; first marriage, 1; origins,
    15–16; response to daughter's
    wedding, 23; second marriage, 16
Rubin, Louis, 244, 251, 264

Salinger, J. D., 185
Samway, Patrick, 55, 74, 87, 169, 185
Saturday Evening Post, 97, 101, 103, 110
Saunders, Lila, 197, 203, 223
Scofield, Trent, 265
Semmes, Ralph, 208
Shales, Tom, 262
Shaw, T. E., 222
Shea, John, 169–72
Shakespeare, 46, 137, 143, 214
Shelby, Isaac, 82, 148
Sheldon, George, 264

Sheridan, Philip, 181, 215
Sherman, William Tecumseh, 11, 107,
    109, 166, 187, 190, 206, 208, 213
Shiloh, Battle of, 10–11, 104, 106
Sibelius, Jean, 232
Simon and Schuster, 224
Singal, Daniel, 164
Smith, Fred, 111, 265
Smothers, Imogene, 117–18, 119
Soloway, Mark, 250
Sons of Confederate Veterans, 2–3
Southern Historical Collection, 245
Spender, Stephen, 196
Squires, Buddy, 259
Stanton, Edwin, 216
Stevens, Wallace, 45
Stevenson, Robert Louis, 45
Stinson, William D., 111–12
Styron, William, 226
Sugg, Redding, 106, 142
Sunnyside, 16–17

Tate, Allan, 100
Thackeray, William Makepeace, 247
Thomas, William, 240, 248
Thucydides, 162
Thurmond, Strom, 99
Tolson, Jay, 35–36, 37, 101, 135, 139,
    185, 201
Toscanini, Arturo, 39, 62
Treaty of Dancing Rabbit Creek, 7
Trollope, Anthony, 247
Trueheart, Charles, 262, 263
Truman, Harry S., 96, 99
Turner Broadcasting System, 235
Turner, Meg, 198–99, 245
Twain, Mark, 247

Université Paul Valéry, 236

Van Ark, Joan, 199
Virginia, University of, 196

Wallace, George, xx, 189, 191–92

Ward, Aileen, 227

Walter, Tom, 262

Warren, Earl, 163

Warren, Robert Penn, 258–59

Washington County. *See* Mississippi Delta

Wasson, Ben, 97, 105, 110

Watergate, 215

Waterston, Sam, 260

Webster, John, 232

Welty, Eudora, 105, 264

Wetherbee, Donald, 52, 71

White, Helen, 106, 142

Wilkes, Ben, 117

Williams, Joan, 188

Williamson, Joel, 54

Willingham, Calder, 224

Wilson, Craig, 262

WJPR, 94, 98

Woodward, C. Vann, 258

Yarbrough, Bill, 105

Zeiser, Mary Jane, 34–35